Medieval
Military
Technology

Medieval
Military
Technology

Kelly DeVries

broadview press

Cataloguing in Publication Data

DeVries, Kelly Robert, 1956–
    Medieval military technology

ISBN 0-921149-74-3

1. Arms and armor — History. 2. Artillery — History.
3. Fortification — History. 4. Warships — History.
5. Military history, Medieval. I. Title.

     U810.D48 1992   623'.09'02   C91-093898-9

broadview press   OR   broadview press
P.O. Box 1243   269 Portage Rd.
Peterborough, Ontario   Lewiston, NY
K9J 7H5   Canada   14092   USA

printed in Canada

Contents

Aan mijn gezin

Acknowledgements

This book was first suggested to me in 1988 when I was a sessional lecturer at the University of British Columbia by my department chairman, Professor Richard W. Unger, whose own works on the history of medieval technology have established him as a "giant" in the field. As he pointed out to me, the history of medieval military technology has been largely left up to amateur historians and antiquarians whose interests in the field are derived largely from their desires to replicate, in museums or in wargames, the arms, armor, and castles of the medieval warrior. Numerous books and articles from professional historians have appeared, it is true, but no one source has been devoted to an overview of all medieval military technology. Moreover, the current profusion of scholarly works on technology and war give little space to the discussion of the Middle Ages, especially in comparison to ancient and modern military technology. To Professor Unger for thus suggesting this to me, I give special thanks.

I also want to thank my mentor in the history of technology, Professor Bert S. Hall, Professor at the Institute of History and Philosophy of Science and Technology at the University of Toronto. In the tradition of Lynn White, Jr., his discussions with me, both in graduate school and since my graduation, have been of untold assistance as I puzzled through the intricacies of studying a historical genre in which one frequently must look beyond the written text. His encouragement of me in this and many other endeavors, as well as his diligence in scrutinizing whatever I send him, has been invaluable.

I also must not forget to praise the Centre for Medieval Studies at the University of Toronto for preparing me for the linguistic and historical necessities which medieval historians must continually face.

Finally, I wish to thank my family, especially my wife, Barbara Middleton, who has stood by me patiently, reading, rereading, and editing every word of this manuscript.

Introduction

Images of the medieval knight in shining armor, the castle, the catapult, and the long- or crossbowman have become the portrait of medieval society most indelibly imprinted on our mind by popular cinema and literature. Even the United States Marine Corps has seen fit recently to use as advertisement the depiction of a medieval knight wielding his sword, hoping by this, I suppose, to gain some sort of historical legitimacy. And, if this were not enough, on almost any given Saturday across North America groups of mock medieval warriors spar and tourney in an effort to recreate what they imagine to have been an age of chivalry, where strict laws of war prohibited unequal military conflict. They are matched by wargamers, who started with *Dungeons and Dragons*, played on 25-cent pads of paper, and have graduated to *Bard's Tale* and *Wizardry*, played on $1,000 computers. For them too, the Middle Ages was a time of intricate (and exciting) military technology.

But they are not alone in their search for the coupling of war and technology. Professional historians are also studying what they view as an unalterable historical dependency. Perhaps responding to Lewis Mumford's question—"how far shall one go back in demonstrating the fact that war has been the chief propagator of the machine,"[1]—recently a number of books have been published concerning the relationship between technology and warfare. Most, however, have taken a wide sweep at the subject, choosing to analyze military technology over the ages rather than focusing on a narrower time. This is certainly the case in the four latest and most prominent works of this genre, namely Bernard and Fawn

M. Brodie's *From Crossbow to H-Bomb*; William McNeill's *The Pursuit of Power: Technology, Armed Force, and Society since A.D. 1000*; Martin van Creveld's *Technology and War from 2000 B.C. to the Present*; and Robert L. O'Connell's *Of Arms and Men: A History of War, Weapons and Aggression.*[2] Consequently, the Middle Ages, as every other period, is dealt with in only a few pages, a short survey insufficient to meet the demands of a reader interested in studying military technology in the years between the Fall of Rome and the sixteenth century.

This book presents a comprehensive look at military technology during the Middle Ages. It concentrates on the invention, manufacture, and use of the technologies which made medieval warfare the material for legends and movies. It discusses the weapons which once brought death and now fill our museums, the castles and fortifications which once protected the population and now serve as tourist havens. While technical when required, this book is directed mainly at the general reader with the intention of serving as a textbook and as a reference guide for medieval scholars.

The book is divided into four parts, each of which is further divided into chapters. Part One discusses the technology of arms and armor during the Middle Ages. Its first chapter focuses on the offensive weapons of the medieval soldier—the spear, lance, mace, ax, sword, composite bow (both short and long), crossbow, and other, less used, miscellaneous weapons. Chapter two addresses the defensive weapons, including the shield, helmet, and body armor. Chapter three, "Stirrup, Mounted Shock Combat, Feudalism, and Chivalry," discusses the debate which arose with Lynn White's article on the stirrup's role in the origin of feudalism.

Part Two examines the technology of artillery. Following a chapter on the history and use in battle and at sieges of non-gunpowder artillery—balistae, trebuchets, and Greek Fire—the second chapter focuses on gunpowder artillery, its invention, proliferation, and use before 1500. Both chapters also discuss the societal and intellectual acceptance of these weapons.

Part Three examines the technology of fortifications. It is divided into four chapters. The first addresses the continued use of Roman fortifications as well as the construction of new fortifications in the early Middle Ages. The second looks at the motte-and-bailey castle, a fortification built from earth and wood. The third, the longest in this section, considers stone castles, while the fourth discusses urban fortifications and fortified residences.

The final section of this book examines the construction of warships during the Middle Ages. Although this section is not divided into chapters, perhaps reflecting how little warfare actually took place at sea during this time, it does note the inventions and innovations in shipbuilding which affected naval warfare. It also deals with the weaponry which was invented or adapted for use in fighting at sea.

What I do not want to be in this book is overly deterministic. It is said that only non-historians of technology believe in technological determinism. Whether this is the case or not is perhaps more easily discussed at professional historical roundtables; I wish only to present here the current historical thought or, in many instances, debate on medieval military technology.[3] Hopefully, such has been done without showing any prejudices, although that may be virtually impossible.

Notes

1   Mumford (1934):86.

2   Brodie (1973); McNeill (1982); van Creveld (1989); O'Connell (1989).

3   One recent article which discusses medieval technological determinism is
     Bartlett (1986).

Part I: Arms
and Armor

Introduction

I t might well be an exaggeration to claim that the Middle Ages would mean little to the modern world without its characteristic offensive and defensive armaments. Yet, certainly for the purposes of modern culture as conveyed by fantasy novels, comics and Hollywood films, is there anything more representative of medieval society than the knight fully outfitted in shining armor, lance couched under his arm, bearing down on his tournament opponent, or the Viking warrior, horns on his helmet, battle axe slicing through defenseless peasants and monks? Could King Arthur be the greatest king of England without his trusty sword, Excalibur, pulled from the rock as a symbol of his right to rule? Or Robin Hood without his longbow, sending its arrow to split an opponent's in the Sheriff of Nottingham's archery meet? Or Roland without his longsword, cutting a Muslim foe (and his horse) clean in half? Or Macbeth without his dagger, murdering Duncan, the king of Scotland? Truly, the Middle Ages without its distinctive arms and armor would lose some of its image, some of its unique character.

Anthropologists have difficulty determining when the first armaments were invented. Some steadfastly adhere to the theory that warfare is a man-made activity, learned but not inherent, and, therefore, that early weapons were initially invented as agricultural implements and not as tools of war. Others take the opposite side of the debate, arguing for an original invention of weapons.[1] Whatever might be the answer, and it will probably never be known for sure, by the beginning of the Stone Age (Neolithic or Early/Middle Paleolithic times—c.70,000 BC) Prehistoric humans had begun to use spears, fire, and stone clubs as protection against animals and other tribes. By the end of the Paleolithic Age (35,000-12,000 BC), cave paintings show that Neanderthals and Cro-Magnons had begun to use strategy and tactics to integrate their weaponry with their combat, thus creating the first organized warfare. Weaponry fit into three categories: clubs, stone axes, and thrusted spears were used for short-range warfare; thrown spears (javelins) for medium-range warfare; and thrown stones for long-range warfare.[2]

The Mesolithic Age (12,000-7000 BC) brought the first arms "revolution." Most significant at this time was the invention of the sling and the bow and arrow. This increased the long-range firepower both in the range of missile fired (generally extending the effective range to 100-200 meters) and in the damage caused by its impact. It also allowed the user to remain concealed and, when used in a group, to unleash a mighty barrage of missile fire. The Biblical story of David and Goliath need only be recalled to exemplify the fatal result of such a missile fired accurately from the smallest warrior against the largest foe. Seemingly of less importance was the invention of the mace and the rudimentary dagger, which also appeared at this time and quickly took the place of the club next to the traditional short-range thrusted spear and stone axe. Cave paintings depict the introduction of protective clothing (proto-armor) worn by some of these late Stone Age soldiers.[3]

As the Ages changed from Stone to Bronze, the types of weapons did not vary, but the material in which they were made did. Neolithic humans began experimenting with the use of copper as early as 6000 BC in Anatolia, but it took 2000 years before the extraction and smelting of metals produced bronze strong enough (and cheap enough) to replace traditional stone tools and armaments. Spears, javelins, arrows, maces, and axes were now crowned by a strong bronze head, which could be sharpened easily. Indeed, archaeological remains from Ancient Mesopotamia and Egypt show that the metallic axe was the most preferred weapon of these civilizations. Daggers became a more viable short-range weapon, especially when lengthened, as bronze now made possible, to produce a sword, which could be used both to pierce and slash an enemy. With bronze weaponry came the invention of stronger, more protective armor: helmets, shields, breastplates, and greaves. Chariots also appeared during the Bronze Age, used primarily as a mode of transportation to and around the battlefield or as mobile missile-launching platforms.[4]

The Iron Age evolved from the Bronze Age, sometime around 1200 BC, and again the material composition of both offensive and defensive armaments changed. Ancient armies began to adopt more systematized armaments policies. Frequently soldiers became known by the name of their armament—the Greek hopelite named after his distinctive shield, the *hoplon*, and the *cataphract* cavalryman called by the name of his heavy armor—while certain lands were known to produce mercenaries especially skilled in the use of a single weapon—Dahae Horse Archers, Numidian Light Cavalrymen, Rhodian or Balearic Slingers, Aetolian Javelinmen, and Cretan or Syrian Archers. The types of weapons, however, remained the same: the spear, sword, and axe were the primary short-range weapons; the javelin was the primary medium-range weapon; and the sling and bow were the primary long-range weapons. The only major changes came with the introduction of the staff-sling (the *fundibalus*), which was capable of throwing a 400 gram stone or a dart over 200 meters, and in the length of the spear, which expanded during the Macedonian period to a length of more than seven meters. This latter weapon (known as a *sarissa*) became the principal offensive armament of the armies of Philip of Macedon and Alexander the Great who used it to conquer Greece, Persia, the Middle East, Egypt, and the western portion of India.[5]

From the beginning of their history, Roman armies too were characterized largely by the use of a single weapon, the *pilum*. The pilum was a heavy javelin, used either as a thrusting or a thrown weapon. Made of a strong but pliable iron, pila when thrown would bend upon impact. This meant that it could not be returned by an enemy, or, if it actually pierced an opponent's armor or shield, it would hinder his fighting or defensive capabilities. The early Roman soldier also carried a dagger, a helmet, and a large, oblong shield called a *scutum*.

This remained the standard equipment for the Roman soldier for more than a thousand years. Styles were changed, torso armor added, and a short sword (*gladius*) replaced the dagger, but otherwise the standard equipment was little modified until the fourth and fifth centuries AD. And why should it have been? The Roman armies dominated the Mediterranean world from the time of their defeat of the Greeks and Carthaginians in the second century BC.[6] Indeed, they conquered so much land using armies equipped in such a manner that their empire has never been equalled.

Trying to link the armaments of the ancient world with those of the medieval world is an impossible task. While the types of armaments varied little between the two periods, and in fact varied little between the Stone Age and the twentieth century, their construction, conception, and tactical use varied considerably. The following three chapters will endeavor to explain these differences, following the development of offensive armaments thematically and the development of defensive armaments chronologically. A chapter will also attempt to summarize the theory, put forth by Lynn White, Jr., that the diffusion of the stirrup to western Europe caused feudalism; both White's thesis and criticisms of it will be discussed.

Arms

The Roman soldiers who faced the barbarian invasions of the fourth and fifth centuries were outfitted with offensive armaments which varied little from those carried by the first-century legionnaires. The spear was still the major Roman infantry weapon, although three different sizes of spear had replaced the earlier pilum: the short *verutum*, having a head with an average measurement of 12.5 centimeters and a shaft measuring 60.5 centimeters; the long *spiculum*, with a head 23 centimeters long and a shaft 167.5 centimeters in length; and the *plumbata*, a short javelin with a barbed and lead-weighted head.

Swords were also carried by infantry soldiers, although the *spathae*, as they were now called, were much longer (72 centimeters) than the original gladii. Support troops continued to use bows, slings, and staff-slings.[7]

Late Roman cavalry, which remained few in number compared with the large number of infantry and generally manned by non-Italian soldiers, were equipped with a long spear (later called a lance) and a long sword. Because the cavalry had no stirrups, both the spear and sword were used only in close-combat situations.[8]

The barbarian soldiers which they faced in the fourth and fifth centuries had different weapons and different attitudes to them than did the Romans. For one thing, there was little standardization among, or even within, the various tribal armies which invaded the Empire. The Visigoths and Ostrogoths, who were successful in their initial conquests largely because of their overwhelming numbers, probably had very few arms, acquiring most of their offensive weapons from the Roman armies they defeated. The Huns, on the other hand, were mostly horsed archers, using the lance only as a secondary weapon. The Franks preferred the axe as their main offensive armament, both as a close-combat, hand-held weapon and as a missile.[9]

Secondly, while first-century Roman writers such as Tacitus had belittled early barbarian armaments, by the time of the invasions, barbarian weaponry had improved both in quality and variety. The infantry still used spears as their chief weapon, but these had been improved with better and stronger iron heads. They also were outfitted with axes, bows with iron-tipped arrows, and swords. The chief weapon of the cavalry was a long two-edged sword.[10] It should also be noted that although the weapons of the barbarians were in most instances not as effective as those of the Romans, the invaders seemed to recognize these limitations and were able to modify their tactics until they could more effectively use their "inferior" weapons. The Romans were unable to do the same, and this tactical failure may have added to their ultimate inability to defeat the invaders of the empire.[11]

Finally, barbarian soldiers generally carried many heavy offensive arms, sometimes equipping themselves with weapons at the expense of armor. This characteristic especially astounded the late Roman chroniclers as it was quite different from the tradition of their own soldiers; many of these authors describe at great length the large number of weapons carried by the barbarians. For example, Sidonius Apollinaris relates his first encounter with Frankish soldiers in 470:

> Their swords hung from their shoulders on baldricks, and round their waists they wore a belt of fur adorned with bosses.... In their right hands they held barbed lances and throwing-axes, and in their left shields, on which the light shone, white on the circuit and red on the boss, displaying both opulence and craftsmanship.

And Procopius, writing a century later, records a similar impression of the Franks:

> The military equipment of this people is very simple.... They do not know the use of the coat of mail or greaves and the

head the majority leave uncovered, only a few wear the helmet. They have their chests bare and backs naked to the loins, they cover their thighs with either leather or linen.... Fighting on foot is both habitual and a national custom and they are proficient in this. At the hip they wear a sword and on the left side their shield is attached. They have neither bows nor slings, no missile weapons except the double edged axe and the angon which they use most often. The angons are spears which are neither very short nor very long; they can be used, if necessary for throwing like a javelin, and also, in hand to hand combat.[12]

In the conquest of Europe the barbarians were the victors, the Romans the defeated. In weaponry this meant that the barbarian tradition became the model for the Middle Ages. Almost all medieval weapons were known at the time of the barbarian invasions—spears, lances, axes, daggers, swords, clubs, slings, and bows—and those which developed later—maces, war hammers, staff weapons, and crossbows—generally evolved from these. The following is a historical catalogue which traces the development and evolution of each of these weapons.

The Spear/Lance

In prehistoric and ancient times the spear was the most important and most widely used offensive armament. Unlike all other weapons, the spear could be used both by the infantry and cavalry, and both as a hand-held thrusting weapon or, when thrown, as a missile. As mentioned above, the spear was the primary arm of the Roman legionnaire; it was also the principal weapon of their fourth- and fifth-century barbarian enemies. And while these barbarian spears were technologically simpler than the pila used by the Romans, they were nevertheless effective on the battlefield. This was noted as early as the first century when Tacitus wrote:

> Only a few of them use swords or large lances: they carry spears—called *frameae* in their language—with short and narrow blades, but so sharp and easy to handle that they can be used, as required, either at close quarters or in long-range fighting. Their horsemen are content with a shield and spear; but the foot-soldiers also rain javelins on their foes: each of them carries several, and they hurl them to immense distances...[13]

Tacitus showed that the barbarians understood the three uses of the spear even before they invaded the Empire, an assessment which was later confirmed by the invasions themselves.

What has not been confirmed, either by archaeological finds or other literary sources, however, is Tacitus' description of the barbarian spears themselves. There is no doubt that the spear was important, but it seems that there was in fact no consistency in these weapons even among, let alone between, the barbarian tribes. M.J. Swanton's impressive study, *The Spearheads of the Anglo-Saxon Settlements*, reveals that twelve different types of spearheads have been found in Anglo-Saxon archaeological excavations. These he has further grouped into four main categories: derivative forms of Germanic spear-types prior to the Anglo-Saxon settlement in England, leaf-shaped blades, angular blades, and corrugated blades. While certain chronological and regional differences can account for some of the variations in spearhead styles, on the whole the conclusion must be that the Anglo-Saxons saw no need for consistency. Each smith probably created his own style of spearhead without apparent official guidelines or influences.[14]

The same must also be true about early medieval spears in continental Europe. Although a study similar in depth and mastery to Swanton's does not exist for continental or Scandinavian Europe, the archaeological remains of spearheads from these regions show a similar lack of consistency.[15] This is further supported by literary evidence. For example, on Frankish spears alone there is a large difference in contemporary descriptions. While Sidonius Apollinaris, Procopius, and Gregory of Tours all note the spear as an important, if not *the* most important, weapon of the Frankish soldiers, none gives a description which might lead to a conclusion that it was a particularly special weapon. Agathias, writing at almost the same time as Procopius and Gregory of Tours, describes a weapon, which he calls an *angon*, which is not only special in its design but also extremely special in its use in warfare:

> The angons are spears which are neither short nor long; they can be used, if necessary for throwing like a javelin, and also, in hand to hand combat. The greater part of the angon is covered with iron and very little wood is exposed. Above, at the top

of the spear, on each side from the socket itself where the staff is fixed, some points are turned back, bent like hooks, and turned toward the handle. In battle, the Frank throws the angon, and if it hits an enemy the spear is caught in the man and neither the wounded man nor anyone else can draw it out. The barbs hold inside the flesh causing great pain and in this way a man whose wound may not be in a vital spot still dies. If the angon strikes a shield, it is fixed there, hanging down with the butt on the ground. The angon cannot be pulled out because the barbs have penetrated the shield, nor can it be cut off with a sword because the wood of the shaft is covered with iron. When the Frank sees the situation, he quickly puts his foot on the butt of the spear, pulling down and the man holding it falls, the head and chest are left unprotected. The unprotected warrior is then killed either by a stroke of the axe or a thrust with another spear.[16]

Is this an accurate description of *the* Frankish spear? Probably not, although most modern historians accept it as such.[17] A similar spear is described in the tenth-century poem, *Waltheri*. It was modified by three cords that were attached to its end so that, if stuck into an enemy's shield, three Frankish warriors could pull and force him to drop it.[18] In fact, the inconsistency of the spear types of the early Middle Ages may mean that there was indeed a spear like the angon used by some Frankish warriors. Anything more, however, cannot be proven.

The first major restructuring of the early medieval army was done by Charlemagne who reigned from 768 to 814. Not only was this a restructuring of command, organization, and tactics, but Charlemagne also insisted on establishing a standardized weapons policy for his troops. The principal weapon, however, remained the spear, and it was to be carried by both infantry and cavalry troops. As early as 792-93 the *Capitulare missorum* (a Carolingian law) required the lance as a weapon for all horsemen. A similar command was echoed in capitularies decreed in 804 and 811. The infantry was to be outfitted likewise with a lance, as directed in the Capitulary of Aachen, decreed in 802-03.[19] This is also evidenced in artistic sources, all of which show the spear as the predominant weapon carried by both the Carolingian cavalry and infantry.[20]

The Carolingian lance was not a missile weapon. Both artistic and literary sources confirm that it was only thrusted at the enemy, whether on foot or on horseback. After the middle of the eighth century, the Frankish javelin or angon is no longer found in archaeological explorations.[21]

With the military changes instituted by Charlemagne, the spear, both as an infantry weapon (the spear) and as a cavalry weapon (the lance), took on a new importance in warfare. It continued to be used sometimes as a javelin but mostly as a thrusting weapon, the soldier either thrusting downward with his spear, in a stabbing motion, or thrusting upwards, in an attempt to strike an opponent under his armor or to lift him from his horse. Yet using the lance only as a thrusting weapon when mounted made the warhorse merely a fighting platform and did not incorporate either its power or speed into the attack. This was accomplished only when the lance was held fixed under the horseman's arm in a couched position. Then, as the horse charged an opponent, the lance blow was delivered by a combination of the lance, the rider and the horse, producing a far greater impact than a manual thrust ever could.

This type of warfare has been called "mounted shock combat" by modern historians, a term which correctly recreates what must have been an extremely forceful and "shocking" attack. It clearly impressed medieval writers, many of whom recount this form of combat in quite graphic detail. Take, for example, the results of such an attack as described in *The Song of Roland*:

> He breaks his shield and bursts open his hauberk, cuts through his bones, and tears away the whole spine from his back; with his lance he casts out his soul; he thrusts it well home and causes his body to swing back and hurls him dead from his horse a full lance-length away.[22]

Although certainly exaggerating the effects of such a blow, the anonymous writer has quite clearly shown the impression that contemporaries had of mounted shock combat, an impression which caused many to flee the battlefield without a blow being made. This too was victory. As R.H.C. Davis has written: "The purpose of a charge was not just to hit one's opponent but to gallop through the enemy ranks so as to make them panic and flee."[23]

To effectively perform mounted shock combat, significant technological changes needed to be made to the lance. No longer would an infantry spear, with its light wood shaft and small iron head, be sufficient to withstand the impact required of the couched lance. The typical cavalry lance was now made of strong, hard wood, about four meters in length; its leaf-shaped metal head had two cutting edges and a sharp point. It was also generally outfitted with a wing attachment behind the lancehead (a *pennon*). This limited the lance's penetration, preventing the weapon from imbedding itself too deeply in an opponent's body or armor to be easily extracted. A flared restraint was attached to the end of the lance to keep it from being driven backward beneath the wielder's arm. Finally, a handgrip was added.[24]

There is, however, some uncertainty about when mounted shock combat was first practiced. Historians for many centuries assumed that the tactic was developed early in the Middle Ages, perhaps even as early as the battle of Adrianople (378). This was countered effectively in 1951, when D.J.A. Ross, in an article entitled "Plein sa hanste" (The Couched Lance), contended that the first couched lance descriptions could not be found before the composition of the early *Chansons de geste*, which he dated 1050-1100.[25] This thesis in turn was rebutted in 1962 when Lynn White, Jr. published his *Medieval Technology and Social Change*. In a chapter entitled "Stirrup, Mounted Shock Combat, Feudalism, and Chivalry" (which will be discussed more thoroughly in chapter three below), White claimed that mounted shock combat was known much earlier than the date which Ross had established, possibly as early as the eighth century, the century which White believed saw the development of stirrups and the origin of the heavy cavalry-based army.[26]

But White's date for the origin of mounted shock combat did not stand long without criticism. Within a year, Ross had defended his 1951 thesis, using not only the *Chansons de geste* but the *Bayeux Tapestry* as evidence,[27] and this was echoed over the next two decades by a number of articles supporting him, all of which established the date of the introduction of mounted shock combat to sometime between c.1050 and c.1150: in 1965, François Buttin used a copious number of original narrative sources to claim a mid-twelfth-century date;[28] in 1980, David C. Nicolle affirmed an early twelfth-century date based on the influence of Crusader couched lance warfare on the Muslims;[29] in 1985, Bernard S. Bachrach established a twelfth-century date based upon the development of the high cantel and high pommel saddle;[30] the same year, Victoria Cirlot, using Catalan artistic, diplomatic, and literary sources, set the date at c.1140;[31] and in 1988, Jean Flori affirmed a date of c.1100 based on Christian and Muslim narratives, epics, and illustrated documents.[32]

Whatever the original date may have been, it seems certain that by the middle of the twelfth century the couched lance had begun to dominate the battlefield, and that from then until the end of the Middle Ages, mounted shock combat was the only use of the lance from horseback. It was also a tactic universally employed throughout western Europe. This is clearly seen in the large number of artistic sources from all western kingdoms which depict the cavalry lance held in a couched position.[33] Contemporary chronicles report that the lance was the principal offensive weapon of the Crusaders in the Holy Land, where the first attack was always a mounted shock combat charge.[34] In England, the 1181 Assize of Arms decreed by Henry II specifies only the lance as a required weapon for horsemen in battle.[35] A similar requirement was ordered of all cavalry soldiers in Florence in 1260.[36] Spain, Germany and France also practiced the battlefield use of mounted shock combat.[37]

Despite its obvious simplicity, however, mounted shock combat was not an easy form of warfare to learn, and cavalry soldiers were compelled to train for many years before they could wield the lance with dexterity and skill. R.H.C. Davis described how the lance was used:

> If one was to hold a lance horizontal and steady while galloping a horse, it was essential to secure the lance at more than a single point. If it was well balanced, one could hold it in one hand and tuck the rear end under one's armpit, but even this position was hard on the wrist, and could not be maintained for long. It was therefore normal for knights to hold their lance upright, not only when on the march, but also at the start of a charge, resting it (from the middle of the twelfth to the four-

teenth century) on a "fewter" or felt butt on the saddle bow. As the charge developed, and at the last moment, the lances were lifted off the fewters and their points lowered or "couched." So as to ensure that the weight of the lance and the force of its blow did not unbalance the rider by being on his right side only, the point of the lance was held to the left of the horse's head with the base secured tightly under the rider's right armpit. Aim was taken by steering the horse and, if necessary, by twisting one's whole body in the saddle.[38]

There was no better place to learn the art of the couched lance than at a tournament, and from the twelfth to the sixteenth centuries there were sufficient tournaments held for everyone to learn their craft well. In the twelfth and thirteenth centuries, jousters at these tournaments generally used the same lances as they would on the battlefield, with the sharp lancehead removed and a blunt *coronal* replacing it if fighting in a tournament *à plaisance*; in a tournament *à outrance*, which more explicitly imitated warfare, the sharp warhead remained. The coronal prevented the lancehead from piercing an opponent's armor, although the impact was still usually forceful enough to knock him from his steed. In the fourteenth and fifteenth centuries, the lances for battle and for tourneying became slightly different. In the place of the flared restraint found on battlefield lances which prevented the lance from slipping under the armpit, the tournament lance was equipped with a cog-like grate which meshed with the lance-rest which all jousters wore on their armor. This also increased the probability of a lance breaking rather than rebounding on impact, thus decreasing the amount of bruising experienced by the jouster.[39]

While the cavalry lance went through several modifications as mounted shock combat developed, the infantry spear remained relatively unchanged between the time of Charlemagne and the fourteenth century. It continued to be rather short, measuring usually no more than two meters in length, and was made of light wood with an inconsistently shaped iron spearhead attached. Still, it remained the primary weapon of the infantry soldier on the battlefield.[40]

In the fourteenth and fifteenth centuries the infantry spear lengthened to become a pike. In this form it continued to dominate infantry warfare until well into the eighteenth century.[41]

The Axe

Technically quite sophisticated and able to smash and pierce armor, the axe (known as a *francisca*), had application both as a weapon and as a tool. Late Roman chroniclers were especially impressed with barbarian axes, reporting that they were used both for close infantry combat and as missile weapons. In their former variant, they allowed the barbarian invaders to create a heavy infantry capable of withstanding and defeating the equally heavy imperial infantry. In the latter case, when thrown in unison as was the custom, they were capable of shattering Roman shields and sometimes killing the soldiers themselves.[42]

Modern experiments have confirmed this. Based on a large number of franciscae excavated from barbarian graves, the average axe weighed 1.2 kilograms, the head accounting for between 300 and 900 grams. The handle measured 40 centimeters in length and the head 18 centimeters. When rotated on its own axis, it could strike an opponent with significant force at four meters with a single rotation, at eight meters with a double rotation, and at twelve meters with a triple rotation.[43]

The throwing axe remained important to barbarian soldiers until the beginning of the seventh century, when for some reason it began to decline in use and eventually disappeared altogether. The hand-held battle axe, however, continued to be favored as an infantry weapon throughout the rest of the Middle Ages.[44] Perhaps nowhere and at no other time was it more popular than when used by the Vikings. It was taken with them as their chief weapon when they first attacked Lindesfarne Abbey in 793, and it continued to be used until at least the end of the eleventh century. To the Vikings, the long-handled, broad-edged battle axe was a symbol of their warrior status, to be buried with them so that they might take it on their journey to Valhalla. To their victims, this axe, typically called a "Danish axe" no matter who was wielding it, was a symbol of the blood-thirsty violence of marauding warriors who felt little compassion for their victims.

There were two types of Viking battle axes. The first was known as the *skeggøx* or bearded axe, because its blade was drawn down like a beard. Archaeological specimens of this type have been dated as early as the eighth century, when they may have been used as tools, and they continued to be used well beyond the end of the Viking raids.

The second type of battle axe used by the Vikings was the *breidøx* or broad axe. These had a much more triangular-shaped head and were used almost exclusively as weapons. They do not appear until 1000, but after this time seem to have been the axe of choice among Viking warriors. The cutting edge of the broad axe was often made of a special hardened iron, welded onto the head, and the blade and neck were sometimes decorated with silver or gold inlay.[45]

Once the Vikings conquered England, the battle axe also became popular among Anglo-Saxon warriors. Moreover, as soon as it became accepted as their principal weapon, Anglo-Saxon armies may have used the axe even more than did those who gave it to them. Their battle axe was precisely the same as the Viking broad axe, although its effectiveness was increased by the organization and training which an Anglo-Saxon army required. It was the chief weapon carried by the Anglo-Saxon army at Hastings. As depicted in the *Bayeux Tapestry*, both professional Anglo-Saxon soldiers (the huscarls) and conscripts (the fyrd) are shown using it. Yet, simply because the Anglo-Saxons favored it so much does not mean that the axe was unknown on the continent, as William the Conqueror himself is shown wielding one in the *Bayeux Tapestry*.[46]

With the loss at Hastings, the use of the battle axe among English soldiers diminished, but it did not die out completely. Norman Englishmen continued to use the weapon, and legend has it that Richard the Lion-Hearted took it to the Holy Land on his Crusade as his main weapon against the Saracens.[47]

Throughout the rest of the Middle Ages, literary, artistic and archaeological evidence shows that the axe was still quite popular as a military weapon. Despite being outlawed for use in tournaments, perhaps because of its violent reputation, the battle axe was still mentioned often in medieval literature. For example, in the chivalric tale *Gawain and the Green Knight*, the axe plays a principal role as the weapon of challenge from the Green Knight to Sir Gawain. (Gawain is challenged to behead the Green Knight with a battle axe and agrees to allow the Green Knight, should he survive this wound, to do the same a year later to Gawain.)[48]

In artistic sources the battle axe also appears frequently, in many styles and lengths. Most are typically shaped like the bearded or broad axes of the Vikings and Anglo-Saxons. Others, however, are shown with spikes, hammers or points at the opposite end to the axe head. Some appear to be nothing more than a pick-axe. Finally, a few are depicted with long axe heads, the tips of which are curved back and either resting on or attached to the haft in what may be a precursor to the staff weapons which became prominent later. Short-handled axes are also frequently depicted, although apparently not for the purpose of throwing.[49]

Finally, there are also a large number of extant examples of medieval battle axe heads. These date from the tenth to the fourteenth centuries and are found in almost all lands of Europe (although it is apparent from the large number of finds in northern and eastern Europe that the axe continued to be favored there more than in other European lands). Most of these reveal little more than what can be learned from artistic sources; they are all similar in size and shape to the axes of the Vikings and Anglo-Saxons, with only slight and limited changes. These include a sharply upward sweep in some axe blades of the twelfth and thirteenth centuries; the addition of a hammer on the back of some axe blades; and an increase in the thickness of some blades as plate armor begins to develop and become more plentiful. However, the latter modification is found only in western Europe where plate armor was most plentiful; those axe heads found in Poland and Hungary remain comparatively thin.[50]

By the fourteenth century, the battle axe began to greatly diminish in popularity as pole-axes, halberds and other staff weapons, all of which had evolved from it, were used more frequently by infantry soldiers. However, at the same time as the infantry began to reject the axe, the cavalry developed a smaller, more light-weight form as a close-combat weapon. The horseman's axe, as it became known, had a small head with a curved blade offset by a hammer at the back. Its pointed haft was the same length as the mace and war hammer, and it was probably wielded in a similar fashion to those other close-combat weapons.[51]

The Dagger

Although limited in use on the battlefield when compared with other weapons, the dagger appears frequently in medieval military history. Although evidence is scarce for all but the most favored weapons of the time, it is known, for example, that the Visigoths, once they settled in Spain during the sixth century, began using daggers of a Hispano-Roman type.[52] The Franks too favored the weapon, with two of Charlemagne's capitularies, decreed in 804 and 811, requiring all cavalry soldiers to carry one.[53] In the north, both the Anglo-Saxons and the Vikings commonly used the dagger; grave sites of both peoples show the weapon buried not only with male adults, but also with women and children. Indeed, according to a study by Heinrich Härke on the appearance of daggers in Anglo-Saxon burials, the size of the weapon buried was related to the sex and age of the corpse: the male adult was buried with the largest daggers, measuring an average of 170 millimeters; the female adult the second largest, an average of 130 millimeters; and children of both sexes buried with the smallest daggers, an average of 100-110 millimeters.[54] Finally, Justinian's sixth-century legal code known as the *Institutes* establishes that at least in the early medieval Byzantine state, the dagger was the preferred weapon of assassins.[55]

It can also be determined from the literary and archaeological evidence of this period that the early medieval dagger was between 45 and 175 millimeters long, made of iron with a single sharp edge and a hilt of wood or bone (preferably from an ox or goat).[56]

Between the tenth and the fourteenth centuries, the dagger remained in use as the *cultellus*. This was larger in length and width than the earlier model, and was in fact similar in both size and shape to the Roman short sword. It was also used almost exclusively as an infantry weapon to dispatch cavalry soldiers who had fallen from their horses, or in close-combat as an auxiliary armament to the sword or staff weapon.[57]

During the late Middle Ages, sometime in the fourteenth century, knights began adding the dagger to their weaponry arsenal. Called a *misericord*, as a pun on the liturgical vestment, this was a short, thin, two-edged dagger which, when attached to the right hip, generally balanced the knight's sword hanging down his left side. While perhaps less frequently used than other of the knight's weapons, on the battlefield it was indispensable, as the misericord was often the only weapon which could easily penetrate between an opponent's plate armor and helmet.[58]

The popularity of the misericord led to the development of other late medieval daggers, namely the *basilard*, the *rondel* and the *ballock*, all of which varied in sizes and shapes with little or no uniformity among them.[59] These weapons were also frequently carried by civilians, with Geoffrey Chaucer outfitting no fewer than five of his characters in *The Canterbury Tales* with one: the Yeoman, the shipman, the murderers of "The Pardoner's Tale," Simkin, and the Monk.[60]

The Sword

While the spear may have been the most popular offensive armament of the Middle Ages, the sword was certainly the most celebrated. Swords were intricately made, expensive to own, and generally passed down from generation to generation. They were also frequently named, with King Arthur's "Excalibur" and Roland's "Durendal" being perhaps the most famous.

Swords were present on both sides of the barbarian invasions. The Romans had both long and short swords, which they used as secondary weapons to their pila. The barbarians too had swords, although only long sizes. The existence of barbarian swords was reported by Tacitus, who in his derisive tone claimed that they had not many of them as their iron "is not plentiful."[61] But if they were not numerous in the first century, they seem to have improved both in abundance and quality by the fourth and fifth centuries, for almost all barbarian soldiers were reported by contemporary chroniclers as bearing one.[62] This can also be seen in the numerous archaeological excavations of barbarian gravesites, almost all of which contain at least one type of sword.

These sites have revealed that barbarian swords were of varying length and description. A few, probably those owned by tribal military leaders, were long (75-100 centimeters), thinly bladed (6 centimeters in width), heavy and two-edged, with a center of gravity near to the point. Most were decorated. Others were shorter, measuring 40 centimeters in length. A third group fits neither of these categories. These could be up to 85 centimeters in length with a width between 4 and 6.5 centimeters. But unlike the long swords whose length they equalled, these were light in weight and were probably meant to be wielded only with one hand. (These swords may correspond to the weapon known to contemporary chroniclers as the *sax* or *scramasax*.) Small versions of the same sword, measuring around 20 centimeters in length, have also been found. All swords ended in an enlarged pommel, of various sizes and shapes, with a hilt covered in wood and leather. They were made of finely forged iron of a quality equal or superior to contemporary Roman swords.[63]

Swords continued to be valued in continental Europe throughout the early Middle Ages. The Code of Ervig (680-87) even made the ownership of a sword mandatory for all men, Goth or Roman, joining the Visigothic army.[64] In Anglo-Saxon England the sword was held in a similar high regard. As H.R. Ellis Davidson has shown in her study, *The Sword in Anglo-Saxon England*, it was an integral part of Anglo-Saxon military society. Relying on both literary and archaeological sources, she has determined that while the axe, spear, and bow were important weapons to the pre-conquest English, "they had none of the richness of association possessed by the sword."[65]

The sword was the weapon of leadership, an effective military tool as well as a ceremonial object. Often it would be given to a boy as a gift at birth or at his naming. The child would grow up playing with it and with other, lighter swords, until it became a weapon he could wield with strength and agility. At other times, the sword would not be presented to the boy until he had reached manhood. As such it stood as a symbol of the end of childhood and the birth of the warrior. Generally in these cases the sword would not be new, but would be a family treasure which had been passed down from one warrior to the next, a token of past wars fought and past victories won. (This need not have been a complete weapon, but could also be the shattered fragments of an ancestor's sword.) The Anglo-Saxon sword could also be won by prowess shown in military affairs: Beowulf received a magnificent sword from the Danish leader, Hrothgar, to reward his defeat of Grendel and Grendel's mother. Finally, a sword might also be given to the Anglo-Saxon warrior by a lord whose army he had joined.

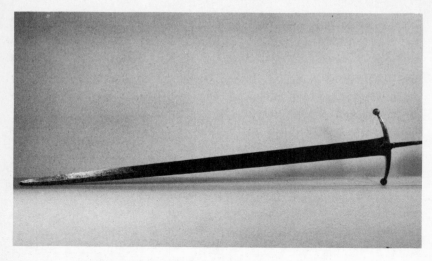

Fifteenth-century French sword. [From the Cleveland
Museum of Art collection.]

Once obtained, the sword became the warrior's constant companion. He carried it into the king's hall or at council, although it could never be drawn. He used it when swearing an oath, and it was the weapon employed for a duel. Of course, it was used in battle. At night it hung above the warrior's bed, and at his death, the sword would either be buried with him, or it would be passed on to his son or another close relative.[66]

The Anglo-Saxon sword was a carefully and intricately made weapon. Forged of pattern-welded steel of the finest ore, its fabrication often took an extremely long time, and was so cherished by its maker that he inscribed it with his name. First the smith, or an associated iron-worker, produced a strong bar of steel. This was accomplished a number of ways, differing, it seems, not with the desired strength of the weapon but with the personal preference of the maker. A bar of pattern-welded steel could be made by twisting a single strip of iron, by twisting a strip with filler rods, by twisting together three equal strips of iron, by twisting one main strip with two filler strips, by forging a twisted rod to close spiral grooves and then adding cutting edges, or by twisting a small central strip with larger filler strips. After this the steel bar was heated until red hot, then reduced in thickness by hammering. At the same time, the edges and a fuller (a groove down the center of the blade which decreased its weight but not its strength) were also shaped. The heating and hammering were repeated a number of times until the desired thickness was achieved. Once the fabrication was completed the sword would be ground, first by a rough grinding stone and then by finer stones and files, until a fine sharpness had been achieved. The crossguard, grip, and handle were added, and the sword polished. Modern attempts at replicating the Anglo-Saxon sword have shown also that it is extremely difficult to reproduce the high quality of this early workmanship, perhaps because the care taken in constructing the weapon is not understood by modern craftsmen.[67]

While Ellis Davidson's work is concerned solely with Anglo-Saxon swords, the social atmosphere which she found surrounding the possession of a sword existed everywhere throughout the early Middle Ages. The technology also differed little, and then only in purity of ore and not in quality of workmanship.

In Charlemagne's many capitularies which refer to weaponry, the sword is always prominent. When a warhorse was owned, so too was a sword; in fact in many sources the sword is reported to be the cavalry soldier's primary weapon. But while a new emphasis on ownership of the sword was present in Carolingian Europe, and the numbers of these weapons increased dramatically, the swords themselves had not changed much from earlier Frankish examples. Both the longsword and the sax continued to be carried, as attested to both in literary and archaeological sources, and both measured and were made the same as the earlier weapons. However, the one-handed sax began to disappear at the end of the eighth century.

The only change which seems to have been made to Carolingian swords was in the shape of the longsword blade. Earlier swords had edges which ran parallel for most of the length of the blade, converging only at the end to form a point. In the beginning of the ninth century, this construction was changed so that the blade's edges began to taper gradually from the hilt to the tip. This shifted the center of gravity closer to the sword grip and made the weapon more maneuverable and easier to handle in combat while at the same time not losing any strength in the blade itself.

Carolingian swords were almost always inscribed with the name of the maker and sometimes, for the most wealthy owners, the hilt was decorated with gold, silver, gems, and jewels. Probably the scabbards were made of wood and leather and also decorated, although none have survived, and they were hung on a sword-belt around the waist; earlier swords were hung either on a belt or from a baldrick across the back.[68]

Carolingian swords became well known throughout Europe; examples have been found everywhere from Iceland to the Holy Land and from Spain to Russia during the ninth and tenth centuries. They were particularly favored among the Vikings who, despite using the axe and spear more frequently as infantry weapons, prized the sword above all other offensive armaments.[69] Carolingian swords also set the technological standard for sword-making for several centuries, although this was mostly because of the large numbers which were then made rather than their comparative quality over earlier swords.[70] The swords on both sides of the Norman Conquest of England were Carolingian-influenced, either by direct diffusion or through the Vikings.[71] Similar swords were used in the Spanish Reconquista and the First Crusade.[72] In all cases the sword was primarily a cavalry weapon, to be used in close-combat, although infantry soldiers also could carry one if they could afford it.[73] The sword was the most expensive offensive armament.

From 800 to 1350 swords did not differ in construction from the Carolingian archetype. This was mostly because of the chain mail armor which they faced, armor which was most easily destroyed by using the sword as a slashing weapon. Thus, sword blades remained flat and light, with sharp edges emphasized rather than a point. Only the size of the blade, the size of the hilt, and the style of pommel, cross-guard, grip, and scabbard changed, although generally for no other reason than personal preference.[74]

With the fourteenth-century change in armor, from chain to plate, a change in sword fabrication was also needed. Plate armor easily resisted the slashing attacks of the Carolingian-style sword, but was more easily penetrated than chain mail had been. Thus the sword needed to be modified in order to take advantage of that handicap. It became a thrusting weapon, its point used more than its edge to attack an opponent. Swords of the late Middle

Ages became shorter and stiffer, often with reinforced, sharp points. Again, size of the blade and the hilt and design of pommel, cross-guard, grip, and scabbard differed according to the preference of each user.[75]

The *falchion*, a variation of the traditional longsword, was also introduced during the late Middle Ages. This was a short, single-edged weapon with a very broad, curved blade, shaped similar to a modern machete. It also was primarily an infantry weapon and was not nearly as popular a sword as the more traditional style.[76]

The importance of the sword did not diminish during the late Middle Ages. Numbers of swords grew—so much so that in 1457 at a War of the Roses muster in England swords were the second most numerous weapon tallied after the bow—and master swordsmen became proficient in the art of fencing, hiring themselves out as tutors or mercenaries. As gunpowder weaponry began to force further changes in armor during the fifteenth and sixteenth centuries, swords once again changed. As plate armor disappeared, swords became lighter. They were still a thrusting weapon, however, and thus the new sword (known as a *rapier*) became more like our modern foil or epee: thin, light, and flexible with an extremely sharp point.[77] The thick, heavy, awkward, but finely crafted medieval sword passed into memory.

The Mace

While Middle Eastern Stone Age humans had constructed a mace by attaching a stone to the end of a club, neither Germanic nor Celtic barbarian tribes had ever developed a similar weapon. They had been satisfied by the fire-hardened club alone, a weapon which they had used at least since the first century AD, if not earlier.[78] It is from this weapon the mace obviously developed, but beyond its evolutionary beginnings, little more can be determined about its origins. While the club is referred to frequently in early medieval artistic and literary sources, there is no indication that these clubs were specially modified by the addition of a separate head.[79]

The earliest indication of a mace separate from, although side by side with, a club is found in the *Bayeux Tapestry*. The Tapestry depicts several clubs being carried by the Normans and Anglo-

Saxons at Hastings, including one being used as a missile weapon; one of these is different from the rest in that it has a tri-colored head. Although primitive in its depiction, because of the difficulty of the art of weaving, it seems certain that this is meant to render a mace, and may in fact be showing the beginning of the transformation from the club to the mace.[80]

By the twelfth century, the club ceased to exist as a military armament, as mace replaced it as a battlefield weapon. Archaeological remains, of which there are several dating from the eleventh to the fifteenth centuries, have shown that mace heads were produced in a variety of shapes and sizes. Two styles in particular predominate. The first and earliest of the two was comprised of a head formed by a number of flanges or wings (generally seven) equally set around a tubular core and made sharp enough to penetrate chain mail armor. The second consisted of a knobbed head, less sharp but thicker than the flanged mace, with the purpose not of penetrating but of smashing shields or plate armor. Most maces of both styles were made in iron or steel, although some were constructed in bronze to lighten the weight of the weapon. All mace heads were attached to a wooden haft, although by the fourteenth century, some maces were being constructed completely in metal.[81]

Artistic and literary sources also establish the popularity of the mace as a weapon. In medieval art of all kinds, the mace is frequently seen. Often, this depiction is very crude, with some artists representing the mace as little more than a rock attached to the end of a stick, something that archaeology has shown to be fictitious. Other artists try to depict the rough and sharp edges of the mace heads.[82]

Literary sources are much more descriptive of the medieval mace. As it became the secondary weapon of the tournament melee, behind the lance, there are many good descriptions of the sounds and destructive capabilities of the mace in military action. The purpose of this weapon was well known to these authors, and they often emphasize its destructive capabilities. As Geoffrey Chaucer writes: "With mighty maces the bones they to-brest." He also records that a mace in combat "todashed" Troilus' shield.[83] But death and broken bones were the infrequent results of a mace attack. More often these resulted simply in a damaged or misshapen piece of armor. Even the great jouster, William Marshal, had to be extricated from his helm, crushed by his opponent's mace, on more than one occasion.[84]

By the end of the Middle Ages, the mace had become fairly sophisticated and often quite handsome, constructed not only in iron, steel, and bronze, but for ceremonial purposes in gold and silver as well. In the fourteenth and fifteenth centuries the most popular style of mace was that known as the "Gothic Mace." It was entirely made of metal and was generally 45 centimeters long weighing an average of 1275 grams, both shorter and lighter than earlier maces. The flanges of the head were thick and acutely pointed, allowing for some penetration, but most often its wielder concentrated on smashing an opponent's armor. The Gothic Mace was fitted with a distinct grip, patterned after a sword grip, thicker than the haft and made of fabric, leather, and wire. The grip had a pommel on the bottom and a guard at the top to keep the hand in place.[85]

One further note should be made concerning the medieval mace. It has always been the tradition that the mace was used, if not entirely created for use, by ecclesiastics in military affairs. Scholars supporting this idea have frequently pointed to the *Bayeux Tapestry* for support, where Odo, the Bishop of Bayeux and half-brother of William the Conqueror, is always depicted with a club in his hand. After all, are not ecclesiastics forbidden from spilling blood, something only the mace can guarantee?[86]

In reality, however, this seems to be more folklore than historical truth. Despite the fact that the mace, as well as every other medieval weapon, almost always "spilled" blood, there is no firm evidence that ecclesiastics did not, or even were not allowed to, carry a blood-spilling weapon. More than likely Odo of Bayeux carried a club or mace not as a weapon but as a symbol of office. The club, and later the mace, symbolized more than military prowess to the medieval warrior; it was, in fact, a symbol of his rulership or feudal nobility. The mace then was the precursor to the scepter. In the *Bayeux Tapestry* everyone who carries a club or mace, including Odo, does so to signify their leadership. Indeed, none, except for the one thrown at the Normans, is pictured as a weapon. In one scene, William the Conqueror is able to identify himself to his troops, who had thought that he had been slain, by raising his visor and grasping his club.[87]

The War Hammer

The medieval war hammer was not a widely used weapon. Probably because of this, it is absent from most written accounts, leaving only a few artistic sources and even fewer extant exemplars to give us an indication that it was used at all. The earliest artistic rendering of the war hammer dates from c.1250 when it is found in the hand of an anonymous English knight's effigy in the Malvern Priory Church. This is a short-hafted weapon with a square hammer head on one side and a short, slightly curved pick on the other.

This single example is unique for the thirteenth century. The next depiction does not appear for more than a hundred years when four can be seen in Spanish paintings dating c.1350-1500. The heads of these weapons are all similar to the English hammer, but two of them have long hafts, both carried by standing figures. This may indicate that the hammer, while not used often in battle, could be carried by both infantry (long-hafted hammers) and cavalry (short-hafted hammers).

The single extant medieval war hammer, dating from c.1450 and currently found in the Wallace Collection in London, differs little from these artistic renderings. The hammer head is still square in shape, although turned at a 45° angle to present a diamond-shaped front; the pick is short, slightly curved, and equal in length to the head. The head is also separate from the haft, which is of modern construction, and is attached to it by a cubical box of steel which is placed over the intersection of the haft and head. The haft may have been metal, but was probably wood, and its length cannot be determined.

While apparently not a popular medieval weapon, the war hammer became much more common in the sixteenth and seventeenth centuries, when its reputation as a chivalric armament caused an increase in production and use.[88]

The Staff-Weapon

The staff-weapon is a generic term which describes an entire category of offensive weapons. In its simplest form, the staff-weapon united the spear or lance with an axe, hammer, or mace to produce a long-hafted infantry weapon which combined the capabilities of a lance during a charge with those of the axe or mace in close-combat melee.

Although most of these weapons date from the late Middle Ages, some earlier evolutionary examples can be discovered. The earliest of these is found in a 977 Catalan document which refers to a *guisarme*, described as a long-hafted weapon with an extremely long, axe-shaped head.[89] A capital of the Church of St. Nectaire in France carved in the late eleventh or early twelfth century, depicts two Roman soldiers carrying long-hafted weapons, one of which is outfitted with an axe head and the other with, what David C. Nicolle describes as "a mysterious *glaive*-like weapon."[90] Five other portrayals of staff-weapons can be dated to the twelfth and thirteenth centuries: a wall painting from the Ermita de San Badilio in Aragon during the early twelfth century depicts a long-hafted trident or military pick carried by a horsed hunter; an illumination from Queen Melisende's Psalter made in the Kingdom of Jerusalem between 1131 and 1143 shows a long-hafted war flail; a carved doorway from San Miguel de Uncastillo in Aragon displays a ball-and-chain on a medium sized haft; a mosaic from the Cathedral of Monreale in Sicily dating from c.1180-90 depicts three long-hafted staff weapons, one with a head similar to the glaive mentioned above and two others with long, hooked blade heads; and, finally, an illumination from the *Roman de Tristan* made in France c.1260, portrays a long-hafted, elongated axe. All these weapons, with the exception of the trident, are infantry weapons, and all, even the trident and the ball-and-chain have later medieval descendants similar enough in size and shape to establish these renditions as early developments or experiments of the later medieval staff-weapons.[91]

In the early years of the fourteenth century, infantry-based armies began to witness their first substantial and constant victories over cavalry-based armies. The Flemings defeated the French at Courtrai in 1302 and at Arques in 1303; the Scots defeated the English at Loudon Hill in 1307 and at Bannockburn in 1314; and the Swiss defeated the Austrians at Mortgarten in 1315 and at Laupen in 1339. Although these victories were not determined by weapons alone—they necessitated a large amount of bravery in the face of a cavalry charge by heavily armed knights atop well-bred and well-trained warhorses, as well as battlefield tactics such as the construction of natural impediments to the charge—the long-hafted weapons which the infantry used at these battles, and the fact that more and more improved long-hafted weapons would continue to be needed was recognized. This led ultimately to the development of many different staff-weapons in the next few centuries.

The most prominent was the *halberd*. In essence, a halberd was the combination of an axe, similar to the Danish Axe, and a spear. Its head consisted of a sharp spear-like point or spike on top with an equally sharp axe head attached beneath it; sometimes a curved pike was added to the back of the axe head. This was then affixed to a long haft, measuring between 1.67 and 2.1 meters in length, by two or four long steel straps forged together with the head which ran down the haft for as much as a meter.[92]

First mentioned in a Swiss poem written by Konrad von Würzburg, the halberd continued to be the most popular late medieval infantry staff-weapon. It also generated several variations. These included the *Ahlspiess*, which was a medium-hafted thrusting weapon with a long quadrangular spike mounted onto its end; the *bardiche* or *vouge* which had a longer, more narrow axe head, the ends of which curved back towards and were sometimes attached to the haft; the *bill* or *billhook* which added a number of spikes and lugs protruding from the blade on all sides; the *chauve-souris*, *couseque*, *partisan*, and *rawcon* which combined a spear head with angular side blades; the *glaive* or *guisarme* which was a large, sharply pointed, single-edged sword blade attached to a long haft; and a *lochaber axe* which was a Scottish weapon similar to both the halberd and the billhook.[93]

A second prominent late medieval staff-weapon was the *pole-axe*. The pole-axe was similar to the halberd and was probably derived from it; it too combined a spear with an axe, although its axe head was generally much smaller than the halberd's. But the pole-axe also added a war hammer to the staff weapon, producing an armament with three offensive capabilities: the point

Fifteenth-century halberds. [From the Tower of London
Armouries Collection.]

Medieval Military Technology

could be used as a spear against a cavalry or infantry charge, the
hammer could smash armor, and the axe could penetrate it. All
other elements, the haft and the method of attaching the head to
the haft, were the same as the halberd.

The pole-axe was developed early in the fourteenth century,
at which time it was little more than an alternative weapon to the
halberd. But in the late fourteenth and fifteenth centuries, it was
adopted as the chief weapon of the dismounted knight who was
accustomed to meeting other dismounted knights in combat and
therefore highly prized the offensive capabilities of the pole-axe.[94]

A third staff-weapon of the late Middle Ages should be mentioned not because of its prominence, as it was used far less than
either the halberd or pole-axe, but because of its uniqueness. The
goedendag combined the spear not with an axe, but with a mace.
Strictly a Flemish weapon, the goedendag, which translates as
"good-day" or "hello," was featured in their early fourteenth-century warfare, and was credited by some French chroniclers as the
reason for the Flemish victory at the battle of Courtrai. It was
employed by the infantry first to pull the French cavalry soldiers
from their horses (using the spear part of the weapon) and then
to crush bones and skulls (using the mace part).[95]

The goedendag saw very limited service, and then only by
the Flemings who themselves abandoned it by the beginning of
the fifteenth century. However, it may have inspired several later
staff-weapons—the Morning Star, the Holy Water Sprinkler, and
the Military Flail—all of which combined the spear with the mace.
The Holy Water Sprinkler and the Military Flail attached their
mace heads to the haft by a chain. These weapons were most
popular during the sixteenth and seventeenth centuries.[96]

A final staff-weapon of importance in the late Middle Ages
was the Military Fork. Little more than a pitchfork, the military
fork consisted of a number of sharp prongs (generally two or
three) which were used to pierce armor. Most also had two down-
turned hooks which could be used to snag a vulnerable seam in
the armor and bring a horseman off his mount or a soldier from
a battlement.[97]

The Sling

Both the hand-held and staff sling were very popular missile weapons in the ancient world. However, the sling seems to have been unknown to the barbarians. It did continue in use among Muslim armies,[98] but there is little evidence for its use in Christian Europe, including Byzantium.

There are very few literary or artistic references to the medieval sling, and most which do exist refer either to ancient or Muslim usage or to the story of David and Goliath.[99] For instance, the sling is listed as a weapon in the laws of Justinian, written in sixth-century Byzantium, but only in a reference which specifies weapons mentioned by Xenophon, who lived in the fourth century BC.[100] It is likewise the answer to one of Aldhelm's riddles, composed in Anglo-Saxon England sometime in the seventh or early eighth centuries, but almost certainly only refers to the weapon used by David to slay Goliath.[101] Finally, Chaucer mentions a staff-sling held by a giant facing Sir Thopas as well as a number of simple slings in his story of Troilus and Criseyde, again referring to the ancient use of the weapon.[102]

Similarly, of the five artistic sources which depict the sling in use, one is an illustration of the fight between David and Goliath, and three show its use by Muslim soldiers against Christians.[103] Only one, found in a manuscript illumination of the *Historia Anglorum* of Matthew Paris made in England c.1255, can be said to picture a sling used by a European soldier. This illumination portrays two staff-slings in the hands of naval soldiers who are operating them in an attack of a coastal fortification.[104] This may be indicative of a continued, but somewhat hidden, use of the sling in medieval warfare. If so, naval combat may have been the perfect place for the sling, both because of its accuracy as a weapon and because it would not suffer the same loss of effectiveness if wet as a bowstring might.

The Bow

A legal document of the reign of Edward II (1307-27) described the three types of bows prominent in England at the time. The most prominent was the longbow, which had an average length of two ells (2.3 meters), a thickness of four thumbs (10 centimeters) and could discharge a "clotharrow" a meter long. It was made of yew, either imported from Spain or grown in England, and was shaped in a characteristic D-shape before stringing. The second was known as a "Turkish bow." This was a composite bow of shorter length, one-and-a-half ells (1.7 meters), which fired a shorter, barbed "wolfarrow." It was made of yew, horn and glue, with its two arms bent forward, against the way they should be curved. The third was known as an "elm bow," denoting the wood used for its construction. Its length is not mentioned but was probably shorter than either the long or the Turkish bows. It discharged a barbed "Scottish arrow."[105]

Although written in the early fourteenth century, this document adequately describes all the bows used in the Middle Ages. The bow simply did not go through the same technological changes that other medieval weapons did. Indeed, the three bows referred to in the document were probably known at the time of the barbarian invasions and were still being used at the close of the Middle Ages.

There is some question among historians about which barbarian tribes used the bow, and how much they used it, at the time of their conquest into the Roman Empire. Ancient authors claimed that the Visigoths were proficient archers, the first to use the bow and the best at it, a claim which the large number of arrowheads found in Visigothic grave sites has confirmed. They carried a Turkish bow, which shot iron-tipped arrows and was frequently discharged from horseback, although it is apparent that the weapon was secondary to the spear in battle.[106] The Huns too were proficient horse archers, avoiding open battle but using the bow for raids and skirmishes against light cavalry.[107]

On the other hand, the Ostrogoths, Franks, Angles, and Saxons, although employing the weapon, did not use it as often as the other barbarians. The Franks preferred the throwing axe as a missile weapon, although a large number of arrowheads have been found in Frankish grave sites, while the Ostrogoths held the bow in such low esteem that Totila, the king of the Ostrogoths during the sixth-century Byzantine invasion of Italy, refused to allow his army to use bows against the invaders.[108] As for the Angles and Saxons, grave sites in England show that they did indeed use the bow, although the small number of arrowheads found in these graves—only 1.1% of Anglo-Saxon warriors' graves contain arrowheads—proves that the weapon was not valued as much as their other offensive armaments.[109] The fact that an internal clue needed to be given to solve an Anglo-Saxon riddle on the bow further confirms this weapon's lack of popularity among those people. (The first word of the riddle, when read backwards, gives an earlier form of the Anglo-Saxon word for bow, *boga*.) Still, the riddle provides an interesting description of the early medieval bow and bears repeating here:

> *Agob*'s my name, if you work it out;
> I'm a fair creature fashioned for battle.
> When I bend, and shoot a deadly shaft
> from my stomach, I desire only to send
> that poison as far away as possible.
> When my lord, who devised this torment for me,
> releases my limbs, I become longer
> and, bent upon slaughter, spit out
> that deadly poison I swallowed before.
> No man's parted easily from the object
> I describe; if he's struck by what flies
> from my stomach, he pays for its poison
> with his strength—speedy atonement for his life.
> I'll serve no master when unstrung, only when
> I'm cunningly notched. Now guess my name.[110]

The Vikings also seem to have had a similar disregard for the bow as a battlefield weapon. Although they used in battle and for hunting, as established by literary and archaeological sources, the bow always played a minor role in Viking military tactics, far less substantial than either the axe or the spear.[111]

By the time of Charlemagne and the establishment of the Carolingian Empire with its professional feudal army, the bow returned to favor, with an importance not previously seen among the Franks. This might have come, as François Ganshof and Simon Coupland insist, as a result of Charlemagne's wars against the Avars and Slavs, tribes which had continued to use the bow since ancient times; their proficiency in the weapon, although not decisive, may have inspired the Carolingians to adopt it. In a decree known as the Aachen Capitulary, pronounced in 802-03, Charlemagne ordered that the bow should become the army's chief infantry weapon, with infantry soldiers ordered to carry it, a spare string and twelve arrows (the contents of one quiver). He followed this in 806 with a decree demanding that each horseman also should be equipped with a bow as well as several quivers of arrows. Both decrees were further confirmed in an 811 capitulary.

The earlier Franks had used D-shaped longbows, perhaps as long as two meters. To these were added the Turkish bows adopted from the Avars and Slavs, with the result that both bows were probably common in the Carolingian army. There was also inconsistency in Carolingian arrows as both barbed and non-barbed arrowheads have been found. The quiver was probably made of wood and leather and was covered with a domed lid to protect the arrowheads although no archaeological exemplar can confirm this; a long strap allowed it to be slung across the archer's back.[112]

The bow had another resurgence in popularity during the eleventh and twelfth centuries. In Spain, the Christian "reconquistadors" had units of mounted archers who, firing in a rearwards position on their horses, discharged arrows from their light, short bows, a tactic which had been adopted from their Muslim enemies. Also Muslim-influenced were the Turkish composite bows, used by the Spanish Christians, and the long, coarse, and clumsy arrows topped by broad, triangular, and sometimes barbed arrowheads, commonly fired from these bows. Infantry archery units were also employed by the Spanish Christians, their weapon being similar, although heavier, to that used by mounted archers.[113]

In France at this time, the bow also played a major military role, with infantry archer units established which were separate from the regular infantry units. Among the French subjects most impressed with the weapon were the Normans; William the Conqueror took several archers to England in 1066. Tradition holds that Harold, the Anglo-Saxon king facing William, died when struck in the eye by a Norman arrow at the battle of Hastings. The *Bayeaux Tapestry* depicts the Normans, all infantry, using a short bow which they drew to their chest to discharge a relatively short arrow. Quivers are attached to their right hips, and they are wearing no armor.[114] The Normans also used archers in their eleventh-century conquests of Sicily.[115]

By the twelfth century, continental European armies were discarding their short bows and adopting crossbows instead. Only in Spain and England would the bow continue to be used for warfare. Spanish soldiers, both infantry and cavalry, would continue to use the short Turkish bow until the end of the Middle Ages. The English too used the short bow and with it achieved several successes in twelfth- and thirteenth-century warfare, most notably at the battle of the Standard fought in 1138 when the English archers decimated the charging Scottish line. By the middle of the thirteenth century, the bow had become so important in England that the Assize of Arms of 1242 named archers as the second most important class of soldiers after the mounted knight.[116]

In fighting with or against the Welsh sometime during the thirteenth century, the English encountered a bow which made them discard their traditional short bow. This was constructed in a similar way and with similar wood as the traditional English bow, but it was longer, and its string was drawn to the ear instead of to the chest, allowing for the discharge of a longer arrow. The range of the arrow extended almost twice as far, to 400 meters, as an arrow discharged from a short bow and delivered a much greater ballistic impact. Arrows fired from the longbow were capable even of piercing chain mail armor at a distance of 200 meters, a feat impossible at any distance by an arrow fired from a short bow. The English army quickly adopted the longbow, recruiting for their army large numbers of Welsh and Cheshire archers proficient in the weapon.[117]

The longbow significantly changed English strategy and tactics, so much so, some historians insist, that England was to gain many victories solely because of its use in warfare. But this is a very disputed point. It seems evident that the longbow altered English warfare from the late thirteenth until the end of the fifteenth century. In 1298, for example, Edward I took a troop of over 10,000 archers with him on his conquest of Scotland (a ratio of three archers to one mounted man-at-arms), an extremely large number in comparison with numbers of archers included in English armies previous to this time. And he was victorious. Also victorious was the English army, again including a large contingent of archers, which faced the Scots at Dupplin Moor in 1332 and at Halidon Hill in 1333. Finally, English archers participated in the decisive victories over the French army at the battles of Sluys (1340), Morlaix (1942), Crécy (1346), Poitiers (1356), and Agincourt (1415). Were not all of these victories brought to the English army because their opponents were unable to face the longbow arrows, fired at a rate of ten flights per minute "like snow on the battlefield?"

Such has been the conclusion of English historians for centuries.[118] Indeed, so much value was placed on the victorious longbow that some English generals in the sixteenth century were reluctant to accept the handgun in the English army, believing that it could never duplicate the successes of the longbow.[119] There certainly seems to be sufficient evidence to support such a theory, especially as the French who faced the English at these battles tried in vain both to buy Scottish mercenaries skilled in the weapon and to train their own soldiers to use it.[120]

However, recently two military historians, John Keegan and Claude Gaier, have cast doubt upon the thesis of English longbow "invincibility." In particular, Keegan, in a study of the battle of Agincourt, has shown that the tactical use of the English archers at this battle, and, for that matter, in all of the battles since the beginning of the fourteenth century, with the longbowmen either skirmishing in a "shoot-out" with their opponents' archers or flanking their infantry troops, could not have caused the losses of life attributed to them by historians. In fact, there is little evidence that the longbowmen, needing to fire with an extremely steep arc to cover the distance between themselves and the enemy and thus unable to penetrate their opponents' armor, did any more damage than the killing of a few horses and the wounding of even fewer men. While the archers did not kill many men, however, they did harass their enemy to such an extent that they broke into a disordered charge, a charge narrowed by continual flanking fire until it reached and stopped at the solid infantry line. This then caused the victory—not the archery fire itself, but the archery-induced disordered charge into a solid infantry line, which was neither penetrated nor defeated.[121]

Whether or not the longbow was decisive becomes an irrelevant point at the end of the fifteenth century when England began to suffer an archery shortage. The kingdom had in the past two centuries weathered several shortages of bows and arrows: on one occasion, the Black Prince was compelled to order the arrest and forced labor of all fletchers in Cheshire in 1356 until his supply of arrows was recouped. The supply of bows and arrows had declined from a total of 11,000 bows and 23,600 sheaves of arrows (each sheaf with 24 arrows) in 1360 to a total of no bows and only 1,000 sheaves of arrows in 1381. This time England did not face a shortage of material but of trained manpower. When Edward IV asked for 20,000 archers to be raised in 1453, he was forced to drop his request to 13,000 archers, and even this number proved too high for the stock of skilled English longbowmen.[122] And despite proscribing the playing of football and golf in 1456 until archers once again became skilled with the longbow, there would never again be either the quantity or quality of longbow archers which had once proved to be so effective in battle.[123]

By the beginning of the fifteenth century another reality of military technology became apparent. The future of missile warfare was not to be archery, but gunpowder weaponry. By this time gunpowder weapons had become small enough to be carried by hand into battle, and before the end of the century, handgunners began to take their place in the ranks of almost all continental European armies. Archers continued to be a part of these same armies, but their numbers began to decline as the numbers of handgunners rose. By the end of the sixteenth century, archery was no longer a part of most military forces.

The Crossbow

The crossbow was a mechanical bow which became the standard archery weapon in continental Europe during the central and late Middle Ages. The basic construction of the weapon was a small bow attached to a stock which provided a groove for the bolt and handle. The bow string was held in place ready for release by a trigger mechanism. The earliest trigger configuration was primitive but effective: a nut, generally made of horn or some other hard surface, protruded from the top of the stock, over which the bowstring would be placed, and was disengaged by squeezing a lever attached to the bottom of the stock. In these early crossbows, the string could be drawn by hand, or with the aid of a simple claw which would be hooked over the string and attached to the bowman's belt. As the bowman stood up, the string would be drawn.[124]

The crossbow was more powerful and more accurate than either a short or longbow, and it could be prepared in a shooting position ahead of time and held there with little effort. On the other hand, loading the weapon took much longer than did the regular bow, no matter what the expertise of the crossbowman was. It was also heavier and required more space in the ranks than did the non-mechanical bow.[125]

The crossbow probably descended from the ancient Greek *gastraphretes* (or "belly bow"), and was also used both in Rome and China. However, it does not seem to have become popular in western Europe until the eleventh century, perhaps because the barbarian invaders were not interested in its technology. Some historians have argued that the crossbow was used, albeit sparingly, by the Franks throughout the early Middle Ages as a defense against sieges. If this thesis is not accepted, however, it is difficult to understand how it was diffused to the western Europeans in the eleventh century. It seems certain that it was not known to the Muslims nor the Byzantines. Anna Comnena, the daughter of the Byzantine emperor, seemed completely overwhelmed by the weapon, which was carried by the First Crusaders. This is her intricate description of the crossbow:

> The crossbow is a weapon of the barbarians, absolutely unknown to the Greeks. In order to stretch it one does not pull the string with the right hand while pushing the bow with the left away from the body; this instrument of war, which shoots missiles to an enormous distance, has to be stretched by lying almost on one's back; each foot is pressed forcibly against the half-circles of the bow and the two hands tug at the bow, pulling it with all one's strength towards the body. At the mid-point of the string is a groove, shaped like a cylinder cut in half and fitted to the string itself; it is about the length of a fair-sized arrow, extending from the string to the centre of the bow. Along this groove, arrows of all kinds are shot. They are very short, but extremely thick with a heavy iron tip. In the shooting the string exerts tremendous violence and force, so that the missiles wherever they strike do not rebound; in fact they transfix a shield, cut through a heavy iron breastplate and resume their

flight on the far side, so irresistible and violent is the discharge. An arrow of this type has been known to make its way right through a bronze statue, and when shot at the wall of a very great town its point either protruded from the inner side or buried itself in the wall and disappeared altogether. Such is the crossbow, a truly diabolical machine. The unfortunate man who is struck by it dies without feeling the blow; however strong the impact he knows nothing of it.[126]

The Church, however, did not have the same affection for the weapon as did the soldiers. Because of its brutality in war, both Pope Urban II (1096-97) and the Second Lateran Council (1139) condemned its use among Christians. Still, this condemnation was rarely heeded, and by the end of the century the crossbow had become quite popular in Europe. In 1200, the Church relaxed its condemnation of the weapon, allowing its use against infidels, pagans, and Cathars, and in the case of a "just war." King Richard I of England was especially taken by the weapon and used it widely; tradition holds that it was he who introduced it to the French, who quickly adopted it. Ironically, Richard himself was killed by a crossbow bolt.[127]

After the twelfth century, use of the crossbow increased markedly especially in continental Europe where most kings and nobles used crossbowmen in their armies, frequently employing mercenary crossbowmen (principally Gascons and Genoese) when they failed to recruit sufficient numbers of these troops from among their own subjects. Crossbowmen were used tactically at the beginning of a battle and on the flanks as harassers of opposing forces.[128]

By the late Middle Ages the crossbow had increased in use and efficiency. The composite crossbow, made of horn, sinew, and glue, which was in use by the thirteenth century, added to the flexibility and therefore to the power of the earlier bows.[129] Other additions to the stock enabled the bow to be strung with greater tension, increasing immensely the power of the pull.

The most common of these additions was a stirrup attached to the end of the stock through which a foot could be placed. This allowed the bowman to use his leg power to draw the string.

Another device added to the stock was the *"goat's foot" lever*, called such because of its similarity to a cloven goat's foot. This lever, which pivoted on a pin, had claws at one end that fixed under the string. As the lever pivoted, the string was drawn.

A further addition, the windlass, was introduced in the fourteenth century. This used pulleys, attached at the butt-end of the stock to a winding device which, when hooked onto the bowstring and wound, would draw it to the trigger. The windlass could quickly draw the string, in only 12 seconds, even though it had a pull of 545 kilograms. (An average longbow pull was only 23 kilograms.)

The final late medieval modification to the crossbow's loading mechanism was the cranequin. This was a sophisticated mechanism which required a metal ratchet bar and a winder that worked by meshing cogs. The ratchet bar's claws fit over the string, and when the handle was wound, the ratchet bar was moved away from the bow, drawing the string with it. The cranequin required very little strength to draw the crossbow string, but it was slower than the windlass, needing 35 seconds to load.[130]

Improvements to the trigger mechanism and to the bolt also added to the efficiency of the crossbow. By the thirteenth century the trigger had become shaped like a duck, the beak of which was the tip which locked the nut into position. As the trigger was pressed upwards toward the stock, the beak was lifted so that the nut would revolve into the bow and the string would be released.[131]

The bolt was made of ash or yew, with a flattened or tapered butt. Goose wing feathers aided the flight. The head was small, sharp, and diamond shaped. Extant examples measure about 40 centimeters in length. Aiming was facilitated by the attachment of a strip of wood with notches in it which was fixed to the butt-end of the stock as a backsight; the right thumb of the crossbowman fit into one of the notches, calibrated for distance, and he aimed by looking down it and along the bolt.[132]

Other areas of military technology were also affected by the rise of the crossbow. By the early thirteenth century, castles were designed with openings for crossbows, allowing for a more systematic flanking fire against besiegers.[133] And ships were also outfitted with the weapon, which greatly improved their ability to engage in naval warfare.[134]

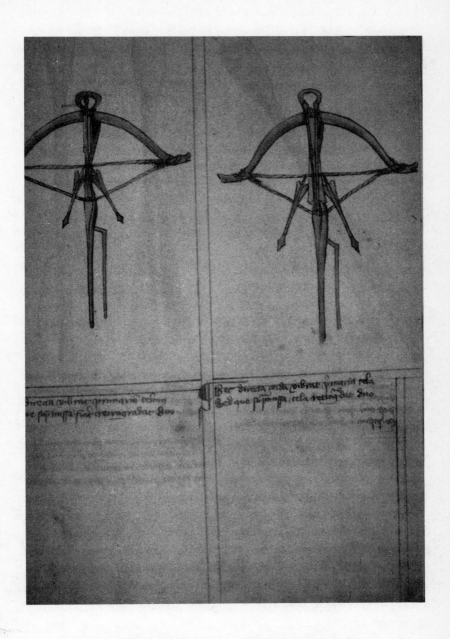

Crossbow found in Conrad Kyeser's *Bellifortis* (c.1400).
[From Kyeser (1967).]

By the fifteenth century, the crossbow was made entirely in steel. This increased its power, giving it a greater range and ballistic impact than any other bow known in the Middle Ages. Estimates as to the range vary from between 370 and 500 meters, with sufficient force to pierce even the best plate armor.[135]

Variations of the crossbow included: the *crossbow à jalet*, used to discharge pebbles and lead balls; the *spring-bow*, a hunting or assassin's trap; and the *crossbow à croc*, which was attached onto a wooden mount.[136]

It should also be noted that although the crossbow was normally an infantry weapon, on at least three occasions the service of mounted crossbowmen is reported: when Philip Augustus of France used them in his early thirteenth-century wars against King John of England; in 1238 when Frederick II of Germany employed a corps of mercenary Hungarian mounted crossbowmen; and in 1239 when Pope Gregory IX used Provençal mounted crossbowmen as defense against the Lombard League.[137]

By the late fourteenth century, gunpowder weapons were beginning to replace crossbows in defense of castles and sometimes on the battlefield; a decline in the skill of shooting a crossbow also became apparent. Steps were taken to halt this decline—in France, Charles V in 1384 prohibited the playing of any game except with a bow or crossbow, and Charles VII in the 1440s set up companies of franc archers who used the weapon—but ultimately the crossbow did not survive the late fifteenth century influx of handguns, and by 1550 the weapon had disappeared from the battlefield.[138]

The Warhorse

While the medieval warhorse itself cannot be called a technological device, and therefore may be out of place in a study such as this, many of the apparatus used to breed and outfit the warhorse, without which its importance might have been less, were indeed products of technology. Thus a brief discussion of the warhorse is warranted.

The warhorse was perhaps the most important military equipment owned by a medieval cavalry soldier. The ownership of a horse not only indicated his military status, but the expense of ownership and the upkeep also established his role within medieval feudal society.

The horse as a bearer of soldiers was known to ancient society, but because of the nature and limitations of its harness, cavalry in ancient military strategy was secondary to the infantry. When cavalry was present on the battlefield, its role was one of skirmishing with the enemy's cavalry or of providing mobile missile fire in an effort to harass an opponent's infantry troops. The horse then needed to be relatively fast, but not particularly well-trained or even well-bred.

Such was the case at the time of the invasion of the Roman Empire. The Roman horsed troops, much smaller in number than their infantry counterparts, were used in just such a manner: not as a front-line force, but as a means of transportation and harassment. Most of the barbarians used their cavalry in a similar way. The Visigoths, Lombards, Burgundians, Vandals, and Ostrogoths all seem to have duplicated the cavalry strategy of their opponents.[139] Others, most notably the Huns, Avars, and Slavs, placed more emphasis on the horse in their warfare, as they preferred the swift raid to open battle.[140] Finally, some—the Franks, Angles, and Saxons—preferred to use their cavalry simply as a royal bodyguard, without involving them directly in combat.[141] The Vikings too restricted their use of cavalry in battle.[142]

Heavy cavalry began to influence the conduct of medieval warfare in the eighth and ninth centuries when the early Carolingian rulers—Charles Martel, Pippin II, and Charlemagne—instituted laws establishing more and better cavalry units and incorporating these into their forces.[143] By the eleventh century, as represented by the Crusades and the conquest of England, heavy cavalry had become the dominant arm of every medieval army. This could not have come about except for the introduction of three technological advances: the stirrup, the nailed horseshoe, and the saddle with pommel and cantel.

The first major technological advance, the introduction of the stirrup into western Europe, came at the beginning of the eighth century. The stirrup (which will be discussed at greater length in a following chapter) was a simple device, the mere addition of a rigid wood, rope or metal tread at the end of a strap descending from the saddle into which the horseman's feet would be placed.

Its impact on cavalry warfare was far greater than its simple technology. Before the introduction of the stirrup, the cavalry soldier was forced to stay onto and direct his horse by pressing his knees into the horse's sides. As can be imagined, this limited both the horseman's ability to ride his steed and his capability to effectively wield weapons while atop it. The stirrup increased the cavalry soldier's stability, as well as adding new dimensions to his fighting tactics; he could now thrust the lance with more power and direction, and, later, he was able to couch it under his arm, using the force of both himself and his horse to "shock" his enemy.[144]

A second technological device which increased the importance of the medieval warhorse was the invention of the nailed horseshoe in c.890. This invention was of limited effect in dryer climates, as in Spain, Italy, and the Holy Land, where the horses' hooves remained hard and capable of galloping over even rocky terrain. But in the wetter northern European lands, where hooves became soft, quickly worn, and sometimes broken, the addition of nailed shoes meant that a horse could travel greater distances at greater speeds over even the most rocky terrains without injury. Battles could be fought at any time of year and over any type of terrain.[145]

The final major technological innovation which improved the medieval warhorse was the invention at the beginning of the twelfth century of the saddle with high pommel and cantel. Prior to this, the saddle had been made of rigid flat leather which replaced the ancient horse-blanket and riding cushions but provided little more lateral stability. It only prevented the rider from falling off his horse, but did nothing to help him in combat. With the addition of a high wraparound cantel, which sat against the rider's back and prevented him from being thrown over the horse's rump, and the addition of an equally high pommel, which protected the rider's genitals and lower stomach as well as keeping him from being thrown over his horse's head, the cavalry soldier was now able to use the full power of his horse to provide a mounted shock lance attack without being toppled from his steed.[146]

At the same time that these innovations were changing the rider's ability to stay onto and fight with his mount, modifications in breeding were changing the horse itself. In the early Middle Ages, there was no need for a specially bred horse. With changes in harness, as well as with the increasing weight of armor, a better bred, stronger, and heavier horse was needed. Known after the twelfth century as a *destrier*, the horse also had to be capable of being trained for either the tournament or the battlefield (rarely would a knight use the same horse for both duties).[147] This meant the selective breeding of a warhorse from Bactrian or Arabian stock through an intricate process over a long period of time, sometimes several years. Eventually this produced a horse, 17 hands tall (173 centimeters), with strong bones and a strong, short back (medieval horses had conventionally measured 12-13 hands in height—122-132 centimeters), one capable of carrying a heavily armored soldier into a battle or a joust.[148]

From the time of the introduction of the first heavy cavalry units, sometime between the eighth and the eleventh centuries, until 1300, victory in nearly every military engagement was tied to heavy cavalry and its tactical use of mounted shock combat. Even after the infantry victories of the early fourteenth century, the mounted warrior, known as a knight in most histories, still remained the dominant part of every medieval army.[149] Off the battlefield, among the noble (or chivalric) class of Europe, the warhorse also played an important role. A knight was expected to own not only his horses for military engagement, but also a number of large, expensive horses on which he rode during jousts and tournaments.[150] In both instances, this would continue to be the case well into the early modern era.

The Arms Industry and Trade

In many ways an attempt to trace the history of the medieval arms industry and trade is an impossible task. Few archival documents on either the industry of, or trade in, weapons survive before the end of the Middle Ages, and even these are incomplete and thus cannot be trusted to give a general impression of what constituted the late medieval arms commerce. Further problems arise in trying to trace the origins of extant weapons, as there was little standardization among any offensive armament during the Middle Ages. Finally, it should also be noted that even if a weapon carried the name of a town (for example, a Damascus steel sword), it did not necessarily mean that the weapon was made there. Indeed, more Damascus swords may have been forged in Spain than in Syria.[151]

It is well known that the Roman Empire had its own centers of arms production which made all weapons in a very standardized way for all the Empire's soldiers. These centers either fell into disuse or were destroyed by the invading barbarians.[152] From then on for nearly a millennium there was no attempt at centralizing the arms industry. Even the great Charlemagne with his numerous capitularies establishing new armament policies did not recognize the need for either standards or centralization. Indeed, because of the industry's diversity, he had to decree extra laws to prohibit arms dealers from selling their wares abroad, a futile effort as swords made by Carolingian smiths quickly made their way throughout all of Europe and even into Russia and the Holy Land. A similar lack of arms trade regulation can be seen in Henry II's 1181 Assize of Arms, where arms for all individuals were regulated by law, but without an indication of where or from whom these were to be purchased.[153]

During these centuries, while the smelting of ore took place at a central location,[154] weapons were manufactured on local forges by local smiths for local warriors. Size, shape, and style were all the personal preference of the maker or the bearer. And while it is true that some smiths, particularly sword smiths, such as Ingelred and Ughtred, became so famous that their signed wares were desired throughout Europe, these individuals were only a very small minority of the number of smiths forging weapons during this time.[155]

However, there are a few conclusions about the arms industry and trade which can be made. First, large stockpiles of weapons acquired by kings especially during the central and late Middle Ages may indicate that there was in many royal courts a centralized arms industry or at least a central arms purchasing bureau.[156]

Second, when towns or regions needed arms, they were able to purchase the services of arms manufacturers who may have wandered from contract to contract fabricating arms for whoever would pay them. For example, the city council of Nuremburg in the late fifteenth century hired a large number of fletchers and smiths to manufacture weapons for the defense of the town.[157]

Third, beyond these itinerant arms makers, there were also a few areas in which an arms industry flourished, supplying all regions of Europe with their weapons. Sometimes the industry was diversified, offering all varieties of arms. For example, according to an extremely detailed and elaborate study made by Claude Gaier, this was the situation with the arms industry in the southern Low Countries, primarily in the region along the Meuse River. At other times, however, a region's industry specialized in one weapon. Eustace Deschamps in the late fourteenth century made a poetic complaint against the arms industry in which he cursed not only the anonymous makers of weapons, but also those in Bordeaux who made daggers, in Clermont who made swords, in Milan who made crossbows, in Flanders who made pikes, and in Damme who made maces.[158]

Fourth, there was an active arms trade which persisted throughout the Middle Ages. This can be seen not only in the large number of weapons whose origin can be traced to far from where they were eventually found, but also in the late medieval documents which establish the existence of an extensive arms trade. As well, towns such as fourteenth-century Avignon served often as markets for this weapons trade, with buyers coming there to purchase weapons made everywhere throughout Europe.[159]

Armor

As soon as prehistoric humans invented weapons for use in battle, they also invented protective garments to defend themselves against opponent's attacks. Evidence of this early armor can be found in cave paintings where distinctive raiment appears on some prehistoric soldiers, most often on archers. Although it is difficult to determine specific details of this early armor from such a medium, some of these garments seem to be protective apparel, made of a coarse material, probably bark or leather, which covered the breast, legs, and genitals.[160]

The veracity of this early armor is disputed—with some historians and anthropologists regarding this apparel as nothing more than shoulder capes, loincloths, and knee-bands—but what is indisputable is that by the time of the Babylonian and Egyptian civilizations, soldiers had begun to concern themselves as much with their defensive, as with their offensive, armament. Those who came into direct conflict with an opponent often covered their breasts, heads, legs and even sometimes their arms with metallic (in this case bronze) armor. As well, most also carried a portable armament which could be wielded to protect a specifically targeted area of the body. Known as a shield, this armor, which was generally made of wood and leather, became the most common defensive armament for the ancient soldier. It was used not only by the regular, front-line soldier, who added its protection to the other armor, but also by the auxiliary soldier, who often carried it as the sole means of defense.

The ancient Greeks placed a particular importance on their armor. Going into battle, most ancient Greek soldiers would be outfitted with a bronze helmet, which covered the head, most of the neck, the cheeks, and the nose, and which also was topped by a plume denoting rank; bronze greaves, which covered the shins and calves; a breastplate, which consisted of front and back pieces of bronze connected at the shoulder; and, most importantly, a large shield.

The shield was wooden, rounded, and concave, and generally measured one meter in diameter, although the size could vary depending on the length and strength of the bearer's arm. Initially, it was also rimmed with a bronze strip around the outer edge, probably to protect against rot, although by the fifth century BC this had been replaced by a solid, thin sheet of bronze which covered the entire shield and was emblazoned by the insignia of the bearer's military unit. While it is not known what wood was used to construct the ancient Greek shield, it is generally thought that it was a hardwood, making the shield a particularly heavy piece of armor, perhaps weighing as much as 7.3 kilograms. To keep from fatiguing the bearer, the ancient Greek shield was outfitted with a special arm and handgrip which distributed the weight along the entire left arm instead of compacting it at the hand or wrist alone. This also meant that it was nearly impossible to remove the shield in the midst of battle.[161]

Not only did the ancient Greeks prize their armor for its protective capabilities, but they also valued its artistic beauty and skill of construction. The best armor was said to have been constructed by the god Hephaestus at a forge fired by the volcanoes inside Mount Olympus, and it contained artistic designs which promised the gods' favor. Such is the description of Agamemnon's armor at the siege of Troy:

> Atreides [Agamemnon] in a loud voice gave his troops the order
> to prepare for battle, and himself put on his gleaming bronze.
> He began by tying round his legs a pair of splendid greaves
> which were fitted with silver clips for the ankles. Next he put
> on his breast the cuirass.... It was made of parallel strips, ten
> of dark blue enamel, twelve of gold, and twenty of tin. On
> either side three snakes rose up in coils toward the opening for
> the neck. Their iridescent enamel made them look like the rain-

bow that the Son of Cronus [Zeus] hangs on a cloud as a portent to mankind below.... Then he took up his manly and man-covering shield, a nobly decorated piece, with its concentric rings of bronze, and twenty knobs of tin making a white circle round the dark enamel boss. The central figure on it was a grim Gorgon's head with awe-compelling eyes, and on either side of her, Panic and Rout were depicted. It was fitted with a silver baldric, round which a writhing snake of blue enamel twisted the three heads that grew from its single neck. On his head, Agamemnon put his helmet, with its four plates, its double crest and its horsehair plume nodding defiantly above.... Beams from the bronze he wore flashed into the distant sky, and Athene and Here thundered in answer by way of salutation to the King of Golden Mycenae.[162]

As well, defeat in single combat meant the surrendering of one's armor to an opponent, who then either donned it himself, if it was superior to his own, or kept it as a trophy of the victory.

The Romans too realized the importance of outfitting their troops in strong, protective armor. Julius Caesar's legionnaires who marched into Gaul and later against the other members of his triumvirate in the first century BC were protected by a solid bronze breastplate (a *lorica*); a bowl-shaped helmet made of solid bronze beaten to shape, which also protected the neck, but not the face; and a large oblong shield, measuring approximately 130 by 65 centimeters (the *scutum*).

Overall the first-century BC Roman armor was not much different from ancient Greek armor, at least in function and design if not in shape. Only the shield differed significantly from its Greek cousin. The Roman shield was not made from hardwood, but was constructed from three layers of glued plywood, each made of strips 6 to 10 centimeters wide, with the outer pieces laid horizontally and the inner piece laid vertically, and covered in canvas and calf hide. A long wooden boss ran the entire length of the shield. There was no metal on the Roman shield, yet even without this added weight it remained heavy, weighing an estimated 10 kilograms. However, because of the shield's shape and size the bearer did not have to wear greaves, and this enabled him to have more speed and freedom of movement.[163]

By the second and third century AD this armor began to change. Replacing the solid and therefore immobile breastplate was a cuirass (a *lorica segmentata*) made of six or seven horizontal strips of bronze attached by hooks and buckles onto a leather undergarment. The shoulders were covered with sets of curved strips of bronze attached to a pair of front and back metallic plates. This allowed the bearer much more freedom of movement than did the solid *lorica* worn by Caesar's legionnaires, and it could also be taken apart easily for transportation and repair.[164]

The solid bronze helmet of Caesar's troops also changed, replaced by a more carefully designed helmet, made in either bronze or iron, which was strengthened inside by an iron skull-plate. The neck was still protected, but now part of the face was covered by ear and cheek pieces. The plume was generally absent from this helmet, although it could still be affixed on top for celebratory purposes.[165]

Finally, the shield changed in shape and construction, not in size. The second- and third-century Roman shield was still quite long, but now it was much more rectangular in shape and curved to fit the body. It was made of plywood, like the earlier Roman model, but now was covered in leather, on which was fastened gilded and silvered bronze decoration and a metallic boss. Around its edges was a rim of wrought iron or bronze. Oval shields, similar to those of the Greeks, also appeared at this time, but were probably used solely by the cavalry.[166]

Sometime around the beginning of the fourth century, the Roman armor changed again, and this time the changes were more dramatic and less defensively efficient than the earlier ones. Recognizing the need to make different helmets for the infantry and the cavalry, Roman armorers began producing two very distinct helmet designs. The infantry helmet was bowl-shaped, made of two iron halves joined together by a metal strip. It was lined by a leather cap, not attached to the outer helmet, on which was affixed an iron neckguard and iron cheek-pieces. The cavalry helmet was also bowl-shaped, but instead of having an inner leather cap on which the neck and cheekguards were affixed, it was constructed of four to six pieces, including a ridge, noseguard and extremely wide cheek-pieces, all of which were attached by rivets or hinges to the helmet itself. Many cavalry helmets were also covered with gilded silver, and some had other decorative designs. Both of these helmet styles were more easily and more cheaply constructed than earlier Roman models, and their existence may indicate a centralization of the late Roman armor industry.[167]

The skillfully constructed, complex *lorica segmentata* was also replaced by more easily constructed and cheaper body armor. Two styles of cuirasses were prevalent in the late Roman empire. The first (a *lorica squamata*) was made of a large number of metallic scales attached to each other by wire or leather laces and affixed to a linen textile undergarment by linen cord. The second (a *lorica hamata*) was constructed of metal rings. Alternate rows of these rings were punched out of sheet metal, with the connecting row in between made from metal wire, the ring ends butted or riveted together; each ring was interlocked with four others, two in the row above and two in the row below—35,000 to 40,000 of these rings were needed to make a cuirass. Both styles covered the torso from the shoulder to at least the middle of the thigh and some seem to have stretched as far down as the knee; both could be worn by either an infantry or a cavalry soldier. Neither of these styles were new to the Romans, and, while both were lighter than the earlier cuirasses, they were also less protective than the breastplates, sacrificing defense for comfort.[168]

However, what may have been the most drastic change in late Roman armor was not a technological modification, but an attitudinal one. At the outset of the barbarian invasions, instead of desiring to be more protected by defensive armament, Roman soldiers wanted to be less encumbered. They took off both their helmets and their cuirasses and began to rely solely on their shields for protection.

How widespread this practice was cannot be determined, although there is ample evidence of it appearing on grave stelae and reliefs throughout Europe. For example, in a relief at Croy Hill in Strathclyde, England, three legionnaires are depicted: none of them is wearing any protective armaments, but are outfitted solely with long, rectangular shields.[169]

That this had an effect on the fighting capabilities of the Romans defending their empire against the barbarian invaders is attested to by Flavius Vegetius Renatus, perhaps the most famous late Roman military writer. Vegetius recounts that it had always been the tradition of Roman soldiers to wear breastplates and helmets, but that this tradition had lately changed with grievous results:

> But when, because of negligence and laziness, parade ground drills were abandoned, the customary armor began to seem heavy since the soldiers rarely ever wore it. Therefore, they first asked the emperor to set aside the breastplates and mail and then the helmets. So our soldiers fought the Goths without any protection for chest and head and were often beaten by archers. Although there were many disasters, which led to the loss of great cities, no one tried to restore breastplates and helmets to the infantry. Thus it happens that troops in battle, exposed to wounds because they have no armor, think about running and not about fighting.[170]

To be fair to the late Roman soldiers, the enemy they faced was not well defended either. Most Germanic warriors had neither breastplate nor helmet, and their shields were not strengthened by either metal or leather. They usually went into battle naked or with a short cloak, protected from their enemies' weaponry by only a light wooden or wicker shield. Therefore, they were perceived from the first military encounter between the two societies to be generally inferior to the Roman soldiers whose armor was more substantial. Such a perception built confidence in the Roman military leadership who often used it to encourage their troops to battle against the Germans.[171]

Whether this disregard for defensive armament was due to the Germans' shortage of metal, as contended by the first-century Roman writer, Tacitus, or whether the barbarians used battlefield tactics which simply did not necessitate the same armor as the Romans, their neglect for defensive armament carried into the fourth- and fifth-century invasions of the Empire. The Germanic soldiers continued to fight without helmet or body protection, although it does appear that their shields had been improved by the addition of a pointed iron boss which also served as a thrusting weapon. However, the shields remained relatively thin and were easily smashed by Roman swords and spears. Some invaders did outfit themselves by stripping the dead Roman soldiers, but the number of armored warriors in the barbarian armies remained small and was most often confined to the nobles or chieftains.[172]

Early Medieval Armor

Initially the Romans were defeated by the barbarians, if we are to believe Vegetius, due to the discarding of defensive armaments by the imperial troops. By the sixth century, the eastern Romans, now known as Byzantines, had begun to arm themselves again with helmets, cuirasses, greaves, and heavy shields. Even horse archers were required to protect themselves with armor. This allowed them to defeat the barbarians in turn and to push them out of Asia Minor and the Balkans; even Italy was recaptured for a while.[173]

In the west, however, warfare continued. There the Empire had fallen, and barbarian tribes frequently clashed with each other in their efforts to establish supremacy and control over the lands and people of that region of Europe. These battles were fought generally with soldiers unprotected by armor.[174]

The only defensive armament which was carried by almost all barbarian soldiers was their shield. The early medieval shield, also known as a *buckler*, was the symbol of warrior status. The soldier received it when entering military service, and it remained with him always; to lose it was tantamount to cowardice. If the warrior was wounded, the shield was used as a stretcher to bear him from the battlefield; if he died, it was buried with him. The most common barbarian shield was convex, round or elliptical and was made from strips of wood and covered by leather. It measured generally 80-90 centimeters in diameter and was 80 to 120 millimeters thick. The metal boss measured 15 to 17 centimeters in diameter with an average height of 6 to 10 centimeters. Some shields were also decorated with symbolic figures and decorations.[175]

Nobles and chieftains did possess helmets and body armor. Sometimes these were quite elaborate—for example, Totila, an Ostrogothic king, had golden armor—but most often they were simple, worn less for protection than for status. Helmets, for example, were usually only simple iron skullcaps and sometimes merely a metal framework covered by leather or another fabric, although some Visigothic helmets were patterned after Byzantine examples. Cuirasses were usually chain mail, fashioned after the Roman *lorica hamata*, or scale armor, like the Roman *lorica squamata*.[176]

The Anglo-Saxon conquerors of England seem to have had a similar disregard for defensive armaments as did their continental cousins. Neither breastplates nor armor were common; only noble warriors and chieftains used them. Only two Anglo-Saxon graves, those at Sutton Hoo and Benty Grange, included helmets and cuirasses among their grave goods, and laws written as late as the tenth and eleventh centuries required only the holders of five hides of land to have helmets and cuirasses. So valuable in fact was a cuirass and helmet that the dead warrior possessing these weapons was generally stripped of them by the conquering enemy, as was Byrhtnoth in the Anglo-Saxon poem *The Battle of Maldon*.[177]

Nor did the Viking conquerors of England improve the Anglo-Saxons' regard for these pieces of defensive armament. The common Viking soldier did not carry anything more than a wooden shield; the nobles were again the only soldiers outfitted with iron mail cuirasses and leather or iron helmets. Indeed, Viking warriors who fought without any armor at all, known as berserkers (or "without shirts"), are quite often mentioned in Old Norse literature and are always praised more highly for their fighting prowess and bravery than are regular soldiers who must rely on a shield for protection.[178]

Anglo-Saxon armor did not differ much from that worn or carried by barbarian soldiers on the continent. Shields were the same shape, size, and material as those carried by Ostrogothic, Visigothic, Frankish, or other barbarian warriors. They also contained an iron boss, although the boss on the Anglo-Saxon shield seems not to have had the extra function of a thrusting weapon. The shields do, however, appear to have been thicker than those made on the continent, as riddles written in both Latin and Old English describe them as scarred, but not broken, by the blows of enemy weapons; as well, they seem to have had a metallic rim, as the *Battle of Maldon* reports that Atherich's shield rim burst under the blow of his enemy's sword. Anglo-Saxon shields were also frequently decorated.[179]

Anglo-Saxon helmets, although adopting the more stylistic details of Roman models, were similar to those worn by barbarian soldiers on the continent. Three prototypes, excavated at Sutton Hoo, Benty Grange, and Coppergate, indicate that they consisted of four parts: the cap, two hinged cheekpieces, and a section of mail protecting the back and sides of the neck. The cap was made of a wide band encircling the head, with a narrower second band attached to the first by rivets and running from back to front. This second band was linked to the wide circular band by two short bands running down towards the ears. The spaces left open by this framework were filled by plates of metal attached to the bands by rivets. Semi-circular holes were cut into the front of the helmet for the eyes, and a long, thin piece of metal descended between these holes to serve as a nose-guard. The cheek pieces, hinged onto the wide brow-band, covered both the ears and cheeks and were probably attached together under the chin by a leather or cloth strap. A mail neck guard, made in a manner similar to a cuirass, was also attached to the brow-band. As well, some ornamentation was frequently included on the Anglo-Saxon helmet: copper eyebrows added above the eye-holes or the figure of a boar on the crown.[180]

Finally, the most celebrated, and probably the least plentiful, armor of the Anglo-Saxons was the cuirass. Again, there seems to be little difference between this armor and that of the continental barbarians. It too was generally a coat of chain mail, descending to the mid-thigh or to the knee and with short sleeves. To the Exeter riddler it was an "excellent garment"; to Beowulf it was a "tangled war-net"; and in Aldhelm's riddles it is described as not fearing "arrows drawn from a long quiver." To all, it was an armament absolutely essential for the protection of a noble warrior.[181]

There was little attempt to regulate armor usage among any soldiers of the early Middle Ages until the late seventh century. The first to do so was Ervig, a king of the Visigoths, who some-time between 680 and 687 wrote a legal code demanding among other things that of his soldiers "some shall wear armor and most shall have bucklers..."[182] This decree was followed in 750 by a similar edict ordered by Aistulf, a king of the Lombards, which required the richest and most powerful of his warriors to be armed with a full set of armor and a shield, as well as his conventional offensive weapons.[183] Whether either of these laws effected any change in the armaments of barbarian armies, however, cannot be ascertained. It is in fact not until the time of Charlemagne that a verifiable transformation or evolution in armor policy can be seen.

Charlemagne recognized very early in his reign that the defensive requirements of his large empire and his desire to conquer lands beyond its borders required a highly regulated professional army. Not only did these requirements and desires necessitate a strict military organization, and a cavalry-based force, but they also demanded an army which was systematically well armed, both offensively and defensively. The first extant law to state this policy was the *capitulare missorum* of 792-93, which demanded that all benefice and office holders in the Carolingian realm possess full armor and shield as well as a horse and offensive weaponry.[184] This was followed in 802-03 by a capitulary again charging these nobles to have their own helmets and cuirasses (known to the Carolingians as *byrnies*).[185] Finally, in 805, the law was made even more specific. In this capitulary, Charlemagne required anyone of his empire who held twelve *mansi* of land to have his own armor and to serve as a horseman in his army; if he failed in his duty, both his land and his armor would be taken from him.[186] Infantry soldiers were not so well protected, although the Capitulary of Aachen, proclaimed in 802-03, did require them all to carry a shield.[187]

The main defensive armament of the Carolingian army remained the shield; it was also the least expensive armor, and thus all soldiers, even horse archers, were required to carry it. (A shield and lance together cost three times less than a helmet and six times less than a byrnie.) Like other early medieval shields, Carolingian shields were round, concave, and made of wood, and at least some were covered, perhaps on both sides, by leather. It was rimmed with metal, and metal strips were sometimes added for extra strength. A dome-shaped metal boss was set in the middle of each shield with a grip running across the underside and attached both to the boss and to the wood; a strap was also connected to the grip allowing the soldier to sling the shield across his back for transportation. However, Carolingian shields were much larger than other early medieval shields, measuring between 52 and 80 centimeters in diameter; thus they protected more of the warrior's torso, with the largest shields covering the body from the neck to the thighs.[188]

While Carolingian shields appear to be little different from other shields of the early Middle Ages, Carolingian helmets differed considerably from their earlier medieval cousins. For one thing, they were not simple leather caps. Most were in fact made of metal, although probably not in a single piece. As well, the design of the Carolingian helmet was unique. The most common of these helmets, as portrayed in artistic sources as no archaeological exemplar has yet been excavated, consisted of a cap encircled by a rather wide rim. The rim rose to a point at the forehead and tapered towards a pronounced neckguard at the rear of the helmet. A strengthening band descended from the top of the helmet and intersected the rim at a button or large rivet. This band also served as the helmet's crest, with some sources showing a feather attached to it.

A less common design was the *Spangenhelm*. More rounded than other Carolingian helmets, the *spangenhelm* consisted of a framework formed by a single headband on which were attached six or more metal bands, known as *spangen*. This framework was then filled with metal or horn plates.[189]

A final unique defensive armament of the Carolingian army was the byrnie. To the Carolingian soldier, the byrnie was his most highly valued piece of armor, not only because of its cost, but also because no enemy he would meet on the battlefield would have one. Indeed, as early as 779, Charlemagne had forbidden the sale of this armor outside the realm; in 803, he added a declaration that soldiers were forbidden even to give it to a merchant, who might sell it to a potential enemy. (It does appear, however, that certain amoral Frankish merchants still sold byrnies to Saracens, Bretons, and Vikings.)[190]

There is some dispute among historians as to what exactly constituted the Carolingian byrnie. Again relying only on artistic and some literary sources because of the lack of an archaeological exemplar, some believe that it was a heavy leather jacket with metal scales sewn onto it. It was also quite long, reaching below the hips and covering most of the arms. This would make the byrnie a unique garment, as scale armor (the *lorica squamata*) had been worn since the fall of the Roman Empire. Other historians claim instead that the Carolingian byrnie was nothing more than a coat of chain mail, but longer and perhaps heavier than

Carolingian horsemen showing typical helmet, byrnie, round shield, and lances. Note also that the saddles are equiped with stirrups. [From *Psalterium aureum* (late 9th century), Stiftsbibiothek, Saint Gall.]

traditional early medieval mail. Without more certain evidence, this dispute will continue.[191]

Leg guards and greaves also appeared during the Carolingian period, worn by the most wealthy of Charlemagne's horsemen. Emerging for the first time were armguards and gauntlets, later to be common armor for knights. Charlemagne also forbade the sale of these armaments to foreigners.[192]

Carolingian military policies remained dominant throughout the ninth and tenth centuries. The army continued to be primarily a well armed cavalry-based force with each soldier protected by a long byrnie (now almost certainly chain mail), a segmented, wide-brimmed helmet, and a large round shield made of wood and leather. Indeed, so influential were these Carolingian policies that they stimulated change in military tradition even beyond the borders of Charlemagne's Empire. Carolingian-style armor became standard for defensive armaments in Spain, Scandinavia, Eastern Europe, and England.[193]

The chain mail byrnie, called by different names, continued to remain the primary body armor into the late Middle Ages. But the shield and helmet changed in design sometime during the late tenth and early eleventh centuries, although the reasons for these changes cannot be known for certain due to the lack of evidence. The shield, being round, did not protect the full body of the horseman, leaving almost his entire leg unprotected from enemy attack. At the same time, its large size made it unwieldy for a cavalry soldier to easily maneuver during battle. These problems were solved by making the shield narrower and kite-shaped.

It is less easy to speculate on the reasons for change in helmet design. Perhaps the wide helmet was too complex in its construction, or perhaps it was simply too difficult to avoid losing it during the pressure of battle. At any rate, the segmented, wide-brimmed Carolingian helmet evolved into a much more simply constructed, more tightly worn conical helmet. The early Carolingian helmet and shield continued to be used until the twelfth century, but only infrequently and, in artistic sources at least, are shown worn most often by non-western European armies, such as Romans and Muslims or, by that special iconographic figure of military evil, Goliath.[194]

Armor in The Bayeux Tapestry

Nowhere are these changes seen more clearly than in the *Bayeux Tapestry*. The *Bayeux Tapestry* is one of the most unique and masterful artistic sources of military history produced during the Middle Ages. While there are certain shortcomings in using it as a source for the study of armor during this period—its small scale and the fact that tapestry as an artistic medium is somewhat inexact—it does depict a total of 201 armed men, 79 of whom are wearing body armor and helmets and even more who are carrying shields. Moreover, there is a consistency among the armor depicted which builds confidence in the historical accuracy of the weavers' work.[195]

The *Bayeux Tapestry* was woven sometime before the end of the eleventh century to celebrate the conquest of England in 1066 by William the Conqueror. It portrays the defensive armaments of the defeated Anglo-Saxon infantry-based army, protected generally by the antiquated armor of barbarian and Carolingian tradition mixed with newer defensive armaments, as well as the Norman cavalry-based army, all wearing new body armor and helmets and carrying new shields.

Almost all of the shields depicted on the tapestry, whether carried by infantry or cavalry, are long, narrow, and kite-shaped with rounded tops and pointed bottoms. Some of these shields appear to curve slightly, although how much and whether all kite-shaped shields had this characteristic cannot be determined. And while, or perhaps because, no kite-shaped shields currently exist, most historians believe that they were constructed in a manner similar to their Carolingian predecessors: of wood probably covered by leather with a metal boss and perhaps a metal rim, although this latter characteristic is impossible to ascertain from the tapestry alone.

The shields are gripped in a variety of ways by a series of leather straps (or *enarmes*) which are riveted onto their insides. The most frequent of these grips consists of a loose strap draped around the soldier's neck, with a shorter strap grasped by his hand. Horsemen carry their shields consistently on the left side, the lance carried by the right hand; infantry also carry their shields in the left hand.

The advantages of the kite-shaped shield for cavalry soldiers have been described above. But this shape also benefitted the infantry soldier. The kite-shape pattern allowed foot-soldiers to plant the sharper bottom edge into the ground while overlapping the wider upper part of each kite to form a rudimentary and temporary battlefield fortification known as a "shield-wall." So effective was this infantry tactic that it became the favorite defensive maneuver of infantry against the cavalry charge during the central Middle Ages.

The shields are also frequently decorated, although there seems to be no consistency, or heraldry for that matter, in these decorations. Among the designs which appear are birds, dragons, wavy crosses, diagonal lines, and saltires, with the boss and rivets also sometimes incorporated into the pattern.

All round shields are carried by English infantry, with one rectangular shield also depicted, carried by an aged Anglo-Saxon foot soldier.[196]

All helmets in the tapestry, both those worn by Anglo-Saxon and Norman troops, are the same pattern: a close-fitting conical crown with a somewhat pointed apex and a wide, flat nasal guard descending over the nose and attached to the brim. While not depicted in the *Bayeux Tapestry*, other artistic sources from the period show that these helmets were secured in place with a leather strap tied under the chin.[197] Surviving helmets from the period show two constructions: some were forged from a single piece of iron and hammered into the desired shape, while others were of a segmented construction with a number of iron plates attached together. These segments either overlapped each other and were riveted together, or they were attached to a metal band framework in a manner similar to the Carolingian *spangenhelm*. The helmets had no cheekguards and, while each was equipped with a noseguard, the efficacy of such a protective device is suspect as one Anglo-Saxon soldier, by tradition King Harold II, is shown pierced through the eye by a Norman arrow, unimpeded by his helmet's nasal guard.[198]

The least innovative defensive armament on the *Bayeux Tapestry* is the byrnie, called a *hauberk* by the eleventh century. Worn by both cavalry and infantry, the hauberks all appear to be chain mail differing little in design or method of construction from

those of the Carolingian tradition. The hauberk was made in one
piece—as indicated by the portrayal along the tapestry's border of
dead soldiers being stripped of their armor by pulling it over their
heads (an indication of the continued value of this defensive armament). A small slit over the left hip accommodated the
warrior's sword. It was also probably worn over, but not attached
to, a heavy, quilted undergarment (known as a *haubergeon*) which
added to the defensive capability of the armor (but which is not
depicted in the tapestry).

Most hauberks are shown descending to the knees and divided
down the front and back by slits which allowed for greater freedom of movement and comfort to a horseman. Although one figure
is depicted with a long-sleeved hauberk, all others have short,
wide sleeves, which leave the forearms bare. Colored bands along
the edges of the sleeves and skirt may mean that cloth was sewn
onto these to soften the roughness of the metal and to guard
against irritation. Only once is a horseman depicted with further
arm protection and then only covering his forearms; there is no
further protection for the arms or hands. However, some leaders
and other important soldiers, including both William the Conqueror and Harold II, are outfitted by mail leggings (or *chausses*).
These may have been mail stockings which covered the entire leg,
even under the hauberk; more than likely they were smaller pieces

Arms and armor from the *Bayeux Tapestry* showing
helmet, kite shield, round shield, and assorted weapons of
the Norman conquest of England in 1066.
[From Stenton (1957).]

of mail, laced up behind the calf. No mail protection for the feet is depicted.

Other figures, again mostly leaders or important soldiers, are also shown to be outfitted with a mail hood or coif over which their helmet sits. Whether this was connected to the hauberk or was an additional piece of mail, like the chausses, cannot be determined from the tapestry.

Finally, several soldiers, all Norman horsemen including William the Conqueror, have colored rectangles shown on the breasts of their hauberks. This design innovation, found elsewhere only in a single eleventh-century Catalan manuscript illumination, has been the subject of debate for many modern commentators on the tapestry. Some, including Charles H. Ashdown, James Mann, and Ian Peirce, believe this to represent the addition of metal plates under the hauberk, and perhaps attached to it, to further protect the vulnerable chest. Others, most notably David C. Nicolle, claim instead that this merely depicts a mail *ventail* (the face covering of a mail coif) which has been unlaced for comfort when not in battle. In either case, and an answer is impossible to arrive at based on the *Bayeux Tapestry* alone, this would have been a characteristic of armor not previously seen.[199]

Twelfth-Century Defensive Armaments

The armor portrayed in the *Bayeux Tapestry* was common throughout the eleventh and twelfth centuries. Not only was it popular in France, Germany, and England, but it also seems to have become the preferred armor design of soldiers in Italy, Spain, Poland, Hungary, and Scandinavia. Furthermore, it was these types of body armor, helmets, and shields which were worn by the Crusaders on their first three crusades into the Holy Land, by the Christian Spaniards fighting to recover their lands from the Muslims, and by countless other soldiers fighting in numerous battles in Europe.[200]

Artistic sources demonstrate, for example, that the kite-shaped shield of the *Bayeux Tapestry* was the most prominent shield carried by troops, infantry, and cavalry, until the beginning of the thirteenth century. The size, shape, and material of the shield remained unchanged, as was the fact that most were decorated and incorporated the metal boss into this decoration. As well, while some shields are shown curved around their carriers' bodies, others are flat, similar again to their depiction in the tapestry. In fact, the only noticeable change in the shield at all through the two centuries following the battle of Hastings was the reduction of the curved top into a flat surface.[201]

Round shields, like those of the Carolingians, also continue to be present in the artistic sources of the eleventh and twelfth centuries. But generally these are seen only in the depictions of evil—Romans, Saracens, Goliath—or of Sicilian and Spanish soldiers who had been influenced earlier by Muslim occupiers. The round shield was always preferred by Muslim warriors.[202]

Helmets as depicted in the artistic sources of the 150 years following Hastings also differ little from those depicted on the *Bayeux Tapestry*. Almost all helmets are conical and segmented, sometimes with a nasal guard and sometimes without.[203] This style is further confirmed by most of the extant exemplars which remain from the period. Of seven helmets preserved in Poland and England (one of German and the remaining of Polish fabrication), made in the tenth to twelfth centuries, all are conical in shape and were constructed by riveting iron plates together and strengthening them by an iron rim. Only two of these helmets have noseguards; two others show signs of being attached to mail ventails. Almost all have evidence of gilded copper decoration.[204]

Two more extant helmets from this period, while conical, are made of a single piece of metal hammered into shape. But these— one said to be the helmet of St. Wenceslaus and now held in the cathedral treasury of Prague and the other, a helmet currently in the Imperial Armoury at Vienna—do not differ in their construction from some helmets depicted in the *Bayeux Tapestry*.[205]

Only one variation in helmet design can be found in these artistic sources: a number of eleventh- and twelfth-century conical helmets have an apex which curves forward instead of rising to a point. While this is a rare occurrence, in comparison to the large number of traditionally-shaped conical helmets, it does appear in artistic sources from France, England, Germany, Burgundy, and Italy; why it occurs cannot be determined.[206]

The body armor depicted in the *Bayeux Tapestry* also varied little before the end of the twelfth century. Most artistic sources show that the hauberks of this period remained chain mail of varying lengths. Hauberks of European armies continued to cover the torso to the hips or lower, while Crusader hauberks were significantly shorter, indicating the difference in battlefield climates. Most of these hauberks hung loose, although at least one manuscript illustration shows them to be gathered around the waist and secured by a belt. Sleeve lengths also varied, with some extending to the wrist and others only to the elbow; some sleeves were loose while others were bound tightly around the arm.[207] All hauberks continued to be worn over quilted haubergeons which provided added protection to the body.[208]

Chain mail chausses, like those worn by the military leaders of the Norman and Anglo-Saxon armies in the *Bayeux Tapestry*, also continue to be depicted in late twelfth-century artistic sources. As well, mail coifs are included with most hauberks portrayed, although whether these were separate pieces of mail or part of the hauberk cannot be determined.[209]

Beyond these similarities, however, there are four types of body armor which are significantly different from those depicted in the *Bayeux Tapestry*. First, in a number of artistic sources foot armor is portrayed. In most cases this is nothing more than an extension of the mail chausses to completely cover the foot, although at times they also include the addition of spurs attached to the heel.[210] Second, in one source, an illumination of the prophet Joshua from a Winchester Bible made in 1160-70, mail mittens can be seen. However, these do not completely cover the hand, but leave the thumb and fingers free.[211] It was not until the beginning of the thirteenth century that full mail mittens were added to the hauberk to protect the hand.[212] Third, not only are there coifs which protect the neck and rest under the helmet, but many also contain ventails. Sometimes these are attached to the nasal guard, while some appear merely to be drawn tightly around the mouth and cheeks without being attached to the helmet.[213] Finally, while hauberks are depicted without outside cover in the *Bayeux Tapestry*, *surcoats*, which were nothing more than cloth coverings placed on top of these hauberks, begin to appear in some artistic depictions of armor of the late twelfth century.[214] It should be noted that all these changes in body armor design appeared in mid to late twelfth-century artistic sources and continued

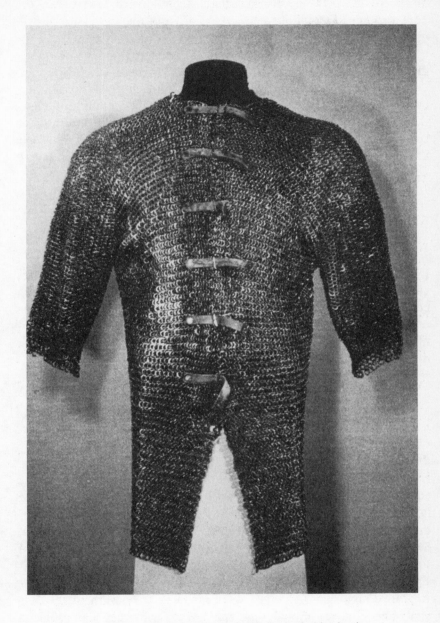

Early thirteenth-century chain mail hauberk (the leather
straps are a post-medieval addition).
[From the Tower of London Armouries Collection.]

to appear more frequently in artistic depictions of armor over the next century, indicating an increase in use among medieval soldiers.

Scale armor (known sometimes as lamellar armor in the Middle Ages) also seems to have remained, at least in artistic renderings of medieval warfare, but these are limited in number, especially when compared to the much larger number of chain mail armor portrayals. Like round shields, they too are most often seen on enemies of Christians: Saracens and Romans.[215] Scale armor continued to be depicted in this way into the thirteenth century.[216]

Shields, Helmets, and Heraldry in the Thirteenth Century

Important changes in the design of almost all defensive armaments came at the end of the twelfth and beginning of the thirteenth centuries. While few changes were made to body armor, with the exception of the rise in use and popularity of the late twelfth-century innovations mentioned above, alterations in the size and shape of the shield, the complete remodeling of the helmet and the introduction of horse armor, and chivalric decorations all signified a new period of armor design.[217]

The kite-shaped shield which had dominated shield design for nearly two centuries evolved into a more triangular shape, shorter, wider, probably lighter, and almost always flat. This was probably not an indictment of the traditional kite-shaped shield which had always provided good protection to its carrier, but reflected the adoption of better leg armor which negated the need for a long heavy shield to protect that part of the body. At the same time, the shape of the new shield allowed for more maneuverability on horseback; infantry troops continued to use the kite-shaped shield for a while until they too switched to the newer triangular design.[218]

More significant changes were made to the design of the helmet. The now traditional segmented conical helmet was replaced during the thirteenth century by what became known as the "Great Helm." Although the conical helmet was used into the thirteenth century, its defensive limitations were evident. Even with the addition of a nasal guard, coif, and ventail, the face and neck remained relatively unprotected. This prompted some experimentation in new helmet designs, especially those which would improve face and neck defense. The most successful of these was the attachment of a face mask, similar in shape to a welding mask, to the front of an iron skull-cap. The shape of the skull-cap mattered little, and there was initially quite a variety. What was of greater importance was the addition of the mask. Pierced with ventilation and sight holes, it immediately cut down the number of facial injuries while at the same time it neither decreased the defensibility nor increased the lack of comfort of the helmet itself. Only the vision of the warrior was impaired, and this obstacle was somewhat overcome by practice and familiarization.[219]

However, despite coming into general use quickly and completely in the beginning of the thirteenth century, the addition of the face mask was but one stage of the evolutionary process which produced the Great Helm. For one thing, a mask for the face did nothing to protect the ears or neck, necessitating still the wearing of a relatively ineffective coif to protect those very vulnerable parts of the body. Therefore, the new helmet evolved one step further, with the addition or attachment to it of a fixed neck guard and fixed ear flaps, and then still one step further with the extension of the helmet to cover the entire head. This produced c.1220 a cylindrical helmet, shaped much like a large can, with a flat-top (also found to be the most convenient shape), which completely enclosed the head. The Great Helm was still worn over a mail coif, to further protect the area between the helmet and the hauberk, but it also required the addition of an extra quilted coif (an *arming cap*) on top of the head and under the helmet both for the comfort of the wearer of the helmet—the Great Helm was both heavy and uncomfortable to wear—and to hold it firmly onto the middle of the wearer's head.[220] Once, the great jouster William Marshal's Great Helm turned around during a joust so that his vision and breathing were cut off; only with difficulty was he able to pull the helmet off in time to save his life.[221]

The Great Helm was quickly adopted by the knight on horseback who needed the added protection it provided, and it soon became the prevalent defensive armament for the head throughout

Fourteenth-century English Great Helm.
[From the Tower of London Armouries Collection.]

all of Europe. But it was simply too cumbersome, too heavy, and too expensive for the infantry soldier to wear. At the same time, as the infantry soldier was also more likely to be involved in more congested melee than the cavalry soldier, whose fights were most often forward charges on horseback, it was more important that he have better vision than the Great Helm accorded.

While the Great Helm became the chosen helmet design for the knight, the infantryman spurned it, choosing instead to wear something more akin to the traditional conical helmet, the *chapel-de-fer* or *kettle-hat*. The kettle-hat was simply a conical-style helmet with a fairly wide brim which protruded out from the cap in an umbrella-shape. Like a conical helmet, it was constructed of segmented metal plates riveted to a metal framework and attached at the bottom to the separate wide brim, which was designed to avoid blows to the face from an enemy on horseback. Also like the conical helmet, the kettle-hat was secured on the head by a leather chin-strap.[222] The kettle-hat would remain the most popular helmet for the common infantry soldier in Europe until the end of the Middle Ages.

The two remaining changes in defensive armament of the late twelfth and early thirteenth centuries, the introduction of horse armor and of chivalric decoration, seem minor in comparison to the introduction of the Great Helm and the kettle-hat. Certainly they did not improve the defensive capabilities of the soldier's armor. However, they too were important.

With the carrying of a shield and the wearing of a hauberk which protected the arms and hands, chausses which included foot protection, and a Great Helm, the only vulnerable part of a horseman was his horse. Up to this time a warhorse had not been outfitted with any defensive armaments and thus could be brought down by a blow to its body. However, in the late twelfth and early thirteenth centuries, some warhorses were outfitted with a quilted cloth or leather blanket (known as a *caprison* or *bard*) which covered the head and body. Although not a complete defensive raiment, the caprison did provide some protection for the cavalry soldier's mount while at the same time not burdening it with too much added weight. Moreover, it provided the owner of the warhorse with a large placard for chivalric emblems. There is a reference in Wace's *Roman de Rou*, written between 1160 and 1174, to metallic horse armor used by William Fitz Osbert at the battle of Hastings; however, this evidence is suspect and cannot be substantiated by artistic sources.[223]

Decorating armor with symbolic illustrations had occurred since ancient times. Indeed, if we are to believe Homer, shield decoration, sometimes with lavish and symbolic art work, was especially favored by both the Greeks and the Trojans during their war. Nor was armor decoration lost after the fall of Rome, for, as was mentioned above, shields of warriors depicted on the *Bayeux Tapestry* were often painted with animals and other designs. Finally, it should be noted that the Crusaders travelling to the Holy Land painted their shields, surcoats and helmets with the sign of the Cross to designate their devotion to the sacred calling of gaining the Holy Land for Christians.[224]

It is, however, difficult to determine what was represented by these early shield decorations. Besides the Crusaders' emblems, which are self-explanatory, there seems to be no reason why someone fighting at Hastings or elsewhere should desire to decorate their armor. Possibly these emblems represented unit organization, or possibly they simply reflected personal warrior artistic tradition, but what seems certain is that they did not have any heraldic meaning.

At the end of the twelfth century, some noble families began to use a variety of symbols to reflect their status. Where this derived from or why it happened at this time cannot be determined. The practice did, however, become popular very quickly, and by the end of the thirteenth century all noble families of any rank had their own heraldic emblems. These symbols were chosen often to represent the traits of the family: a lion might represent courage, a dragon strength, a fox cunning, etc. When two families intermarried, their emblems reflected this by combining the two heraldries.[225]

There was no better place to display these heraldic emblems than on the armor of the family's warriors, and during the thirteenth century, such emblems began to appear frequently. While this occurred especially on parade or tournament armor—armor never meant to be used in combat—it also appeared on some battlefield armor. The shield, of course, continued to be the primary surface for the display of heraldic symbols, but soon it was joined by other armor surfaces serving a similar purpose: surcoats, helmet crests, banners (carried by squires), and warhorse caprisons.[226]

Thirteenth-Century Body Armor

Chain mail continued to be used and favored by soldiers in the fourteenth century,[227] but as high-powered crossbows and long-bows were able to break the rings and penetrate the armor, new, more capable defense was needed.[228] This led to the next significant change in defensive armaments: plate armor. This change was initiated in the late thirteenth and early fourteenth centuries and lasted well into the sixteenth century.

There had been some tendency to use plates of metal as body armor since ancient times, with the Greek breastplate an excellent example of this. Furthermore, lamellar or scale armor had endured throughout the Middle Ages, although it appeared infrequently and was, at least in artistic sources, mostly associated with evil. Clearly, medieval soldiers up to the end of the thirteenth century preferred chain mail armor for their battlefield protection.[229]

The earliest reference to plate armor appears in a written source, Gerald of Wales' *Topographica Hibernica et expugnatio Hibernica* (The Topography and Conquest of Ireland), written in the late twelfth century, which claims that in a Danish attack on Dublin in 1171 the Danes were clad in long hauberks made of both chain mail and "plates of iron stitched together skillfully." Certainly this could be the earliest indication of plate mail, but as it stands alone as the single reference to plate armor in the twelfth century—even Danish sources of the attack on Dublin do not corroborate it—it may also be simply a reference to scale armor.[230]

More certain evidence for plate armor does not come until the early to mid thirteenth century. Both artistic and written evidence mention the introduction of this new design of armor at this time. For example, one chronicler, Guillaume le Breton (d.1225), writes about a fight between Richard I of England (at the time only Count of Poitou) and William de Barres, which describes each combatant as wearing "molded iron plates" as an extra protective garment under the chain mail hauberk.[231]

The plate armor worn by Richard I and William de Barres was most certainly not a primary but a secondary defensive armament. However, it may well show the evolutionary process which produced the first plate armor, a process whereby the suit of armor was made in pieces of plate attached to the existing chain mail or leather armor as added defensive protection. Such might also be the case with a manifesto written from the German Emperor Frederick II to King Henry III of England in 1241 which mentions leather armor strengthened by iron plates sewn onto it.[232]

Artistic sources also add evidence of metallic plates attached to other parts of the thirteenth-century armor-clad soldier. Principal among these were the metallic kneepads (*poleyns*) which were placed over chain mail chausses. At first these were very small, almost insignificant in the defense of the soldier, but after c.1270, they became much larger and began to play a more integral role. These were followed shortly after by plate armor added to the elbows of the hauberk (known as *couters*) and to the shins.[233] The poleyn, couter, and shin-guard (known as a *jamber* or *shynbald*) remained in use throughout the rest of the Middle Ages.[234]

The evolution of early torso armor is difficult to determine. Written sources are almost non-existent, and artistic sources are of little more assistance since early plate armor was kept hidden under the surcoat until the middle of the fourteenth century. Indeed, there is some indication that initially it may even have been attached to the surcoat itself, producing a *coat of plates* or *brigadine*, which was worn over the chain mail hauberk.[235] There is also some evidence that the initial plates worn to protect the torso were not made of metal only, but that a variety of materials were used including whalebone, horn, and *cuir-bouilli* (leather hardened by wax), as well as iron, steel, and latten (a rigid form of brass).[236]

By c.1350 the coat of plates was replaced by a more solid and independent breastplate, separate from other torso defensive armaments. The breastplate was made from a solid metal piece fashioned to cover the chest, back, and sides to the top of the diaphragm, with the rest of the torso—stomach, waist, and hips—protected by a flexible horizontal coat of plate hoops (*waist-lames*) riveted to a fabric cover. Later, c.1370, these too would disappear, replaced by a metallic hoop skirt which covered the same area. At first, this skirt (called a *fauld* or *tonlet*) was attached to the breastplate; however, later in the century the breastplate was separated entirely from any waist or hip armor and from the back-plate.[237]

By the end of the fourteenth century, the independent breast-plate had become the primary piece of plate armor and was fa-vored by both cavalry and infantry soldiers. For the soldier on horseback, two features were added to the breastplate to make it even more popular. First, a hinged bracket was attached to the right side of the chest, and served to support a couched lance. Second, a V-shaped bar was riveted to the armor just below the neck and was designed to prevent an opponent's weapon from sliding up along the slippery plate surface into the throat. These innovations were known as a *lance-rest* and a *stop-rib* respectively and became prominent features of the knight's breastplate through-out the fifteenth century.[238]

While the poleyns covered the knees and the shynbalds the shins, there was also the need to protect the foot and the rest of the leg. For the foot, *sabatons* were developed in the second decade of the fourteenth century. The most popular sabaton design consisted of a series of narrow overlapping plates shaped like a pointed shoe which covered the top of the foot and was attached by laces to a leather base. Later sabatons would cover all but the heel of the foot, and most could also be fitted with spurs.[239]

For the leg, shynbalds, and poleyns were usually accompanied by plate *cuisses* which covered the front of the leg below the hauberk to the knee. These too date from the early decades of the fourteenth century and were also initially constructed by a series of overlapping plates riveted together. By c.1370 this had changed, however, with cuisses constructed of a single metal plate which was fashioned to the shape of the thigh. It kept this con-struction and shape until c.1500. Cuisses were always accompa-nied by shynbalds and generally by poleyns; sometimes, however, a knight might not wear sabatons, choosing instead to wear a more comfortable mail or leather shoe.[240]

Plate armor for the arms and hands also developed in the late thirteenth and early fourteenth centuries. The earliest plate gauntlet appeared in the last quarter of the thirteenth century and was probably made in a manner similar to the coat of plates: metallic plates attached to the top of a leather or cloth housing, in this case a glove. Unlike the coat of plates, the plate gauntlet was almost immediately accepted, quickly replacing the chain mail mitten.

This method of constructing gauntlets continued until the end of the fourteenth century, although the plates became fewer in number and began to get larger. Eventually, the gauntlet consisted of only a single plate which protected the back and sides of the hand, molded in the shape of the knuckles and the base of the thumb, and separate, smaller plates to protect the fingers and the thumb. All plates were still attached by rivets to a leather glove. While earlier gauntlets favored a loose, flared cuff, the later fourteenth-century cuff became more close-fitting (the so-called "hourglass" gauntlet). Sometimes the gauntlet was also decorated by iron spikes (*gadlings*) or by the heraldic symbols of the knight.[241]

Plate defenses for arms, beyond the couter mentioned above, were not developed until c.1330, much later than plate armor for legs and hands. After this date, however, a number of arm defenses (collectively called the *bracer*) emerged: the *rerebrace* covering the upper arm from the elbow to the shoulder, the *vambrace* covering the lower arm from the wrist to the elbow, and the *spaudler* or *pauldron* protecting the shoulder. Each arm defense was constructed of a single plate of metal formed to fit the arm of the wearer. The couter continued to protect the elbow.[242]

During the period c.1275 to c.1350, plates known as *ailettes* were sometimes attached to the top of the shoulder plates at a 90° angle. Most often these were rectangular, although other shapes are also known, and all were decorated with heraldic symbols. Because of their placement, most often near the head, these may have been used to provide extra defense to the neck and cheeks; however, as not all were made of metal, ailettes may have had no defensive purpose, serving instead only as a symbol of office or as a placard for heraldry. After c.1350 they cease to appear on suits of plate armor, although why they were discarded remains a mystery.[243]

Finally, in the last decade of the thirteenth century plate armor was also invented for the chin and the neck. Up to this time, a chain coif had generally been used to protect these very vulnerable parts of the body. But with the utilization of plate as armor, this was quickly replaced by a metal collar (known as a *gorget* or *bevor*), made of a single piece of metal formed to cover the neck from the shoulders to the chin. However, the gorget appears to have been the least used of the fourteenth-century plate armors, with most soldiers choosing to continue protecting their necks with chain mail coifs.[244]

Plate Armor

By c.1330 plate armor began to dominate the armor industry. By the middle of the fourteenth century, it became clear that chain mail was no longer favored by knights who preferred the brilliant shine of the plate, often referred to as "shining like the sun," and the added status that ownership of this very expensive armor could bring in parades or tournaments, coupled with its added defensive strength. Plate armor (sometimes erroneously called plate mail) would continue to be used into the early modern age.

Initially at least, a full suit of armor included all of the pieces mentioned above: armor for the torso, neck, throat, legs, feet, arms, and hands. Over this, the soldier usually wore a surcoat, which added no extra protection, but did serve his heraldic purposes.[245] However, the making of plate armor was still not a perfect technology and experimentation with designs, forms, and metals continued throughout the fourteenth century. Large armor industries also began to form, with huge centers located in every kingdom, although the regions of Lombardy and the southern Low Countries (especially along the Meuse River) were generally recognized as producing the choicest plate armors.[246]

By c.1410 most experimentation in plate armor had ceased, and armor industries everywhere in Europe were producing excellent and very expensive "suits" of plate armor formed to outfit perfectly any wealthy noble and aristocratic soldier or jouster.[247] So distinct were each center's armor that by style alone the provenance of a suit of armor could be determined, and with it the social status of the wearer determined. In general, during the fifteenth century two styles of armor predominated: the Italian and the German, although Italian-style plate armor was not always made in Italy, nor was German-style plate armor always made in

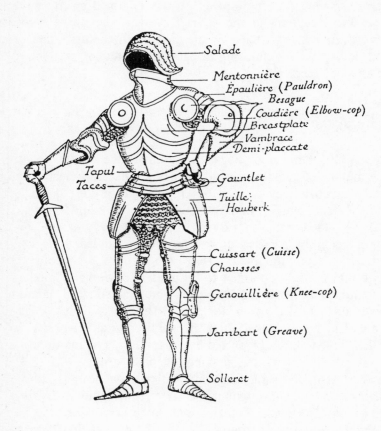

Salade
Mentonnière
Épaulière (Pauldron)
Besague
Coudière (Elbow-cop)
Breastplate
Vambrace
Demi-placcate
Tapul
Taces
Gauntlet
Tuille
Hauberk
Cuissart (Cuisse)
Chausses
Genouillière (Knee-cop)
Jambart (Greave)
Solleret

Fifteenth-century plate armor. [From Ashdown (1925).]

Germany. As well, both styles were worn throughout Europe, with Italian-style armor also worn often in Germany and German-style armor often in Italy.

Also, new carburizing processes and the use of the blast furnace allowed steel to become the principal metal for armor construction. Not only were the defensive capabilities of the plate armor thus improved, but steel could be polished to a high shine which impressed both the wearer and those who saw him. The shine was so brilliant in fact that plate armor became known as

"white armor" in contemporary sources. This was further emphasized at the beginning of the fifteenth century by the removal of
the surcoat worn by knights, leaving the bare, brilliant armor to
be viewed by all.[248]

Torso armor continued to be the primary part of the suit, the
foundation of which was a strong, well-designed breastplate. Two
styles of breastplate were present in the fifteenth century: the
Italian style was rounded in shape, covering the front and sides
of the torso, and was cut off at the waist, while the German style
was more boxed. Below the waist, the torso was protected by a
narrower lower breastplate (known as a *plackart*) which overlapped the main breastplate and was attached to it by a number
of leather straps and buckles. Most plackarts also supported a
fauld, made of a various number of waist-lames, which were
joined to it by rivets and straps. Later in the century, faulds were
accompanied by sometimes quite long oblong plates hanging from
the lames as added protection for the groin and thighs. A backplate
completed the torso defense. It was constructed in the same design
as the breastplate, with an upper plate overlapped by a lower plate
to which a fauld was affixed (although generally containing fewer
waist-lames). The backplate was attached to the front armor by
shoulder straps and a waist-belt.[249]

The shoulders continued to be protected by pauldrons in the
fifteenth century. These were made in various styles, although the
most common in the early part of the century was a large square-
shaped plate on the left shoulder and a smaller, similar shaped
one on the right shoulder. As the century continued, pauldrons
became less angular and more spread out in the back, forming
what looked like an overlapping set of "wings." Also, c.1430,
they began to be covered by reinforcing plates (*gardebraces*) attached to the pauldrons which continued to grow in size until the
left one had become so large that it extended as high as the ear.
The right gardebrace remained small to allow for ease in using
the couched lance. Sometimes pauldrons were decorated with in-
scriptions, such as invocations *Ave Maria* and *Ave Domini*.[250]

Very few changes were made to plate arm defenses in the
fifteenth century, although they were almost exclusively known as
vambraces. Other alterations were merely stylistic, varying generally between German and Italian designs. For example, the Ital-

ian-style armorers made larger upper vambrace cannons while the Germans enlarged the lower portion; German-style armorers made their vambraces fluted and more decorative than did their Italian-style counterparts; and Italian-style armorers preferred smooth, undecorated surfaces of plate armor, which tended to be more radiant when polished.

While vambraces remained relatively unchanged between the fourteenth and fifteenth centuries, the couter changed significantly. What had in the century previously been merely an elbow-guard now had added to its outside a large plate which formed a distinctive side-wing. This was especially massive on the right elbow, in the arm which carried the lance and thus did not have the benefit of a large protective pauldron, although the left side-wing was also quite large. The Italian-style couter was larger than the German-style one, although again the German-style armorers preferred more decoration.[251]

The gauntlet changed only after c.1430 when it evolved from protecting the hand with only a partial plate covering to an entire plate mitten. This was achieved by surrounding the entire hand with armor and by extending the metacarpal plates to the tips of the fingers. The number of plates depended on the flexibility desired—the more plates the better flexibility—with the right hand always more flexible than the left. At the same time, the "hourglass" shape of the cuffs fell out of fashion, with the new cuffs extending up the forearms until they eventually, c.1450, stretched to just below the couters.[252]

Early fifteenth-century leg defenses (called collectively *legharnesses*) also differed little from their fourteenth-century predecessors. Only two significant changes were made in legharnesses and both came about c.1430. The first was the addition of a side-wing to the poleyn. This developed similar to and often as a mirror image to the couter side-wing, growing larger and fancier in design and decoration as the century progressed. Again, as with the couter, the German-style was smaller and more decorated than the Italian-style. The second change was the addition of an articulated plate to the top of the cuisse which protected the space between the main cuisse plate and the groin.

Sabatons also remained the same in construction as fourteenth-century models with the exception that some extended only to the end of the foot and were rounded, while others had added, and sometimes detachable, extensions which were pointed and stretched several inches beyond the end of the foot.[253]

The gorget also did not change much in function from the fourteenth century, although it did increase in popularity among German-style armorers after c.1430. The Italian-style armorers continued to use mail coifs for neck defense. The fifteenth-century gorget did however change in style, with new models made of two main plates, front and rear, which enclosed the base of the neck and extended over the top of the breast- and backplates. The two gorget plates were hinged together on one side and secured by a pin on the other.[254]

While the gorget was sometimes disregarded, it was a very important piece of armor. Indeed, the absence of the gorget may have caused the throat wound of the count of Burgundy, Charles the Bald, at the battle of Montlhery in 1453, when contemporary chroniclers report that his throat guard had fallen off, and that he had not bothered to replace it.[255]

The defensive strength of plate armor precluded the need to wear a heavily quilted haubergeon under the armor for added defense, as had been the custom with chain mail. Still, there was the need to wear something under the armor to protect the wearer against the discomfort of the plate metal. Therefore, a haubergeon continued to be worn in the late Middle Ages, although it shrunk both in size—extending only to the hips and elbows—and in thickness. Even this was too large, and the haubergeon began to disappear in the fifteenth century, with soldiers choosing to use an *arming doublet* instead. This was a thinly padded garment with mail attached in places not covered by the plate armor: the neck (even if a gorget was worn), the armpits, the elbow-joints and the tops of the thighs and groin. In the latter case, the Italian-style arming doublet was a relatively long, loose skirt, while in the German-style, the arming doublet was a short, tight-fitting pair of mail breeches which contained a genital protecting cod-piece. A quilted arming cap, like those used in the thirteenth century, continued to be worn under the helmet; sometimes it also extended around the cheeks and chin to keep the skin there from being irritated, although the late medieval helmet was generally lined.[256]

The weight of a suit of armor was immense. It has been estimated that a complete suit of plate armor (including helmet and shield, to be discussed below) for use on the battlefield weighed between 23 and 28 kilograms, while a suit of plate jousting-armor, much heavier because of the definite geography and chronology of the tournament against the uncertainty of the battlefield, weighed between 41 and 46 kilograms.

However, this is a bit overstated, as plate armor probably hampered the body less than did chain mail, because of its even distribution of weight; the weight of chain mail was unevenly distributed with most of the weight carried on the shoulders. Indeed, the chief discomfort of plate armor may not have come from its weight, but from its lack of ventilation, and from its heat in the summer and cold in the winter.[257] As well, this armor took a tremendous amount of time to put on, a fact made light of by many late medieval authors, including Geoffrey Chaucer. Describing the arming of Sir Topaz, Chaucer writes:

> They covered next his ivory flank
> With cloth spun of the finest hank,
> With breeches and a shirt,
> And over that (in case it fail)
> A tunic, then a coat of mail,
> For fear he might be hurt,
> And over that contrived to jerk
> A hauberk (finest Jewish work
> and strong in every plate)
> And over that his coat of arms,
> White as a lily-flower's charms,
> In which he must debate.[258]

Nevertheless, with the changing style, rules, and weaponry of warfare in the late Middle Ages, it was absolutely essential that everyone who could afford to do so should be outfitted with the finest plate armor. Defensibility with this armor was impressive; it was capable of withstanding penetration by crossbow bolts, longbow arrows, and handgun shots, not to mention the spears, halberds, swords, and other weapons used at the time. Failure to wear this armor could cost a soldier his life. The most prominent example of this was John Talbot, the Earl of Shrewsbury, who was slain when dressed only in a brigadine at the battle of Castillon in July 1453.[259]

Late Medieval Infantry Armor

Naturally, the late medieval plate armor discussed here was used principally by noble or aristocratic knights who commonly fought on horseback. The expense of plate armor, coupled with its discomfort and lack of flexibility, made its use by infantry soldiers rare, although in the fourteenth and fifteenth centuries a few wealthy footsoldiers did venture to clothe themselves in the armor of knights on horseback.[260] It is also true that many infantry soldiers commonly wore some pieces of plate armor, most notably the breastplate and the gauntlets. Still, even this was beyond the financial capabilities of most individual infantry soldiers; nor could the wealthiest late medieval state be expected to outfit all their infantry in plate armor.

Some infantry soldiers continued to use chain mail hauberks,[261] and some, especially archers, simply went without. However, it seems that many footsoldiers did opt for the less expensive and more flexible coat of plates. And these armors, while patterned similarly to those worn by cavalry, had some marked changes made to them to accommodate the infantry soldier.

This in itself would be difficult to describe, as few artistic sources of the late Middle Ages depict anything other than knightly plate armor, except for the 25 examples of infantry armor excavated from mass graves found at the site of the battle of Wisby, in Götland, fought on July 27, 1361.[262]

Although there are six different styles of armor found at Wisby, some of which may have been worn by cavalry, all 25 suits of armor have the same basic characteristics: all are sleeveless hauberks consisting of overlapping iron plates which had once been rivetted or laced onto the inside of a leather covering, with the covering alone the only connection between the plates. Only two armor suits have plates riveted to the outside of the covering, and in both cases these were only small shoulder plates.

The hauberks vary in size and number of plates and in general appearance; the plates to form a hauberk vary in number from eight to almost 600, and in size from 15 to 50 centimeters to less

Pre-1361 infantry armor from the battle at Wisby
excavations. [From Thordemann (1939).]

than 2 to 10 centimeters. On some, plates are placed vertically; on others, horizontally and vertically. Most cover the torso with a skirt to the hips, while others are more tight-fitting and extend only to the waist; extra shoulder plates appear to have been added to some, if not all. Most cover the entire torso, front and back, although at least five may have covered only the front and sides of the torso leaving the back without plate protection. Almost all opened in the back, with two opening on one side, two on both sides and one in the front. Finally, some hauberks were decorated, either with other iron plates in scutiform, scallop and semicircular shapes, or with bronze mountings in the shape of heraldic shields, fleur-de-lis or shells.[263]

Other armors were also found at Wisby. These included chain mail hauberks, mail and plate gauntlets, arm and leg guards made of plate, plate sabatons, and almost 200 mail coifs. Interestingly, although these coifs should have been used under helmets or iron caps, no traces of these were found, and this may indicate that infantry soldiers did not always wear head protection beyond the neck.[264]

Perhaps the Wisby finds only indicate a Scandinavian tradition of infantry defensive armaments. Nevertheless, the mass graves at this battle do contain the most numerous examples of infantry armor yet found. Moreover, the fact that the basic characteristics of this armor are so similar, yet without apparent systemization, establishes what may be a pattern of late medieval infantry armor.

Late Medieval Helmets

The Great Helm remained the chief armor for the heads of cavalry soldiers in the fourteenth century and of tournament jousters into the sixteenth century. It also remained relatively unchanged in function from that of earlier times although stylistically a few significant changes must be noted.

The first design change came at the end of the thirteenth century, when the Great Helm lost its traditional "can" shape and began to taper more. The crown resembled the earlier conical helmets, truncated at the top and sometimes ending in a slight point. It also lengthened to rest on the shoulders and on the chest and was attached to the armor there.

The second design change followed soon afterwards and had perhaps the longest enduring consequences for helmet design in the next two centuries. This was the addition of a moveable visor, where the whole or part of the face mask was attached by hinges to the helmet so that it could be opened on a side or pivoted upwards.

At the end of the fourteenth century, the Great Helm became higher in the skull with the lower edge slightly curved forward to form a pair of lips; the lower lip was longer than the upper lip with an eye-slit open in between. This in turn evolved into the famous "frog-mouthed" form of helmet which developed in the early fifteenth century and became extremely popular for use in tournaments for the next hundred years.[265]

Throughout the late Middle Ages, crests were mounted on top of the Great Helm and sometimes became quite ornate, especially for parade and tournament armor. Ailettes, such as those which appeared on early fourteenth-century torso armor, horns, plumes of feathers, crowns (for royalty), and heraldic symbols were all common. All seem to have been made of molded leather and attached to the helmets by laces. Crests remained in use until the middle of the sixteenth century.[266]

From the end of the thirteenth century as well, the Great Helm was often equipped with *guard-chains*. These attached the helmet at first to the surcoat, but after c.1300 by rivets or staples to the breast- and backplates. Initially, they were used probably to keep the helmet attached during battle, but they also allowed the soldier to carry the helmet slung over a shoulder by the chain.[267]

Infantry soldiers continued to wear the kettle-hat, and, like the Great Helm, it too retained a stylistic constancy during the thirteenth and fourteenth centuries. Indeed, only three changes in design can be noted. First, after c.1300 the kettle-hat was constructed from only one plate or from only a few plates riveted together. Second, its brim grew wider and flaired out away from the head more. Finally, while the kettle-hat in many instances continued to be worn over a hood-shaped mail coif, the style in the late thirteenth century was to attach the coif directly to the helmet. This was known as a *mail tippet* and would soon become the style for all late medieval helmet designs.[268]

The kettle-hat was worn until the sixteenth century, and evolved into the conventional helmet of the early modern period, so frequently portrayed on the heads of Conquistadors.

However, the Great Helm and the kettle-hat were not the only, nor even the most popular, helmets of late medieval soldiers. That honor may in fact fall upon the *bascinet*. Three types of bascinet were prevalent during this period. The first was a small globular helmet, usually pointed on the crown, which curved down on each side to cover the ears. Sometimes these were fitted with, and sometimes without, a moveable visor which could extend below the chin, but usually only covered the face; a mail coif covered the neck and cheeks. Quite often this visor was in the shape of a snout, giving rise to the term "pig-faced bascinet," made popular by modern collectors. The second was a large, but tight-fitting conical helmet which extended to the shoulders on the sides and back. It too was sometimes fitted with a pivoted visor and, if not, at least with a triangular-shaped nasal guard. When the visor was closed, it looked much like a Great Helm. The third type was a tall conical helmet with a straight lower edge at a level below the ears, in a design not dissimilar, although not derived from, the conical helmets of the tenth to the thirteenth centuries. All three types of bascinet were developed in the early fourteenth century and were popular for over 200 years.

By c.1350 all bascinets had become more tight-fitting and conical, stretching down the back of the neck and covering the cheeks. The apex of the helmet also moved more to the rear until, in the fifteenth century, it formed almost a vertical line with the back of the helmet. This helmet was known sometimes as the Great Bascinet and was used by both cavalry and infantry troops, although the latter soldiers generally used it without a visor.

After 1330 the bascinet was fitted with its own mail tippet, attached, like that of the kettle-hat, by rivets to the bottom rim of the helmet. It surrounded the helmet, covering the neck, cheeks and chin, and was laced together in the front of the face. Sometimes a solid metal gorget replaced the tippet around the neck.[269]

Three further late medieval helmet designs evolved from the bascinet. The first was known as the *barbuta* (also known early on as the *celata*), and it appeared initially in mid fourteenth-century Italy. The barbuta consisted of a visored helmet made from

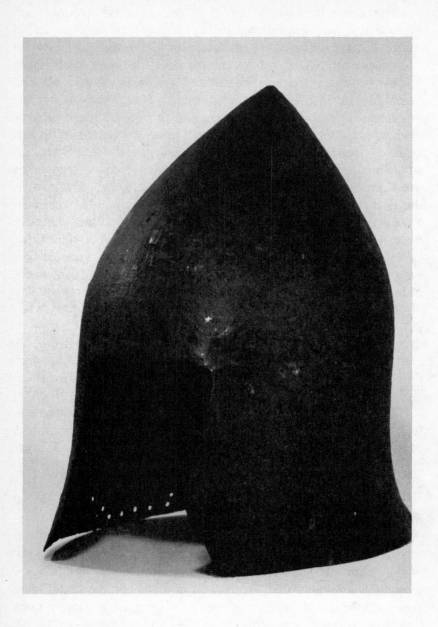

Italian bascinet (c.1400).
[From the Cleveland Museum of Art Collection.]

a single piece of metal. Like a bascinet, its skull was rounded and curved to the shape of the neck, although so much so that it almost formed a tail in the back. The facial opening of the two styles was distinctly different. The barbuta's facial opening was quite narrow, covering the cheeks and fitting tightly around the eyes. In this way, it was very much like an ancient Corinthian Greek helmet; in fact, that prototype may have inspired it in the true Renaissance spirit.[270]

From the barbuta evolved the *sallet* (or *salade*) which appeared in Italy early in the fifteenth century, becoming especially popular after c.1430. In essence, the sallet was little more than a combination of the barbuta and the kettle-hat: it was a conical helmet like the barbuta and had a wide brim like the kettle-hat. Indeed, sometimes the brim was so exaggerated in its width, especially among late fifteenth-century German-style armorers, that it extended far to the rear to form an extensive downward sloping tail. It also harkened back to earlier helmets, affixed to the head not by its shape, but by a chin-strap of leather; this allowed for more flexibility of movement as well as greater air circulation.

As with other late medieval helmets the sallet was often visored. However, unlike others, this visor did not cover the entire face. Instead, it covered only the forehead and the eyes, allowing the wearer to see through an eye-slit in the helmet's brim. The neck and cheeks were protected by a gorget or bevor of plate.

The sallet was initially popular among Italian-style armorers, but by the late fifteenth century, German-style armorers also constructed them frequently. They also seem to have been used by both cavalry and infantry soldiers.[271]

The final late medieval helmet style which grew out of the bascinet was the *armet*. It too originated in the fifteenth century and was similar to other tight-fitting visored helmets, most notably the Great Bascinet. And like the barbuta and sallet, the armet was conceived and produced first by Italian-style armorers, not becoming popular among German-style armorers until the sixteenth century. The armet comprised a skull cap of one metal piece which reached only to the level of the tops of the ears, except at the back where it reached to the neck. Cheekpieces were then riveted onto this cap so that they overlapped both each other and the back strip; all these pieces were then riveted together. A bluntly pointed visor was then hinged to the cap as a facemask which could be raised or lowered when desired. At times a metal gorget was also added to the armet to protect the neck, and on some exemplars a metal rondel was attached at the rear, although the reason for this is difficult to ascertain.[272]

Late Medieval Shields and Barding

The flat or slightly curved, triangular shield of moderate size, popular in the thirteenth century, continued to be popular in the fourteenth and fifteenth centuries as well, but, it seems, only among cavalry soldiers. As such, however, the placing of the lance in couched position on top of the shield generally meant that it was too low in the charge or joust to provide much defense to the soldier holding it. To rectify this trouble, at the end of the fourteenth century the right hand top corner of the shield often had a notch cut into it to support the couched lance without losing the shield's defense.

After the turn of the fifteenth century, the triangular cavalry shield was supplanted by a variety of shapes and sizes. The most common of these was an oblong, either rounded or pointed on the lower edge, and often bent forward at the top and bottom (although what defensive advantage such a shape might give is not known). Leaf-shaped and round shields were also known. All cavalry shields of any shape were usually made of metal, and sometimes, if used exclusively in tournaments, they were reinforced by extra metallic plates.

In the early fifteenth century, shields of all shapes and sizes began to fall into disfavor among the cavalry, already well protected by a massive amount of body armor. This trend continued until after c.1450 when the shield continued to be used only in jousts.[273]

Infantry soldiers rejected their thirteenth-century triangular shields, returning sometime in the early fourteenth century to the round shield not seen in regular use in western Europe since Charlemagne's day. Three styles of late medieval infantry shields developed:

1) the *target* or *targe* which was fairly large, flat, and equipped with a number of enarmes for gripping by the forearm and hand,

2) the *buckler* which was small, often concave, with a hollow metal boss and gripped by a single crossbar across the inside, and

3) the *pavise* which was a large oblong shield generally propped up by a wooden brace to provide protection to archers and crossbowmen.

Most infantry shields continued to be made of wood covered by leather, and all styles were used well into the sixteenth century.[274]

Finally, the late Middle Ages also saw significant changes in armor for horses. In the middle of the thirteenth century horse armor was nothing more than a quilted fabric or leather bard, used infrequently, which covered almost the entire horse but offered little protection against an enemy's attack. While this style continued into the fourteenth century, its defensive ineffectiveness led to constant experimentation. Among these was the invention of a plate bard, made in metal or *cuir-bouilli*, which appeared initially in the last decade of the thirteenth century. It too had limitations, mostly because it was almost impossible technologically to form plate armor which would comfortably fit a horse while not hindering its speed and maneuverability. This was in part deflected, however, by the production of plate armor not to cover the entire animal, but only its most vulnerable parts, the chest and head. A coat of plates, made similar to a human coat of plates, was also developed and served as an evolutionary step in the construction of metal plate armor for the entire horse which came at the end of the fourteenth century, although most examples date from the fifteenth and sixteenth centuries. When complete— and horses were not always clothed in their complete armor, especially on the battlefield—the horse's bard included: a *chanfron*, which covered the head; the *peytral*, a large piece of metal curved to the shape of the chest; a *crupper*, which consisted of three oblong plates of metal riveted together, one of which lay across the horse's back and two hanging down each side; and the *flanchards*, oblong plates suspended on each side of the horse from

the lower edge of the saddle. The chanfron, which was the most
intricate piece of the horse's armor, was usually constructed from
a single plate of metal, carefully formed to fit the horse's head,
with holes for the eyes, ears and nose. All pieces of the bard
were separable and connections between them were protected by
a mail or laminated defense known as a *crinet*.

There was some attempt at various times during the fifteenth
and sixteenth centuries to increase the length of the bard, covering
the horse to its hooves. But each of these attempts proved to make
the horse less fast and maneuverable, and consequently was never
put into general use.[275]

There is also a late medieval reference to dog armor. On
October 18, 1371, the duchess of Burgundy ordered armor made
for six of her dogs. However, what this armor might have been,
if it was ever made, or whether it was to be used in military
enterprise or only for parade, cannot be determined by this single
reference.[276]

Plate armor continued to be made in the sixteenth and, to a
limited extent, in the seventeenth centuries.[277] However, its "hey-
day" was clearly the late Middle Ages, when chivalry reigned,
tournaments were fought, knights in shining armor were revered
(and feared) and gunpowder weapons had not yet effected a change
in military attitudes.

The Stirrup, Mounted Shock Combat, Chivalry, and Feudalism

Perhaps one of the most important debates of the last century among scholars of medieval history is focused on the socio-economic system known as *feudalism*. Not only do modern historians argue about what constituted feudalism and about what its origins were, but some even question the historical validity of the system itself. These historians choose to see it as a "tyrannical construct," to use the words of Elizabeth A.R. Brown, which "must be declared once and for all deposed and its influence over students of the Middle Ages finally ended."[278]

However, for the sake of argument, and for a review of the role of military technology in the debate, it is necessary to look at feudalism as a system defining the society, economy, and polity of the medieval world. In its basic form, feudalism, a word derived from the Latin *feodum* (meaning fief), describes the structure of medieval society which gave the king "ownership" of all the lands and the peasants who lived on them. The peasants served the king by working his lands and giving him a portion of the produce derived from them. The king promised to protect the peasants from outside invasion. Between the king and the peasants was a group of individuals who "administered" the king's lands and the peasants on them. They were the holders of fiefs, and their titles varied from area to area; they were, for lack of a better general term, landlords (or lords for short).

Ideally, the feudal structure was quite simple. The kings gave the fiefs to the lords, who then served as his *vassals*, providing an administrative organization and watching over the economic yields of the kingdom. The lords derived their own livelihood from the fiefs by taking an amount of the yields produced by their vassals, the peasants. In turn, the lords promised the king to deliver a certain amount of the produce of their fiefs for his maintenance, as well as to provide him with security, in the form of an army, to protect his combined land-holdings. Naturally, this system did much to benefit those individuals who, for whatever reason, gained the fiefs; and it also served the king by giving him some administration and security. The peasants too derived a few benefits from the system, although these were far fewer than either those of the lords or the king. In return for working the lands, the peasants received a promise of peace and security from their landlords.

But the ideal was rarely reached in the Middle Ages. Viking, Hungarian, and Muslim invasions, as well as the constant medieval European warfare, proved that few lords were able at all times to protect their peasants. And, while strong kings had little difficulty in holding the loyalty of their lords, the more numerous weak kings frequently faced noble insurrections or indifference. There was also a constant struggle among the lords to increase their fiefs, often at the expense of a neighbor, which escalated the upheaval of feudal society.[279]

Why the lords were there, how they came to gain their status and what their responsibilities were regarding the king and the peasants are the questions most asked in the feudalism debate. The answers vary. To Marc Bloch, they are socially determined. Feudalism was constituted by

> a subject peasantry; widespread use of the service tenement (i.e. the fief) instead of a salary, which was out of the question; the supremacy of a class of specialized warriors; ties of obedience and protection which bind man to man and, within the warrior class, assume the distinctive form called vassalage; fragmentation of authority—leading inevitably to disorder; and, in the midst of all this, the survival of other forms of association, family and State...[280]

To François Ganshof, they are political. Feudalism was

> a body of institutions creating and regulating the obligations of obedience and service—mainly military service—on the part of

a free man (the vassal) towards another free man (the lord),
and the obligations of protection and maintenance on the part
of the lord with regard to his vassal. The obligation of maintenance had usually as one of its effects the grant by the lord
to his vassal of a unit of real property known as a fief.[281]

To Joseph Strayer, they are jurisdictional. Feudalism was "a
fragmentation of political authority, public power in private hands,
and a military system in which an essential part of the armed
forces is secured by private contracts."[282] And, finally, to Georges
Duby, the answers to these questions can only be reached by
considering the *mentalité* of the Middle Ages. To him, feudalism
was

a psychological complex formed in the small world of warriors
who little by little became the nobles. A consciousness of the
superiority of a status characterized by military specialization,
one that presupposes respect for certain moral precepts, the practice of certain virtues; the associated idea that social relations
are organized as a function of companionship in combat; notions
of homage, of personal dependence, now in the foreground,
replacing all previous forms of political association.[283]

One of the earliest and most constant explanations for feudalism is that it was created for military purposes, and that it survived
as long as the king had no other option for acquiring a military
force. This theory was expressed if not first, certainly with the
most impact in 1887 by Heinrich Brunner. In an article entitled
"Der Reiterdienst und die Anfänge des Lehnwesens" ("Knights'
Service and the Origin of Feudalism"), Brunner claimed that feudalism began as a military organization, a socio-economic structure
for producing and supporting a cavalry-based force.[284] He explained that while the barbarian tribes had had a history of fighting
on horseback, by the time they invaded the Roman Empire, because their economy had shifted from a herding emphasis to an
agricultural one, cavalry warfare was almost non-existent. Among
these tribes, the Franks, who later came to dominate most of
western Europe, had little use for horses; their chief weapon, the
francisca, was efficient only when used by infantry.

The Franks encountered numerous enemies in the early Middle
Ages, most of whom fell to defeat at the hands of this infantry

force. Chief among these enemies were the Muslim armies which invaded the Frankish lands until 732 when Charles Martel defeated them at the battle of Poitiers and later pushed them below the Pyrenees Mountains. The Muslims fought on horseback, and although defeated, Brunner contends, put up such a virulent opposition to the Franks that it forever changed the latter's military strategy. So quick and decisive was this change that when chroniclers describe the Frankish army at the battle of the Dyle, fought in 891, they report that "the Franks are unused to fighting on foot."

Brunner thus determined that sometime between the two battles a shift in military opinion was effected. Working through a number of sources, he judged that the change could be dated from the mid-eighth century, principally during the reigns of Charles Martel (who ruled as Mayor of the Palace until 742) and his son, Pippin III (who ruled as King of the Franks from 751 to 768). Among other evidence, Brunner discovered that in 755, Pippin had changed the time of the Marchfield, the traditional Frankish mustering of the army, from March to May, when forage was more readily available to horses. He further found that, in 758, Pippin had replaced the Saxon tribute of payment in cattle to payment in horses. Most importantly, he proved that Charles Martel seized a large number of church lands after the battle of Poitiers and distributed them to retainers in exchange for military service.

Why would Charles have done this unless it was to provide his retainers with the ability to gain extra income? And why would they need this extra income if it was not to supplement their military might by adding expensive warhorses to their military equipment? Evidently, Charles gave fiefs of church lands to his retainers so that they might serve him as a force of horsed warriors. Failure to do military service meant the forfeiture of these lands and the added income they might bring. Feudalism was born.

Brunner's article was almost immediately attacked. Many military historians argued that the German scholar had no basis for his thesis because his facts were wrong. Some claimed that cavalry was known among barbarians, especially among the Visigoths, before the time of Charles Martel, and therefore that the institution of a Carolingian cavalry-based force had not created feudalism;

others contended that Frankish armies even as late as the reign of Charlemagne were not composed of a large, nor even a primary body of cavalry, that horsed troops were in fact far fewer in number and importance than the infantry. Therefore, if cavalry was the basis for feudalism, feudalism could not be considered a Carolingian innovation.[285]

Brunner's thesis outlived these criticisms; there was simply no reliable evidence to rebut his argument that the Frankish army during the eighth century had transformed from an infantry-based force to a cavalry-based one. Nor could it be proven that cavalry warfare had been conventional among earlier barbarian armies. Finally, while a number of scholars also charged that Brunner was wrong in naming such a late date for the origin of feudalism, contending instead that the union of fief and vassal was much older than the eighth century, these scholars found it extremely difficult to counter Brunner's evidence of the seizure of church lands, the first datable grant of lands for use as benefices.[286]

In 1962, in a chapter entitled "Stirrup, Mounted Shock Combat, Feudalism, and Chivalry" of his important study, *Medieval Technology and Social Change*, Lynn White Jr. challenged Brunner's thesis.[287] He did not, however, level his critical barrage on the conclusion of Brunner's argument, as other historians had done. Indeed, White agreed with the nineteenth-century German historian's view that feudalism originated out of military necessity. What White disagreed with was Brunner's contention that it was the Muslim invasion of Francia, and in particular the battle of Poitiers, which caused Charles Martel to change his military strategy by instituting a cavalry-based force and with it feudalism. For one thing, White found little supporting evidence for the claim that the Muslim invasion had been such a crisis for the Franks. Charles Martel "turned his attention to Islam only after he had consolidated his realm," and in fact "made little effort for several years to follow up his victory."[288] White also questioned the use by Spanish Muslims of cavalry in their attacks on the Franks, citing other studies which showed that the Muslim armies did not fight with large numbers of cavalry until the second half of the eighth century, perhaps responding to their encounters with the Frankish armies and not the other way around.[289]

Most importantly, White added, the date of the battle of Poitiers, which Brunner had placed in 732, had recently (1955) been discovered to be actually 733. This in itself was of little consequence to the thesis, except for the fact that Brunner had placed so much emphasis on the seizure of church lands as evidence of the importance of the Poitiers battle, an action which occurred in the earlier year:

> Poitiers, therefore, cannot have inspired Charles's policy of confiscations for the improvement of his cavalry. His military reforms had begun a year earlier, although doubtless they had not yet greatly modified the structure of the Frankish forces when he met the Muslim invaders.[290]

Still, White could not find any other reason why these lands had been confiscated except to establish a cavalry-based force, and thus he was unwilling to completely discount Brunner's military rationale for feudalism. But if the Muslim invasions of Charles Martel's realm had not prompted this change in military strategy, what had? White contended that the cause was not strategic change, but was instead technological change: the invention of the stirrup.

Stirrups seem small and insignificant. Yet they may be the most important invention for the military use of a horse. A cavalry soldier might be uncomfortable without a saddle, but he could still ride; and he might find guiding the horse difficult without reins, but by grasping the horse's mane he could still steer it. However, without stirrups, the rider had no capability of using his mount as little more than a mode of transportation or a mobile missile launching pad. If he was to mount a charge in the customary fashion against an enemy without them, the force of his blow would just as likely unseat him from the steed as deliver the desired impact to his opponent.

Yet, despite their importance, stirrups were a relatively late invention. With the exception of an isolated illustration of stirrups from the ninth-century BC Assyrian Empire, there is no ancient tradition of stirrups. And even though they were well known in China, India, Korea, and Japan during the early Middle Ages,[291] they seem not to have diffused to Europe or the Middle East until at least the seventh or even the early eighth century. It was at that time that the stirrup first appeared in Persia and from there was carried to other Muslim lands.[292]

From there the stirrup spread almost immediately to Byzantium and then, either from the Byzantines or by direct diffusion, to the Franks. This White substantiates with archaeological, linguistic and, to a lesser extent, artistic evidence, all of which places the use of the stirrup among the Franks in the early eighth century.

He also found that at the same time there was a change in weapons' policy among the Franks which led them to discard their battle axes (*francisca*) and barbed spears (*ango*), both of which were only infantry weapons, and adopt longswords (*spatha*) and heavier and longer wing-spears or lances, the most distinct feature of which was their prominent cross-piece which prohibited the impaling of an enemy so deeply that the weapon would be stuck. The purpose of this could only have been to allow the horsed warrior the ability to couch his lance under his arm during the charge, adding the momentum of the horse's movement to the lance's thrust, a tactic which White called "mounted shock combat."

These changes in military technology could only have been induced by the use of the stirrup by the Franks. When Charles Martel realized the true military worth of the stirrup, and he alone did so, he began to insist on its use by his soldiers. The effect was quickly seen and Charles's conclusions verified; a cavalry force was demanded, one which was expensive to initiate and maintain. Therefore, changes in the structure of society were needed and put into effect. The result was feudalism.[293]

Fighting as a cavalry-based force was much more expensive than as an infantry-based army. The warhorse was extremely expensive, and more than one horse was usually needed by the soldier; the maintenance of these horses was also costly. Equally expensive were the new arms and armor needed to fight upon that horse, as the cavalry now had to expect to do most of the fighting. To attack effectively with mounted shock combat also required an immense amount of training, beginning usually at puberty. This meant that the soldier was unable to work in the fields or elsewhere. Thus, while the soldiers initially chosen to form this new cavalry core of the Frankish army may have been so selected because of their inherent wealth or bravery in battle, their continued presence in the cavalry necessitated some endowment which would extend their ability to afford the weapons and training time needed to be an effective cavalry soldier. They became owners of fiefs, feudal elite, nobles, knights, and the *chivalric* class (which, after all, derives its name from being wealthy enough to fight on horseback).[294]

Charles Martel began feudalism, but his son, Pippin, and grandson, Charlemagne, took it throughout Europe. Italy accepted the new military and socio-economic reforms with the defeat of the Lombards, as did Eastern Europe with the conquest and defeat of the Saxons and Avars. A century later, the Byzantines, in constant contact with the Carolingians, adopted feudalism, and two centuries later it was taken by the Normans to England and Sicily and by the Crusaders to the Holy Land and Spain.[295]

Lynn White concludes his article:

> Few inventions have been so simple as the stirrup, but few have had so catalytic an influence on history. The requirements of the new mode of warfare which it made possible found expression in a new form of western European society dominated by an aristocracy of warriors endowed with land so that they might fight in a new and highly specialized way. Inevitably this nobility developed cultural forms and patterns of thought and emotion in harmony with its style of mounted shock combat and its social posture; as [N.] Denholm-Young has said: "it is impossible to be chivalrous without a horse." The Man on Horseback, as we have known him during the past millennium, was made possible by the stirrup, which joined man and steed into fighting organism. Antiquity imagined the Centaur; the early Middle Ages made him the master of Europe.[296]

Although initially praised by reviewers for its insight and novelty, Lynn White's thesis was not allowed to stand without criticism for long. His use of military technology as the determining factor in the origin and rise of feudalism almost immediately produced a stir among those historians who believed in an economic, social, political, or *mentalité* cause. Several criticisms were quickly written. The first which appeared was published in 1963 in the prestigious, leftist historical journal *Past and Present*. Written by P.H. Sawyer (and combined in a "review article" with a criticism of another of White's chapters in *Medieval Technology and Social Change*, on the invention of the plough, by R.H. Hilton), the article, entitled "Technical Determinism: The Stirrup and the Plough," condemned White's use of technology to determine anything in social history, especially feudalism.[297]

The criticism was harsh:

> The technical determinism of Professor Lynn White, Jr., however, is peculiar in that, instead of building new and provocative theories about general historical development on the basis of technical studies, he gives a misleadingly adventurist cast to old-fashioned platitudes by supporting them with a chain of obscure and dubious deductions from scanty evidence about the progress of technology.[298]

In particular, Sawyer argued that White had not produced enough evidence to prove that the introduction of the stirrup could have made such radical social changes as those of feudalism. He also attacked White's conclusion that it was Charles Martel's genius which allowed the stirrup to be exploited in the Frankish army, while being ignored elsewhere, namely in Anglo-Saxon England. And he argued that White had not sufficiently traced the diffusion of the stirrup from China, something which was needed before going further in his hypothesis.[299]

But it was White's sources which fell under the greatest amount of criticism by Sawyer. He contended that because of the meagerness in finds, difficulty in dating and the fact that it was impossible to use evidence from graves further to the east as evidence for Frankish customs, archaeological remains could not be used as conclusive substantiation for either the dating or the significance of stirrups in early Carolingian military strategy. Artistic and linguistic sources were also suspect. Most of the artistic material cited by White, Sawyer claimed, were made at least a century later, and the written work also dated from the same later period. Finally, Sawyer criticized White's discussion of the Frankish movement from infantry to cavalry arms and armor, arguing that again there was imprecise dating and a lack of significant change as seen by later sources (in particular in the *Bayeux Tapestry* which shows a number of horsed soldiers using non-wing-spears as cavalry lances).[300]

Sawyer further went on to criticize White's contention that mounted shock combat was adopted by the Franks in the eighth century and by others within a century or two later: "There is no evidence to support this claim and there is much against it." And he criticized White's understanding of the expense of mounted warfare.[301]

Sawyer's article was written quickly and with much, sometimes undue, emotion. And while it asked some very important questions of White's thesis, it did not often offer evidence to show that White was wrong in his conjectures. Indeed, Sawyer too often answered accused generalizations with other equally sparse arguments. Furthermore, despite not saying so directly, it was impossible not to read in the harsh tone taken by the author of his obvious dislike for the military explanation of the origin of feudalism defended by White, a point which tended to decrease his objectivity.

Yet another criticism of White's thesis appeared three years later in the relatively obscure *The University of Colorado Studies: Series in Language and Literature*. Entitled "The Stirrup and Feudalism," and written by literary historian, J.D.A. Ogilvy, this article in many regards was an embarrassment of historical criticism which probably should not have been published.[302]

Ogilvy approached White's thesis on two levels: criticism of White's understanding of military matters and criticism of his linguistic evidence. In the latter, Ogilvy was competent, showing where White made mistakes in his discussion of the linguistic changes in describing the mounting of horses. But none of these linguistic criticisms was new, and in fact all Ogilvy's examples had been pointed out by Sawyer.

Of his criticisms on White's understanding of military history, however, Ogilvy fell into the trap of having perhaps too much zeal with too little knowledge. Deriving most of his material from Sir Charles Oman's *A History of the Art of War in the Middle Ages*, written in the early twentieth century, Ogilvy began by stating, without substantiation, his belief that stirrups did nothing more for a horseman than allow him a more convenient means of mounting his steed and of remaining in the saddle; certainly they were not necessary for effective couched lance warfare. In this he followed Oman's statement that the Byzantine Cataphract and the Tamberlaine horse-archer were far more formidable than the lancer, and that the Frankish lancer only gained his reputation because of the lack of first-class infantry to oppose him.

Second, again following Oman, Ogilvy tried to show that victory in medieval warfare came not by the adept use of mounted shock combat, but rather by the leaders of these victorious armies or the ineptitude of the opposing force. However, almost all of the battles he chose as examples—Hastings, Falkirk, Louden Hill, Bannockburn, Crécy, Poitiers, Rosebeek, Agincourt, Joan of Arc's battles, and the fifteenth-century Swiss battles—took place in the fourteenth and fifteenth centuries, some 600 years after White's date for the rise of mounted shock combat.

Finally, Ogilvy questioned the date of the invention of the winged-spear (an Utrecht Psalter drawing shows a winged-spear used by an infantry soldier); the date of the appearance of mounted shock combat (it had occurred earlier, used by Alexander the Great, Hannibal, Caesar, and the Visigoths at Adrianople); and the belief that the stirrup was somehow more important in the formation of heavy cavalry than heavy armor. In the last criticism, Ogilvy held that it was the necessity for heavy, expensive armor which brought about the land endowments given by Charles Martel to his military elite. Whereas cavalry had no advantages in sieges, armor did, and armor also defended a knight from horse archers when a horse was of little help. Since these were the manner of the battles and the opponents facing Charles Martel, Ogilvy could only conclude that cavalry at the time was merely an adjunct to infantry, that mounted shock combat occurred before the eighth century, and that the stirrup played only a minor role in warfare and none at all in the origins of feudalism.

Ogilvy's use of Oman, whose classical work on medieval military history is constantly being reworked by military historians, showed his inherent lack of understanding of the field, a criticism which he hypocritically directed at White. Had he done any research, he would have recognized his flaws and rewritten (or perhaps withdrawn) his article. Even if his linguistic criticisms were valid, placed as they were next to his many military historical errors, they too looked suspect.

Thus it seemed that White's article met at least the initial onslaught of criticism and passed these tests suffering only a modicum of historical bruises. Then came the publication of two articles in 1970, both of which seriously harmed White's thesis with their criticisms.

The first was only a small part of a larger article written by D.A. Bullough and published in the *English Historical Review*. Entitled *"Europae Pater*: Charlemagne and His Achievement in the Light of Recent Scholarship," it reviewed current studies on Charlemagne and the Carolingians.[303] Although relatively short, Bullough's criticisms cast significant doubt on three of White's primary arguments: the change of the army muster from March to May in 755 (or 756 as Bullough contended the date should rightly have been), the evidence for Carolingian cavalry successes in narrative sources, and the absence of stirrups from pre-eighth-century Frankish graves and their presence in later graves.

Bullough dismissed moving the month of Marchfield as unimportant both because there was little evidence to support the idea that armies in the Frankish world had ever been mustered in March—*Campus martius* meant "field of war" not "field of March"—and because in 755 (or 756) the explanation for a late muster was that the snows blocking the Alpine passes had not yet melted.[304] He dismissed Carolingian cavalry successes because he found no evidence in the narrative sources that the armies of Charles Martel, Pippin, Carloman, or even Charlemagne succeeded against their enemies because of their mounted shock combat tactics; Bullough contended that they succeeded because they were able to fight in a number of different ways, willing to adapt their strategy and tactics to whatever military need presented itself.[305] Finally, on the presence or absence of stirrups in Frankish grave-finds, Bullough first agreed with White that there had been no stirrups found in pre-eighth-century warriors' graves, but at the same time he demonstrated that there had also been no stirrup finds in any eighth-century grave. Furthermore, Bullough showed that the only artistic source used by White to support his claim of eighth-century stirrups, the illuminations found in the Valenciennes Apocalypse, was actually misdated, with the correct date being post-800.[306]

Bernard S. Bachrach's lengthy article, "Charles Martel, Mounted Shock Combat, The Stirrup, and Feudalism," was also published in 1970 in *Studies in Medieval and Renaissance His-*

tory.[307] Bachrach, a military historian, approached his criticism of White's argument in a manner similar to Bullough, although in much greater depth. He preferred to criticize point by point the evidence on which White built his thesis, thereby destroying its foundations. He also preferred to attack these points not by using generalizations or secondary sources, but by using what he believed was superior, or at least contradictory, primary evidence. At the same time, he also sought to refute Brunner's theory which he saw as irrevocably intertwined with White's both in their basic arguments and their flaws.

After almost cavalier mention in a footnote of new evidence from Arabic sources which returned the date of the battle of Poitiers to 732, destroying perhaps White's most central attack on Brunner,[308] Bachrach began by criticizing three pieces of literary evidence which both used to date their theses to the mid-eighth century: Pippin's changing of the Saxon tribute from cattle to horses in 758, the 755 shifting of the Marchfield to May (also criticized by Bullough), and the fact that at the battle of the Dyle in 891 the Franks fought on horseback.

With each of these issues Bachrach questioned the evidence used by the authors as well as the logic which led them to their conclusions. In all three cases he showed that other conclusions were equally if not preferably possible. The 758 Saxon tribute, which had been in cattle in 748, nearly a decade and a half after the purported switch was made to cavalry, was so low that it may in fact be merely "a mayor or king who needed horses only for his household." The Marchfield, which several scholars and one contemporary writer, Hincmar of Reims, claimed only meant the "field of Mars," might only have been a "general muster for war which might be held at any time of the year." And the Latin linguistic evidence used by Brunner and White to show that at the Dyle the Franks were "unused to fighting *on foot*," might just as easily have meant that the Franks were "unused to fighting *step by step*," indicating that they were not used to advancing on an enemy as slowly as they had to on the swampy terrain of the Dyle battlefield.[309] Taken alone, the problems that Bachrach pointed to in these pieces of evidence might not detract from the earlier theses, but they did show that these authors' conclusions were built on rather weak foundations.

From these smaller issues, Bachrach next moved to a more significant question (and one also raised by Bullough): were there horsemen in Charles Martel's armies? This he answered: "A detailed review of Charles Martel's post-733 military campaigns suggests serious reservations as to whether heavily armed horsemen engaging in mounted shock combat were in fact the decisive element of his armies." Most of the military engagements were sieges, naval expeditions, or campaigns with too little tactical information to substantiate the claim that cavalry was a main factor in their outcome.[310]

If Charles Martel's armies were not cavalry-based, what then about those of his sons, Pippin and Carloman? Again Bachrach answered: "A detailed review of the campaigns of Pepin and Carloman show them to have been very like those of their father, Charles." Most were either sieges or expeditions for which too little tactical information was known to substantiate Brunner's and White's theses.[311] Bachrach wrote:

> From the many campaigns of Charles, Pepin, and Carloman described by contemporaries and near contemporaries there is not a shred of evidence to suggest that heavily armed horsemen engaging in mounted shock combat were the decisive element of their armies.[312]

In addition, Bachrach looked at White's contention that changes in weapons by the Franks, with the adoption of the longsword and the winged spear, signified a move away from an infantry-based army to a cavalry-based one. In both cases, however, Bachrach could not find archaeological evidence to substantiate White's dating of these changes to the eighth century; both date from much earlier.[313]

Having shown that the eighth-century Carolingian armies were not cavalry-based, Bachrach next shifted his focus to the existence of stirrups among the few horsed warriors who did fight with these armies. First, he established that the linguistic arguments for a mid-eighth-century date for stirrups were inaccurate, for the same philological evidence used to prove White's date also appeared in the sixth century. Second, the earliest artistic depiction of stirrups could not be dated until sometime between 863 and 883, and even after this time there was an inconsistency in the artistic sources, some showing stirrups, others without. Third, stirrups were also absent in inventories of military equipment found in historical documents, literary sources, military manuals, and descriptions of Charlemagne's military regalia.[314] If nothing else, stirrups failed to impress Carolingian artists and authors with their innovation.

Finally, Bachrach questioned White's archaeological evidence for the prominence of stirrups in the Carolingian world. Archaeological evidence did substantiate the existence of stirrups in the late seventh or early eighth centuries, but, Bachrach contended, at the same time it did not show "that the use of the stirrup was common among horsemen or that it helped bring about the development of mounted shock combat." This could be proven by citing the archaeological excavations of 704 Frankish warriors dating from the seventh to the ninth centuries. Of these 704, 135 can be identified as possible cavalry soldiers (85 sure identifications and 50 likely identifications); and of these 135 only 13 have stirrups buried with them. Not only did this show that stirrups were not common among Frankish horsemen, but it also established the fact that horsemen did not make up a significant proportion of the fighting troops of the Frankish armies.[315]

With White's and Brunner's theses effectively denounced, Bachrach attempted to provide his own theory as to the reasons for Charles Martel's seizures of church lands. To Bachrach, the occurrence of these seizures was undeniable, although it was not solely church lands which were confiscated, but also lands and moveable wealth of laymen. All of this was then dispensed for the service and support of military retainers. However, Bachrach excused this not as the origin of feudalism but simply as the existence of military *honores*. Military *honores* were nothing more than gifts given to armed retainers to reward their service. They did not originate with Charles Martel—in fact, they had been a tradition among Frankish leaders at least since the time of Clovis (481-511) and probably before—nor did they represent the purchase of "mercenaries" or feudal warriors.[316]

With all of this evidence, Bachrach concluded:

> ...some doubt has been cast upon the allegedly creative or innovative genius of Charles Martel. He did not grasp the importance of the stirrup, he did not make heavily armed horsemen

using mounted shock combat the decisive arm of his military forces, nor did he even make cavalry the decisive arm of his military forces, and he did not provide for the explosive development of a new or little used technique for the securing of armed support called feudalism by some. In both military tactics and military organization Charles essentially continued to use techniques which were prevalent under his predecessors.[317]

Bullough's and Bachrach's criticisms were not later answered by Lynn White, nor has any other historian risen to White's defense. Evidence of this can be seen by the fact that in a 1985 article entitled "Animals and Warfare in Early Medieval Europe," Bachrach repeated most of his criticisms against White, although no one had rebutted them in the fifteen years since his first attack.[318]

These arguments, principally those put forth by Bachrach, cast so much doubt on the credibility of White's evidence that his thesis on the stirrup causing feudalism, at least for the moment, seems to be dead. General histories of medieval warfare or military technology written since Bachrach's critical article have chosen either to mention the invention of the stirrup without linking it to the rise of feudalism,[319] or they supply summaries both of White's thesis and of his critics, principally the criticisms of Bachrach.[320] Most do recognize the necessity of the stirrup for mounted shock combat, although they generally refuse to give a date for this technological development.[321] More specific studies on medieval cavalry also spend little, if any, space on the question of the stirrup and feudalism. Most focus on other aspects of White's thesis: the couching of lances for mounted shock combat, the use and breeding of warhorses, and the transformation of cavalry to knighthood and chivalry.[322]

Notes

1   Ferrill (1985):15-16.

2   Ferrill (1985):16-17.

3   Ferrill (1985):18-26.

4   Ferrill (1985):38-44.

5   On the weaponry of the Greek armies see Hanson (1989):55-88 and Ferrill (1985):99-102. On the weaponry of the Macedonian army see Ferrill (1985):175-80. For both see A. Hall (1957):II:695-700.

6   See Bishop and Coulston (1989):17-62; Webster (1985):127-29; and A. Hall (1957):II:703-07.

7   Bishop and Coulston (1989):63-65. On the *plumbata* see also P. Barker (1979) and Sherlock (1979).

8   Ferrill (1986):48-49.

9   E. Thompson (1958):6-7; Ferrill (1986):143-44; and Bachrach (1970b):436-37.

10   E. Thompson (1958):3-6.

11   Contamine (1984):12.

12   Apollinaris is translated in Davis (1970):108-09, Procopius in Bachrach (1970b):436-37. See also Agathias in Bachrach (1970b):436.

13   Tacitus (1970):105-06.

14   Swanton (1973).

15   J. Cirlot (1967):8-14; Bruhn de Hoffmeyer (1972):86-88; and Brønsted (1960):122-23.

16   Bachrach (1970b):436-37.

17   See Contamine (1984):176-77.

18   Contamine (1984):177.

19   Coupland (1990):30; Ganshof (1968):65; and Beeler (1971):14.

20   Coupland (1990):47.

21   Coupland (1990):47.

22   Ross (1951):10.

23   Davis (1989):19.

24   Ascherl (1989):271.

25   Ross (1951).

26   L. White (1962):1-38.

27   Ross (1963).

28   Buttin (1965).

29   Nicolle (1980).

30   Bachrach (1985):744-48.

31   V. Cirlot (1985).

32   Flori (1988).

33   See the numerous examples in Nicolle (1988).

34   Smail (1956):112-13 and Contamine (1984):67.

35   Contamine (1984):67 and Beeler (1971):186.

36   Contamine (1984):67.

37   For Spain see Bruhn de Hoffmeyer (1972):168-70 and Powers (1988):130-31.
      For France and Germany see Buttin (1965) and Gaier (1983):36-38.

38   See Davis (1989):19-22.

39   Juliet Barker (1986):178-79 and Ascherl (1989):271-72.

40   See Mann (1957):66-67 and Bruhn de Hoffmeyer (1972):126-31.

41   Oakeshott (1980):44-47 and Contamine (1984):135-36.

42   E. Thompson (1958):5; Bachrach (1970b):436-37; Contamine (1984):12,
      176; Ferrill (1986):145; and Ashdown (1925):19.

43   Contamine (1984):176. See also Härke (1990):34.

44   Contamine (1984):20.

45   Brønsted (1960):122; Poertner (1975):150; and Foote and Wilson (1970):272-
      73.

46   Mann (1957):66 and Härke (1990):34.

47   Ashdown (1925):31-32 and Powicke (1962):56, 86, 92.

48   Loomis and Loomis (1957):324-89. See also Herben (1937):483.

49   See the many examples in Nicolle (1988).

50   Nicolle (1988):#876, 919, 992, 1003-05, 1021-22, 1035, 1055, 1067-68,
      1098, 1110-12, 1125, 1145, 1458, 1479, 1506-07, 1526-29.

51   Oakeshott (1980):72-74.

52   Bruhn de Hoffmeyer (1972):77.

53   Beeler (1971):14.

54   Härke (1989):144-48 and Brønsted (1960):123.

55   Justinian (1987):55, 145.

56   See Härke (1989); Brønsted (1960):123; Ashdown (1925):18-19; and Stork
      (1990):#61.

57   Ashdown (1925):38.

58   Mann (1958):322-23.

59   Mann (1958):323. Evidence for this lack of uniformity can also be seen in
      four fourteenth-century daggers preserved in Germany. See Nicolle
      (1988):#1227-30.

60   Herben (1937):483-84.

61   Tacitus (1970):105. See also E. Thompson (1958):3.

62   See, for example, Sidonius Apollinaris', Procopius' and Agathias' descrip-
      tions of Frankish warriors found in Bachrach (1970b):436-38 and Davis
      (1970):108-09.

63   Contamine (1984):12, 177-78 and Bruhn de Hoffmeyer (1972):78-86.

64   Contamine (1984):19-20. See also Bruhn de Hoffmeyer (1972):78-86.

65   Ellis Davidson (1962). The quote is found on page 211. This work has since
      been supplemented by Wilson (1965) who provides an additional catalogue
      of Anglo-Saxon swords.

66   In addition to Ellis Davidson (1962), on the sword in relation to the status
      of the Anglo-Saxon warrior see Brooks (1978):82-87, and on swords found
      in Anglo-Saxon gravesites see Härke (1990).

67   See Ellis Davidson (1962), in particular Appendix I, pp. 217-24; Engstrom,
      Lankton and Lesher-Engstrom (1990); Fino (1964):47-66; Peirce
      (1986):154-55; and Williams (1977).

68   Coupland (1990):42-46; Ganshof (1968):65; and Beeler (1971):14.

69   Brønsted (1960):119-22 and Contamine (1984):28.

70   Bruhn de Hoffmeyer (1961):46-50.

71   Mann (1957):65-66; Peirce (1986):154-55, 162-64; and Ashdown (1925):23.

72   For Spain see Bruhn de Hoffmeyer (1972):119-25, 160-68 and Powers
      (1988):131. For the Crusades see Smail (1956):112-14.

73   Beeler (1971):26.

74   Oakeshott (1964):25-55 and Bruhn de Hoffmeyer (1963):5-18. See also the
      large number of swords from this period illustrated in Nicolle (1988).

75   Oakeshott (1964):56-79 and Bruhn de Hoffmeyer (1963):18-25. On differ-
      ences in pommel, cross-guard, grip, and scabbard designs see Oakeshott
      (1964):80-138 and the illustrations in Nicolle (1988).

76   Mann (1958):318-19; Ascherl (1988):273; and Ashdown (1925):67.

77   On the sixteenth-century sword see Oakeshott (1980):125-45 and Bruhn de
      Hoffmeyer (1963):25-66.

78   E. Thompson (1958):5 and Thorne (1982):50.

79   See, for example, Justinian (1987):54, 143.

80   Mann (1957):66; Thorne (1982); and Ashdown (1925):127.

81   Nicolle (1988):#918, 1122-23, 1446, 1480, 1510, 1516, 1536.

82   See the numerous examples in Nicolle (1988).

83   Herben (1937):483.

84   J. Barker (1986):179-80.

85   Oakeshott (1980):62-72.

86   See, for example, Ashdown (1925):127-28.

87   This is the thesis behind Thorne's article (1982). See also Oakeshott (1980):62-64 and Mann (1958):66.

88   Oakeshott (1980):69-72.

89   Bruhn de Hoffmeyer (1972):170.

90   Nicolle (1988):#707.

91   Nicolle (1988):#686, 819, 676, 1416, 788.

92   Oakeshott (1980):47-48; Ashdown (1925):128-29; and Deuchler (1963):341-42.

93   Oakeshott (1980):51-56 and Ashdown (1925):125-35.

94   Oakeshott (1980):49-51 and Ashdown (1925):131-32.

95   Verbruggen (1977); Ashdown (1925):125-26; and Nicolle (1988):#974.

96   Oakeshott (1980):53-56 and Ashdown (1925):126-27.

97   Oakeshott (1980):53 and Ashdown (1925):128.

98   Bruhn de Hoffmeyer (1972):105.

99   For an argument against this view see Ashdown (1925):50-51.

100   Justinian (1987):55, 145.

101   Stork (1990):#74. This seems to be the case as the manuscript copier, or someone nearly contemporary with him, has written the gloss *goliam* above the word *tyrannum* in the riddle.

102   Herben (1937):486.

103   Nicolle (1988):#1212, 671, 696, 1423.

104   Nicolle (1988):#1606.

105   Prestwich (1980):70. See also Nickel (1982):350-51.

106   Bruhn de Hoffmeyer (1972):72.

107   Ferrill (1986):145.

108   On the Franks see E. Thompson (1958):11; Bachrach (1970b):438; and Coupland (1990):49. On the Ostrogoths see E. Thompson (1958):9.

109   Härke (1990):34.

110   Crossley-Holland (1979):#23.

111   Brønsted (1960):123.

112   Coupland (1990):48-50; Ganshof (1968):65; and Beeler (1971):14.

113   Bruhn de Hoffmeyer (1972):131-33 and Powers (1988):75, 131.

114   Mann (1957):67-68.

115   Contamine (1984):55.

116   Bradbury (1985):39-57; Beeler (1966):89, 91, 140, 274; and Powicke (1962):44, 88-89.

117 On the adoption of the longbow see Bradbury (1985):71-90 and Powicke (1962):119. For an alternate view of the adoption of the longbow see Ashdown (1925):34-36. On the range of the longbow see McKisack (1959):241; Prestwich (1980):70; and Ashdown (1925):34-36.

118 See McGuffie (1955); Bradbury (1985):91-138; Prestwich (1980):59, 70, 173, 197; and Ashdown (1925):121-25.

119 See Esper (1965).

120 Bradbury (1985):141.

121 Keegan (1978):78-116 and Gaier (1978).

122 Prestwich (1980):192 and Allmand (1988):101.

123 Powicke (1962):244 and Allmand (1988):52.

124 Bradbury (1985):8, 147-48 and Nickel (1982):353.

125 Bradbury (1985):8 and Ashdown (1925):88.

126 Comnena (1969):316-17. See also Bradbury (1985):8-10 and Contamine (1984):71.

127 Contamine (1984):71-72, 274.

128 See Contamine (1984):72; Allmand (1988):61; and Bradbury (1985):45, 76-77.

129 Bradbury (1985):146-47 and Foley, Palmer and Soedel (1985):105-07.

130 Bradbury (1985):148-49 and Ashdown (1925):85-86. See also the illustrations in Nicolle (1988):#654, 656, 772, 833, 945, 1247, 1259.

131 Bradbury (1985):149. See also Nicolle (1988):#686-87.

132 Bradbury (1985):149-50.

133 Contamine (1984):110.

134 Lane (1969-70).

135 Bradbury (1985):150; Foley, Palmer and Soedel (1985):107-09; Vale (1981):113; and Payne-Gallwey (1903):20.

136 Bradbury (1985):11 and Ashdown (1925):86-87.

137 Contamine (1984):71.

138 Contamine (1984):202, 274 and Bradbury (1985):143.

139 Bachrach (1985):709.

140 Bachrach (1969).

141 Bachrach (1985):710-11. E. Thompson (1958):11-12 contends that neither the Franks nor the Anglo-Saxons used the horse in military affairs.

142 Brønsted (1960):125.

143 Ganshof (1968):65.

144 See Bachrach (1985):737-42. For other references to the stirrup, see chapter three of this section.

145 L. White (1962):19, 110, 287.

146 Bachrach (1985):746-48; L. White (1962):7-8; Davis (1989):23-24.

147 On the training of a warhorse see Bachrach (1988):188-93.

148 Davis (1983); Davis (1989):49-98; and Bachrach (1988):176-77.

149 Lyon (1987); Verbruggen (1947); Contamine (1984):126-32; Allmand (1988):58-59; and Vale (1981):122-27.

150 Juliet Barker (1986):173-76; Keen (1984):23-26, 103-04; and Vale (1981):121-27.

151 See Bruhn de Hoffmeyer (1972):113-14.

152 Bishop and Coulston (1989):69.

153 Contamine (1984):87-88.

154 Fino (1964).

155 Contamine (1984):188-90; Bruhn de Hoffmeyer (1972):96-97; and Powers (1988):127-28.

156 Contamine (1984):189-90.

157 Eltis (1989):91.

158 Deschamps (1897):VII:34-36. See also Giraud (1895-99).

159 Brun (1951). See also Giraud (1895-99).

160 Ferrill (1985):22.

161 Hanson (1990):55-88.

162 Homer (1950):197-98.

163 Bishop and Coulston (1989):19-20 and Robinson (1975):11-25, 147-52.

164 Bishop and Coulston (1989):55; Robinson (1975):174-86; and Webster (1985):122-25.

165 Bishop and Coulston (1989):55-57; Robinson (1985):125-26; and Robinson (1975):26-107.

166 Bishop and Coulston (1989):57-61, 67-68 and Webster (1985):126-27.

167 Bishop and Coulston (1989):66-67.

168 Bishop and Coulston (1989):65 and Robinson (1975):153-73.

169 Coulston (1988):1-15.

170 Ferrill (1986):128-29.

171 E.A. Thompson (1958):3-4.

172 E.A. Thompson (1958):4-8; Bruhn de Hoffmeyer (1972):89-90; Ferrill (1986):144-45; and Bachrach (1970):436-37.

173 E.A. Thompson (1958):8.

174 E.A. Thompson (1958):11-12.

175 Contamine (1984):178; Bruhn de Hoffmeyer (1972):93; and Enlart (1916):447.

176 Contamine (1984):178; Bruhn de Hoffmeyer (1972):90-93; and Burns (1984):185.

177 Hamer (1970):48-69. See also Brooks (1978):82-92.

178 Brøndsted (1960):123-25.

179 Ashdown (1925):13-14; Stork (1990):#87; Crossly-Holland (1979):#5 and Hamer (1970):67.

180   Bruce-Mitford (1974a):198-209; Bruce-Mitford (1974b):223-52; Addyman, Pearson and Tweddle (1982):189-94; Ashdown (1925):13; Brooks (1978):93-94; and Crossley-Holland (1979):#61.

181   Ashdown (1925):11-12; Brooks (1978):94-96; Mann (1958):316; Stork (1990):#32; and Crossley-Holland (1979):#35.

182   Contamine (1984):19-20.

183   Contamine (1984):19.

184   Coupland (1990):30.

185   Coupland (1990):38-39.

186   Ganshof (1968):66 and Bachrach (1974):29.

187   Coupland (1990):30.

188   Coupland (1990):35-38 and Enlart (1916):450-51.

189   Coupland (1990):32-25 and Enlart (1916):448-50.

190   Coupland (1990):39 and Ganshof (1968):66.

191   Coupland (1990):38-41. See also Ganshof (1968):52 and Enlart (1916):448-49.

192   Coupland (1990):41-42 and Enlart (1916):450.

193   Mann (1933):286.

194   Nicolle (1988):#722 and 742 for helmets, and #618, 687, 715, 726, 727, 729, 737, 743, 1120, 1393, 1417 and 1418 for shields.

195   Mann (1957):56-58.

196   Mann (1957):63-65; Peirce (1986):160; Ashdown (1925):29-30; and Nicolle (1988):I:344.

197   Nicolle (1988):#742.

198   Mann (1957):58-60; Peirce (1986):159-60; Blair (1958):25-27; Ashdown (1925):28-29; and Nicolle (1988):I:344.

199   Mann (1957):60-63; Peirce (1986):155-59; Blair (1958):23-24; Ashdown (1925):23-28; Enlart (1912):451-53; and Nicolle (1988):I:344-45.

200   Contamine (1984):67, 73, 88, 188-89.

201   See the large number of illustrations of kite-shaped shields in Nicolle (1988). See also Bruhn de Hoffmeyer (1972):138-40, 179-85.

202   Nicolle (1988):#618, 687, 715, 726, 729, 743, 1387, 1393, 1396, 1397, 1399, 1417 and 1418 and Bruhn de Hoffmeyer (1972):138-39.

203   See the large number of helmets illustrated in Nicolle (1988). See also Bruhn de Hoffmeyer (1972):170-72 and Enlart (1912):457-60.

204   Nicolle (1988):#1094, 1095, 1107, 1108, 1109, 1144 and Peirce (1986):159. Another helmet, now in the collection of the Metropolitan Museum of Art, was also made in a similar manner to these helmets and may also date from this period. However, its date and provenance have yet to be determined. See Peirce (1986):159.

205   Peirce (1986):159-60.

206 Nicolle (1988):715, 752, 887, 888, 1149, 1280, 1299, 1300, 1301, 1304 and 1309.

207 Enlart (1912):453-57; Mann (1933):286-87; Bruhn de Hoffmeyer (1972):172-79; and Juliet Barker (1986):168. See also the numerous examples of the chain mail hauberk from this period in Nicolle (1988).

208 Juliet Barker (1986):166-67.

209 See illustrations in Nicolle (1988). See also Blair (1958):32-36; Bruhn de Hoffmeyer (1972):172-79; Enlart (1912):453-57; and Mann (1933):286-87.

210 Nicolle (1988):#747, 906, 1161, 1163 and 1165.

211 Nicolle (1988):#905. See also Blair (1958):29.

212 Blair (1958):28-29 (illustrated pp. 206-07).

213 See, for example, Nicolle (1988):#626, 634, 635, 707, 708, 714, 725, 1293, 1305.

214 See, for example, Nicolle (1988):#747. See also Blair (1958):28-29.

215 Nicolle (1988):#715, 716, 758, 1154, 1404, 1409, 1412, 1417. See also Contamine (1984):187.

216 Nicolle (1988):#763, 768, 1134, 1320.

217 Contamine (1984):67, 89.

218 See the illustrations in Nicolle (1988). See also Mann (1957):65 and Ashdown (1925):48-49.

219 Blair (1958):29-30; Enlart (1912):471-73; and Ashdown (1925):42-43. See also the illustrations in Nicolle (1988):#759, 827, 829, 901, 1166, 1203, which all show evolutionary steps in the creation of the Great Helm.

220 Blair (1958):30; Enlart (1912):472; and Ashdown (1925):43-35. There are a large number of illustrations in Nicolle (1988) of the Great Helm. As well, there are a number of extant Great Helms, from both the thirteenth and the fourteenth centuries. See Nicolle (1988):#761, 1179, 1219, 1220, 1222, 1223, 1225, 1318. For illustrations of the arming cap, see Nicolle (1988):#926, 933, 934, 1187, 1321.

221 Juliet Barker (1986):164.

222 Blair (1958):31-32 and Enlart (1912):474-75. For the artistic sources of the kettle-hat see Nicolle (1988):#772, 833, 834, 835, 837, 840, 955, 956, 1193, 1213, 1214, 1313, 1325.

223 Blair (1958):184; Bruhn de Hoffmeyer (1972):187; and Nicolle (1988):#1197, 1198, 1335.

224 Contamine (1984):190.

225 Keen (1984):125-31.

226 Blair (1958):30-31; Ashdown (1925):45-47; Enlart (1912):473-75; Juliet Barker (1986):164-65, 180-86; and Nicolle (1988):#831, 1196, 1197, 1198, 1200, 1201, 1202, 1208, 1322, 1323, 1335.

227 See, for example, Mann (1933):288-90 and Nicolle (1988):#613, 664, 697, 700, 703, 1217.

228 Vale (1981):104-05.

229 Blair (1958):37.

230 Blair (1958):37.

231 Blair (1958):37-38.

232 Thordemann (1939):I:289-92. See also Blair (1958):38-39.

233 Blair (1958):38.

234 Blair (1958):42-43, 62-63; Ashdown (1925):80-81; Mann (1933):288-89; and Nicolle (1988):#958, 962, 964, 968, 980, 982, 983, 1238, 1240, 1241, 1242, 1352, 1357, 1376.

235 Blair (1958):39-41; Ashdown (1925):81-82; and Nicolle (1988):#1244, 1373, 1626.

236 Blair (1958):41 and Nicolle (1988):#1352, 1430, 1431.

237 Blair (1958):56-58, 61; Ashdown (1925):89-90, 101-02; Juliet Barker (1986):169-70; Brun (1951):219-20; and Nicolle (1988):#1372.

238 Blair (1958):58-61.

239 Blair (1958):43-44, 62 and Nicolle (1988):#979, 980, 981, 1242, 1244, 1576, 1590.

240 Blair (1958):43, 64-65; Ashdown (1925):105; Juliet Barker (1986):171; Brun (1951):221-22; and Nicolle (1988):#979, 980, 981, 982, 1241, 1242, 1244, 1346, 1431, 1576, 1590.

241 Blair (1958):41-42, 66-67; Enlart (1912):484-87; Ashdown (1925):103-05; Thordemann (1939):230-44; Brun (1951):222-23; and Nicolle (1988):#799, 962, 1243, 1576.

242 Blair (1958):44-45. 64-66; Ashdown (1925):102-03; Mann (1933):288-91; Juliet Barker (1986):170-71; Brun (1951):221-22; and Nicolle (1988):#962, 1238, 1576.

243 Blair (1958):45-46; Enlart (1912):476-79; Ashdown (1925):63-65; Juliet Barker (1986):181-82; and Nicolle (1988):#978, 1237, 1615.

244 Blair (1958):42 and Brun (1951):221.

245 Blair (1958):53 and Enlart (1912):479-83.

246 Blair (1958):53-54; Vale (1981):120-21; Nicholas (1987):268-70. For specialized studies on the armor industry and trade see ffoulkes (1912); Gaier (1973); Larsen (1940); and Brun (1951).

247 For the cost of this armor see Contamine (1984):95, 116-17; Vale (1981):125-26; and Gaier (1973):67-69, 73, 89, 343-52.

248 Blair (1958):77-78 and Enlart (1912):503. For a discussion of the technological processes of making plate see Vale (1981):105-07; Gaier (1973):189-98, 254-79; Williams (1980); and Larsen (1940):52-53. And for a table listing the metallurgical anaylsis and strength of plate armor, see Vale (1981):186.

249 Blair (1958):80-82, 92-96 (illustrated pp. 218-21); Oakeshott (1980):85, 88-96; Enlart (1912):503-08; Ashdown (1925):144-46; Vale (1981):109-12, 119-20; and Mann (1933):293-305.

250 Blair (1958):80-83 (illustrated pp. 210-11); Ashdown (1925):146-51; Oakeshott (1980):87; and Vale (1981):110.

251 Blair (1958):83-84, 96-99 (illustrated pp. 210-11) and Oakeshott (1980):86.

252 Blair (1958):84, 99-100 (illustrated pp. 206-09); Oakeshott (1980):87; and Enlart (1912):509.

253 Blair (1958):81, 84-85, 100-02 (illustrated pp. 214-17); Oakeshott (1980):87; and Enlart (1912):508-09.

254 Blair (1958):96 and Oakeshott (1980):87.

255 Vale (1981):76.

256 Blair (1958):74-79; Juliet Barker (1986):166-68; and Herben (1937):479-81.

257 See the charts of armor weights in Vale (1981):184-85; Blair (1958):191-92; and ffoulkes (1912):119.

258 Chaucer (1951):199. See also Herben (1937):479.

259 Vale (1981):76.

260 See Contamine (1984):132.

261 See Nicolle (1988):#1244, 1245, 1247, 1265, 1377, 1378, 1614.

262 Thordemann (1939); Blair (1958):55-56; and Nicolle (1988)#1063-1066.

263 Thordemann (1939):245-84.

264 Thordemann (1939):93-117.

265 Blair (1958):47-48, 73; Enlart (1912):489-91; Ashdown (1925):62-63, 91-93; and Nicolle (1988):#611, 970, 1222, 1223, 1225, 1276.

266 Blair (1958):48, 74 (illustrated pp. 196-97); Enlart (1912):493-98; Juliet Barker (1986):164-66; Herben (1937):478; and Nicolle (1988):#847, 976, 1251, 1257, 1272, 1273, 1353, 1358, 1359, 1362, 1371, 1615.

267 Blair (1958):48 and Nicolle (1988):#1359.

268 Blair (1958):52, 70, 91, 105, 110-11 (illustrated pp. 198-99); Ashdown (1925):76-77; Mann (1933):296; and Nicolle (1988):#661, 976, 1074, 1075, 1245, 1274, 1276.

269 Blair (1958):51-52, 67-70, 102-05, 109 (illustrated pp. 194-95); Oakeshott (1980):117; Enlart (1912):491-93; Ashdown (1925):74-76, 82-84, 97-100; and Mann (1933):291-92. See also the numerous archaeological and artistic sources illustrated in Nicolle (1988).

270 Blair (1958):73-74, 85; Oakeshott (1980):109-11; Enlart (1912):513; Ashdown (1925):100; and Mann (1933):296-97.

271 Blair (1958):85-86, 105-07, 110 (illustrated pp. 200-01); Oakeshott (1980):111-16; Enlart (1912):513-15; and Ashdown (1925):141-42.

272 Blair (1958):86-91, 105 (illustrated pp. 202-03) and Oakeshott (1980):118-23.

273 Blair (1958):181-82 (illustrated pp. 224-25); Enlart (1912):519-20; Ashdown (1925):106-07; Juliet Barker (1986):176-77; and Nicolle (1988):#979-82, 1237-44, 1274, 1371, 1372, 1590.

274 Blair (1958):182; Enlart (1912):499-500; Ashdown (1925):106-07; Herben (1937):484; Deuchler (1963):332-34; and Nicolle (1988):#660, 1363.

275 Blair (1958):184-87; Juliet Barker (1986):175-76; Gaier (1973):365-67; Herben (1937):484-85; and Deuchler (1963):338-40.

276 Gaier (1973):87, 367.

277 For a survey of post-medieval armor see Blair (1958):112-55; Enlart (1912):521-26; Ashdown (1925):163-84; and Oakeshott (1980).

278 E. Brown (1974):1063-88. The quote is from page 1088.

279 An adequate, although far from comprehensive survey of feudalism is found in Strayer (1985). More extensive studies of the subject are Stephenson (1942), Bloch (1961) and Ganshof (1964).

280 Bloch (1961):II:446. See also E. Brown (1974):1071.

281 Ganshof (1964):xvi. See also E. Brown (1974):1071.

282 Strayer (1965):13. See also E. Brown (1974):1073.

283 Duby (1958):766 as quoted in and translated by E. Brown (1974):1074.

284 Brunner (1874).

285 See L. White (1962):5.

286 See L. White (1962):6-11.

287 L. White (1962):1-38.

288 L. White (1962):11.

289 L. White (1962):12-13.

290 L. White (1962):12.

291 See Littauer (1981):99-105.

292 L. White (1962):14-20.

293 L. White (1962):25-28.

294 L. White (1962):28-33.

295 L. White (1962):33-38.

296 L. White (1962):38.

297 Hilton and Sawyer (1963):90-100.

298 Hilton and Sawyer (1963):90.

299 Hilton and Sawyer (1963):90-92.

300 Hilton and Sawyer (1963):92-94.

301 Hilton and Sawyer (1963):94-95.

302 Ogilvy (1966):1-13.

303 Bullough (1970):84-90.

304 Bullough (1970):85-86.

305 Bullough (1970):88-90.

306 Bullough (1970):86-87.

307 Bachrach (1970a):47-75.

308 Bachrach (1970a):50n.2.

309 Bachrach (1970a):50-53.

310 Bachrach (1970a):53-54.

311   Bachrach (1970a):54-57.

312   Bachrach (1970a):57.

313   Bachrach (1970a):57-58.

314   Bachrach (1970a):58-62.

315   Bachrach (1970a):62-66.

316   Bachrach (1970a):66-72.

317   Bachrach (1970a):72.

318   Bachrach (1985):737-42.

319   See, for example, McNeill (1982):20; van Creveld (1989):18; Beeler (1971):9-10; and Keen (1984):23.

320   See Contamine (1984):179-84; O'Connell (1989):86-87; and Gillmor (1982):201-02.

321   See Davis (1989):51.

322   For works discussing the couching of the lance see Ross (1963); Buttin (1965); V. Cirlot (1986); and Flori (1988). For works on the medieval warhorse see Bachrach (1969); Bautier (1976); Davis (1983); Bachrach (1985); and Davis (1989). And, for works on the rise of chivalry from cavalry see Verbruggen (1947); Duby (1980); Hunt (1981); Barber (1982); Keen (1984); Mortimer (1986); Lyon (1987); and Nelson (1989).

Part II:

Artillery

Introduction

Personal arms and armor were important in battlefield warfare, but most medieval military engagements were not fought on the battlefield but were against castles or fortified towns. Without the means to capture these fortifications, conquest of foreign lands was impossible. There was therefore a need for weapons which could breach fortifications. Swords, spears, and other hand weapons could do no damage against them; nor could the most powerful bowman firing the heaviest bow destroy even the most basic fortification. Starvation could be and was used frequently, often with success, depending on the abundance of food supplies in the besieged fortress and on the availability of relief troops. But the procedure of driving a town or castle into starvation—known customarily as a "siege"—was protracted, requiring often more than a year and sometimes longer to gain victory. The ten-year siege of Troy was not created by Homer simply as a literary metaphor, but also reflected ancient reality. Even after ten years it required a trick, the Trojan Horse, to take the heavily fortified city and end the confrontation.

Other ancient methods of conquering fortifications were also extremely inadequate. Chief among these was mining the besieged fortress. An attacking force would attempt to tunnel under the fortification's walls and then collapse the tunnels in order to bring down a section of those walls above. In some instances mining was successful, but more often, especially when encountering inaccessible terrain or effective countermining from the defenders, this procedure failed.

Also nearly always ineffective was the direct assault of a fortification using scaling ladders and battering rams. Either these attacks were easily countered by defenders inside the fortress, or the fortification was built on terrain which could not be easily surmounted, such as the Judean fortress at Masada in the first century AD which held out nearly three years before the Romans could construct an earthen ramp to reach its walls.

Early in ancient times the need for the construction of heavy weapons, artillery pieces, with power enough to breach the gates and walls of fortresses was recognized. From these a missile, stone or bolt, could be launched with enough propellant force either to cause a break in the wall or to weaken a part of the wall so that continual impact would eventually cause a break in it. In this way, the fortress would eventually yield to the attacker. Later it was found that these weapons, although continuing to be used against fortifications as their main targets, could also be used on the battlefield as long-range anti-personnel weapons.

The following two chapters will discuss the technology of medieval artillery. The first discusses the pieces that have come to be known generically as catapults; a small section also surveys the history of Greek Fire. The second chapter discusses the invention and early use of gunpowder artillery.

Non-Gunpowder Artillery

The word *catapult* is a generic term which describes all ancient and medieval non-gunpowder propelled missile-throwing artillery. The first catapult is thought to have been invented in 399 BC at Syracuse. There King Dionysius I, threatened by the Carthaginians and other enemies, assembled a large group of engineers to create an arsenal of weapons. Among these was the first non-torsion artillery piece (the *gastraphetes*). In essence the *gastraphetes* (which in Greek means "belly-bow") was little more than a large, powerful, and flexible bow. The flexibility of the weapon came from the bow itself which was a composite of wood, horn, and animal sinew: a wood core covered by a tension layer of sinew in front and a compression layer of horn in back. This, using a sinew bowstring, supplied the propulsive force to the missile.

In this there was little variation from the hand-held composite bow, which by the fourth century BC had been known for several centuries. However, the difference between the hand-held weapon and the *gastraphetes* was its power, which was supplied by the latter's elaborate stock apparatus. The *gastraphetes* was mounted on a heavy stock, made in two sections. The lower section (or case) was fixed solidly to the bow. The upper section (or slider), with approximately the same dimensions as the case, fit in a dovetailed groove in the case and was able to slide freely back and forth. On each side of the case was a straight ratchet with two pawls fit into the ratchets and attached to a claw-like trigger mechanism.

At the end of the stock was a concave withdrawal rest which could be used by the operator to place against his stomach and, with the front of the bow fixed on the ground, allowed him to withdraw the slider, attach the string to the trigger, load a missile and discharge it. A man could thus withdraw the bowstring and discharge a missile with much greater power than was possible with the traditional hand-drawn bowstring.

The *gastraphetes* added between 50 and 100 meters range to the hand-drawn composite bow (estimated to have been 500 meters at maximum range). It also added a propellant force to a missile so that few pieces of armor could withstand it, although the force was probably still too weak to breach many fortification walls.[1]

Non-torsion artillery technology spread quickly throughout the ancient world, and soon some improvements were made to the original *gastraphetes'* design. By 360 BC winches had been added to the stock allowing for easier and greater drawing power; this ultimately brought increased propellant force to the missile discharge. A base too was added, increasing both the stability and size of the weapon.[2] Still, non-torsion artillery continued to be limited in force and power, both of which remained dependent on the strength and flexibility of the bow. If these were exceeded, the bow simply broke. As well, while some *gastraphetes* were equipped to fire stone balls, most fired only heavy arrow-shaped bolts, and this also limited the force of impact.

Thus it was necessary to change the bow part of this early artillery to allow for an increase in the force of projection and also for a change in missile type and size. After some experimentation, the flexible bow was replaced with torsion springs. The users of the *gastraphetes* were probably aware that it was the sinew in the bow composition which gave it its resiliency, so that by stressing the role of the sinew, in the formation of tightly twisted springs, the power of the artillery could be increased.[3] And with the anchoring of rigid bow arms in these springs, the bow could effectively be replaced.

Otherwise the rest of the torsion catapult remained little altered from its non-torsion predecessor, with a heavy sinew string, slider, winch, ratchet apparatus, and trigger mechanism. The springs were the only significant change in technology, and yet this alone allowed for much more power given to the propelling of missiles, now almost always stone balls (weighing from 13 to 26 kilograms, although stones as large as 162 kilograms are known to have been used). When the bowstring was drawn back on a torsion catapult, the tension of the springs was applied to the bow arms which in springing forward discharged the missile. This resulted not only in a much longer range for the artillery, but also in a much greater force given to the discharged missile. This weapon could breach fortification walls.[4]

It is believed that the first torsion-spring catapults were made by Macedonian engineers between 353 and 341 BC and used afterwards by Philip II in his conquest of Greece.[5] The technology was then passed to Philip's son, Alexander the Great, and used in his conquest of Persia, the Middle East, Egypt, and India. Alexander seemed to have been particularly impressed by his catapults' power and used them successfully to take towns, like Tyre in 332 BC, which would have been nearly impossible to conquer by other siege methods.

After Alexander's death, torsion artillery technology, which had by then clearly supplanted non-torsion pieces, passed to his successors and from them to Carthage, Rome, and other ancient lands. Improvements in the technology were also made. Most important among these was the addition of washers to the springs to permit the adjustment of the tension thereby extending or limiting the distance that the arms of the catapult could be drawn back. In this way the amount of force delivered to the missile discharge could be varied: a close target could be struck by a looser tension on the springs, while a more distant target needed a tighter tension. The springs could also be loosed when not being used in military campaign to keep the sinew from weakening.[6] Other important innovations were the addition of bronze coverings over the springs, which kept them dry during rain or river crossings, and tripod swivel mounts, which allowed for a rapid change of direction in discharging missiles.[7]

Improvements were also made in the operation of torsion catapults. Training, practice, and even competition of catapult operators was encouraged and several schools, especially those at Samnos, Ceos, and Cyanae, encouraged increased skill in catapult use. Rhodian operators were particularly highly prized for their skill in catapult firing, and they were frequently employed by both Greece and Rome as mercenary artillery operators.[8]

In the ancient world the most sophisticated artillery was made at Alexandria under the Ptolemies. Their machines were sought by almost every other land. In fact, it is highly plausible that both Carthage and Rome during the First and Second Punic Wars faced each other using Alexandrian catapults. This gave Alexandria impetus in the construction of some highly experimental catapult models. One of the most curious examples is a chain-driven repeating catapult described by Philon in the last part of the third century BC. In this machine, bolts were fed one at a time from a magazine into the slider trough by means of a revolving drum. The chain-link drive, operated by a winch, then fired the bolt and recocked the weapon by engaging the lugs on the chain links with a pentagonal gear. A trigger claw was locked and fired at the appropriate time by pegs mounted in the stock of the weapon, past which the slider moved.

There were, however, many problems with this machine. First, because it was so elaborate, the need for it to be constantly repaired must have been great. Second, it fired only along fixed lines, and thus would have been useful only against fixed targets, like a fortification wall. Finally, there is no indication that this weapon was ever constructed, and it may in fact have been only an engineer's dream design.[9]

The Romans made two important alterations to the traditional torsion catapult (which they called a *ballista*). First, they made it smaller and more portable. Known as the *cheiroballista*, this variation of the older torsion model contained all of the former's parts and was probably not too much lighter. But it was more compact, easier to assemble, and easier to transport. The springs were set further apart, and this gave a wider field of view and made aiming easier. The bow arms also seem to have been capable of greater range than larger torsion artillery. Clearly, this weapon was meant to be used on the battlefield (or at sea) rather than against fortifications.[10]

The second alteration to the traditional ancient torsion catapult was much more extreme. Rather than simulating a bow using two vertical sinew springs with two arms swinging horizontally, the *onager* used only one horizontal spring and one arm swinging upwards. There was no bowstring; at the end of the single arm was a sling in which a missile, presumably a stone ball, could be placed for launching. The trigger was a piece of rope used to anchor the arm for loading. The arm was in turn mounted on two large and heavy main horizontal beams held apart by a number of crossbeams. As such the *onager* was much more like our modern perception of a catapult than other ancient models. However, it should be noted that this weapon was infrequently used by the Romans, who continued to prefer traditional torsion artillery. Apparently, it appeared only at the end of the Empire and is mentioned only by one author, Ammianus Marcellinus (330-390 AD).[11]

That torsion catapults were effective in sieges and on the battlefield is without question. Although their range seems not to have differed much from non-torsion catapults or even from strong bowmen without a substantial decrease in accuracy—most stone throwing artillery needed to be within 150 meters of a fortification to be effective[12]—the force of impact of a missile fired from one of these weapons was astonishing. At the siege of Gaza, Alexander the Great was wounded in the neck by a catapult bolt which pierced both his shield and his breastplate. A skull unearthed at Maiden Castle in Dorset was entered by a catapult bolt moving at such a high velocity that it pierced the skull without smashing it; had the missile been an arrow from a hand-held bow, the skull would surely have shattered.[13] Perhaps the most vivid picture of the awe-inspiring power of these weapons comes from the pen of Josephus, the Jewish historian of the first-century Roman conquest of rebellious Judea, who details their use by the Romans at the siege of Jotapata in 67 AD:

> The force with which these weapons threw stones and darts was such that a single projectile ran through a row of men, and the momentum of the stones hurled by the engine carried away battlements and knocked off corners of towers. There is in fact no body of men so strong that it cannot be laid low to the last rank by the impact of these huge stones.... Getting in the line of fire, one of the men standing near Josephus [the commander of Jotapata, not the historian] on the rampart had his head knocked off by a stone, his skull being flung like a pebble from a sling more than 600 meters; and when a pregnant woman on

?? leaving her house at daybreak was struck in the belly, the unborn
.· child was carried away 100 meters.[14]

When the barbarian tribes invaded the Roman Empire in the
fourth and fifth centuries, they were met by a large amount of
artillery—*ballistae, chieroballistae,* and *onagers.* Indeed, the Romans might have had catapults defending nearly every fortification
besieged by the invaders, and it is reported that several arms
factories continued to supply artillery pieces for military use during the early invasions.[15] It is similarly recorded that in some
engagements these catapults were successful in thwarting barbarian
attacks against Roman fortifications. For example, Ammianus
Marcellinus describes how one Gothic attack was halted when a
single large stone fired from an *onager,* despite hitting no one,
caused such mass confusion that it eventually routed the attackers.[16] And Procopius, writing about the defense of Rome in 537-
38, provides a colorful witness to catapult destruction:

> ...at the Salerian Gate a Goth of goodly stature and a capable
> warrior, wearing a corselet and having a helmet on his head,
> a man who was of no mean station in the Gothic nation...was
> hit by a missile from an engine which was on a tower at his
> left. And passing through the corselet and the body of the man,
> the missile sank more than half its length into the tree, and
> pinning him to the spot where it entered the tree, it suspended
> him there a corpse.[17]

Ultimately these catapults were not successful in defending the
Roman fortifications against the besiegers. Indeed, there were
likely many problems with their technology and use. First, many
towns and fortifications probably did not have a large arsenal of
catapults in stock at the beginning of the barbarian invasions,
primarily because their security, especially that of the western
imperial towns, had not often been threatened. Second, at this
time many military detachments seem to have been unfamiliar with
catapults and untrained in their use, a fact attested to by many
contemporary authors. Finally, many of these machines were probably not in good working order. It has been estimated that the
life of sinew springs was no more than eight to ten years, and
many of the existing artillery pieces undoubtedly had strings which
could not function properly.[18]

Traction Trebuchet

While the Romans used their catapults against the barbarians with some success, once the barbarian tribes had overrun the Empire, they do not seem to have been able to acquire this technology from their conquered foes. Why this was the case has been the subject of debate among modern historians. Some, led by Kalvero Huuri, E.A. Thompson, and Lynn White, Jr., have contended that barbarians were simply unable either to use or to continue to construct Roman-style catapults.[19]

They argue that although there is some evidence of early barbarian use of artillery, at the siege of Thessaloniki by the Goths in 269 and at Tours by the Alemanni or Franks a century later, in both instances the use of artillery failed to prove significant as defenders were able to burn the catapults by hurling blazing missiles at them.[20] Moreover, by the sixth century there is no further mention of them. Whether this was, as Thompson surmises, "owing to the low technical level of their [the barbarian] society generally,"[21] or whether they simply did not feel the need for the use of artillery against fortifications which fell relatively easily to them by other means, cannot be known. For whatever reason, these historians contend, catapult technology seems to have passed into obscurity.

However, this thesis has lately come under attack by a number of historians, namely David Hill, Carroll M. Gillmor, and Paul E. Chevedden, who argue that the reason for the barbarians' rejection of Roman catapult technology is that they had accepted an alternative: the *trebuchet*.

It is well established that trebuchets originated in China between the fifth and third centuries BC, and from there diffused westward to the Islamic lands by the end of the seventh century AD, where they continued to be used until the fifteenth century.[22] The earliest of these artillery pieces were quite large and were designed with a rotating beam placed on a fulcrum which was supported by a wooden tower and base. The beam was positioned unevenly on the fulcrum (at a ratio of 5-6:1 for a light trebuchet and 2-3:1 for a heavy trebuchet) with the largest end of the rotating beam holding a sling in which projectiles, generally stone boulders, would be placed. On the opposite, small end of the beam were 40 to 125 ropes which were pulled by a team of men estimated to number between 40 and 250. By pulling in unison, the team generated a strong force which discharged a projectile weighing between one and 59 kilograms in a relatively flat arc for a distance of between 85 and 133 meters.[23] It is this source of power which gives the artillery piece its modern name, the *traction trebuchet*.

None of these points are questioned by any of the historians mentioned above. But whereas the first group maintains that the traction trebuchet was not introduced to western Europe until it was seen by the Crusaders when they attacked the Muslims on the First Crusade, the second group contends that trebuchets were known and used by western Europeans as early as the sixth century. As evidence, they point to an eyewitness account of the siege of Thessaloniki by the Avaro-Slavs in 597 written by John, the Archbishop of Thessaloniki. In this account, John describes some siege machines of the Avaro-Slavs (known to him as *petroboles* or "rock throwers"), a description which seems to indicate that they were traction trebuchets:

> These *petroboles* were tetragonal and rested on broader bases, tapering to narrow extremities. Attached to them were thick cylinders well clad in iron at the ends, and there were nailed to them timbers like beams from a large house. These timbers had the slings from the back and from the front strong ropes, by which, pulling down and releasing the sling, they propel the stones up high and with a loud noise. And on being fired they sent up many great stones so that neither earth nor human constructions could bear the impacts. They also covered those tetragonal *petroboles* with boards on three sides only, so that those inside firing them might not be wounded with arrows by those on the walls. And since one of these, with its boards, had been burned to a char by a flaming arrow, they returned, carrying away the machines. On the following day they again brought these *petroboles* covered with freshly skinned hides and with the boards, and placing them closer to the walls, shooting, they hurled mountains and hills against us. For what else might one term these extremely large stones.[24]

It can be further established that the technology for these weapons was transferred to the Avaro-Slavs by a captured Byzantine soldier named Bousas a decade before the siege of Thessaloniki.[25]

Besieged city from *Le chevalier du cygne* showing a
traction trebuchet. [Bibliotèque Nationale, Paris.]

Other references to siege machines appear frequently among the chronicles of the early Middle Ages, indicating perhaps a continual use of the trebuchet.[26] Two riddles in the Anglo-Saxon riddle collection known as the *Exeter Riddle Book* have also been interpreted as describing catapults.[27] But none of these references are descriptive enough to allow such a claim to be validated. Indeed, it is not until the 885-86 siege of Paris by the Vikings before a more detailed description of siege machines can be found, and, like the machines described at the siege of Thessaloniki, those at Paris also may have been traction trebuchets.

At this siege, according to the poem *De bello Parisiaco* (The Attack on Paris) by Abbo of Saint-Germain-des-Prés, the defending Franks deployed a type of defensive apparatus known as a *manganum* or *mangonel*, the mechanics of which were similar to the traction trebuchet—a rotating beam engine throwing huge stones against the opposing Vikings:

> The Franks prepared some heavy pieces of wood each with an iron tooth at the end, so as to damage the Danish machines more quickly. With coupled beams of the same length they built what are commonly called mangonels, machines for throwing vast stones, which could blast the lowly race of barbarians often blowing out their brains, crushing crowds of them and their shields. Not one shield that was hit did not break; not one unfortunate who was hit did not die.[28]

Yet the lack of collaborative evidence (despite the large number of sources on this siege, only Abbo's poem makes reference to the presence of mangonels), the lack of an elaborate description (there is no reference either to the shooter holding the sling or to a team pulling on ropes to discharge the stone), and the lack of a definitive conduit for the diffusion of this artillery technology from either the Avaro-Slavs or the Muslims (although some historians suggest that Charlemagne's forces may have learned it from their numerous attacks against the Spanish Muslims or from the Byzantines in Sicily) attack the credibility of this reference. More importantly, despite the possibility of similar weapons appearing again at the siege of Angers in 873, they appear to disappear from western Europe until the twelfth century. Thus if these were indeed traction trebuchets, their use seems not to have had an enduring influence in European military strategy.[29]

In 1147, two traction trebuchets were reportedly used by the
Crusaders to capture Muslim Lisbon. They were operated by
crews organized in shifts of 100 pullers which fired 5,000 stones
in 10 hours (250 shots per hour or one shot every 14.42 seconds).[30] After this, traction trebuchets appeared at many sieges
throughout western Europe. Not only can this be seen in numerous
narrative references, but also through a large number of diverse
artistic sources as well. Traction trebuchets are depicted in a relief
carving of the late twelfth-early thirteenth centuries found in the
church of St. Nazaire in Carcassonne and in illuminations found
in the *Maciejowski Bible* (Paris c.1250), the *Le chevalier du cygne*
(French c.1200), a *Histoire du Outremer* (French c.1300), another
Histoire du Outremer (Jerusalem c.1280), the *Liber ad honorem*
of Peter of Eboli (Sicily or southern Italy c.1200-1220), and the
Skylitzes Chronicle (Sicilian or Byzantine, twelfth-early fourteenth
centuries).[31]

Still, despite their frequent usage, there was often an inconsistency in the accuracy and power of the missiles discharged from
this artillery. Primarily, this was due to the fact that the accuracy
and force of the missile was dependant on the strength and unity
of a team of pullers. When a team was well trained in the firing
of these catapults, their efficiency must have been excellent. However, when a team of pullers was not well trained or had suffered
losses in numbers, accuracy and power of discharge diminished.
Consequently, there was a search for an alternate power source,
and this ultimately led to the creation of the counterweight trebuchet.

The Counterweight Trebuchet

The counterweight trebuchet differed little from its technological
cousin. The only significant change was the substitution of the
pulling ropes with a fixed counterweight, usually a box filled with
stones, sand or some other heavy body, which provided the power
to discharge the missile.[32] Not only did the counterweight allow
for a more balanced discharge force, but as it was estimated to
have weighed as much as 4500-13,600 kilograms, it could propel
rather heavy projectiles (45-90 kilograms) an estimated 300 meters. Larger projectiles might also have been used; what are es-

timated to be fourteenth-century trebuchet balls made of marble and excavated at Tlemcen measured 2 meters in circumference and weighed 230 kilograms.[33]

The counterweight trebuchet appeared as early as the mid-twelfth century in the Mediterranean area and then spread into northern Europe, the Middle East, and North Africa. It may have a Byzantine provenance, as the earliest recorded use of the counterweight trebuchet was at the Byzantine siege of Zevgminon in 1165; but the Byzantines themselves may have learned it from elsewhere.[34] After this time it appeared frequently, and was probably used initially in conjunction with the more technologically primitive traction trebuchet. The Muslims seemed to have especially favored this weapon, and it appeared often in the Holy Land where they used it frequently against the Christians, including against the strongholds of Hims in 1248-49 and Acre in 1291 where it is reported that they had 92 counterweight trebuchets.[35] The weapon appeared as far north as Flanders, where a counterweight trebuchet is depicted in an early fourteenth-century illumination of the *Roman de Saint Graal*; England, appearing in Northumberland in 1244; and Scotland, where it is found in a Carlisle Charter illustration of 1316.[36]

Counterweight trebuchet from Conrad Kyeser's *Bellifortis* (c.1400). [From Kyeser (1967).]

As Lynn White jr. contends, the counterweight trebuchet was "the first important mechanical utilization of the force of weight."[37] As such, it was of great interest to many technical writers and draftsmen of the late Middle Ages and the Renaissance, and led to detailed descriptions and drawings of the mechanism by such eminent authors as Villard de Honnecourt and Giles of Rome in the thirteenth century; Conrad Kyeser, Marino Taccola, Roberto Valturio, and the "Anonymous of the Hussite Wars" in the fifteenth century; and Leonard da Vinci and Agostino Ramelli in the sixteenth century.[38]

Both traction and counterweight trebuchets seem to have been effective siege weapons. Although they were never used in large numbers—the 92 counterweight trebuchets at Acre in 1291 being an exception—sometimes they brought a more rapid conclusion to a siege by breaching the fortification's walls. Indeed, some of these victories were quite dramatic. For example, at the siege of the abbey of Holyrood near Edinburgh in 1296, Edward I had three trebuchets which fired 158 stones in three days causing its surrender, and in 1304, at the siege of Stirling, the same king used 13 trebuchets which fired 600 stones and within days breached the walls of the castle.[39] However, the best description of the destructive capabilities of these catapults can be found in the *Chanson de la croisade albigenoise* which discusses the siege of Castelnaudry by the Occitans in September 1211:

> The besiegers set up their trebuchet on a road but all around they could only find stones which would have fragmented under the impact of firing. In the end they found three which they brought from a good league away. With their first shot they knocked down a tower. With their next, in everyone's sight, they destroyed a chamber. With the third shot they fired the stone disintegrated but not before causing great injury to those who were inside the town.

With this display of force, the town was compelled to surrender.[40]

Trebuchets were used not only to breach fortification walls, but also often to intimidate and destroy the morale of the besieged. At these times stone missiles were replaced by incendiaries, the carcasses of putrefying and diseased animals or even the bodies or body parts of compatriots of the besieged. For example, at the siege of Schwanau in 1332, the besiegers from Strasbourg massacred 48 prisoners and placed their bodies in barrels which were catapulted into the castle in an effort to frighten the besieged inhabitants.[41]

The time of the trebuchet was, however, short-lived. By the mid-fourteenth century, it became apparent that gunpowder weapons would quickly make the catapult extinct as a siege weapon. Still, because of the novelty of gunpowder technology, it was not until the 1380s that there was a decline in the use of trebuchets in sieges. Almost all of the early sieges of the Hundred Years War included them.[42] Sometimes they were used side-by-side with early gunpowder weapons in both attacking and defending fortifications. Indeed, they were present with gunpowder weapons as late as 1373 in defense of Queensborough Castle.[43] Even during Charles V's reign (1364-80), the French continued to build counterweight trebuchets and produce trebuchet balls while at the same time increasing their supply of gunpowder weapons.[44]

Trebuchets continued to be used into the fifteenth century: at the siege of Mortagne in 1405, at St. Omer in 1406, in Saint-Pol in 1419-20, in Touraine in 1421, at Paris in 1421-22, and in Picardy in 1422. Trebuchets continued to appear in some French arms inventories until c.1460, but in all these instances it is clear that the use of this artillery technology was becoming more infrequent and sporadic.[45] Trebuchets were replaced by the new, and ultimately more powerful, gunpowder artillery.

Greek Fire

Only one other non-gunpowder artillery technology was used in the Middle Ages: Greek Fire. Because of its limited use, and then only by the Byzantines and Muslims and not by western Europeans, it will be dealt with only briefly here.

Although it is uncertain precisely where Greek Fire originated, or even what it was or how it was discharged, all the evidence indicates that it was an incendiary device which was ignited and pumped through tubes at short range onto attackers. Most certainly the substance itself was a crude oil, a mixture of olefins and naphthalenes, or a distillation of crude oil which was obtained naturally from the region northeast of the Black Sea. The oil was thick and viscous. It was heated to increase its flammability and then pumped by air pressure through a nozzle over a match or lamp to ignite it. Once ignited, the oil was discharged as a jet stream onto opposing ships or people, burning all that was in its path (including all that was on water as it continued to burn while floating.) Although the range of the stream of fire was small, all that came within its range was easily destroyed.[46]

Greek Fire first made its appearance in the Byzantine navy in the seventh century. Between 674 and 678 the Arab fleet made a number of attacks against Constantinople. Although these were unsuccessful, contemporary historians Theophanes and Cedrenus reported that the Byzantine emperor, Constantine Pogonatus, was so concerned with the safety of his capital that he ordered a number of fireships to be equipped with siphons of Greek Fire. These were then sent against the Arab fleet which was attacked and defeated.[47]

From then on Greek Fire was used infrequently, perhaps because of the danger to the host ship, and when it was, it succeeded only in naval battles. In 941, it was used to annihilate a fleet of Russian ships attacking across the Black Sea from Kiev; and in 1103, it caused a Pisan fleet near Rhodes to flee.[48] Even as late as 1453, on the eve of the fall of Constantinople, the Byzantine navy was using Greek Fire with success, chasing off a Turkish attack in the Sea of Marmora near the Bosporus Strait.[49] The sole example of the use of Greek Fire on land may be the siege of Constantinople in 1453 where it is reported that the Byzantines sent Greek Fire against the Turks in a final desperate attempt to defend their city.[50] Greek Fire was so infrequently employed that it appears in only one artistic source, an illumination found in the twelfth-early fourteenth-century *Skylitzes Chronicle* (f34v), which shows a Byzantine warship discharging the weapon from its afterdeck.[51]

Despite the seeming success of Greek Fire for the Byzantine navy, and the seeming accessibility of the weapon as evidenced by a large number of recipes in western European and Islamic sources,[52] the weapon was not used much beyond the Byzantine Empire. In fact, only the Arabs appear to have experimented with Greek Fire, and then exclusively on land, using it as early as 807 against the Byzantines at Heraclea and later against the Crusaders at Nicaea and Jerusalem in 1099, at Acre in 1191, at Damietta

in 1208, and at Mansura on the Nile delta in 1249.[53] Even then
the Arabs did not have the same technological capabilities with
the weapon as did the Byzantines, as Greek Fire did not play a
significant role in the outcome of the above-mentioned battles or
sieges.

Perhaps more intriguing is the question of why the western
Europeans failed to use this technology. Whether it was because
they lacked the natural materials to make the substance or whether
they denied its effectiveness cannot be known. It is however apparent that the western Europeans had heard of Greek Fire and
were intrigued by its destructive capabilities. For example, in
1340, at the siege of Tournai, after a lengthy and fruitless siege
of the town by Edward III's English and Low Countries' forces,
the situation had become so dire that the *Chronique des Pays-Bas*
reports that Edward called an expert in siege artillery to him to
discuss tactics to be used against the fortifications of the town.
Among other things which this man proposed was a "dragon"
made of wood which would spew out Greek Fire. The dragon
was then made "using magic" and was in fact successful in destroying some of Tournai by fire (although it seems not by Greek
Fire). The English King then paid the engineer a great sum of
money to build more of these machines, but incapable of fulfilling
his promises, he fled, and despite a fervent search for him by
the army, he was never seen again. The anonymous chronicler
does assure us, however, that the engineer died "an evil death"
for his sins.[54]

Gunpowder weapons, having some of the same incendiary results, quickly replaced Greek Fire. In only one engagement did
the two weapons meet each other. This occurred in 1455 when
Turkish cannons easily destroyed Byzantine ships outfitted with
Greek Fire before the latter vessels could come within close
enough range to use their incendiary weapons.[55] The age of the
gun had arrived.

Gunpowder Artillery

Perhaps the greatest and certainly the most enduring invention in medieval military technology was gunpowder weaponry. Invented in China, gunpowder was probably discovered by an alchemist in the eighth or ninth century AD. Shortly thereafter its military potential was recognized, leading to its use in bombs, grenades, rockets, and fireworks during the tenth to twelfth centuries. It was not until the late thirteenth or early fourteenth centuries that the Chinese developed cannons, being content merely to use gunpowder as an explosive rather than as a propellant. There is, however, some evidence that the concept of "guns" was known in India in the early twelfth century.[56]

By the middle of the thirteenth century, gunpowder made its way to western Europe, although by a means yet to be ascertained. The most likely conduit was through the Islamic lands to Byzantium or to Spain and then on to western Europe. In c.1267 a recipe for gunpowder appeared in Roger Bacon's *Epistola de secretis operibus artis et naturae, et de nullitate magiae* (Letter on the Secret Workings of Art and Nature, and on the Vanity of Magic). This was followed by similar recipes written c.1275 in Albert the Great's *De mirabilibus mundi* (Concerning the Wonders of the World) and c.1300 in Marcus Graecus' *Liber ignium ad comburendos hostes* (Book of Fires for the Burning of Enemies). These recipes varied slightly, but all combined saltpeter, sulphur, and charcoal in a mixture which when lit combusted with a forceful explosion.[57] Still, none of these authors described a weapon which could use their gunpowder mixture.

When this weapon was invented in Europe, it was not in the form of a bomb, grenade, or rocket, as in China. It was instead a tube-shaped weapon which used gunpowder to discharge a missile from it; and it was commonly called a "cannon" from the French *canon* or "gun" from the English *gynne* or *gunne*.

It is difficult to determine when the first cannon was made in Europe. Written evidence from the early fourteenth century is scarce and often disputed. References to guns appearing at the defense of Forli in 1284 and in the armory of Ghent in 1313 are suspect and unsubstantiated.[58] More trustworthy are the later references to guns at the siege of Metz in 1324, in a Florentine armory in 1326, and at the siege of Cividale (Friuli) in 1331, but even these references have been questioned.[59] Less controversial are two artistic sources, an illumination found in Walter de Milemete's *De notabilibus, sapientiis et prudentiis regum* (Concerning the Majesty, Wisdom and Prudence of Kings), made in London c.1326, and a second illumination, obviously inspired by the first, found in a companion volume to the Walter de Milemete treatise known as the *De secretis secretorum Aristotelis* (The Secrets of Secrets of Aristotle), also made in London in the last

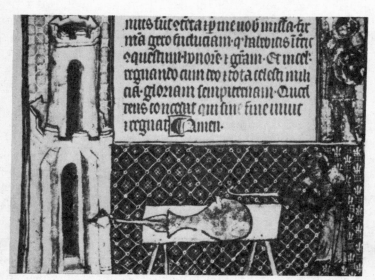

Early gunpowder weapon from Walter de Milemete's *De notabilibus, sapientiis et prudentiis regum* (c.1327).
[Christ Church, Oxford.]

half of the 1320s. Each of these depicts a large vase-shaped cannon lying on its side. In the first, a soldier, dressed in armor, is igniting the gun with a hot iron through a hole in the breech of the weapon, propelling a large arrow-shaped bolt from its opening towards what appears to be a fortification.[50] The second illustration is similar to the first in the shape and mount of the cannon and in the missile it fires, but differs in that no target is depicted and that a squad of four armored soldiers assist in the ignition of the weapon.[61]

In the late 1330s and 1340s references to gunpowder weaponry multiply. Guns were included in armories in Lille, Lucca, Aachen, Deventer, London, Siena, and St. Omer. They appeared at the sieges of Tournai in 1340 and of Calais in 1346-47, and almost certainly, although disputed, at the battle of Crécy in 1346, where they were used on the battlefield solely "to cause panic."[62]

The beginnings of gunpowder weaponry were thus quite modest, but their evolutionary progress was spectacular. Over the next 150 years guns were made larger, and they were made smaller. Eventually they became hand-held. The methods of manufacture also changed, as guns became less frequently made on the forge and more frequently at the foundry. Transportation methods, metallurgy, and powder chemistry were subjected to experiment and eventually improved. More importantly, gunpowder weaponry led to significant changes on the battlefield and at sieges. It was, in the words of William McNeill, "an arms race," which affected every kingdom and principality and which would eventually lead to the so-called "military revolution."[63]

As can be judged by the target depicted in the Walter de Milemete illumination, the first and most enduring impact of gunpowder weapons was on siege warfare. Early gunpowder artillery pieces were heavy cannons with large calibers which fired heavy projectiles.[64] Huge guns were ideal for this type of fighting as the walls of castles were easily damaged by the ballistic force of gunshot, and by the middle of the fourteenth century nearly every siege was accompanied by gunpowder artillery bombardment. By the end of the century, cannons were even breaching fortification walls. The first of these victories came in 1377, at the siege of Odruik, when Philip the Bold, Duke of Burgundy, used cannons which fired 91 kilogram balls to bring down the walls of the castle.[65] At the siege of Oudenaarde in 1382, it is recorded that the rebellious Philip van Artevelde "made a marvelyous great bombard shotying stone of marvelyous weyght and when this bombard shot it made suche a noyse in the goygne as though all the dyvels of hell had been in the way."[66] With this weapon, he captured the fortification.

In the siege warfare of the fifteenth century, gunpowder weaponry continued to be significant. By 1412 and the siege of Bourges, the Duke of Berry, who was defending the city, was forced to vacate his residence no fewer than seven times to avoid the persistent and accurate gunfire of the French and Burgundian cannons.[67] At Harfleur, in 1415, Henry V had to rely on his guns to bring down the walls of the town when his mines were continually countermined. Eventually he moved his guns on clumsy platforms next to the walls of the town before the siege was effective.[68] Fortepice was flattened in 1433 by a single great bombard, the Bourgoigne.[69] And the town of Bouvignes fell in 1466, when, as contemporary chronicler Philippe de Commynes states, "two bombards and other large pieces of artillery, [shattered] the houses of the town...and [forced] the poor people to take refuge in their cellars and to remain there."[70] Finally, in August 1466, the town of Dinant, which had resisted 17 sieges during the Middle Ages, fell to Charles the Bold, the Duke of Burgundy, after only a week of gunpowder artillery bombardment.[71]

Sometimes it was a long and heavy bombardment which was required to defeat a besieged fortification. For example, at the siege of Maastricht from November 24, 1407 to January 7, 1408, the town received 1514 large bombard balls, an average of 30 per day; at the siege of Lagny in 1431, 412 stone cannonballs were fired into the town in a single day; at Dinant in 1466, 502 large and 1200 smaller cannonballs were fired; and finally, at the siege of Rhodes in 1480 over 3500 balls were shot into the town.[72] At other times, simply the presence of large gunpowder weapons among the besieging army intimidated the inhabitants of a town or castle. An example of this came at the siege of Bourg, in June 1451, which Charles VII captured in just six days after his heavy artillery was brought up to the walls of the castle, although they never fired a shot.[73] At the siege of Ham in 1411, only three shots were fired from the bombard known as "Griette." The first passed over the town and fell into the Seine; the second destroyed a tower and two adjacent walls; and the third made a breach in the wall itself. Before a fourth shot could be fired, the town capitulated.[74]

At other times gunpowder siege artillery was unsuccessful, especially since many commanders, trained in the old tactics of siege warfare, did not recognize the capabilities of these new weapons and were thus unable to use them effectively. Such a lack of recognition occurred even as late as 1472 when the lord of Cordes besieged Beauvais. Philippe de Commynes reports:

> My lord of Cordes...had two cannons which were fired only twice through the gate and made a large hole in it. If he had had more stones to continue firing he would have certainly taken the town. However, he had not come with the intention of performing such an exploit and was therefore not well provided.[75]

As well, misuse of the guns by inexperienced operators continually caused problems. Frequently these early gunpowder weapons exploded, and sometimes more bizarre accidents occurred. At the siege of Poeke in July 1453 the Ghentenaars broke ranks and fled because one of their cannoneers inadvertently allowed a spark from his ignitor to fly into an open sack of gunpowder which burst into flames. All the nearby cannoneers panicked and ran; when the rest of the army saw this, it also took flight.[76]

Gunpowder weapons had less impact on late medieval battlefield warfare. Despite the use of cannons on the battlefield of Crécy in 1346, other fourteenth-century battlefield uses of gunpowder weaponry were infrequent, and even then rarely did they play a role in the outcome of the battle. In the fourteenth century, it may in fact have been only at the battle of Bevershoutsveld, fought outside the walls of the town of Bruges in 1382, where guns may have decided the outcome. Here gunpowder weapons brought by the Ghentenaars to besiege the town were turned against the attacking Brugeois militia which had ventured outside of the protective walls of the town to fend off a Ghentenaar onslaught. As the anonymous author of the *Chronique de Flandre* describes the scene: "The Ghentenaars moved themselves and their artillery forward. This artillery fired a blast with such furor that it seemed to bring the [Brugeois] line directly to a halt."[77] Other late fourteenth-century battles in which guns were used on the battlefield were Aljubarrota in 1385 and Castagnaro in 1387.[78]

With the adoption of smaller cannons in the early fifteenth century as well as improved accuracy, the destructive capabilities of guns rose until it became, according to M.G.A. Vale, "patently obvious that the gun could not only batter down fortifications, but could kill, and kill selectively, from afar."[79] These guns began to appear more frequently on the battlefield: at Tongres and Othée in 1408, at Agincourt in 1415, at Cravant in 1423, at the battle of the Herrings in 1429, at Bulgneville in 1431, at Formigny in 1450, at Castillon and Gavere in 1453, at Blore Heath and Ludford Bridge in 1459, at St. Albans in 1461, at Montlhery in 1465, at Huy and Brusthem in 1467, at Grandson and Murten in 1476, at Nancy in 1477, and at Bosworth in 1485.[80]

As in siege warfare, sometimes these guns were quite effective. For example, at the battle of Castillon, a letter written to "my beloved friends" by a now anonymous author describes the destruction: "Girault the cannoneer and his assistants and companions directed their artillery against the enemy. And it was very sorrowful, for each ball hit five or six men, killing them all."[81]

More often, however, battlefield gunfire was extremely ineffective. At Othée, for example, the guns fired too slowly to create a non-penetrable barrage.[82] At Montlhery, the Burgundian cannons were positioned strongly on the field but still were unable to fire more than ten salvos at the French army.[83] And at Brusthem it is reported that,

> The battle began with an artillery duel. The Burgundians...advanced their pieces up to the dikes at four or five spots and from there fired at the Liégeois. Moreover, they managed to unleash a considerable bombardment (the Burgundians are said to have fired seventy rounds.) But the trees and hedges impeded their line of fire.[84]

Smaller weapons which could be easily transported and maneuvered on the battlefield were needed. The solution was hand-held gunpowder weapons. These may have appeared as early as 1334 at the battle of Este, although this is a highly questionable date.[85] More probably they were invented in the late fourteenth

century, although the earliest evidence of their existence is again
an artistic source, a drawing appearing c.1400 in Conrad Kyeser's
Bellifortis. It shows a cannoneer firing a weapon held at the front
by a tripod and at the rear by the cannoneer's hand.[86] After this,
uses of hand-held gunpowder weapons, initially called
"coulevrines à main" and later "haquebusses," increase. Especially attracted to these weapons were the dukes of Burgundy,
beginning with John the Fearless, who by 1410 may have included
as many as 4000 hand-held gunpowder weapons in his arsenal.[87]

Other armies soon followed this example, and by the middle
of the fifteenth century most battlefield engagements included
hand-held gunpowder weapons. So conventional had they become,
in fact, that in January 1456, when Philip the Good, Duke of
Burgundy, was planning a crusade against the Turks, he included
500-600 gunners outfitted with hand-held gunpowder weapons
under the command of a master of artillery.[88] And by the 1460s
and 1470s, Philip's successor, Charles the Bold, had forces
equipped with haquebusses "without number," guns which he continually used in his military engagements against the French, Germans, and Swiss. For example, at the siege of Neuss in 1475,
one eyewitness reports: "It was pitiful how culverins were fired
at [the people of Neuss] thicker than rain..."[89] They were also
used at the battles of Grandson, Murten, and Nancy. At Nancy,
the Burgundians were defeated and Charles the Bold was killed
by Swiss forces equally well equipped with their own hand-held
gunpowder weapons.[90]

Before the fifteenth century, gunpowder weaponry also began
appearing on board ships. While small gunpowder weapons may
have been added to ships shortly after they began to be used on
land, most references to shipboard gunpowder artillery before the
end of the fourteenth century are questionable.[91] After the beginning of the fifteenth century, however, it seems that few ships
left port without carrying a complement of cannons. They were
probably used by Spanish ships at the battle of La Rochelle in
1372 and at the battle of the Seine in 1416, and they were certainly
found on board English ships of the 1410s and 1420s and on
Italian ships in the Lombard Wars of the 1420s and 1430s.[92] As
well, by 1410 Christine de Pisan wrote in her *Le livre fais d'armes
et de chevalerie* (The Book of the Feats of Arms and Chivalry)

advocating "greeting" attacking ships "ryght well with gode bombardes" when encountering them.[93]

Naval guns also seem to have been different from those used in land engagements. They were smaller; more standardized in barrel length, caliber and chamber size; and capable of being loaded with both powder and ball from the rear. Hand-held gunpowder weapons also frequently appeared on board ships. Still, these guns may not have been very effective in naval warfare. Although there are many contemporary reports of naval gunfire bombarding coastal fortifications and opposing ships, it is not until 1513 that the first sinking of a naval vessel by shipboard guns is recorded, and this may indicate that these naval gunpowder weapons were still a long way from the intensive ship-to-ship bombardment of the early modern period.[94]

Early Cannons

The earliest medieval gunpowder weapons were known simply as cannons or ribaudequins, and it is uncertain what they looked like or how they were made. Even the illuminations found in and inspired by Walter de Milemete's manuscript cannot help here as it is impossible to determine the technological make-up of the weapon from the illustrations alone, and in fact they may only be an illuminator's vision of a cannon as described by another witness. But as the technology became better known and more common, gunpowder weapons began to be made in many different sizes and a few different shapes.[95]

The largest, best known, and most impressive of all of these weapons were the bombards. They measured as much as 5.2 meters, weighed as much as 16,400 kilograms and had calibers as large as 71 centimeters. This made them extremely difficult to transport and to maneuver on the battlefield, confining their use to sieges alone. But at these sieges, the presence of one or more bombards was significant, for they fired stone cannonballs weighing as much as 386 kilograms (although most fired balls weighed much less). They also often impressed medieval eyewitnesses with their sounds "like devils out of hell" and their destructive capabilities. This is seen clearly in a contemporary account of the siege of Bourges in 1412:

[The besiegers]...caused a cannon called Griette, which was bigger than the others, to be mounted opposite the main gate. It shot stones of enormous weight at the cost of large quantities of gunpowder and much hard and dangerous work on the part of its expert crew. Nearly twenty men were required to handle it. When it was fired the thunderous noise could be heard four miles away and terrorized the local inhabitants as if it were some reverberation from hell. On the first day, the foundations of one of the towers were partly demolished by a direct hit. On the next day this cannon fired twelve stones, two of which penetrated the tower, thus exposing many of the buildings and their inhabitants. At the same time, other batteries at the siege were also making breaches in other parts of the wall.[96]

Bombards were also frequently named, unlike most other gunpowder weapons. Often these names indicated the city of their construction or ownership, i.e. the Brucelles, Dijon, Paris, Montereau, Valexon, etc.; other names denoted their regional origins: Cambray, Artois, Bourgoigne, St. Pol, Brabant, Luxembourg, etc. Some bombards carried the names of classical heroes, such as Jason and Medea, or of contemporary military leaders. For example, the French had La Hire, Barbazin, Flavy, and Bon-

The late fourteenth-century bombard Dulle Griete, now located on the market place of Ghent.

iface, while the English christened theirs Bedford, Robin Clement, Brisebarre, and Herr Johan. Other bombards seem to have had feminine names such as Katherine, Griette, and la petite Liete. Still other etymologies—Prusse, Ath, Bergier, Bergière, Le Damp, or La plus du monde—simply cannot be known with the little information given in the inventories.[97]

However, bombards were expensive to make and their use in non-siege encounters was limited. Moreover, by the middle of the fifteenth century, when fortifications began to be outfitted with their own gunpowder weaponry, bombards or the mounts on which they stood were frequently easy targets of defensive gunfire. Therefore, in western Europe they began to be replaced by smaller weapons, as cannoneers discovered that at a siege a larger number of more easily maneuverable smaller guns could provide the same and sometimes more offensive power as a single large bombard, and without the possibility of defensive fire easily destroying their firepower. The Ottoman Turks, however, continued to prefer using large bombards in besieging the fortifications of Byzantium, including the city of Constantinople, where they seem to have been largely unopposed by defensive gunpowder weapons. Smaller weapons could also be used on the battlefield.

Measurements for medium-sized gunpowder weapons, known as veuglaires, crapadeaux, mortars, bombardelles, courtaux, falcons, and serpentines, vary greatly. Weights as small as 48 kilograms are reported, but so are weights of 3584 kilograms. Lengths and calibers are more standard, with lengths averaging between 1.22 and 1.83 meters and calibers between 7.6 and 17.8 centimeters. Stone cannonballs fired from these weapons weighed between 1 and 14.5 kilograms. They were used both at sieges and on the battlefield and would eventually become the most common type of non-hand-held gunpowder weaponry of the early modern army.

The smallest gunpowder weapons of the late Middle Ages were known most often by the name culverin, and their use was almost strictly limited to the battlefield. There great numbers of these weapons were sometimes used. This is certainly evidenced by the large numbers of culverins captured by the Swiss from the Burgundians after the battles of Grandson, Murten, and Nancy fought in 1476 and 1477. Indeed, at the battle of Murten in 1476,

Early handgun from Conrad Kyeser's *Bellifortis*.
[From Kyeser (1967).]

if it is possible to believe Philippe de Commynes' numbers, as many as 10,000 culverniers may have participated on both sides of the battle.[98]

Weights for these guns, averaging between six and 23 kilograms, were often very small in comparison with other gunpowder weapons. Lengths too were small, averaging between 15 and 122 centimeters. Calibers are never recorded, but they must have been quite small as most culverins fired lead instead of stone cannonballs; it was easier, and ultimately cheaper, to found small lead cannonballs than to carve stone ones. It is also in the culverins that the origin of hand-held guns may be seen, as many of the smallest of these were capable of, and often depicted as, being attached to a stock, wooden or metal, and were transported and operated by hand.

Construction of Gunpowder Weapons

Three types of metal were used for gunpowder weapons in the fourteenth and fifteenth centuries: bronze, forged iron, and cast iron. Bronze was the most highly prized metal for constructing cannons, but its large expense limited its use in most armies, with the result that there were many more iron cannons than bronze ones made during this period.[99] This expense also limited their size, with few large bombards and many more medium and small weapons being made in this metal. It seems to have been especially preferred in the construction of hand-held weapons. All bronze cannons were also cast at a foundry and were probably less heavy, but much stronger than their iron counterparts.

Iron was a more plentiful and less expensive metal for the making of gunpowder weapons.[100] However, it was also far more difficult to cast, especially since methods of iron founding in the late Middle Ages were expensive and primitive.[101] Still, some cast iron cannons were made during this period; indeed, this may have been the chief method of gun manufacture before 1375. This is seen in the drawing of Walter de Milemete's manuscript, which appears to depict a cast iron cannon, and in the earliest extant gunpowder weapons, four Italian *bombardellas*, weighing between 10 and 60.5 kilograms and measuring between 29 and 58 centimeters in length, all of which were founded between 1325 and

1375.[102] Cast iron cannons continued to be made during the fifteenth century, but their numbers diminished after 1442. They did not appear again until after 1543, when a breakthrough in iron founding cut the costs of casting, and cast iron cannons became the most common gunpowder artillery.[103]

Most iron cannons were not made at the foundry but on the forge. They were constructed by soldering several iron bars together to form a tube, adding a strong, solid piece of metal to the rear of the tube and reinforcing the whole weapon with a number of iron rings soldered around it. The lack of strength in such a weapon was easily made up by its low cost of construction and its relatively quick production time. Using this method of construction also made it possible to build a gun of any weight or length, and it was especially popular for the construction of large bombards; all the extant bombards from this period were built in this manner. Forged gunpowder weapons were able to be repaired on the siege or battlefield site, and late medieval artillery trains always contained a number of forges, smiths, and pre-fashioned rings and bars for this purpose. Forged iron cannons continued to be the most popular method of construction for gunpowder weaponry into the sixteenth century.

This method of constructing gunpowder weapons was not however practical for making hand-held guns. Breaks in the solder between the iron bars which emitted hot gases, and the possibility of rupture was too dangerous for cannoneers firing these weapons, and therefore most hand-held guns were made either in cast iron or cast bronze.

Most cannons in the late Middle Ages had removable chambers to hold the gunpowder which fitted in an opening near the breech. Like most of the guns they fitted into, removable chambers were also constructed using strips of iron forged together and bound by iron circles. These chambers were fixed solidly in place with a wedge of iron or wood, and several chambers accompanied each artillery piece allowing for a rapid rate of fire, presuming of course that the weapon was able to cool down fast enough to warrant such speed.[104]

Although removable chambers are not pictured in the Walter de Milemete manuscript illumination, nor do the extant Italian *bombardellas* mentioned above have removable chambers, this innovation in gunmaking was known as early as 1342 when an account of a St. Omer bailiff lists gunpowder weapons with separate chambers at the castle of Rihoult in Artois. After this date and into the sixteenth century, most cannons were built with separable and removable chambers.

Gunpowder weapons of all sizes, bombards to culverins, bronze or iron, had removable chambers. However, removable chambers were most frequently found in medium and small guns. Sizes of these chambers varied with the size of the weapon; those whose lengths are recorded measure sometimes as small as 15 centimeters, but most were twice that size. The amount of gunpowder included in the chambers also varied. Generally, the chamber was completely filled, although sometimes it is recorded as being only partially filled; whether this was to vary the range of fire or for some other reason is not known.

Gunpowder, Transportation, Mounts, and Aiming

While gunpowder weapons themselves varied in weight, length and caliber, and whether they had removable chambers or not, what went inside these weapons—projectiles and gunpowder—varied little. As far as gunpowder was concerned, although there was some experimentation with amounts, the three main ingredients— saltpeter, sulphur, and charcoal—remained the same. The ideal proportions of these substances—74.64% saltpeter, 11.85% sulphur, and 13.51% charcoal—were rarely achieved; however, most gunpowder recipes did approximate these ideal percentages, resulting in a combustion satisfactory enough to propel a projectile to its target.[105]

The quality of gunpowder depended more on its purity than on its mixture. In the fourteenth century, gunpowder was kept fine by milling it at a horse-powered mill, and it was kept pure and stable by transporting the saltpeter apart from the rest of the powder and combining it only at the last moment at the site of the battle or siege. Still, this rarely produced an even combustion, and later, sometime after 1420, milling was discontinued, and gunpowder became engrained or "corned." Using brandy, vinegar, or the urine of a "wine-drinking man" to corn the powder, this allowed oxygen to circulate around the granules and to produce an even combustion and thus a more precise and systematic missile discharge. Eventually, corning also allowed for the production of a cheaper, more stable gunpowder.[106]

The projectiles of gunpowder weapons also varied little in substance. Because of the imperfection of early cannon bores, gunpowder weapons often misfired. If the bullet was too tight, the cannon might explode, and if the shot fit too loosely, in the days before wadding became frequently used, the cannon lost propulsion pressure and produced an inadequate discharge.[107]

As indicated in the Walter de Milemete manuscript illumination, the first projectiles may have been large bolts, complete with specially constructed points which stoppered the muzzle sufficiently to allow for the build-up of gases needed to discharge it. However, other evidence for the use of bolts as projectiles is scarce and may lead to the conclusion that if bolts were initially used as gunpowder weapon projectiles, their use did not last long. Certainly such a projectile's offensive capabilities were limited, and they may in fact have not withstood the explosion of gunpowder behind them without disintegrating.[108]

Most gunpowder-propelled projectiles were instead, like trebuchet projectiles, round balls made in stone or cast metal. Stone projectiles were generally used by the largest cannons because of their cost.[109] These balls were fashioned by masons either in a central masonry or on site. Masons frequently accompanied the artillery trains on their military expeditions and were there not only to fashion new cannonballs but also to shave existing balls to correctly fit their artillery muzzles.[110]

Metal balls, on the other hand, were used chiefly in medium-sized and smaller guns. Both lead and iron were used to make these cannonballs, although probably because of the poor quality of cast iron in the late Middle Ages, lead was the preferred metal for making them. The first reference to the use of metal cannonballs was in 1325-26, but they do not seem to have been frequently used until the fifteenth century. Eventually, they supplanted stone cannonballs.[111] Metal cannonballs could also be made at the battlefield or siege site, as there is evidence of forges, cannonball molds, and blacksmiths present in late medieval artillery trains. However, most metal cannonballs were probably cast at an arsenal and transported to the battle or siege.[112]

There is also some evidence for the existence of incendiary cannonballs in the fifteenth century. They are recorded to have been at the sieges of Breteuil in 1356, Oudenaarde in 1379, and both Beaulieu and Dinant in 1465.[113] They are also found in the French armory in the Bastille in 1428.[114] What the incendiary mixture in these cannonballs was is unknown, as is the reason for its use when plain cannonballs could have caused fires on their own without an added incendiary mixture. Moreover, exploding cannonballs, while intriguing several late medieval engineers,[115] are never mentioned in fourteenth- and fifteenth-century military adventures and were probably too dangerous to use in actual fighting. They likely would have exploded inside the cannon barrel before they were discharged.

At the siege of Neuss in May 1475, it is reported that cannonballs were used in an even more unusual manner. There, gunpowder-propelled projectiles were used as messengers to the inhabitants of Neuss to delivering letters reporting that a German relief army was on its way.[116]

As for the transportation and mounting of these weapons, in the fourteenth and early fifteenth centuries gunpowder artillery was transported to the site of a siege or battle by water or on carts. The guns were then placed on mounts especially constructed there by carpenters who always accompanied artillery trains.[117] By the middle of the fifteenth century, however, this had changed. Cannons were mounted permanently on wheeled carriages which also carried their ammunition and gunpowder. Sometimes these mounts featured protection for the guns and their operators by way of mantles, shields, palisades, etc. As well, also at this time, cushions were added to the back of these guns to absorb the recoil of the weapon.[118]

Even with these improvements, the easy movement of guns to and on the battlefield or at a siege was not fully achieved until the middle of the fifteenth century, when better technology improved gun carriages. Until then, the strategic and tactical agility of these weapons was not fully realized. Sometimes gunpowder weapons, despite their wheeled carriages, were too heavy to transport across existing bridges and roads. Such was the situation in 1411, when the large bombard Griette fell through a bridge in Flanders landing in the ditch below, and in 1436 at Châtillon in

Burgundy, when the passage of heavy cannons en route to the siege of Calais badly damaged the bridge on the main road.[119] At other times, again despite their wheeled carriages, cannons were unable to maneuver on the battlefield. At the siege of Neuss, on May 23, 1475, the Burgundians under Charles the Bold were able to pass around the German artillery set up along the Rhine river because of its inability to quickly change its direction.[120]

Bombards and other large gunpowder weapons were mounted alone, but small and medium-sized cannons were frequently mounted together as a battery of artillery on the same carriage. Artillery batteries as large as five guns were known, and sometimes two different types of gunpowder weapons were mounted on the same carriage.[121]

The mount also set the aim of a cannon. This could be accomplished in a number of ways: first, by placing a fixed mount on terrain angled to provide the correct aim; second, by mounting the cannon on a fixed axle to provide its aim; third, by using the terrain and axle together to aim the weapon; fourth, by using a wall or rock under the carriage to move the aiming angle; and last, by adding a calibrated aiming device to the mount to change the aiming angle.[122] Although these methods seem simple in comparison with modern techniques, medieval cannoneers became quite adept at the aiming of their weapons. Philippe de Commynes reports an incident in 1465 near Paris which shows that sometimes these artillerymen were able to reach far distances with good accuracy: "The king [Charles VII] had a train of artillery mounted on the walls of Paris, and they fired several shots which reached as far as our [the Burgundian] army; this is no small distance, for it consists of two leagues; but I believe that their muzzles were raised very high."[123]

The Effect of Gunpowder Weapons

The invention of gunpowder weapons not only had an impact on warfare, but on society and the state as well. Most knights, nobles, and princes did not welcome the introduction of gunpowder weapons. Traditional medieval warfare respected their social status, leading frequently to ransom rather than death in a battlefield defeat. But gunpowder weapons had no such respect for class, and nobles risked death as did non-noble soldiers. Eventually, they too began to fall to the power of the cannonball. In 1383, at the siege of Ypres, a "very brave English esquire," Louis Lin, was killed by a cannon shot. In 1414, the Bastard of Bourbon was killed by gunshot at Soisson. In 1428, Thomas Montagu, Earl of Salisbury and leader of the English forces in France, was killed at Orléans when a stone cannonball fired from a bombard shattered and mortally wounded him in the head. In 1438, Don Pedro, the brother of the King of Castile, was decapitated by a cannonball during the siege of Capuana at Naples. Four years later, John Payntour, an English squire, was killed by a culverin at La Reole. In 1450, two prominent French military leaders, Pregent de Coetivy, Lord of Rais and Admiral of France, and Tudal le Bourgeois, Bailiff of Troyes, were killed at the siege of Cherbourg; and in 1453, two more prominent individuals lost their lives by gunshot: John Talbot, Earl of Shrewsbury, who was killed at the siege of Castillon in July, and Jacques de Lalaing, "le bon chevalier," who was killed that same month at the siege of Poeke, near Ghent. Finally, in 1460, King James II of Scotland died when one of his large cannons exploded next to him.[124] These deaths did not, however, keep nobles from using the weapons, and by the end of the fifteenth century, nearly every noble had introduced gunpowder weapons into his armies.[125]

At first, non-nobles too were reluctant to accept these weapons. Their sounds were thunderous, and the ground shook when they fired. To the common soldier, such weapons could not have come from God, despite a tradition which developed that they were invented by a German monk named Bernard Schwarz. John of Mirfield, an English surgical writer of the late fourteenth century, described guns as "that diabolic instrument of war", and a title page of a 1489 Basel edition of St. Augustine's *De civitate dei* (The City of God) showed two towns, one guarded by angels and the other by devils, one of whom is armed with a gun.[126]

However, this was not the image of gunpowder weapons held by the Catholic Church. The same church which had banned the use of the crossbow at the Second Ecumenical Lateran Council in 1139 did not hold a similar dislike for guns, especially since it became apparent even before the end of the fourteenth century that the Ottoman Turks showed no hesitation in using them against

Christian armies. If the Islamic God had given guns to His people, the Christian God would also want His people to defend themselves with the same powerful weapons.[127]

As well, in Christian Europe, gunpowder weapons were seen to provide justice. A bombard made in 1404 for Sigismund of Austria was so inscribed: "I am Katerine. Beware of what I hold. I punish injustice."[128] Pope Pius II was so impressed by the weapons that he even possessed his own gunpowder weapons, naming them after himself, Enea and Silvia, and after his mother, Vittoria.[129]

Early in the history of gunpowder weapons the church also furnished cannoneers with their own patron saint, Saint Barbara. She was a fitting patron for those who operated gunpowder artillery, for at her martyrdom, her father, who had denounced her Christianity, was struck down by a clap of thunder and a lightning bolt. Icons of Saint Barbara were painted on guns, and her name was invoked by gunners in battle, as they believed that she would protect them from death.[130]

Kings and important princes also became interested in the use and procurement of gunpowder weapons. Edward III of England (1328-77) may have been the first sovereign to see the future uses of guns, as he stockpiled a small number of the relatively new weapons at the Tower of London, using them both at the battle of Crécy and at the siege of Calais.[131] His interest was succeeded by the dukes of Burgundy, Philip the Bold (1363-1404), John the Fearless (1404-19), Philip the Good (1419-67), and Charles the Bold (1467-77). The Burgundian dukes amassed large quantities of gunpowder weapons, and they used them on almost all of their numerous military expeditions. They also refused to allow their gunpowder technology to remain stagnant, and they experimented with sizes of weapons, methods of manufacture, modes of transportation, metallurgy, and powder chemistry. In some instances, Burgundian guns were even painted different colors, although the reason for this is unclear.

It was also during the reign of these dukes that gunpowder became an official part of the military organization. Philip the Bold supervised the construction and testing of guns, and he organized their use in war under the leadership of an *artilleur*.[132] John the Fearless further increased the number and quality of the

Burgundian gunpowder weapons, appointing Germain de Givery
as the first ducal master of artillery and ordering him to bring all
the gunpowder weapons of the duchy "which were not actually
in use in his castles" together at a special arsenal in Dijon, the
duchy's capital. During John's reign, artillery operators were even
given separate uniforms, including a blue hat, for use in ducal
processions.[133]

Philip the Bold continued the artillery program of his father
and grandfather by adding even more gunpowder weapons to the
Burgundian artillery stores. Philip fought against the French, English, and Germans, and he was also involved in putting down
several insurrections in his ducal holdings, principally in the southern Low Countries. In all of these conquests he used his large
and elaborate artillery train. He also recognized the threat of an
enemy's artillery and is reported to have kept a spy in England
solely for the purpose of assessing the strength of the English
gunpowder artillery holdings.[134]

Philip's son, Charles, could not follow in the footsteps of his
ducal ancestors, for he possessed none of their military or diplomatic skills, nor was he able to defend successfully the lands
which he inherited. He was still interested in continuing the now
traditional Burgundian gunpowder artillery plan. At one time, he
even went so far as to import a particularly experienced cannoneer
from Nuremburg, known as Master Hans, paying the gunner's
wife to watch his children during his absence (October-November
1467).[135] But Charles's enemies—the Germans, Swiss, French,
and Liègeois—had also increased their artillery holdings, equalling
the quality and quantity of the Burgundian gunpowder weapons.
Eventually they used these weapons to defeat the Burgundian
forces and to end Burgundian power.

It was the French under Charles VII (1422-61) who ultimately
established the most "modern" artillery train. Charles increased
the royal budget to procure a larger number of new guns, and he
added heavier new taxes to his kingdom's inhabitants to pay for
this increase. He also took a special interest in the construction
of new and often unworkable inventions related to his gunpowder
weapons. An example of this is recorded in 1449-50 when Charles
requested the design of a new carriage for his artillery, the object

of which "was to create a gun-carriage which was not drawn by horses..."[136]

But perhaps the most important feature of Charles VII's gunpowder artillery train was its intricate organization and superior leadership. Under masters of artillery, Jean and Gaspard Bureau, the French artillery holdings grew in number and efficiency. Duties of cannoneers were established, officers were appointed, competency was improved, and pay was increased. This allowed Charles to take his artillery on every military expedition, and this use ultimately contributed to the eventual French victory over the lesser armed English in the Hundred Years War.[137] Moreover, after Charles VII's death, the French artillery holdings grew consistently larger, improving under both Louis XI and Charles VIII, the latter using it to invade and easily conquer Italy in 1494.

By the end of the fifteenth century and the beginning of the early modern era, gunpowder weaponry had simply become a feature of everyday life. Guns had become so conventional that they began to be used in celebrations, in fashion, and in crime. Ultimately, guns even became virility symbols.[138] A musical instrument took the name "bombard" because of its shape and sound, both of which resembled the gunpowder weapon of that name. Engineers became interested in guns and designed new ones.[139] Even new surgical techniques were developed to heal the new wounds created by gunshot.[140]

Perhaps no other weapon in the history of humanity has had the impact of gunpowder weapons. Even before the end of the sixteenth century Francis Bacon recognized them as one of the three inventions which changed the medieval into the modern world. (The other two were the compass and the printing press.) At the very least, gunpowder weaponry "revolutionized" warfare. From its meager beginnings in the fourteenth and fifteenth centuries developed a force so effective that almost all other medieval military technological innovations disappeared from use. Arms, such as the bow, sword, spear, and lance, were quickly replaced. Armor, even the heavy plate armor of the fifteenth century, provided little protection. Trebuchets propelled their missiles too weakly against fortifications. And castles and town walls proved to be too large and too flat to withstand the constant battering.

Notes

1   Marsden (1969):5-12 and Landels (1978):99-104. The only ancient writer to describe this catapult is Heron (c.350-270 BC). See Marsden (1971):17-60.

2   Marsden (1969):13-16.

3   Marsden (1969):16.

4   Marsden (1969):16-47 and Landels (1978):104-30. A number of ancient writers describe these torsion catapults. See Marsden (1971).

5   Marsden (1969):58-61.

6   Marsden (1969):29-33; Landels (1978):112-15; Baatz (1978):1-17; and Soedel and Foley (1979):153.

7   Landels (1978):119 and Baatz (1978):1-17.

8   Marsden (1969):73-76.

9   Landels (1978):123-26; Soedel and Foley (1979):155-56. For Philon's description of this catapult see Marsden (1971):146-53.

10   Landels (1978):130; Marsden (1971):206-32; and Marsden (1969):189-90. Heron's description of the *cheiroballista* is found in Marsden (1971):215-27. For a description of the use of catapults on the battlefield and at sea see Marsden (1969):164-73.

11   Landels (1978):130-32; Marsden (1969):190-91: and Marsden (1971):249-65. Ammianus Marcellinus' description of the *onager* can be found in Marsden (1971):250-254.

12   On the ranges and accuracy of these weapons see Marsden (1969):86-95.

13   Marsden (1969):95-98 and Soedel and Foley (1969):153.

14   As quoted in Hacker (1968):45.

15   Marsden (1971):234-48.

16   Lander (1984):259.

17   As quoted in Hacker (1968):45-46. See also Wolfram (1988):345.

18   Johnson (1983):79 and Lander (1984):259.

19   Huuri (1940); E.A. Thompson (1958):13-17; and L. White (1962):102-03.
      For a more complete listing of other authors who agree with this contention
      see Gillmor (1981):1 n.1.

20   E.A. Thompson (1958):13-17 and Johnson (1983):78.

21   E.A. Thompson (1958):13.

22   On the Chinese origin of the trebuchet see Needham (1976). On the diffusion
      to and use of these weapons in Islam see Donald Hill (1973):100 and
      Chevedden (1990):20-27.

23   Szwejkowski (1990) and Donald Hill (1973):102-03.

24   Chevedden (1990):10-11 and Vyronis (1981):384.

25   Chevedden (1990):12-13.

26   See David Hill (1979):112-13.

27   Crossley-Holland (1979):#17 and 53. See also David Hill (1979):116-17.
      These have also been interpreted as describing fortresses, ovens and bat-
      tering rams.

28   David Hill (1979):113-15; Gillmor (1981):2-5; and Fino (1972):27-28.

29   Gillmor (1981) believes that these were traction trebuchets, while Donald
      Hill (1973) and L. White (1962) contend that the introduction of the traction
      trebuchet comes later.

30   Donald Hill (1971):102; Chevedden (1990):16-17; and L. White (1962):102-
      03.

31   Nicolle (1988):#723, 772, 774, 787, 830, 1423, and 1427.

32   Donald Hill (1971):105.

33   Donald Hill (1973):105-06; Payne-Gallwey (1903):309; and L. White
      (1962):103. On the dynamics of trebuchets see Hill (1973):106-14.

34   Chevedden (1990):28-31. For a discussion as to whether the counterweight
      trebuchet was a Byzantine, Islamic or Western invention see Chevedden
      (1990):44-47.

35   On the Muslim use of the counterweight trebuchet and the number of their
      technical treatises describing the weapon see Chevedden (1990):31-76.

36   Fino (1972):25, 35-41; Donald Hill (1973):104; Nicolle (1988):#977 and
      1261; and Contamine (1984):104-05.

37   L. White (1962):103.

38   On Villard de Honnecourt see Contamine (1984):103-04 and Nicolle
      (1988):#798, 1587. On Giles of Rome see Giles of Rome (1968):357v-358r
      and Fino (1972):29. On the "Renaissance" engineers see Gille (1966),
      Prager and Scaglia (1972) and B. Hall (1971).

39   Contamine (1984):104-05.

40   As quoted in Contamine (1984):104.

41   Contamine (1984):104.

42   Contamine (1984):194.

43   Brown, Colvin and Taylor (1963):II:801-02.

44   Contamine (1984):194.

45   Contamine (1984):195.

46   Haldon and Byrne (1977); Ellis Davidson (1973):68-74; Forbes (1955):100-
      03; and Partington (1960):28-32.

47   Ellis Davidson (1973):62; Forbes (1955):102; and Partington (1960):12-15.

48   Ellis Davidson (1973):62-64; Forbes (1955):103; and Partington (1960):18-
      20.

49   Ellis Davidson (1973):65.

50   Ellis Davidson (1973):65-66 and Partington (1960):27.

51   Bruhn de Hoffmeyer (1966):140-52 and Nicolle (1988):#1427.

52   Partington (1960):42-61.

53   Ellis Davidson (1973):64-66; Partington (1960):22-27; and A. Hall
      (1957)III:377.

54   DeVries (1987):226.

55   Ellis Davidson (1973):65-66.

56   Needham (1985); Needham (1986); and Gwei-Djen, Needham and Chi-Hsing
      (1988).

57   Partington (1960):42-81 and Needham (1986):39-50.

58   Contamine (1984):139; Partington (1960):97-98; and Clephan (1911):55-56.

59   Contamine (1984):139; Clephan (1911):56-57; Partington (1960):100 and
      Carman (1955):18-19.

60   James (1913):140. See also Nicolle (1988):#976; Contamine (1984):139;
      Needham (1986):fig. 82; Clephan (1911):57; Partington (1960):98-100; and
      Carman (1955):17-18.

61   James (1913):181. See also Needham (1986):fig. 83.

62   On the disputed reports of cannons at Crécy see Burne (1955):192-202.

63   McNeill (1982):80.

64   Vale (1975):59.

65   Froissart (1888):248-50.

66   As quoted in Cipolla (1965):22.

67   Vaughan (1966):150-51.

68   Burne (1956):42-46.

69   Garnier (1895):98-99.

70   Commynes (1969):149.

71   Vaughan (1970):397.

72   Contamine (1984):200-01.

73   Vale (1981):138.

74   *Livre des trahisons* (1873):96.

75   Commynes (1969):236.

76   Vaughan (1970):34.

77   As quoted in DeVries (1987):339. See also Contamine (1984):199.

78   Contamine (1984):199.

79   Vale (1975):64 (translation author's).

80   Burne (1956):235, 319, 333-41; Goodman (1981):28, 30, 47, 93, 121;
     Vaughan (1966):60; Vaughan (1970):26, 328-30, 385; Vaughan (1973):20-
     22, 223, 376-77, 387-88, 423-24; and *Livre des trahisons* (1873):169-70.

81   "Lettre" (1846-47):246 (translation author's).

82   Contamine (1984):199.

83   Vaughan (1970):387-89.

84   As quoted in Contamine (1984):199.

85   Brusten (1953):108.

86   Gille (1966):61 and Fino (1974):24.

87   Brusten (1953):108.

88   Vaughan (1970):361.

89   As quoted in Vaughan (1973):322-23.

90   Deuchler (1963):302-03.

91   DeVries (1990):818-21.

92   DeVries (1990):821-22.

93   DeVries (1990):821.

94   Unger (1980):234 and DeVries (1990):828.

95   An understanding of what the types of gunpowder weapons were, their ac-
     cessories and how they were manufactured can be gained in Gaier
     (1973);Contamine (1984):137-50, 196-207; Fino (1974); Clephan (1911);
     Vale (1981):129-46; Partington (1960):91-143; and by studying the original
     documents in Garnier (1898).

96   Religieux de Saint-Denis (1839-52):IV:652 (translation author's).

97   Vale (1981):145.

98   Commynes (1969):308 and Deuchler (1963):342

99   Cipolla (1965):24-25.

100 Gaier (1973):195-99.

101 B. Hall (1983):70.

102 Nicolle (1988):#1342-45.

103 B. Hall (1983):70.

104 Contamine (1984):144; Fino (1974):22; and Brusten (1953):101.

105 See the chart displaying the percentages of saltpeter, sulphur and charcoal
     for several late medieval gunpowder recipes found in Contamine
     (1984):196.

106 Contamine (1984):197-98.

107 Fino (1974):21.

108 Fino (1974):24-25; McNeill (1982):83; and Clephan (1911):65-67.

109 For a comparison of the costs between iron and stone cannonballs see Contamine (1984):198.

110 See Gaier (1973):285 for a discussion of the duties of an artillery mason. Garnier (1895):135 mentions masons in the artillery train at the siege of Villy in 1443.

111 Fino (1974):24.

112 Garnier (1895):126.

113 Fino (1974):26; Vaughan (1962):70; and Brusten (1953):113.

114 [Inventaire] (1855):333.

115 See, for example, Kyeser (1967):f.110v.

116 Vaughan (1973):300-01.

117 Brusten (1953):109.

118 Brusten (1953):109 and Gaier (1973):200.

119 Vaughan (1970):79.

120 Vaughan (11973):200-01.

121 Garnier (1895):129.

122 Brusten (1953):110.

123 Commynes (1969):I:133.

124 DeVries (1991):131-46. See also Contamine (1984):206 and Vale (1981):136-37.

125 Hale (1966):123-24.

126 Contamine (1984):138 and Hale (1966):18-19.

127 Hale (1966):125-26.

128 Hale (1966):117.

129 Vale (1981):145.

130 Hale (1966):126; Lombares (1984):29-30; and Cipolla (1965):23.

131 See note 62 above.

132 Vaughan (1962):124, 204.

133 Vaughan (1966):151, 168 and Brusten (1953):108.

134 Thielmans (1966):71.

135 Vaughan (1973):16.

136 Vale (1974):127, 141.

137 Dubled (1976) and Contamine (1972):230, 238-39, 311-17, 534.

138 Hale (1966):131-33 and Contamine (1984):206-07.

139 See Gille (1966).

140 DeVries (1991).

Part III:

Fortifications

Introduction

Medieval military technology did not only serve to protect (or to harm) the individual, but also served to protect the masses. The desire to protect one's lands, family, and possessions, the idea of defense, may be an innate trait carried through evolution, for it appears in animals as well as humans. Where the difference between the species lies is not in the idea of defense itself but in what is done with this defense. For animals, defense may be accomplished through aggression, through flight or, in some instances, through the protective strength of specialized members or castes whose function in the animal community is to guard it.[1]

While humans may try to protect themselves by these means, they also use other methods: alliances or confederations with their enemies and the construction of fortifications behind which they and much of their land and possessions may be defended. Historically, it is this latter non-animalistic method of defense which has been preferred. While diplomacy has been frequently tried, it has not been as successful in defense as have fortifications. Nor has it left any archaeological remains. Indeed, it is the large number of fortification remains which has convinced some anthropologists that Neolithic humans were deeply involved in warfare, perhaps more than any other activity, and that warfare, or at least the defense against warfare, may have been the reason for the foundation of Neolithic villages. Certainly this is evident in the existence of a very large number of fortified sites built around the eastern Mediterranean between 8000 and 4000 BC.[2]

The singular purpose for these early fortifications was defense. Humans needed to protect themselves by keeping attackers out. This meant choosing a site that was in the first place geographically and physically difficult to reach and then improving those hindrances with the addition of artificial barriers. Often these were impressively large and wide. For example, the fortifications of Jericho, built between 8350 and 7350 BC, consisted of an earth and stone wall 3 meters thick, 4 or more meters high, and 700 meters long, surrounding an area of 10 acres. There was also a large solid tower inside the wall which was 10 meters in diameter and 8.5 meters high with a stairway through the center and access through a door at the bottom. There may also have been other towers. This fortification protected a population estimated at 2000 with 500 to 600 fighters capable of defending the walls with archery. That these walls provided substantial security for Jericho's inhabitants is evident from the fact that the town itself did not fall until 1250 BC, more than 6000 years after the walls were constructed.[3]

While it is difficult to compare medieval fortifications to those of Jericho, the motive for building similar structures was the same in both periods. During much of the Middle Ages there were additional reasons to construct fortifications, for it was implicit in the feudal contract that the noble would protect the peasants living on and farming his lands. (This may have been the only benefit of feudalism for the peasants.) When the noble was unable to provide this protection, the feudal system broke down.

The following few chapters will discuss the construction of medieval fortifications. They will determine where they were built, why they were built, how they were built and ultimately, if history warrants, how they were taken. For ease of study a chronological approach will be followed, with chapters devoted to early medieval fortifications, motte-and-bailey castles, stone castles, and, finally, urban fortifications and fortified residences.

Before going further, however, it should be explained that one generalization of fortification study, "castellogie" as it is now called, is not pertinent when discussing the Middle Ages. Historically during times of peace, fortifications have fallen into disuse and ruin, as they were deemed unnecessary. However, in many cases this "peace dividend" backfired on the civilizations who promoted it, as the weakened defenses allowed later attacking armies easy access to the land and people behind them. This may have been the determining factor in the fall of both the Old and Middle Kingdoms of Ancient Egypt, Sparta-controlled Ancient Greece, and perhaps even Troy, if one wishes to discount Virgil's romantic story of the Trojan Horse.[4] Except for a brief period during and shortly after the reign of Charlemagne, there was simply not enough peace during the Middle Ages to allow civilization to neglect its fortifications. Consequently, there are still a large number of these fortifications which are in marvelous condition, although now serving more as tourist spots than as protective deterrents against attacking forces.

Early Medieval Fortifications

The Roman Empire was a society of builders. Although some scholars may insist that none of this construction was inventive or even unique, that the Romans merely utilized the more original and creative work of others, what they utilized and how they utilized it produced remarkable results.[5] Roman temples, fora, theaters, baths, ceremonial arches and columns, roads, aqueducts, bridges, tombs, palaces, villas, and gaming arenas have all impressed numerous historians with their size, beauty, and durability. But not to be neglected are the Roman imperial fortifications. Rome's peace and stability relied upon its defenses, a fact well understood by its leaders, and perhaps no other civilization has ever devoted so much effort or money to the construction and upkeep of its defenses. By the second century AD the very extensive Roman empire was nearly surrounded by fortifications. Fortresses were built along the Danube, Rhine, and Euphrates Rivers, and walls were built in Scotland, Numidia, and Germany. These were supplemented with watchtowers, outpost forts, and signal towers. Within these borders were walled towns and fortified garrisons. All of these fit into the grand military strategy of the Roman Empire, one that by the second century was less interested in outside conquest than in preserving internal peace and prosperity.[6]

By the reign of Emperor Hadrian (117-28 AD) the boundaries of the Roman Empire had been established. Rivers and seas provided some natural barriers while land borders became defended perimeters, fortified with walls and trenches. The stone fortifications comprising Hadrian's Wall split the Roman-controlled province of Britannia from the Pict-controlled Scotland. In Germany, between the natural boundaries of the Rhine and Danube Rivers, lay a series of trenches and wooden palisades which separated the Empire from a number of barbarian tribes, generically called the Germans by contemporary Roman historians. Another fortress, this a stone wall, was built between the Danube and the Black Sea, also to keep out barbarian invaders. In North Africa, a trench-and-earthen wall system known as the *fossatum Africae* ran over a distance of more than 750 kilometers separating the province of Numidia from marauding Bedouin tribes living in the Sahara desert. Finally, a double ditch, 24 kilometers long, separated Roman-held northern Mesopotamia from the Sassanid Persian south between the Khaber River and the Jebel Sinjar mountains. These fortifications, together with their nearby natural barriers which were also lined with fortresses, formed the Roman *limes*, or defended borders, the network which protected the peace and stability of second-century imperial life.

The most complex and elaborate of these border fortifications and also the one which most easily shows how earnest the Romans were about construction was Hadrian's Wall. Built between 122 and 125 AD, Hadrian's Wall crossed Britain for 117 kilometers between Bowness in the west and Newcastle in the east. It was not the first set of fortifications built along this route, but roughly followed the system of wooden stockades and trenches built in 81 AD by Agricola, the famous governor of Britain. While Agricola's fortresses were meant to be only temporary barriers against the Picts, Hadrian's construction was meant to be a permanent frontier, consisting not only of the wall itself but also of a number of watchtowers, fortresses, signal towers, and outpost forts.

For most of the wall's length it was 2.3 meters thick, but for a 37-kilometer portion, crossing between North Tyne and Newcastle, it measured nearly 3 meters in thickness. It was constructed of stone with a rubble and mortar core. It is estimated that Hadrian's Wall stood 5 to 6 meters high, although this varied with the terrain. It had a rampart walk at a height of 4 to 4.5 meters. In front of the wall, for most of its length, was a V-shaped ditch, 8-9 meters wide and at least 3 meters deep.

At intervals of 494 meters along the wall, raised turrets, made to hold only a few men, were constructed to serve as watchtowers.

At every Roman mile (1480 meters) along the wall, a small fortress, known as a milecastle, was built, 80 in total. Erected in stone and earth, these rectangular fortresses measured 21.3 by 18.3 meters. Inside were two barracks made to hold approximately 50 soldiers. A larger fortress, known as a Homestead, was built every 5 Roman miles along the wall. The 16 Homesteads were enclosed on three sides by a stone wall, 1.5 meters thick, supported by an earthen rampart 4.5 meters thick; the fourth side was the wall itself. Square towers were placed on each of its angles and along its walls. The Homestead was built in the traditional garrison manner enclosing several barracks, meant to hold perhaps 600 men, and a number of official military buildings. Only four gates, each guarded by two towers, allowed access into these fortresses. Finally, within 240 kilometers of Hadrian's Wall were two fortified legionary garrisons, at York and Chester. These could quickly come to the aid of the wall garrisons, if needed, as a series of signal towers linked them.[7]

All of this provided a formidable defense against opposing forces in Britain. Other Roman border defenses were not so sophisticated; the German wall was simply a wooden palisade 3.7 to 4 meters high, while the *Fossatum Africae* was nothing more than a ditch, 4 to 6 meters wide and 2.3 to 3.4 meters deep, in front of an earthen wall, 2 to 2.5 meters high.[8] Still, these were not meant to provide an impenetrable border for the Empire, but, combined with the natural protection provided by rivers, mountains and deserts, all of which were also lined by fortresses, they did impede any invasion of the imperial lands until a contingent of soldiers could arrive to put an end to the assault. The Empire remained protected from outside invaders for more than a century.

Even if invaders were able to break through these border defenses, they still had another fortification to breach before reaching the major cities of the Empire: the walls which surrounded most large urban areas. After a description of the elaborate fortification system at Hadrian's Wall, it may seem unusual to contend that it was not the border fortifications which the Romans trusted for their ultimate protection. It was instead the walls of their towns which most Roman citizens relied on for their protection against outside invasions.

Town walls were always important to the Roman people. The city of Rome itself was first enclosed by walls, a defensive structure of earth and later stone, as early as the fifth and fourth centuries BC, and this system was added to and rebuilt several times over the next 700 years. This early Roman wall was massive, measuring 3.6 meters wide at the base fronted by a ditch 29.6 meters wide and 9 meters deep. It was also effective, holding off Hannibal for more than 14 years during the Second Punic War.[9]

But Rome was not the only fortified city within the Empire. By the early part of the third century AD no fewer than 54 towns in western Europe were fortified by walls, 17 alone in Britain. Most of these walls enclosed large areas, some as big as 200 hectares. Many of the walls were rectangular, reflecting the traditional shape of the legionary camp from which many towns had sprung. Other walls took on the shape of the towns at the time of construction. While their height is often difficult to estimate, these walls were probably not more than 10 meters high. They were primarily built in stone and measured between 1.5 and 2.5 meters wide; all, except those at Cologne, were also supported by an earthen rampart upon which a single soldier could stand.

Towers were constructed along the walls at wide intervals. The towers could be round, semicircular, polygonal, trapezoidal, or rectangular, and some measured as much as 9 meters in diameter. Ditches surrounded the walls. At Cologne, for example, the ditch measured 8 to 12 meters wide and 5 meters deep and stood nearly 4 meters from the walls.[10]

All these walls were built with great technological sophistication. They were freestanding, built throughout with very precise small blockwork, mixed occasionally with patches of *opus reticulatum* and mosaic work. The towers contained windows facing the exterior. Those of the lower register were narrow slits while those of the upper levels were the larger keyhole type. The gateways, usually flanked by towers, were built to emphasize their monumental aspects. They allowed passage for at least one vehicle, with flanking passageways allowing pedestrian traffic as well. In many instances these monumental gateways, some of which have survived, were also decorated with ornamented cornices, mouldings, architraves, and pilasters.[11]

The peace of the second century was to be short-lived, however, as the third century brought invasions from outside and civil war from inside the Empire. Some of the problems of the third century in fact may be attributed to a neglect of the fortifications built earlier. For example, there was a lull in new fortification construction, especially in the construction of new town walls, after the death of Hadrian because of the sense of security which attended the peace.[12] Moreover, when new fortifications were built, like the Antonine Wall, constructed north of Hadrian's Wall in 139-43 AD, they were built in a far less elaborate manner, and did not have the durability of their older counterparts. The Antonine Wall was an earth-and-timber structure and was much narrower and shorter than Hadrian's Wall, with fewer attached fortresses. It was abandoned less than 20 years after its construction because of its ineffectiveness against the Picts.[13]

However, more important perhaps for the dwindling peace of the third century was the large numbers of civil wars which took place within the Empire. Between the reign of the "five good emperors" (one of whom was Hadrian) which ended in 180, and the reign of Constantine, which began in 312, there were 36 different Roman Emperors, many of whom reigned for less than a year. Frequently, one army and its candidate for emperor opposed another; this generally meant that the two armies left their posts guarding the imperial borders and fought each other on a battlefield in Italy.

Invading forces pushed more strongly against the borders of the Empire; the political upheaval of the Roman armies allowed for invasions to come through holes in the *limes*. In 249, for example, the Goths broke through the Danube River fortifications and invaded the Balkans. This was followed in 256 by the Franks who broke through the Lower Rhine River fortifications into Gaul. At the same time, the Saxons ventured across the English Channel and invaded Britain. Sometimes the Romans defeated these invasions, but as the number of incursions increased, the number of Roman victories decreased. By 262, the Goths had completely overrun Greece and had reached Athens, although they were eventually driven back before they could sack the city. Six years later, another German tribe, the Heruli, followed the Goths and in fact did sack Athens.

Not only in Europe, but everywhere in the Empire, boundary fortifications failed. In 256, the Borani, a tribe living in southern Russia, raided the Black Sea Coast; in the same year the Sassanid Persians, from Mesopotamia, overran Syria and even captured and imprisoned the inept Emperor Valerian who died in captivity.

Finally, in 269, Rome regained its military strength. This was largely the work of four emperor-generals: Claudius Gothicus (268-70), Aurelian (270-75), Probus (276-82) and Diocletian (284-305). Claudius Gothicus, as the name implies, in 269 pushed the Goths out of the Empire and stopped the holes in the Danube *limes*. Aurelian both conquered and destroyed Palmyra, the Sassanid Persian capital, pushing the Sassanids behind the borders of Syria, and recovered Gaul from the Franks, before he was murdered in 275. Probus once again secured the Rhine and Danube Rivers as fortified borders. And Diocletian rebuilt and reorganized the army and began a program of repairing and strengthening old fortifications as well as building new ones.

The problem with the border fortifications was not that they were too few or too weak. They had never been built to withstand invasions, merely to impede the progress of invading armies until the legions garrisoned behind them could respond. Thus it was understood by Diocletian and others that the reason for the failure of the border fortifications in the third century was that the support armies were too involved in selecting and defeating emperors instead of guarding the borders of the Empire. Diocletian planned first to rebuild the army, and then to re-establish the old, effective border fortifications, especially along the Rhine and Danube Rivers and in Syria.

Diocletian accomplished both of these goals. He increased the size of the army, which had been depleted by plagues as well as by warfare in the third century, and he also reorganized it in order to increase its mobility. During the invasions of the third century, one part of the Empire was often left without defensive garrisons when another part was attacked. This produced problems, especially in the middle of the century when several borders of the Empire were invaded at the same time. As some border troops went in support of others, they left their own defenses nearly empty, and this resulted in several successful invasions. In order to resolve this problem, Diocletian reorganized the army to provide more support troops more quickly to the borders which were in danger of invasion. He divided his troops into two distinct branches, the Garrison armies and the Field army. Both consisted of cavalry and infantry, but in the Field army the cavalry took precedence. It was the responsibility of the Garrison legions to guard the borders, while the Field army would come to the aid of the Garrison troops when needed. The fact that the Field army was primarily on horseback meant that it could travel more quickly to the border and also meant that no new border fortifications were needed.[14]

However, the problems of the third-century invasions pointed out three areas inside the imperial borders that needed the construction of new fortifications. First, there was a need to fortify important highways leading from the borders to the interiors. Once the invading armies penetrated the borders of the Empire, they easily cut off the internal lines of communication and supplies. Therefore, in the late third and early fourth centuries, both conventional-sized fortresses and small road forts were constructed along the highways in the Empire. Their primary responsibility was to hinder the very deep penetrations of the Empire like those which had occurred in the third century, keeping valuable supply and communication lines open. But they also served another purpose: they provided refuges for the inhabitants of these mostly rural regions against bands of barbarians, whose intent was less to invade the Empire than to pillage its isolated villages and farms.[15]

A second area that needed more fortifications was the coast of Britain. As detailed above, Hadrian's Wall had given Britain a very elaborate border fortification against the Picts in Scotland. But the third-century invaders had been the Saxons from across the Channel who landed on the coast between the Isle of Wight and Norfolk. Therefore, it was necessary to build fortifications along the "Saxon Shore," as it came to be known. A number of fortresses were built along this shore. They were quite large, covering an area which varied in size between 1.5 and 4 hectares, with an average size of 3 hectares. They also varied in plan from earlier fortresses. Although a number were of the traditional rectangular shape, others, such as those at Pevensey and Sussex, differed from this tradition; Sussex, for example, was oval. The walls were also much thicker than earlier fortresses, measuring 4.3 meters, and they were not always backed by an earthen rampart. They were also built much higher, for those walls that still exist, for example at Pevensey, Richborough, and Lympne, all exceed 7 meters in height. Finally, the walls were also frequently, although not always, supported by large D- or U-shaped bastions which were designed to support Roman artillery. There were two large, main gates on opposite sides of each fortress, with two smaller gates on the remaining two sides. Eleven of these structures still exist, several in excellent condition, although two more may also have been built.[16]

The final and perhaps most pressing need for new fortifications was in the towns. While those towns fortified by walls in the first and second centuries had largely escaped damage from the invaders of the third century, several other large urban areas, not so fortified, fell victim to pillaging and looting. Therefore, beginning in the reign of Diocletian, a concerted effort was made to rectify this situation. Moreover, while there was some reconstruction of existing town walls, mostly in an effort to make them more capable of sustained resistance, the primary effort in this regard was for the construction of new town walls. The city of Rome, seen to be open to attack by Emperor Aurelian constructed a new fortified wall with a circumference of 18 kilometers, a thickness of 4 meters and a height of 6 meters. Included also were 381 gates and towers equipped with artillery.[17]

The number of these late Roman walled towns is impressive. While only 54 can be identified in Europe from the second century and earlier, most of those built along the borders, more than that number were built in the province of Gaul alone between 286 and 306. In total, several hundred European towns constructed walls during this period. The walls were built wherever there was a town and not just along the borders of the Rhine and Danube Rivers.

These walls also were not built with the same technological sophistication as were their earlier counterparts. The normal type was constructed of rubble and concrete, 3 to 4.3 meters thick, set on a foundation of re-used stone blocks, fitted together often without mortar, and with a facing of small ashlar cubes banded horizontally with tiles. Their towers, like those on the Saxon Shore forts, also became bastions, for use with artillery. Most were semi-circular in plan, 6 to 9 meters in diameter, except for those at the angles of the walls which were round or square in shape.

These changes in the method of fortification building in the late third and early fourth centuries indicate an urgency in the construction of town walls. This is certainly evident in the re-use of earlier masonry. While this could simply indicate the large amount of destruction caused by the invasions, more likely it signifies that the inhabitants of these towns felt that they did not have the time to wait for finely cut masonry.

The use of tiles on these walls also demonstrates the urgency of their construction. They were built in stages, and a course of tiles was laid when each stage was finished in order to level out the irregularities in the facing blocks, to fasten the two stages together, and to serve as support for the scaffolding of future stages. The absence of ramparts and deep ditches also indicates how quickly they were built. While ditches were usually present, they were narrow and shallow rather than the deep V-shaped trenches of earlier town walls.

Finally, the most obvious evidence for urgency in fortification building is in the construction of gateways. While second century gateways were massive and often ornately decorated, built mostly to impress the person travelling through them, the late Roman gateways had none of these features. They had become only a part of the defensive function of the wall. They were not decorated, and many had shrunk in size, becoming narrow, and therefore easily guarded, access points for pedestrians entering the town. Larger gates, usually only one or two per town, through which vehicular traffic travelled, were heavily guarded on both sides by rectangular or semi-circular guard towers or bastions which extended beyond the walls and could be outfitted with artillery.[18]

It is important to examine the Roman imperial fortifications for two reasons. First, these were the fortifications which failed to keep the barbarian invaders from overrunning the Empire during the fourth and fifth centuries. Second, these fortifications continued to remain the primary defensive strongholds of Europe during the early Middle Ages.

Diocletian's reorganization of the Roman army and construction of new fortifications provided some security for the Empire against outside invaders. The possibility of invasion, however, remained an ever present threat, especially after yet another civil war, this one to decide Diocletian's successor, further depleted the numbers of soldiers along the Empire's borders. With this in mind, Constantine's decision to move the imperial capital from Italy to Constantinople in 330 certainly can be interpreted as a retreat from the sparsely populated and poor western part of the Empire to the more populous and wealthier east. If he, or his successors, could only defend one portion of the Empire from invasion, it was undoubtedly more important to protect the eastern portion.

The awareness of imminent invasion is also reflected in several written sources of the fourth century. In a threatening letter written in June 365 by Emperor Valentinian I to the military commander of the *limes* of *Dacia Ripensis*, the emperor urges his military leader to "not only restore the fortifications which are crumbling, but also [to] build each year further towers in suitable locations."[19] The anonymous author of the *De rebus bellicis* urged that there be "a continuous line of forts constructed at intervals of one mile with firm walls and very powerful towers...so that the peaceful provinces may be surrounded by a belt of defenses, and so remain unimpaired and at peace."[20]

On the other hand, despite this awareness of problems with the border fortifications in the face of possible barbarian invasions, there was very little new fortification construction after Diocletian's reign. For example, the *Notitia dignitatum et administrationum omnium tam civilium quam militarium in partibus Orientis et Occidentis*, an early fifth-century administrative list of fortresses and garrisons in the Empire, records few fortifications which had been built after Diocletian.[21] In fact, the city of Constantinople did not receive its walls until 413, long after the barbarian invasions had already begun.[22]

If a date must be assigned to the beginning of the barbarian invasions, most scholars agree that it should be 376, for it is on this date that the Visigoths, with the Huns encroaching on all sides of their territory, asked Emperor Valens to allow them to cross the Danube River and to cultivate the wastelands of Thrace as *foederati*, or confederates of the Empire. Valens agreed to their request as he felt that not to do so would mean certain invasion; besides the Visigoths would then provide him with a defensive deterrent in the unpopulated Thracian regions. What Valens did not realize, however, was how many Visigoths would actually want to cross the borders into the Empire. When an estimated 200,000 Visigothic refugees passed over the Danube River, Valens found that he could not feed them, and the Visigoths were forced to challenge the Roman army, defeating it at the battle of Hadrianople in 378. The proverbial "floodgate" had opened, and the imperial borders began to crumble as on all sides barbarian tribes began to cross into the Empire.

The fall of the western portion of the Roman Empire took very little time. By 406 the Alans, Suevi, and Vandals had crossed the Rhine River and entered Gaul. Three years later they crossed the Pyrenees into Spain. By 410 the Visigoths had moved into Italy and sacked Rome, moving two years later into Gaul and finally, two years after that, into Spain. By 416 they had crushed the Alans and Siling Vandals and set up the Visigothic Kingdom of Toulouse. By 428 the Asding Vandals, split from their Siling cousins, had crossed over the Mediterranean and invaded North Africa.

In the mid-fifth century another wave of barbarian invaders entered the Empire, again because of the Hunnic threat. By 436 the Burgundians had invaded the region around Geneva. By 449 the Angles, Jutes, and Saxons had raided and settled in Britain. And by 451 the Franks, Ostrogoths, and Alemanni had entered Gaul, the Ostrogoths eventually moving into Italy. The western part of the Roman Empire remained so only in name, and even that was lost in 476 when the last western Roman Emperor, Romulus Augustulus, was removed by Odovacar the Ostrogoth.[23]

Because of the large number of successful barbarian invasions into the Roman Empire, it might be assumed that the fortifications were to blame for not protecting the Empire and its inhabitants. Certainly this seems to be a valid criticism in looking at the border defenses in Britain and along the Rhine and Danube Rivers. For although the Visigoths were freely allowed to cross the Danube and enter the Empire in 376, later invasions crossed through territory protected by the border fortifications without such permission. The Burgundians and Ostrogoths crossed the Danube without hindrance from the fortifications along that river; the Alans, Suevi, Vandals, Alemanni, and Franks did the same across the Rhine; and the Angles, Saxons, and Jutes were similarly unhindered by the Saxon Shore fortresses in their conquest of Britain.

However, while the fortifications themselves were overrun, the fault for this does not necessarily lie with the late Roman fortification technology. Again, their planned purpose had never been to provide strict deterrence to invasion. The fact remains that there were simply not enough Roman soldiers to provide this reinforcement. This is attested to as early as the fourth century by the anonymous author of *De rebus bellicis* and repeated a century later by the historian Zosimus who placed the blame on Constantine who "withdrew from the frontier the great majority of soldiers to install them in towns which had no need for protection."[24] Without those reinforcing troops, the border fortifications could do (and did) little against the large number of barbarians overrunning them.

Furthermore, the barbarians were extremely incompetent in conquering the walled towns of the Empire. Despite possessing what should have been adequate siege technology, the barbarians suffered some spectacular failures in attempting to take the towns of the Empire. These failures began as early as the late fourth century when the Visigoths, led by Alaric, were unable to capitalize on their victory at Hadrianople by advancing on the major towns of the Empire. Although they were able to conquer the largely unfortified towns of Greece—Piraeus, Corinth, Argos, and Sparta—they were unable to take the walled town of Thebes. Even the small, but ably fortified town of Tegea defended itself against the Visigoths.[25] Similar problems with walled towns accompanied Alaric's attack on Italy in 401-10. Although he was able to conquer and sack Rome, he was unable to capture the towns of Hasta (Asti), Pollentia (Pollenzo), and Ravenna.[26] In 441, Palermo successfully defended itself against a siege by the Vandals.[27] In 451, Attila the Hun was unable to take Orleans.[28] In 501, Avignon withstood the attacks and siege of the Merovingian king, Clovis, and six years later, Arles was able to do the same, also against Clovis.[29]

Clovis' sons and grandsons faced similar problems in taking towns fortified by walls: in 532, Theuderic was unable to take the town of Vitry; in 542, Saragossa withstood the attacks of Chlotar and Childebert; in 581, Chilperic failed to take Bourges, and that same year Guntram Boso was unable to take Avignon; finally, in 585, Childebert was unable to take Bellinzona, Pavia, or any other fortified Italian town.[30] In the sixth century, the Ostrogothic king, Witigis, also had difficulty capturing fortified towns, failing first in 536 to take Rome and then in 537-38 to take Arminium.[31] Even as late as the eighth century, would-be conquerors of towns fortified during the late Roman Empire still faced problems in capturing them as witnessed in the inability of the Muslim leader al-Samh to take Toulouse in 721 and in the similar inability of Charles Martel to take Narbonne in 737.[32]

The frustration of these failed conquests can be seen no better than at Arles in 568. In that year the Merovingian king, Chlotar, died leaving the town of Arles divided between his two sons, Sigibert and Guntram, who immediately began to fight over it. Ultimately, Sigibert was able to enter Arles unopposed, but when Guntram heard of his brother's occupation of the town, he sent his own forces to besiege it. Sigibert became convinced that he could not hold the town against a siege, so he advanced out of the gates against Guntram's army. However, he was forced to retreat back to Arles where he discovered that the gates of the town were locked and the inhabitants turned against him. In final frustration, Sigibert and his remaining troops were forced to abandon their equipment and swim across the Rhone River to safety.[33]

Still, the inability of barbarian invaders to take strongly fortified towns only affected those towns for a short time. In the end, most did fall, some by surprise attacks, some by treason, and some by prolonged siege leading to starvation. Others, like Rome in 537-38, opened their gates in the hope of being granted mercy.[34] Again the lack of defending troops must be cited, for without being able to count on a relief army to come to their aid, few towns desired to suffer the starvation and death that accompanied a prolonged siege.

The fifth-century siege of Rome by Alaric and the Visigoths is an example of why strong fortifications were not a factor in a prolonged siege. Despite having perhaps the best fortifications of any city in the late Roman Empire, Rome finally fell in 410 after several attacks and a siege of nearly two years. Rome was certainly the largest prize in the western Empire, and Alaric had had designs on it since he first attacked Italy in 401. But after two military defeats at the hands of the great Roman general, Stilicho, Alaric had not even reached the outskirts of the city. The situation changed drastically in 408 when the Roman military and political leadership turned against Stilicho and he was killed. The path to Rome was now clear for Alaric who quickly moved to the walls of the city. Unable to take Rome by force because of its superior fortifications, he besieged it, blockading all land and river routes into the city. For two years the Roman inhabitants held out against their Visigothic foes, until finally hunger and plague filled the city with corpses. With their walls still intact, but without hope of a relieving army to aid them, the Romans surrendered on August 24, 410. Even this is disputed as several contemporary sources claim that the city would have held out even longer against Alaric, except that a gate was opened by traitors hoping to buy leniency from the Visigoths.[35]

Perhaps because of their problems in taking the walled towns of the Empire, the barbarians grew to respect them as defensive fortifications. Most barbarian leaders refused to destroy the walls of a captured town unless they feared that the walls might harbor later resistance against them.[36] At the same time, while they may have respected the walled towns as fortifications, it is also clear that they did not completely understand their function. In the presence of an army which could wage effective siege warfare, such as Belisarius' Byzantine force which reconquered Italy in 535-40, the walls provided little security for their occupants.[37]

After the Empire: The Carolingians and Vikings

The late Roman town walls outlived the Empire and were in fact the chief fortification of the early Middle Ages. The Goths, Lombards, Franks, and other barbarian occupiers of the western Empire did not add any town walls of their own.[38] However, they did keep the existing walls in good repair. Gregory of Tours, describing the mid-sixth-century walls of Dijon, depicts fortifications not much changed from their first construction three centuries earlier:

> It is a fortress girded round with mighty walls and set in the center of a pleasant plain.... The four entrances of the town are placed at the four quarters of the compass, and thirty-three towers adorn the circuit of the walls which are made of squared stones rising to a height of twenty feet, with smaller stones placed above to reach in all some thirty feet, the whole being fifteen feet thick.[39]

Even as late as 890 the towns fortified during the third century elicit comment. Chartres, for one, is described in the *Cartulaire de Saint Père* as being "famous for the thickness of its walls."[40]

What the barbarian conquerors of the western Empire added instead of new town walls was the rural fortification, the precursor of the archetypal medieval castle. Details about these early castles are at best limited. There is really no way of even determining exactly how many of them were built in the early Middle Ages. Because there was little stone construction involved, few archaeological remains survive. However, there are some written references to these castles which can give us some idea to how many there were, who inhabited them, what purpose they served, and even, to a certain extent, how they were constructed.[41]

There are several aspects of these fortifications which are the same in almost all cases. First, they were strictly a barbarian structure with no Roman precursors. In fact, they appeared so early in the barbarian invasions (at least as early as the late fifth century) and were so numerous, particularly in the regions of western Europe dominated by the Franks, that there is some possibility that their concept actually preceded the invasions themselves. Although there is no way of being certain about this, these early castles may have been a part of the Frankish civilization before their entrance into the Roman Empire. Certainly by the early sixth century there were so many of these fortifications that their numbers impressed several contemporary writers, among them Sidonius Apollinaris, Sulpicius Severus, and Gregory of Tours.

They also relied not on walls or towers for their protection, but on the inaccessibility of their location. Many were built on

high places, some on rocky promontories or isolated buttes. Sometimes, such as in the fortresses of Grèze, Chastel-Marlhac, and
Ronzières, this provided their only security. At other times this
defense was aided by a wall or rampart. Only rarely was this a
stone wall; more frequently it was an earthen rampart crowned
by stacked stones and wood. In two instances, at Piègu and Nicet,
the castles themselves were actually built on top of an earthen
rampart.[42]

To outsiders this natural defense seemed formidable. Sidonius
Apollinaris was so impressed with the castle at Avernie, built on
a jagged rock promontory and nearly surrounded by water, that
he was "fain to keep silence about it."[43] Gregory of Tours was
another contemporary fan of the rural fortification. Describing the
fortress of Chastel-Marlhac, he writes:

> The people of Chastel-Marlhac were besieged, but they retained
> their liberty, for they bribed the invaders not to take them cap-
> tive. It was only because of their own stupidity that they had
> to pay anything at all. The place was a natural fortress, for it
> was surrounded not by man-made walls, but by cliffs which
> rose sheer for a hundred feet or more.[44]

These castles also stood apart, and in some instances quite a
distance apart, from the urban areas already defended by town
walls, making them in effect the protectors of the rural regions
of western Europe. Several were constructed to protect agricultural
and economic centers, serving as refuges for farmers and other
agricultural workers during times of war. Others were sanctuaries
or ecclesiastical centers. However, many castles were built and
controlled by wealthy individuals, and in these cases served as
proto-feudal manors, both as residences for these "nobles" and
as defenses for the people who worked on their nearby agricultural
lands. It was, after all, Sidonius Apollinaris' wealthy friend, Pon-
tius Leontius, who controlled the castle at Avernie, at the confluence of the Garonne and Dordogne Rivers, an area of prime
agricultural land, and he undoubtedly used his fortification in a
way similar to those used by later medieval feudal lords.[45]

These fortifications continued to be built and used, together
with the Roman town walls, as a means of defense for the people
of Francia during the turbulent and unstable Merovingian era.

Some areas even embraced them as official and legal defensive structures. However during the eighth-century attempts of Pippin II to unite the realm under his Carolingian rule, these castles provided not an aid but a hindrance to stability. Pippin was forced to subdue each of these fortresses, and frequently, because of their superb natural defenses, this task was difficult to achieve. In particular, he was required to spend significant time and troops in subjugating the castles of Aquitaine. He was in fact so pressed by his attempts to conquer them, that he was forced to impose sanctions on anyone who participated in their defense, sanctions still in effect nearly 100 years later.[46] Pippin also may have built a few rural fortifications himself, although their numbers were probably quite small.[47]

Pippin died in 768 leaving the Carolingian realm to his son, Charlemagne. The father had made a kingdom; the son would make the kingdom an empire. In almost every one of his 42 years of rule, Charlemagne summoned his army for conquest outside of the kingdom's borders. By 814 this included the whole of modern France, Belgium, Holland, and Switzerland, most of Germany, and a large part of Italy and northern Spain. He defeated the Avars in the east, the Lombards in Italy, the Saxons in the north, the Muslims in northern Spain, and the Danes in southern Denmark.

Yet there is some dispute over whether this great conqueror built fortifications. Certainly he knew their worth, for on a number of occasions the people he defeated were lodged behind their defenses, and their subjugation sometimes took a very long time. Two towns in particular, the Lombard-controlled Pavia and the Muslim-controlled Barcelona, both defended by strong Roman fortifications, necessitated sieges of longer than a year before they fell to him. Charlemagne also had to capture Avar and Saxon fortresses.[48]

Still, it is uncertain whether Charlemagne himself prized fortifications. Scholars argue both sides of the debate. On the one hand, Bernard S. Bachrach and Charles Bowlus maintain that Charlemagne built many fortifications during his reign. Bachrach insists that Charlemagne "did appreciate the significance of fortifications and utilized them as a basic element in the military organization in several parts of his kingdom, including Saxony and

the Spanish March." He notes that in many instances after Charlemagne captured a fortress or a walled town, he repaired the
existing defenses and then garrisoned a number of troops inside
it. He also built several new fortifications, although most of these
were small rural fortresses or castles. In particular, Saxony and
Aquitaine were filled with fortifications built under Charlemagne's
direction.[49] Bowlus agrees with these conclusions noting in his
specific study of the eastern frontier of the Carolingian Empire
that "by the end of the ninth century the entire frontier region
was studded with fortifications," many of which were built during
Charlemagne's reign.[50]

On the other side of the debate, Gabriel Fournier and
Rosamond McKitterick conclude that Charlemagne did not build
many significant fortifications. Neither denies that he did construct
some in Saxony, Aquitaine, or on the Ostmark as claimed by
Bachrach and Bowlus. However, they do not agree that these were
significant in their number, size, or defensive capabilities. Fournier insists instead that at best these fortifications were but transi-
tory measures and only used for the submission of the lands in
question. On campaigns Charlemagne neither used the existing
fortifications in a systematic manner nor built new ones. In fact,
he also neglected town walls, although Fournier is uncertain
whether this was a conscious act or done simply because the
Roman walls were still in good repair. He claims further that
Charlemagne preferred to use other means to provide military
security: the isolation of hostile lands, hostage taking, the creation
of large dependencies, feudalistic administration, Christianization,
and the implantation of a solid religious foundation.[51] To all of
this McKitterick agrees. She writes:

> It seems that once an area with fortified sites had been subdued,
> the Carolingians retained only a limited interest in this form of
> military organization.... Town walls were not repaired or re-
> built; indeed, they were often destroyed for the sake of the
> masonry.[52]

There may be no correct answer to this dispute, and for
Charlemagne's rule it <u>was not especially important</u>. His lands were
never invaded, and he in fact never lost a battle, unless one wishes
to count the rather small affair at Roncesvalles, which is so blown

out of proportion in *The Song of Roland*. What makes it important is that within 100 years of Charlemagne's death his realm was invaded numerous times by both the Vikings and the Hungarians, and the ease with which these "new barbarian" invaders sacked numerous towns leaves the historian searching for reasons.

The first and perhaps most "barbarous" of these invaders were the Vikings. Their initial attack was in 787 when they landed and pillaged the southern coast of England. Six years later they returned to England and sacked the wealthy Lindesfarne Abbey. These successes led to further, larger raids. By 834 they had swept through both England and Ireland and had turned their wrath on the continent. By 840 they had raided the Low Countries' towns of Noirmoutiers, Rhé, Dorestad (four times), Utrecht, and Antwerp. In 843 they wintered for the first time in Gaul, capturing Nantes and ravaging the valleys of the Loire and Garonne Rivers; they even threatened the Muslim towns of Lisbon and Cadiz. In 845 they sailed up the Seine with an estimated 120 ships and destroyed Paris. In the following 30 years they raided up the Rhine, the Meuse, the Scheldt, the Somme, the Seine, the Marne, the Loire, the Charente, the Dordogne, the Lot, and the Garonne Rivers. One expedition even sailed through the Straits of Gibralter and raided Nekur in Morocco, the Mercian coast of Spain, the Balearic Islands, and Rousillon. These Vikings then wintered on the Rhone delta and the following year raided upstream as far as Valence, sacking Pisa and Luna (which they mistook for Rome) before returning to Brittany. In 879 the Vikings sacked Ghent. A year later they destroyed Courtrai and numerous towns in Saxony. In 881 they sacked Elsloo and Aachen where they raided Charlemagne's palace; in 882, Condé; in 883, Amiens; in 884, Louvain; and in 885-86, they besieged Paris, but were bought off by King Louis the Fat who paid them 700 pounds of silver and gave them permission to spend the summer sacking Burgundy, an area which he did not control. Choosing to avoid combat, only twice were the Vikings defeated in battle: in 878 at Edington by Alfred the Great and in 891 at the Dyle by Arnulf, King of the East Franks. After the second defeat, the Viking raids dissipated, although they continued to a lesser extent until 1066.[53]

The Hungarian raids lasted a shorter time and were perhaps less destructive. They were, however, still devastating to late Carolingian Europe. These raiders were first used as mercenaries by Arnulf, King of the East Franks, against the Moravians in 892. Enticed perhaps by this legitimate warfare, they returned to raid the west in 899, when they advanced south into Italy and attacked Pavia. The following year, they moved to Bavaria and in 901 to Carinthia. From 906-09 they raided Saxony, Carinthia, Bavaria, and Thuringia. The attacks then stopped until 917 when the Hungarians reappeared in the eastern Carolingian Empire and proceeded for the next seven years to raid Basle, Alsace, Burgundy, Saxony, Lombardy, and Provençe. After 924 their power waned although they continued to remain a menace until Otto the Great decisively defeated them at the battle of Lech in 955.[54]

While some of the details of these raids are disputed, such as the number of participants and the composition of their forces, a predominant characteristic was that the raiders successfully sacked many supposedly fortified towns and palaces. Both England and continental Europe appear to have been unprepared for the Viking and Hungarian onslaughts. The question that must be asked then is what happened to the fortifications that were supposed to protect their inhabitants from this very thing?

In England the answer is simple. There were no new fortifications; there is no record of any new defensive construction taking place after the fall of the Roman Empire. The only fortifications left, mostly town walls, were those which the Romans had built more than 600 years previously. These had been poorly maintained and provided little protection to their inhabitants. This is no better expressed than in an Old English poem entitled "The Ruin," written during the Viking invasions:

> splendid this rampart is, though fate destroyed it,
> The city buildings fell apart, the works
> Of giants crumble. Tumbled are the towers,
> Ruined the roofs, and broken the barred gate
>   ...Often this wall
> Stained red and grey with lichen has stood by
> Surviving storms while kingdoms rose and fell.
> And now the high curved wall itself has fallen.[55]

In the Carolingian Empire the question of fortification failure is more difficult to answer. However, if Charlemagne himself was not to blame, the fault may be his son's and grandsons'. For not only was there so little fortification construction in the ninth century that chroniclers of the period describe such building as "novel"—not even the emperor's palace at Aachen had been fortified[56]—but some fortresses were actually dismantled. For example, in 814, Louis the Pious, Charlemagne's son, gave permission to the Bishop of Langres to destroy the walls of the town so that he might use the masonry to construct a church. This was repeated a number of times: in 817-25 when Ebbo, the Archbishop of Rheims, was allowed to demolish his town gates and walls to build the cathedral; in 859 at Melun when Archbishop of Sens, Wenilo, was given permission to use the town walls to build a church there; and finally in Charles the Bald's *Edict of Pitres*, proclaimed on June 25, 864, in which he commanded that all fortresses which were not built with the permission of the king be dismantled. Thus, even though the Vikings were already raiding the countryside, some fortifications were being destroyed.[57] Other fortifications had been so neglected that they were easily overrun.[58]

The Viking and Hungarian raids did eventually force the building of new defensive structures. By 900 almost all of western Europe threatened by continual invasion had responded with some new fortifications. However, because of the speed required in the construction of these defenses, they were usually not elaborate, tending to be less technologically sophisticated than simply utilitarian. They were built in order to protect the more urban regions of a kingdom as these were often the chief targets of the raiders. Finally, they were also primarily projects funded and supported by kings rather than by feudal lords.

England and the Viking Invasions

England was the earliest land hit by the Viking invaders, and it also endured their attacks the longest. There were very few fortifications with which the Vikings had to contend in their late eighth- and early ninth-century invasions. Moreover, the disunity of the Anglo-Saxon kingdoms on the island, resulted in a very slow defensive response. The Vikings generally found that there was very little or no opposition to their continual onslaughts. Even

London was easily conquered, falling into their hands easily in 872. It was not until the late ninth century when Alfred the Great, the King of Wessex, began to unite the kingdoms of England under his leadership that the Vikings began to encounter opposition. In 878 Alfred defeated what became known as the "Great Danish Army" at the battle of Edington, and in 886 he freed London from Viking control; in response to these military feats, the rest of England recognized his rule.[59]

But the defeat of the Vikings at Edington and in London was not the limit of Alfred's military exploits. He recognized that the failure of England to withstand the invasions was caused not only by the disunity of offense against them, but also by the lack of defensive fortifications. Therefore, after uniting his neighboring kingdoms and also momentarily halting the invasions, Alfred set out to improve the fortifications of England. This meant more than simply repairing the old Roman walls, but the building of new ditch and earthen rampart fortresses known in Old English as *burhs*.

Alfred was not the first to construct a *burh*. They may instead have originated in Mercia during the reign of King Offa (758-96). As well as Offa's Dyke, a 192-kilometer long ditch dug between Wales and Mercia, he constructed a small number of these fortifications to house his own residences. Only two of these Mercian *burhs* have been excavated, but, they are very similar to those of Alfred and may have provided the archetype.[60]

Because of an early tenth-century list of Alfred's *burhs*, known as the Burghal Hidage, which delineated their administrative and economic role in the kingdom, much is known about the locations and responsibilities of these fortifications.[61] And this, coupled with the large number of archaeological excavations of the sites, has provided a unique opportunity to understand what these structures were and how they were used.[62]

Alfred built 30 of these fortifications. They were distributed widely throughout his kingdom and evenly placed so that no more than a single day's march separated one fortress from the next. They were mostly constructed along the kingdom's routes of communication—roads, navigable rivers, and trackways—and in several instances reused the sites of earlier Roman or Iron Age fortifications. They were also frequently constructed near the king's fortified residences and permitted him better military control over his kingdom.[63]

Although the *burhs* had some administrative and economic functions, ultimately their most important purpose was to give military protection. They were first and foremost to provide a refuge for the inhabitants of the kingdom against the Viking invaders, including, if needed, the necessary supplies to withstand a prolonged siege. Second, they were to provide an offensive threat to the Vikings by housing a large garrison of troops. These troops could be summoned to encounter any invading army or band and perhaps thwart attempts at raiding the kingdom.[64]

The *burhs* were quite large. Estimates garnered through a study of the Burghal Hidage indicate that the garrison in each fortress could number nearly 900;[65] refugees increased the number which needed to be housed. The Wareham *burh*, a rectangular fortress, measured roughly 700 by 610 meters and the Wallingford *burh*, also rectangular, measured 760 by 550 meters. Even the smallest *burhs* excavated, such as that at Crickdale, measured 412 meters square. The area enclosed was between 20 and 40 hectares.[66]

Their defenses were relatively simple. All *burhs* were surrounded by a large ditch, sometimes 34 meters wide and between 5 and 8 meters deep. They were also protected by a 3-meter high wedge-shaped earthen rampart with a timber facing or revetment at the front. Above this rampart was a stone wall at least 1.5 meters in height.[67]

Their construction was expensive, both initially and in their later maintenance. The expenses were paid for by the landowners of the kingdom, who naturally profited by the physical and economic protection they received against the invaders. There was, however, no lack of defenders to garrison these fortifications, as early charters place the defense of the *burhs* together with bridge-building as the highest obligation of Alfred's subjects.[68]

The *burhs* were relatively effective in halting many Viking raids of the period. Although some raiders were able to avoid them and attack the interior of the island, this was a dangerous plan, as it meant that a large number of armed troops were stationed between the raiders and their ships. Such an event occurred in both 893 and 914 when the Vikings initially bypassed the

Anglo-Saxon *burhs* only to be defeated later as they tried to return to their vessels. The Vikings also were unable to take the *burhs* by attack or starvation. On numerous occasions—at Pilton in 893, Chichester in 894, and Bedford and Wingamere in 917—their attacks on the *burhs* failed; in only one instance, in 892 at Lympne, were the Vikings able to capture a fortress, and this may have been because of its poor construction and small number of defenders.[69]

The building of *burhs* continued after Alfred's death in 899, especially during the reign of his son, Edward the Elder (899-924), who maintained the *burhs* built during the reign of his father and added several more himself. It was also during his reign that the Burghal Hidage was written. However, during the tenth century the number of newly-constructed *burhs* dwindled and the maintenance of older *burhs* declined. Garrisons of troops also abandoned these fortifications. In turn, the Vikings, who knew the value of fortifications and had always fortified their raiding camps, began to seize Alfred's *burhs* to use against the nearby population. These defensive fortifications had become offensive threats, and by using them the Vikings eventually gained control of all England.[70]

Continental Anti-Viking Fortifications

The fortifications on the continent constructed to check the Viking and Hungarian raids were neither as systematic nor as extensive as were Alfred's *burhs* in England. Nor have they been studied as thoroughly. For example, there is evidence of a fairly large program of fortification construction in the Carolingian Ostmark (lower Austria and Carinthia), built primarily as protection against the Hungarians. But so few archaeological excavations have been done and so little documentary evidence survives that very little can be determined about them. Those that have been excavated, at Freisach and Mosaburg, show that they were constructed of earth and timber and were situated in rather harsh terrain— Freisach in a marshy area near a river and Mosaburg in an impenetrable swamp—which provided a natural protection. Also because of their location, near communities of free peasants, they may have provided refuges to the nearby farmers, although their small size would have precluded a large refuge population.[71]

The situation in Italy was similar to that of the Ostmark with very little known about the fortifications constructed there between the ninth and eleventh centuries. Although the major urban areas still relied on their old Roman walls for protection against the raiders, walls which they struggled to repair and rebuild, some with the addition of new towers, a few new fortifications were also constructed. According to several early tenth-century charters, these fortresses were to have been elaborate structures, made of stone and incorporating elevated platforms, apertures for archery, defensive towers, and ditches. If these architectural formulae were used, then these fortifications indicate that castle building in late Carolingian Italy had far surpassed any other in Europe during this period. But archaeological excavations have yet to confirm this.[72]

In Carolingian France and Germany much more is known about the fortifications erected to halt the Viking and Hungarian incursions. The construction of fortifications in the wake of the ninth- and tenth-century raids can effectively be divided into four chronological phases. The first, dating between the start of the continental raids (c.830) until 862-64, represents a period of little organized opposition to the raids, either by the kings or by their feudal lords, despite a rather strong raiding schedule by the Vikings. It was also a period of little fortification construction. In fact, the erection of only one fortress, built in 830 by the abbot of the monastery of St. Philibert de Noirmoutiers, is recorded in the documents of this period.[73]

The second phase of anti-Viking fortification construction, dating between 862 and 879, represents a complete reversal of earlier policy. During this period there was an extensive, royally-supported, fortification construction program, which ultimately saw a number of different defensive structures built against the northern raiders.

During the third period, between 879 and 887, there was little new defensive construction, as the Carolingian kingdoms were filled with dynastic quarrels and civil war. Even the maintenance of older fortifications was neglected. As such, little effort was given to the protection of the land against outside invaders, and the Viking raids increased in intensity and destructiveness.[74]

Finally, the fourth phase of anti-Viking construction, which began in 887 and continued into the eleventh century, returned to a more intense construction program. However, this phase was not royally supported, but was carried on by the feudal lords whose overall power had increased during the struggles of 879-887.

It is then the second and fourth phases which should be explored in an effort to understand what was done to try and curtail the Viking and Hungarian raids into Germany and France. The increase in fortification construction between 862 and 879 was largely the work of Charles the Bald, King of the West Franks. Why he changed his policies in 862 is not known. He had been the king of his region since 840 when his father, Louis the Pious, died, and yet for 22 years he had shown no desire to try to curb the Viking incursions into his land. France, which was essentially Charles' kingdom, was especially hit hard by the invasions, and this may be why he was forced to change his defensive strategy against them. However, initially this strategy was not to build new fortresses or town walls, although these would later be built, but instead to construct fortified bridges.

This was in fact a very logical strategy. If the Vikings were travelling upstream to raid the towns of France, including Paris, why not try to stop them on the rivers before they reached those towns? But fortifying bridges had never been done before and its success as a strategy had yet to be proved. Nevertheless, Charles the Bald commanded in 862 that two fortified bridges be built, one at Pîtres on the Seine River and a second at Treix on the Marne.

The bridge at Pîtres, which has been the most completely excavated, was chosen because of its particularly favorable strategic location. It was situated at the confluence of the Seine and two of its tributaries, the Andelle and the Eure: this removed the possibility of portaging from the Seine to one of its tributaries and thereby avoiding the fortification. It took between 6 and 15 years to complete, and consisted of two stone bridgeheads, large enough to garrison troops, with a wooden span extending across the 400-meter width of the river. Surrounding the bridgeheads on each bank were earthen fortresses, which measured 600 meters in perimeter, and probably served as refuges for the nearby population. The size of the bridgeheads is not known, but they have been estimated to have covered an area measuring 25 by 5 meters and to have been at least 3.5 meters high and 1.3 meters thick.[75]

Later fortified bridges were planned on the Seine at Charenton, on the Oise near Pontoise, and on the Loire at Les Ponts de Cé, but they may not have been completed. Charles the Bald may also have constructed a fortified bridge in Paris, but this too is uncertain.[76]

The fortified bridges seem to have been remarkably successful in their defense of the Seine and Marne. No Viking fleets are recorded to have passed beyond the bridge at Treix after its construction, and between 879 and 885 no ships sailed up the Seine past the bridge at Pîtres. Moreover, although the Vikings did successfully row up the Seine to besiege Paris in 885, the four months it took for them to reach their destination, a distance of only 234 kilometers, indicates a continued strong defense waged against them by the troops garrisoned at Pîtres. Perhaps the greatest measure of success can be seen also in 885 when the Vikings chose to besiege the uncompleted bridge at Pontoise, contrary to their usual custom. Although the fortress did eventually capitulate, and afterwards may not have been completed, it did hinder the Viking advance towards Paris for several weeks, allowing the Parisians more time to strengthen their own defensive structures.[77]

Other fortifications were also constructed by Charles the Bald during this period, at Le Mans, Orleans, Tours, and St. Denis. However, they were smaller undertakings than the fortified bridges, and were probably only earthen fortresses providing refuge for the local populations. Again, whether the fortifications themselves were effective in halting Viking raids is not known, although these raids did in fact diminish during this period. They did provide security to many in the Parisian and Loire regions of France who had for so many years felt the brunt of attack.[78]

Perhaps the most important characteristic of the fortification construction during this period was that it was done at the behest and with the support of the king. As mentioned, Charles the Bald in 864 even went so far as to order the destruction of all fortresses built without his permission. It was then perhaps fitting that among his last commands concerning fortification construction, as expressed in the Capitulary of Quierzy-sur-Orge of 877, was the order to build a fortified palace for himself at Compiegne.[79]

During the civil wars which followed Louis the German's death in Germany in 876 and Charles the Bald's death in France a year later the feudal lords took over the building of fortifications. The confusion of civil war had given them power over a series of inept kings, but with this power came the responsibility to protect the people, especially against the Viking raids, which increased and remained a constant menace, as well as the later Hungarian raids.

There was certainly nothing systematic in the lords' efforts to fortify their own domains. Every lord was responsible for the defenses of his own lands; the stronger and more wealthy lords built the strongest and most numerous fortifications. Powerful lords, like the counts of Flanders and the lords of Luxembourg-Trèves, covered their lands with fortifications, while weaker lords left their lands almost unprotected.[80] Some of these fortifications were improved or newly constructed town walls and fortified monasteries,[81] but most were smaller, more rural and more localized fortresses, not unlike the rural fortifications of the Merovingian kingdom. Most of these were constructed of earth and timber and relied, also like their Merovingian archetypes, on the harshness of the terrain for protection. Because of their small size, the fortresses throughout Flanders averaged only 200 meters in diameter and appear to have been used less as refuges for the population and more as private noble residences and as garrisons for troops.[82]

This was a response to the tenor of the times. Civil wars continued as did the Viking and Hungarian raids, and most of these fortifications were used in several military situations. For example, between 930 and 948 the fortress at Mouzon, built on land owned by the archbishop of Rheims, was taken and retaken no fewer than five times; between 938 and 945, the fortress at Montigny, built on land owned by the abbey of St Crispin at Soissons, was fought over three times and destroyed twice.[83] It was obvious that these earth and timber fortifications were no longer providing the protection they were built for. Other more defensible and stronger fortifications were needed, and by the end of the tenth century stone castles, in their "truest" medieval form, began to appear throughout Europe.

The Motte-and-Bailey Castle

Before embarking on a study of stone castles in the Middle Ages, it is necessary to look at the motte-and-bailey castle, for, despite overlapping chronologically with the first stone castles, it provides a technological evolutionary link between the fortifications of the early and later Middle Ages. Although the motte-and-bailey castles were not made in stone, they involved similar intricate techniques of construction. More importantly, the motte-and-bailey castle was used by William the Conqueror to subjugate England after his conquest in 1066. This then marks the first deliberate and systematic attempt to use fortifications in an offensive military sense: for the garrisoning of troops as a threat to the inhabitants of a region.

In its simplest form, the motte part of the motte-and-bailey castle was little more than an earthen mound topped by a superstructure of wood. The bailey was an enclosed yard surrounding the motte and separated from it by a ditch. As such, the motte-and-bailey castle provided protection to its inhabitants from the size of the bailey, the depth and width of the ditch and from the height of the mound.

As with all innovations in medieval fortification construction, it is difficult to trace the origin of this castle. Most of them were located in the northwest regions of Europe, and some historians have argued that their origin is geographical: they were built to raise the ground above marshlands and floodplains.[84] Others contend that their origin is strictly military, that they were descendants of similar Roman, Merovingian, or Viking fortifications.[85] These are merely conjectures. Remains of motte-and-bailey castles have

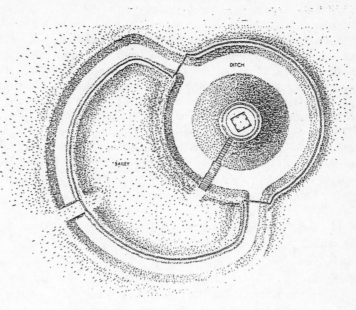

Motte-and-bailey castle (top view).
[By Eric Mose; from Hope-Taylor (1958).]

been found in Denmark, the Low Countries, the Rhineland, Northern France, Southern Italy, and England, and most date from the
late tenth and eleventh centuries.[86] Therefore, their origin might
be linked to the last phase of French and German fortification
construction against the Vikings and Hungarians.

This is certainly a logical conclusion as this period of castle
building, lacking royal domination and systemization, allowed for
some variations and experimentation in fortification construction.
Furthermore, the motte-and-bailey castle seems to have been particularly attractive to the most powerful lords of northern Europe,
lords who benefitted much from the civil wars of the late Carolingian age; they are found in great numbers on the lands of the
dukes of Normandy and the counts of Flanders, Brittany, Blois,
and Anjou. Indeed, the best literary description of a motte-and-
bailey castle is found in the early twelfth-century writings of Walter of Therouanne who describes the castle of Merkem in Flanders:

There was near the *atrium* of the church a fortress, which we
may call a *castrum* or *municipium*, exceedingly high, built after
the custom of that land by the lord of the town many years
before. For it is the habit of the magnates and nobles of those
parts, who spend most of their time fighting and slaughtering
their enemies, in order thus to be safer from their opponents
and with greater power either to vanquish their equals or suppress their inferiors, to raise a mound of earth as high as they
can and surround it with a ditch as broad and deep as possible.
The top of this mound they completely enclose with a palisade
of hewn logs bound close together like a wall, with towers set
in its circuit so far as the site permits. In the middle of the
space, within the palisade, they build a residence, or, dominating
everything, a keep.[87]

It is, however, the use of motte-and-bailey castles in Normandy which provides the link to those in William the Conqueror's
England. The Norman motte-and-bailey castle may be traced to
Count Fulk Nerra of Anjou. Fulk Nerra, who will be discussed
later, built a number of fortifications during his reign as the powerful Count of Anjou (987-1040). As attested to by literary and
archaeological evidence, many of these were motte-and-bailey castles, and they were used by both Fulk Nerra and his son, Geoffrey
Martel, for the defense of their realm and the conquest of neighboring regions, including Maine and Normandy.[88]

It is in this contact with Normandy and Maine that William
learned the value of the motte-and-bailey castle. Even before his
conquest of England, he began building a number of these, both
in the eastern part of his duchy, where he resided, and in the
western part, where he was still fighting for control.[89] In these
castles William placed his most trusted lieutenants, his *vicomtes*,
and in this way he extended his control over the whole of Normandy.[90] Four of these motte-and-bailey castles—at Dol, Rennes,
Dinan, and Bayeux—are depicted in the *Bayeux Tapestry*.[91]

After subduing his own duchy of Normandy and the neighboring county of Maine, William used the motte-and-bailey castle
to conquer England. On October 22, 1066, the Norman army, led
by William, defeated the English army at the battle of Hastings.
Harold Godwinson, the King of England, was killed and his entire
army was either destroyed or dispersed. However, William's conquest was not complete. Although their military defense was gone,

the English people were not willing freely to embrace Norman rule. The English were a proud people who, although having been conquered several times by invading armies, nevertheless desired the relative autonomy and independence which they had enjoyed under the reigns of Edward the Confessor and Harold Godwinson. The invading Norman army was a threat to this autonomy.

William realized the difficulty of subduing such a people, and he also realized that he had few soldiers with whom he could accomplish this task. He recognized that a series of fortifications would be needed to aid him in this subjugation. He chose the motte-and-bailey castle system, a system which was relatively quick and easy to build. Moreover, in addition to controlling the English, the motte-and-bailey castles would also provide protection against invading armies and a control over William's own feudal lords. He could thus consolidate his rule over all of his new kingdom.[93]

The motte-and-bailey castle was not entirely new to England. The Normans had earlier entered England in 1051 at the request of Edward the Confessor, when the powerful Earl Godwin, Edward's chief advisor and father-in-law, had been banished from the kingdom. These Normans had replaced Godwin and his sons as advisors to the king. One of the first problems they encountered was the continual raiding along the Welsh marches by bandits and insurgents. To stop these raids, the Normans constructed three castles along the border between England and Wales. These fortifications, known by the names Hereford, Ewias Harold, and Richard's Castle, were all motte-and-bailey castles, and even after the return of Earl Godwin in 1052, they supported a small Norman garrison.[93]

Even before the battle of Hastings, William the Conqueror began to build the motte-and-bailey castles, perhaps fearing a need to retreat to their protection. Immediately after landing on the southern coast of England, he built the first at Pevensey, on the site of the Saxon Shore fortress; it was followed two days later by another at Hastings, a construction recorded by the *Bayeux Tapestry*.[94]

After the victory at Hastings, William continued to build motte-and-bailey castles until a skeleton of castles covered England. Each area of conquered territory was immediately viewed from a military perspective; the possibilities of outside invasion and inner discord were assessed; and castles were built. This was likely the most extensive and rapid castle-building program in history.[95]

In March 1067, after the construction of several motte-and-bailey castles, and immediately following the erection of the castle at Winchester, William returned home to Normandy. As soon as he left, rebellions occurred in Dover and Hereford. William's administrators, Odo, Bishop of Bayeux, and William FitzOsbern, newly appointed Duke of Hereford, were unable to put down these revolts, and the king was forced to return to England in December 1067.[96] His response to the growing dissatisfaction with Norman rule was to construct more motte-and-bailey castles. From 1068 to 1070, the greatest number of these were built. As well, the construction of these fortifications marked the transition from what might have been an Anglo-Norman partnership to an outright military occupation of England by the Normans.[97]

Several revolts followed William's return, but each was put down handily by the Normans. Frequently, a motte-and-bailey castle played a role in their suppression. An example of this took place in the town of York, which was the most important northern English town in 1066. It was the provincial capital of Northumbria and had remained a point of conflict between the Vikings and Anglo-Saxons for several centuries. On the very eve of the Norman invasion, the Vikings, under the command of the Norwegian king, Harald Hardrada, had taken possession of the town, only to be later defeated by Harold Godwinson at the battle of Stamford Bridge. The Yorkish people, mostly Anglo-Scandinavians, had supported the English king in this battle, and they were not very willing to accept his conqueror's rule. Therefore, a number of revolts met Norman governance, beginning in 1068. William answered the first by building a motte-and-bailey castle to guard against further insurrection. It was a particularly large fortress, garrisoning more than 500 soldiers. Still, in early 1069, the inhabitants of York revolted once again, even attacking the castle which William had constructed to guard over them. It held until William arrived with reinforcements, and the uprising was put down. William then constructed a second motte-and-bailey castle across the Ouse River from the first, building the fortification in eight days. But even this did not secure the town against rebellion. A few months later, in September 1069, the citizens of York, aided by some Danish mercenaries, again rose against Norman rule, and again they attacked the castles. On this occasion the Yorkish rebels prevailed, capturing and burning both castles. Again William was forced to come north with his army, and in 1070 the two motte-and-bailey castles were rebuilt. Finally, the people submitted to their new king.[98]

York was unusual only in the frequency and obstinacy of its revolts. England was a very large kingdom and provided an ideal target for the invasions of foreign soldiers or the marauding of domestic rebels. In order to prevent further military altercations which were costly and could potentially lead to defeat, William was forced to systematize his construction of motte-and-bailey castles.

All of these castles were built in strategic locations, guarding roads, streams, and ports.[99] More importantly, they were each built by individuals, barons, who like the *vicomtes* in Normandy had been entrusted with their construction by William who in turn granted them jurisdiction over the lands the castles protected. The barons were given permission to confiscate any lands needed for the construction of these defenses, and the motte-and-bailey castles always ruled the most favorable and strategic positions in England. Moreover, no motte-and-bailey castle was to be built without William's permission.[100] This measure was designed to protect the king from baronial revolt. As a result then of involving a number of nobles in the fortification construction process, but at the same time limiting the number and power of these fortifications, William established the subjugation and feudalization of the English people, while at the same time protecting his own power of rule.[101]

William the Conqueror died in 1087. There is no accurate means of knowing how many motte-and-bailey castles had been built during his years as King of England. The only land survey of William's realm, the *Domesday Book*, is incomplete and often in error when it mentions castles. Indeed, it misses the well-known motte-and-bailey castles of Dover, Nottingham, Durham, and even the White Tower in London.[102] It has been estimated, however, that between 500 and 550 were built between 1066 and 1087, although the number may actually have been higher.[103] If nothing else celebrated his reign in England, the large number of motte-and-bailey castles which stretched across William's kingdom provided a fitting monument.

After William's death his sons continued his policies of fortification construction, although they did so with less urgency and commitment than had their father. There had not been a foreign invasion for several years, and, more importantly, the people of England were now much less intent on rebelling against their Norman occupiers. Therefore, the need for new construction had diminished. Besides, even before William died, it had become apparent that the motte-and-bailey castle would be replaced, sometimes using the motte as a foundation, by a stone castle. William himself built two of these, at London (the White Tower) and at Colchester, and more would follow during the rule of his successors.[104]

Because of the large number of English motte-and-bailey castles, and also because of the large amount of attention that has been paid to them by modern historians and archaeologists, there is much known about them. There is also the rather unique portrayal of them as found in the *Bayeux Tapestry*, where no fewer than five motte-and-bailey castles are depicted.[105] While the tapestry detail is primitive, it does show the nature in general of the motte-and-bailey castle design, as well as several variations.

While the *Bayeux Tapestry*'s depictions of the motte-and-bailey castles can help to illustrate what they were and even how they were built, ultimately archaeological evidence must be added to this source before a more complete picture of this type of fortification can be determined. Fortunately, there have been many recent excavations of motte-and-bailey castles, and from them it is possible to gain an accurate idea of the technological sophistication required to build a castle of this type.

Contruction Techniques

The motte part of the castle structure was made entirely of earth, and unless destroyed by later construction, it still remains. As a result, it is the easiest part of the castle to see in detail. The simplest form of earthwork defense has always been a ditch dug around the area to be protected. On a motte-and-bailey castle, when a ditch was dug in such a fashion, the removed earth was piled high in the center. As the ditch grew deeper, it also grew wider; the greater the width and depth of the ditch, the greater the defensibility of the structure. For example, the ditch at Baile Hill in York measured 21 meters wide and 12 meters deep.[106] As the ditch grew, the mound in the center of the ditch also grew in size. Some ditches were water-filled, as at Abinger and Baile Hill, but this was an infrequent addition and usually required a nearby natural water source.[107]

Mottes varied greatly in size and shape. On average they measured between 5 and 11 meters high and between 6 and 30 meters in diameter across the top. The larger mottes probably contained a hall, and may be considered "residential mottes," while the smaller, and more common, mottes contained only a tower and may have served to garrison just a few soldiers.[108] The angles of the mottes' sides also varied considerably depending on the soil which was used in its construction. If the motte was built in clay soil, its sides would be very steep; if built in sand, it would have a gentler slope.[109]

While none of the wooden motte superstructures remain, post-holes provide an idea of the size and design of these buildings. Some were quite large. For example, the structure on the motte at Bayeux, as depicted in the *Bayeux Tapestry*, is shown as a massive building with windows, a domed roof, and a forebuilding near its bridge.[110] In other cases, at the castle of Abinger for example, these post-holes reveal a small tower of large height. This means that the size of these towers was not as important as was their height.[111] The walls of the towers were not solid to the ground, but were on stilts, as revealed in the *Bayeux Tapestry*. This provided added defense to the inhabitants of the castle, an elevated fighting platform, and an excellent view of the surrounding countryside.[112] Also adding to the defense of the structure may have been tiles of hide or thick bark attached to the sides of the towers. Such a protective skin appears on the motte tower at Dol in the *Bayeux Tapestry*.[113]

Archaeological evidence has shown that there were four prevalent substructure constructions in the motte-and-bailey castle.[114] First, there was sometimes no substructure. The tower was merely erected on top of the motte. This was certainly the situation when a natural knoll was used as a motte, which occurred infrequently, but also indicates a hastily built fortification not meant to provide permanent defense.[115]

Second, a substructure was built on the old ground surface with the motte then constructed above it. This appears to have been the type of substructure built at Hastings, for the *Bayeux Tapestry* shows men building the motte with the stilts of the tower already erected.[116] This may also indicate that the towers used by William in his pre-battle motte-and-bailey castles were prefabricated in Normandy and transported to England on board William's ships.[117] Archaeological excavations have confirmed this as a frequent substructure construction, as the post-holes at the Burgh motte-and-bailey castle in Suffolk descend through the entire motte.[118]

A third type of substructure was erected on the ground surface, its exterior only being buried, while the interior was retained as a cellar. While the first two types of substructure were prevalent

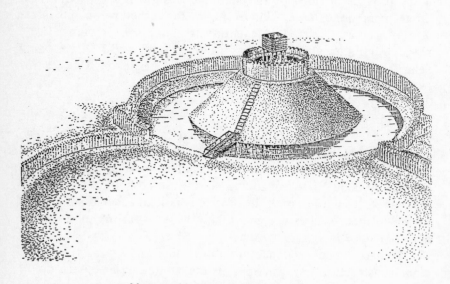

Motte-and-bailey castle (side view).
[By Eric Mose; from Hope-Taylor (1958).]

during the eleventh century, this type seems to have been a later innovation of the early twelfth century. Examples have been found at South Mimms, where the substructure was built in wood, and at Farnham, Ascot Doilly, and Wareham, where the substructure was constructed in stone.[119]

Finally, the fourth type was a free-standing tower to which a mound was later added. This may indicate that the motte was not in the castle-builder's original plan, but was a later protective addition to the already constructed tower. Certainly, this must have been the case at the castle of Lydford in Devonshire, where the motte covers windows in the base of the tower. As with the third category of motte substructure, this type was not common and may have existed only in the early twelfth century. As such, both could represent transitional ideas in castle building, marking the end of the motte-and-bailey castle age and the beginning of stone castles.[120]

As shown in both the *Bayeux Tapestry* and in archaeological excavations, a palisade was built around the top edge of the motte. The post-holes discovered during the archaeological excavations at Abinger showed that the palisade there consisted of two uprights, the outermost much taller than those inside. It is thus assumed that the palisade included a fighting platform which gave added defense and some offense to the motte. This is confirmed by the *Bayeux Tapestry* where the motte palisade at Dinan is provided with two external fighting platforms.[121]

Outside the motte and separated from it by a ditch was a large bailey. Most often this was kidney-shaped, but sometimes its shape took advantage of the terrain at the site.[122] On the outside edge of the bailey was another palisade, probably just a simple single-log fence. Sometimes there was yet another ditch beyond it.[123] The bailey was so fortified that it too provided a defensive fortress, and as such could have provided refuge to the nearby population or shelter to the horses and cattle belonging to the inhabitants of the castle. There is evidence of buildings constructed within some baileys. Usually it simply protected the inner motte structure.[124]

The bridges from the bailey to the motte were also important in the defense of the castle. Two types seem to be most prevalent. First, except for the castle at Dol, the motte-and-bailey castles

pictured in the *Bayeux Tapestry* all have a flying bridge leading
directly from the bailey edge to the top of the motte. These bridges
were all stepped with transverse bars of wood at regular intervals
for safer passage. There are gates at one end of the bridge.[125]
Second, the excavations at Abinger revealed a small bridge across
the motte ditch followed by small steps up the motte itself. If an
attack occurred, this bridge would simply have been destroyed to
prevent easy crossing.[126]

It must be noted that there were certain variations within the
motte-and-bailey castle design. The mottes are square-shaped at
the castles of Cabal Trump and Aughton.[127] Double ditches enclosed the motte-and-bailey castles at Berhampstead, Corbets,
Llanstephan, and Penrhos. Two baileys are attached to a motte
set midway between them at Windsor and at Arundel. Finally,
two mottes are attached to one bailey at Lewes and at Lincoln.[128]

Strategically, the motte-and-bailey castles were very effective.
They were quickly constructed and could be built by unskilled
labor using material available at the site.[129] They also played a
strong role in stopping large armies.[130] However, they did have
some disadvantages. Timber was ill-suited for warfare. It could
not withstand heavy assaults, and because it was not seasoned, it
needed constant repair. It was also very susceptible to fire.[131]
Perhaps this is the reason why motte-and-bailey castles were
quickly replaced by stone structures throughout England and on
the continent.

Nevertheless, for William the Conqueror's purpose of subduing the English people, the motte-and-bailey castles were perfect.
Frequently Englishmen were pressed into the service of building
them.[132] Sometimes they were also constructed on sites which
were previously occupied by other dwellings: 166 houses were
destroyed in Lincoln, 113 in Norwich, 27 in Cambridge, and in
York one-fifth of the town was razed to build castles. Even the
Catholic church was not safe from destruction. For example, part
of the cemetery of the monastery at Ely was dug up to build the
ditch of the castle there.[133] More importantly, the motte-and-bailey
castles of the Norman conquest destroyed not only dwellings, but
also the rebellious spirit of the English. They became the symbols
of defeat and subjugation.[134]

Stone Castles

Earth-and-timber fortifications had proven entirely inadequate in protecting western Europeans from the Viking and Hungarian incursions of the ninth and tenth centuries. And although the motte-and-bailey castle was successfully used by William the Conqueror to subdue England in the late eleventh century, even he recognized that these earth-and-timber structures were but temporary defenses for his newly conquered kingdom. More permanent fortifications, made of stone masonry, were needed to better defend the lands of Europe and their inhabitants from outside attack.

Yet, despite the obvious need for stone castles and the fact that by the end of the twelfth century they dotted the landscape of every medieval duchy, county, and kingdom, one of the most difficult dates to determine in the history of medieval military technology is their origin. Unless the historian of fortifications is willing to accept the early tenth-century Italian charters for stone castles discussed in the first chapter of this section, which are without archaeological confirmation, there is neither written sources nor archaeological evidence which proves the existence of a stone castle before the late tenth century.

This was a period of instability and weakness of central rule throughout all of Europe, a condition which led to much experimentation in fortification construction; experimentation which probably produced some stone castles. As in the case of the motte-and-bailey castle, the late tenth- and early eleventh-century Count of Anjou, Fulk Nerra, may be the initiator of this new defensive construction.

During Fulk's reign he was faced with almost continual military conflict which he countered by building fortifications. Fulk fortified all of his borders with castles, at least 30 major strongholds in all. Frequently, these became the targets of Fulk's enemies, but rarely did they fall. Moreover, Fulk's own offensive forces, quartered in these fortifications, were able to make extensive attacks into his enemies' lands, ultimately giving him much more territory than his neighbors.[135]

Most of Fulk Nerra's fortifications were constructed using earth and timber, and some of them were motte-and-bailey castles. However, at least two, at Langeais and at Montbazon, may have been constructed in stone. Both of these castles played important roles in Fulk Nerra's castle building strategy. Langeais was built on the Loire River, and together with the fortress at Amboise, which had been constructed upstream by Fulk's father, Geoffrey Greymantle, it controlled the entire region. Montbazon was built to the east of Langeais, on the Indre River, and provided defense for a southern route of communication with the fortresses of Amboise, Langeais, and Loches (which lay even further south).[136]

There are also stone ruins at both sites which may date from Fulk's reign. The stone ruins of Langeais reveal a tower keep (also called a donjon) originally 15 to 16 meters high with an outer rectangular perimeter measuring 17.5 by 10 meters. The walls were built on a shallow crushed rock foundation which in places is only .7 meters below the surface. The walls were made of ashlar blocks, perhaps as many as 144,000, and measured between 1.2 and 1.7 meters thick. The fill between the ashlar frame was composed of limestone and mortar. It was built not on a man-made motte, but on a natural rise of relatively short height. There are no wooden elements which survive, but it is apparent that the tower was divided by wooden floors into three levels and that access was gained by a wooden door and staircase.[137]

That these ruins are those of Fulk Nerra's castle is disputed. Fulk's castle at Langeais dates from 993-94, and two historians, J.F. Verbruggen and Marcel Deyres, claim that that fortification was nothing more than a wooden fortress; the stone keep, which now lies in ruins, did not replace it until the late eleventh century, and then not as a military structure, but as a domicile.[138] On the other side of the dispute is Bernard S. Bachrach who contends that the stone tower built at Langeais was indeed Fulk Nerra's late tenth-century fortress and that it was constructed solely for defensive purposes. As proof, Bachrach claims that the extensive and unsuccessful siege operation which Odo I of Blois undertook there in 996 could only have occurred if the structure was a stone fortress.[139]

The fortress at Montbazon also presents problems to the historian attempting to place the date of its stone ruins within Fulk's reign. It was built in a similar rectangular pattern to Langeais, but was much larger. It measured at the base 19.65 by 13.75 meters and stood between 28 and 30 meters high. The walls were also thicker than at Langeais, measuring between 2 and 2.4 meters. There may also have been an exterior (or curtain) wall with a tower built on its northeast corner.[140]

Fulk Nerra's Montbazon castle also dates from the late tenth century, as a written reference of 1005-06 attests to its completion by that time. Again it is Bachrach's contention that the stone castle which now lies in ruin there is Fulk Nerra's, while Deyres asserts that it should be dated after 1050, although even he must admit that stylistically it could have been built earlier.[141]

The dispute is perhaps inconclusive, but what may ultimately shift the argument in Bachrach's favor is the large number of stone ruins which can be found on the sites of other of Fulk Nerra's castles. Most of these have not been examined as well as the keeps at Langeais and Montbazon, but at least some appear to date from the early eleventh century and may have actually been built by Fulk Nerra himself or by some of his retainers. These include the castles at Loudun, Argenton-sur-Creuse, Melle, and Brosse.[142] More importantly, other unexamined stone castles in lands adjacent to Fulk Nerra's also seem to date from the early eleventh century and may have been influenced by the Angevin count's building strategy. Odo II of Blois, William II of Angoulême, Odo of Déols, Boso the Old of La Marche, and even King Robert II of France may all have followed Fulk Nerra's example and built stone castles. Moreover, not only is there archaeological evidence to support these early stone constructions, but many of these fortresses also successfully withstood lengthy and harsh sieges during this period, sieges which could only have been endured if the castles were built in stone.[143] Fulk Nerra then may ultimately be the pioneer who is responsible for this major innovation in fortification construction.

However, if Fulk Nerra was not the originator of the medieval stone castle, it may be that it was first built in another area of the western Frankish kingdom: the south-eastern portion known as Catalonia. There, after Charles Martel halted the Muslim invasion of France at the battle of Poitiers in 732, and later, after Charlemagne pushed them below the Pyrenees Mountains and captured Barcelona, a royal province was established along the Spanish March to protect the lands of Provence and Aquitaine from further Muslim conquests. After 809, when offensive action by the Franks against the Muslims ceased, this province became a defensive "buffer-zone" between Carolingian France and Muslim Spain. The counts of this region were drawn from the Carolingian aristocracy and were strong military leaders whose responsibilities in administering the province extended beyond the simple protection of its boundaries alone to the protection of the Carolingian kingdom as a whole.

By the middle of the tenth century the situation in Catalonia had changed dramatically. The counts of that province had gained the same freedoms from central rule that other French nobles enjoyed, and, more importantly, the Muslims in Spain began to fight a civil war among themselves, a war which would destroy the once great unity of the Muslim Spanish Umayyad dynasty. This also allowed the Christian Visigoths in the northeast to revolt against their Muslim rulers and to establish their own Leonese kingdom. By 911 the Christians had conquered one-fifth of Spain, and although the more populous and powerful southern portion remained in Muslim hands, the call for "Reconquista" (reconquest) spread throughout the rest of Europe.[144]

Catalonia was to play a major role both offensively and defensively in the early years of the Reconquista. To do so, the counts of the region first had to increase their military strength and then had to build permanent garrisons to hold these soldiers. By the end of the tenth century, a large number of castles were built throughout Catalonia. They performed a dual purpose: by merely existing they provided a defensive formation against any Muslim attacks, and at the same time, by harboring soldiers, they also provided an offensive threat to the Muslim principalities across the border.[145]

It is not known exactly when these castles began to be built of stone. It seems that initially they were built of earth and timber, although they were not motte-and-bailey castles. But by the beginning of the eleventh century (or maybe even earlier) most of these fortifications had been built or rebuilt of stone. They were tower keeps, like the castles of Fulk Nerra, but rather than being rectangular in shape, most were circular. They were also massive structures, and in fact dwarfed most castles of northern France. For example, the tower of Vallferosa was 38 meters in circumference and more than 30 meters high. Most also contained at least three and sometimes as many as five stories which were open to the outside by round and elliptical windows.[146] However, despite some similarities in structure, there is no apparent connection between the castles of Catalonia and those of Fulk Nerra.

Whether Fulk Nerra or the counts of Catalonia first originated the stone castle is not historically important. Of far greater importance are the facts that by the end of the eleventh century stone castles began to be built everywhere in Europe, and that by 1300 almost all of the castles which would be built in the Middle Ages had been built. In France, the increase in the number of fortifications was incredible. In Poitou, the number of castles increased from 3 before the tenth century to 39 in the eleventh century, and in Touraine, the increase was from 9 to 26 during the same period. In other regions even more stone castles were built in even less time. For example, in Auvergne, the number of castles grew from 8 to 34 during the 50 years between 1000 and 1050, and in Maine, the number increased from 11 to 62 between 1050 and 1100.

By the twelfth century the total number of castles which had been or were being built reached a very impressive total. In France, during the reign of Philip II "Augustus" (1180-1223), the king alone held more than 100 castles with his nobles holding several hundred more. And in England, at the beginning of the reign of Henry II in 1154, there were an estimated 274 castles held by the king and his barons. While this number cannot compare with the more than 500 motte-and-bailey castles built during the reign of William the Conqueror, considering the more sophis-

ticated and elaborate building technology required to construct
stone castles, the number is still quite impressive.[147]

Early Stone Castles

During the eleventh and twelfth centuries, the stone castle established itself in medieval society as a representation of power,
strength, and defense. Even popular literature began to use the
castle as a metaphor both for aristocratic and noble strength, and
also, to a lesser extent, for the evil oppression of the poor and
of the church.[148] The castles themselves at the end of the eleventh
century had changed little in style and function from those built
earlier. They remained simple tower keeps built solely to garrison
troops for defensive and offensive military operations.

However, at the end of the eleventh and beginning of the
twelfth centuries the function of castles began to change. Instead
of being simply fortified barracks for soldiers, they began to be
built and used as royal and feudal residences. This in turn changed
their structural and technological requirements. No longer would
the simple tower keep, built more for its size than for its comfort,
satisfy the needs of its owner. Apartments, halls, chapels, kitchens, storage chambers, and even latrines had to be incorporated
into the new castle structure, and all changes had to meet the
station and comfort of a royal or noble inhabitant and his family.
At the same time, the primary responsibility of the fortress, providing protection to the lands and population surrounding it, necessitated that a continued military strength be present. This often
led to a compromise in the comfort of the residents to benefit the
defensibility of the structure, a situation which meant that at least
until the late Middle Ages few medieval kings or nobles would
live in the opulent style of Charlemagne or his immediate descendants.

Although this move to castle residency occurred everywhere
throughout Europe in the late eleventh and early twelfth centuries,
it is perhaps most easily evidenced in the stone castles of the
Norman kings of England and their barons from 1077 to 1154.
The motte-and-bailey castles built by William the Conqueror had
performed their function well. Anti-Norman revolts were quelled
throughout the kingdom and by 1077 had nearly disappeared, and

the few outside invasions which occurred, all of them quite small in size, had little effect. Indeed, because of their success, motte-and-bailey castles continued to be built for the conquest and subjugation of Wales, Scotland, and Ireland; but in England proper they were no longer needed.[149]

Rather than building tall stone barracks like those on the continent, what replaced the motte-and-bailey castles in late eleventh-century England were stone residential castles. In some ways these new castles were merely the evolutionary extension of William the Conqueror's motte-and-bailey castle building strategy. For one thing, their military functions were the same, providing both defense against outside invasion and domestic stability. At the same time, with the English kingdom now effectively subject to Norman rule, it was time to replace the obviously weaker earth-and-timber motte-and-bailey castle with a stronger stone masonry fortification. Therefore, while some motte-and-bailey castles continued to function in their earth-and-timber state—one of the York castles remained a wooden fortress until the end of the thirteenth century[150]—often new stone castles were built on top of and replacing the old conquest structures.

These new castles were built in two distinct styles. The first style has been characterized by R. Allen Brown simply as the "keep-and-bailey castle." These were the easiest and probably the most economical castles to construct, for they made very few alterations to the old motte-and-bailey castle design. As the name implies, the bailey remained relatively intact with a stone keep added to replace the old wooden fortress on top of the motte. The keep was the strongest and most important part of this castle. Called a shell-keep, because of its usual circular shape, it was constructed on top of the motte, if it was large enough, or around it, if the motte was small. In the latter case, the motte was usually leveled or hollowed out, although in some cases it was actually incorporated into the shell-keep structure.

The keep contained the lord's apartment and sometimes also a hall, chambers, and a chapel. Other residential buildings—kitchens, storehouses, stables, barracks, and, if not included in the keep, the hall and chapel—were built away from the motte in the bailey enclosure. This meant that the bailey too needed more than ditches and wooden palisades to protect its perimeters, and often

a stone wall was added. Only a few keep-and-bailey castles—
among them Framlingham, Helmsley, and Pickering—did not add
a stone wall to their baileys, and then only because their defenses,
wide double ditches, were perceived to provide the necessary defense for the bailey buildings.[151] Large and often quite intimidating
stone gatehouses and stone towers were also added to protect the
bailey enclosure.[152]

A good example of a keep-and-bailey castle is the one constructed at Farnham. Built c.1138 by Henry of Blois, the Bishop
of Winchester, as his residence, Farnham Castle was erected on
a D-shaped motte-and-bailey castle with the motte lying slightly
off-center but apart from the bailey wall. A stone motte substructure, 11.3 meters square, provided the foundation for a keep, 15.6
meters square. The height of the keep is not known, although it
could not have been very large judging from the difference in the
sizes of the substructure and of the keep built on top of it; it also
may not have been completely finished. The motte and keep were
further surrounded by a circular stone shell-wall entered only by
a wide and shallow gatehouse. Four rectangular towers were also
built along the shell-wall. The bailey was enclosed by a stone
wall, and there were at least three bailey buildings, including a
rather large hall and a chapel.[153]

This style of Norman residential castle was not very popular,
although there are several examples, and its presence may in fact
represent a situation in which little capital was available for castle
building. However, the keep-and-bailey castle continued to be built
into the thirteenth century with the most famous example being
that constructed by Henry II at Windsor.

The second style of stone castle built by William the Conqueror and his heirs was the rectangular tower keep. Rectangular
tower keeps were extremely large castles, much larger than shell-
keeps of the keep-and-bailey type. Many of them covered an area
more than 30 meters square, with two of the largest being the
White Tower in London, which measured 36.5 by 32.5 meters,
and Colchester Castle, which measured 46.5 by 35 meters. They
were also quite tall, having at least two or three stories and a
basement.[154]

This gave ample room inside the keep for all the rooms needed
for residency: the lord's apartment, halls, chambers, staircases,

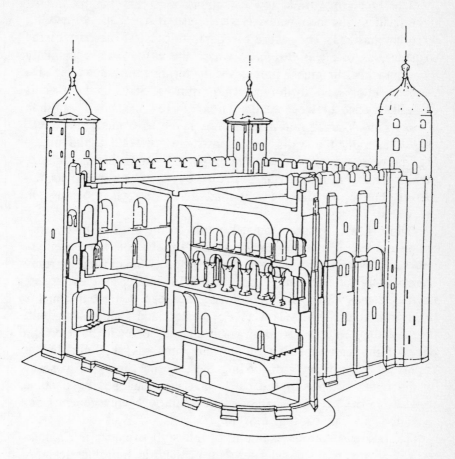

Tower keep: White Tower cutaway.
[From Brown (1989g).]

kitchens, chapels, fireplaces, storerooms, latrines (which at times opened directly onto the outer keep walls), and sometimes even a dungeon. It also usually contained a fighting gallery, which opened to the outside through arrow-loops, and one or more watchtowers. Forebuildings and gatehouses, many equipped with drawbridges and portcullises, were also attached to the keep and limited access to it. The roof, which was sometimes pitched but most often flat, was made of wood and sometimes contained a rampart or battlemented parapet.

The most important and technologically complex feature of
these castles was their walls. Here defensive strength and stability
were emphasized. They were of course thickest at the base of the
structure, as this was the place where the castle was most likely
to be attacked by picks, bores, and battering rams, but their size
was also impressive in the uppermost stories. Sizes of these walls
naturally varied between castles, although few measured less than
3 meters thick and some measured as much as 6 meters in thickness. Generally the walls were constructed of solid ashlar dressings between which was stuffed large amounts of stone rubble.
Stability was brought to the structure by its substructure, its numerous buttresses and the fact that there were few openings in
the walls.

These keeps were customarily built on the sites of motte-and-
bailey castles. Sometimes they replaced exactly the wooden motte
structure, as at Castle Acre and at Lydford, but most often they
were simply too large to fit on the smaller motte. In these cases,
the motte was either discarded, with the keep being built on the
bailey, as at the White Tower, Colchester, and Canterbury; built
on the bailey wall, as at Kenilworth and at Corfe; or built on the
edge of the mound rising out of the ditch, as at Clum and at
Guildford. The bailey surrounding these keeps continued to serve
as the outer defense of the castle and was enclosed by a stone
wall, as in the keep-and-bailey castles, although enlargements beyond the old bailey often took place.

There are numerous examples of this style of castle in England
as it was the most popular of Norman castle building designs.
Perhaps the most famous of these are the two earliest constructed,
the White Tower and Colchester. Both were built under the direction of William the Conqueror, and they may have been completed before his death. Both may also have been the work of the
same architect, Gundulf, the Bishop of Rochester.

The White Tower, called such because it was white-washed
during the Middle Ages, was begun c.1078. It rose nearly 27.5
meters, not including the extra height of the three turrets, and
enclosed two stories and a basement. Each story was divided into
two large halls, the largest of which measured 28 by 11.3 meters;
a further subdivision enclosed the chapel of St. John, which rose
from the basement to the roof and included a crypt and sub-crypt.

The first story contained the halls and chambers for conducting the kingdom's affairs, with the second story, which was later divided into two, probably containing the chief residential chambers. The second story was quite lofty and contained a fighting gallery built halfway up the halls. Finally, the basement, which was only partially below ground level, was not divided into separate chambers and may have served only for storage and as a prison. Spiral staircases in each of the turrets led between the stories and also gave access to the watchtowers and roof, except for the basement which was serviced by only a single staircase.

The walls of the White Tower were quite thick, measuring between 3.5 and 4.5 meters at the base, and were constructed with ashlar dressings filled with a rubble core. On each face of the keep and also on the largest turret a number of flat and narrow pilaster buttresses rose from the ground nearly to the top of the castle. Also, unlike most castles of this design, there were many large windows. There was, however, only a single entrance to the keep's first story, through a forebuilding which is now missing.

The White Tower was probably intended by William the Conqueror to be his primary personal residence. In contemporary writings it is rarely described simply as a castle or a tower; instead, as in the writings of William Fitzstephen, it is described as a "fortified palace." Still in excellent condition, it continues to be the grandest example of Norman stone castle building.[155]

Although larger, the Colchester castle was built in a style similar to that of the White Tower. It stands on the ruins of an old Roman temple, which may have influenced its large size, and reused some of the Roman masonry in its construction. Its walls were of similar size and construction as those at the White Tower, although the three turrets at Colchester were larger and square-shaped, adding more stability to its immense structure. As well, Colchester was entered only by a single entrance through a forebuilding equipped with a portcullis and a large wooden door.

The interior was similar to the White Tower; however, the chapel and one hall were smaller than those in the London keep. There was also the addition of a small room on the first story, the purpose of which is unknown, and there were only two turret staircases, with the third turret containing the building's latrines.

Tower keep: Hedingham Castle, Essex.

As well, there was a third story at Colchester, although it was destroyed in 1683.

Although this keep was built in the residential style, it may not have served as one. At least it was not regarded as a royal residence by William the Conqueror. Built on the East Anglian coast to guard against Scandinavian invasions, it appears to have been a military barracks, which explains the large latrine facilities.[156]

In England, the Norman rectangular castle style was used in later fortification construction and was especially favored by Henry II in his numerous late twelfth- and early thirteenth-century castle building projects. They were kept in repair throughout the Middle Ages and thus remained an active defensive consideration in the kingdom. However, by the middle of the thirteenth century, its popularity as an architectural style had diminished, replaced by a round-shaped castle style which nevertheless still retained the residential aspects introduced by the earlier Norman castles.[157]

While this discussion of residential castles has focused on England in the late eleventh and early twelfth centuries, there were numerous examples of this type of fortification found in continental Europe. Moreover, with few exceptions, they followed the two styles in which English castles were constructed. For example, the castle at Gisors in Normandy, which was built in 1123-24, and the Pfeffengen Castle in Switzerland, built later in the twelfth century, were very much like the keep-and-bailey castles of England.[158] And the castles built at Arques in Normandy (1125), Loches in Touraine (early twelfth century) and Ghent in Flanders (mid-twelfth century) were much like the English rectangular keeps. The only difference between these continental castles and those in England were their smaller size. For example, Loches measured only 25 by 13 meters, although it rose more than 37 meters high, while Ghent measured only 28 by 17 meters. At Ghent, the walls were also narrower than most English castles, measuring at most only 1.7 meters thick.[159]

Castles of the Crusaders

A second important development in medieval European castle construction came with the Crusades to the Holy Land at the end of the eleventh century. Called initially at the Council of Clermont on November 27, 1095, by Pope Urban II, the First Crusade attempted to regain the lands where Jesus Christ was born, lived, and died, lands then under Muslim control. The response to Urban's call was enthusiastic, and a large army gathered to set out on Urban's declared day, Assumption 1096. After a bumbling journey to the Holy Land which saw the Crusaders fighting more against the harsh conditions of the Middle East than against the Muslims, the Crusade was successful. The first prize, Antioch, fell on June 28, 1098, and it was followed a year later, on July 13, 1099, by the fall of Jerusalem.

By 1101 the Crusaders had secured their presence in the Holy Land. Their initial success resulted to a large extent from a civil war which was being fought within the Islamic lands between the Seljuk Turks and the Egyptian Fatamids. This civil war had both depleted the fighting strength of the Muslims and brought disunity in the defense of their territories. For a while then the Crusaders met almost no military reaction to their conquests. However, they realized that they eventually would be forced to defend their newly won territories. And they would have to do it with fewer soldiers than they had in the initial conquests, as many of the First Crusaders, perhaps as much as one-half to two-thirds of the initial force, returned to Europe following the fall of Jerusalem.[160]

Four Crusader kingdoms were carved out of the captured Holy Land territory: Edessa, Antioch, Tripoli, and Jerusalem. Kings were elected and a feudal structure created. In order to ensure the security of the kingdoms against Muslim attacks from outside and Muslim/Jewish uprisings from inside these kingdoms, two practices were instituted. First, the Crusaders negotiated with the Muslims and Jews for peace. Treaties were made, bribes paid, and alliances formed; some Muslims and Jews were even used as tax collectors and policemen. Second, numerous castles were built throughout the four kingdoms. The Crusaders realized the need for building castles, and for building them quickly, and within three decades after the fall of Jerusalem most of their castles were completed, a feat that had not been equalled in Europe.[161] Of the two practices, the building of castles was the most effective. Treaties, alliances, and even bribes all failed to keep the peace during the century following the First Crusade. But the castles rarely failed, and when they did, it took a long time and necessitated a large number of men.

Of initial concern to these castle builders was the security of the Crusader Kingdoms' frontiers. Three were especially vulnerable, and the Crusaders concentrated their initial castle construction in these areas. The first, and perhaps most important, was the sea coast. The Crusaders had conquered almost all of the coast from Antioch to the Sinai Desert, with the exceptions only of Tyre (which was captured in 1124) and Ascalon (which was captured in 1153), and it needed to be protected. The second was the frontier facing Damascus. The third protected the kingdom of Jerusalem in the south against incursions from the Fatamids in Egypt. These frontiers all received numerous castles. A fourth border, west of Antioch and facing Aleppo, might also have been filled with castles, except that negotiations between the Crusaders and the Seljuk Turks led to a "demilitarized zone" without either Muslim or Crusader fortifications.[162]

Castles were built along all major routes and in every major mountain pass, along the deserts, the mountains, the rivers, the lakes, and the sea. But protecting the frontiers was only one obligation undertaken by the Crusaders, and it was a responsibility which they could not completely fulfill. There was simply a limitation to the defensibility of the kingdoms' frontiers, especially when so few soldiers were available as reinforcements should a border or a castle be attacked.[163]

The function of many other castles built by the Crusaders was not the protection of the kingdoms' boundaries, for they were built deep inside the Crusaders' lands. These served as garrisons for soldiers who could be used offensively to besiege nearby Muslim towns, such as Tyre and Ascalon, or to raid unfriendly Muslim lands. Defensively they served as refuges against the attacks of strong Muslim leaders, like Saladin, until relief could come from elsewhere in the Crusaders' kingdoms or from Europe. They served as centers of authority and police posts for the governance and security of the kingdoms against the insurrections of Muslim rebels.[164] Finally, these castles were administrative centers and hubs of economic development and colonization.[165]

With the exception of a few castles built to defend the larger towns of the Holy Land, at Tripoli, Tortosa, Tyre, Beirut, Acre,

and Jerusalem, most Crusader castles were built in the countryside. It was here that the Crusaders could use the harshness and
inaccessibility of the Middle Eastern terrain to add to the defensibility of their structures. The castles were built on the summits
of precipitous rocks or next to steep ravines. At two places, Tyron
and Habis, the Crusaders even fortified caves. Most castles had
thick walls faced with large stones. Because their inhabitants an-
ticipated long sieges that might last until reinforcements could
arrive from Europe, the castles were provided with reservoirs for
water supply and large cellars for food storage. For example, at
the castle of Margat it is estimated that there were sufficient food
and water supplies to feed a garrison of 1000 men for 5 years.[166]

In general, two types of castles were built by the Crusaders.
The first followed the style which began to be common in Europe
at the end of the eleventh century. These were large rectangular
keeps enclosed by a stone wall. They shared with their European
counterparts the same simple utilitarian character and the same
solid construction. As well, they were often as large in area as
were their European cousins, but were usually only two stories
high instead of three. At the same time, their overall defensibility
was improved by the harshness of terrain on which most stood.[167]

Two of the best examples of this type of Crusaders' castle
were built at Safita and Jebail, and were known to the Crusaders
as Chastel Blanc and Giblet respectively. Lying in the southern
coastal region of Syria, the castle at Safita was built on a rocky
knoll nearly 1000 feet above sea level. At this height and with
the precipitousness of its slope, defense was secured. The keep
measured 30.5 by 18.3 meters and stood more than 25 meters
high. It had two stories: in the upper story was a large, vaulted
room, presumably the living quarters, which filled the entire extent
of the keep and was lit by only a few arrow-slits; below it was
a hall, also filling the extent of the keep, which was used as
chapel. The flat roof had a battlemented parapet. Around the keep
was an oval wall with a large polygonal tower at its south-west
end. There may also have been a gatehouse near this tower, although it has now disappeared. On the lower slopes of the knoll
was another polygonal wall with a fortified gateway which added
to the defense of the castle above.

It is not certain when the castle at Safita was originally built, although it must have been before 1166-67 as the Muslim general, Nur ad-Din, is said to have captured it then. It is also known to have been a Templar castle, although whether that Order was the initiator of the construction is uncertain.[168]

The castle at Jebail is also a good example of a rectangular keep castle, but it is unlike Safita in many ways. For example, it was built not on a precipitous location, but at the southeast corner of a wall surrounding a town and a small harbor, the site of the ancient Phoenician sea-port of Byblos. It was also much smaller than the Safita Castle, measuring only 17.7 by 22 meters. It too had two stories. The castle of Jebail was one of the strongest Crusader castles, built much more solidly than the keep at Safita by reusing large blocks of ancient stone masonry with old marble columns cut up and used for bonding. Surrounding the castle was a rectangular curtain wall reinforced with small corner towers. An extra tower in the center of the north face guarded the gate. The Jebail Castle was constructed as early as the first decade of the twelfth century and served as a part of the fortifications of the Kingdom of Tripoli.[169]

However, most of the Crusaders' castles were not built in the rectangular keep style. These castles simply could not sufficiently meet the military needs of the Christian force occupying the Holy Land. For one thing, they were too small. They could not house enough troops to stand in the way of an attacking force, nor could they store enough food and water for a prolonged siege. As well, rectangular keeps often took a long time to construct, and as they were the focal point of the castles' defense, there was little protection until they were completed. The Crusaders needed a fortification which was both larger and more quickly built. Thus they chose to build most of their castles in the style of the older Byzantine fortresses already prominent in the Holy Land.

On their journey to Jerusalem the Crusaders saw and were impressed by the majestic walls of Constantinople. Afterwards they besieged the Muslim-held Byzantine fortresses at Nicaea and Antioch. When they reached the Holy Land they confronted other Byzantine defensive structures, structures which were so strong that they had been repaired and imitated by the Muslims who had inhabited them since the seventh century. These clearly influenced the Crusaders, and they began to imitate them.[170]

These fortresses can be most easily described as castle complexes, for they did not rely on a single rectangular keep for their defense. Instead, they imitated urban fortifications with walls strengthened on the sides and in the corners with towers. The buildings inside the complex, none of which duplicated the European rectangular keeps, became less important in the defense of the castle. They were meant simply to provide housing and storage. These castles were also larger and could be more quickly constructed than rectangular keep castles.

The Crusaders built many castle complexes, most of which were impressive in their size and structure. Walls, sometimes double walls, surrounding a large bailey dominated each castle. As they were the primary means of defense, the walls were very tall and made of the strongest masonry. They were also protected at intervals by a number of battlemented towers. Entrance into the castle was through a single large gatehouse equipped often with heavy wooden doors, portcullises, and, occasionally, a drawbridge. Buildings in the bailey varied in size, shape, and purpose. There were halls, barracks, kitchens, magazines, stables, baths, latrines, storehouses, and, especially in the cases of castles held by the monastic military orders, chapels and chapter houses. In some castles there were also keeps or citadels, built as residences or barracks, and meant to stand as a final line of defense should the outer walls fail. Many castles contained large, deep wells and/or rain-water reservoirs.

The shape of these castles was determined by the terrain on which they were built. The harsher the terrain, the more defensible the castle. Thus most Crusader castles were located on high, precipitous hill-tops or ridges. Often added to this defense was a deep and steep ravine or ditch, sometimes natural and sometimes hewn out of solid rock. The terrain also determined that some castles, among them Saône, Beaufort and Toprakkale, were divided into two separate baileys or fortresses accessible to each other only by means of a small drawbridge. However, in spite of the harshness of terrain on which most of these castles were located, this did not seem to limit their size, as most covered quite large areas. For example, the castles at Saône and Subeibe covered an area of 5 and 6.5 hectares respectively.[171]

Perhaps the most impressive of these castles, and certainly the one most studied by modern historians and architects, was Krak des Chevaliers. Krak des Chevaliers remains to this day one of the best preserved and most awe-inspiring medieval castles in the world. No less a historical figure than T.E. Lawrence (Lawrence of Arabia) was struck by its beauty and endeavored to make a study of it. He described it as "...perhaps the best preserved and most wholly admirable castle in the world, [a castle which] forms a fitting commentary on any account of the Crusading buildings of Syria."[172] Built in the mountainous regions of southern Syria not far from the castle at Safita, Krak des Chevaliers was constructed using the terrain to improve its defensibility. It was erected on a hill-top over 640 meters high and surrounded on all sides by moderately steep slopes. Yet its area measured nearly 140 by 210 meters, making it one of the largest of the Crusaders' castles.

The outer defenses consisted of a polygonal wall, which contained several defensive galleries and semicircular towers. A small

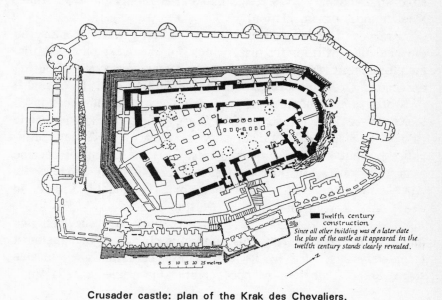

Crusader castle: plan of the Krak des Chevaliers.
[From Smail (1956).]

gate in the northern face of this wall was guarded by two adjacent towers. Between the outer and inner defenses was a forecourt, 16 to 23 meters wide, with a deep rock-hewn ditch in the southern section serving as a reservoir. The stables, magazine, baths, and latrines were also located in the forecourt.

The inner stronghold of the castle lay on top of a steep revetment rising from the forecourt. It was large and spacious and contained a range of buildings serving different functions, including more water tanks and food storehouses. As the castle eventually came under the control of the Knights Hospitallers, the inner stronghold also included a cloister and chapel.

The entrance to the fortress was protected by three fortified gateways between which lay sharp-turning narrow corridors. For greater defense, the stronghold was topped by five massive towers, one on the northern, one on the western, and three more on the southern perimeters. All five towers also contained many chambers in their several stories and were probably the living quarters of the knights. They were separated from each other and from the main fortress by a series of stepped bridges. All the buildings in the inner stronghold, like the outer walls, were built using the most proficient of architectural and masonic skill. The stone was solid—pierced only by arrow slits—and smoothly cut with some, albeit minor, ornamentation.

Krak des Chevaliers was built in the early twelfth century on the site of a Muslim fortress, which for the most part was dismantled, and it remained a formidable defensive stronghold during the entire Crusader occupation of the Holy Land. It was also important in the number of combatants which could be housed there. In 1212 Wilbrand of Oldenburg estimated that the castle held more than 2000 soldiers, although most of these were probably Maronite or Syrian mercenaries. This meant that it became a target of many Muslim sieges and attacks. It survived sieges by Alp Arslam, the Sultan of Aleppo, in 1125 and by Saladin in 1188, and it withstood further Muslim attacks in 1163, 1167, 1207, 1218, 1229, 1252, 1267, and 1270. It also survived two major earthquakes during this time. Finally, after being almost completely evacuated by its inhabitants, and after an extensive siege, Sultan Baibar of Aleppo captured the castle in 1271.[173]

Crusader castle: Krak des Chevaliers, Syria.

After the initial conquests, the Crusaders had little military success. At the same time, nearby Muslim rulers began to unite and threaten the Crusader kingdoms. The first major setback for the Crusaders came in 1144 when the poorly protected kingdom of Edessa fell to the Muslim leader, Nur ad-Din, leaving the other kingdoms open to conquest. In response, the Second Crusade was immediately called by Pope Eugene III. However, it was a miserable failure. Arriving in the Holy Land in late 1147 the Second Crusaders began to quarrel with the resident Crusaders, primarily over the latter's willingness to make alliances and treaties with the Muslims. This divisiveness brought a lack of offensive military unity which ultimately led to failure on the battlefield against the more unified Muslim army.

With the failure of the Second Crusade, Nur ad-Din began to extend his power to the south. Damascus was taken in 1154 and Egypt fell in 1168. Nur ad-Din died in 1174, but he was succeeded by his nephew, Saladin. Saladin was an even more capable general than his uncle. When he succeeded to the throne he controlled all of the land surrounding the remaining Crusader kingdoms, and it was only a short time before he began to think about extending

his power there as well. By 1187 he began to move into the
Crusader lands, and on July 4, 1187, he met and defeated a large
Crusader army at the battle of Hattin. The road to Jerusalem lay
open to him, and the city fell on October 2. Only Tyre, the
kingdom of Antioch, and the kingdom of Tripoli remained in
Crusader hands.

This again brought an immediate response from the papacy.
Jerusalem, the gem of the Holy Land, had fallen to the Muslims,
and it was the responsibility of the kings and princes of Europe
to retake it. The Third Crusade brought large armies from the
three most powerful kingdoms of Europe: Germany, France, and
England. All three armies were led by their kings. However,
despite the royal and papal influence in this Crusade it also met
with abject failure. The German army, choosing to travel overland
to the Holy Land, never reached its target. Its emperor, Frederick
Barbarossa, then probably 68 years old, drowned on the journey
when he fell off his horse while crossing the Saleph River in Asia
Minor, and his army was shortly thereafter decimated by disease
and Muslim attacks. The French and English armies, choosing to
travel overseas, did arrive at the Holy Land. But once there, the
two kings, Philip II (Augustus) of France and Richard I (the Lionhearted) of England, never could agree on any military action.
No major campaign was ever launched, and no battle ever fought;
only Acre fell to the Crusaders after a rather lengthy and unevent-
ful siege. Finally, in October 1191, Philip went back to France
and began attacking Richard's territory there. A year later Richard
returned home.

With the failure of the Third Crusade came the end of defensible borders in the Holy Land; now there were only defensible
areas, all of which were protected by castles.[174] Soon they too
fell to Muslim armies. Later Crusades met with similar failure,
and while both Frederick II of Germany and Louis IX of France
(Saint Louis) eventually retook some of the lost Holy Land, by
the end of the thirteenth century the remaining territory and all
castles held by the Crusaders fell to the Muslims. In 1268 the
kingdom of Antioch surrendered; in 1289, Tripoli capitulated; and
finally, in 1291, when Acre fell, the last vestiges of the Crusaders'
conquest returned to Muslim control.

During these defeats, until the Crusaders were finally forced out of the Holy Land, castles continued to be built. But these fortifications, most of them erected in Crusader-controlled towns, were not nearly as elaborate or sophisticated as those constructed during the first half of the twelfth century. Indeed, there seems to have been an air of desperation in much of their construction.[175] One feature prominent in these later fortifications is important. The Crusaders had discovered during their attacks on Muslim fortifications and then later in the defense of their own castles that there were many disadvantages to rectangular keeps and towers. For one thing, the straight walls of a rectangular keep were relatively easy to destroy by a battering ram or siege machine. They also presented virtually unprotected corners to attackers, as there was no potential for flanking fire. A circular or multangular keep or tower was much more easily defensible than a rectangular structure. It presented no unseen or shielded cover to the enemy and often offered no straight walls to his battering machines.[176]

[handwritten margin note: adoption of rounded Towers]

The "Golden Age" of Castle Construction

Perhaps no other event in medieval history had the impact on European fortification building as did the Crusades. Because most Crusader Castles were built larger and more capable of a sustained defense than their European counterparts, they tended to impress everyone who saw them. This, added to the fact that so many soldiers of different European kingdoms and principalities served in the Holy Land, many of whom would authorize and control the construction of castles when they returned home, meant that the Crusader Castles greatly influenced late twelfth- and thirteenth-century castle building throughout all of Europe. This in turn created a "golden age" of castle construction which produced perhaps the finest examples of what modern students see as the archetypal medieval castle.

While it is true that the rectangular keep castle continued to be built until the end of the Middle Ages, by the beginning of the fourteenth century its numbers had been surpassed by the construction of non-rectangular keep castles. These were built in a style which differed radically from that used in the construction of European castles during the late eleventh and early twelfth

centuries, but was very much like that used in building the
Crusaders' castles. In particular, these new castles were built as
complexes which relied on walls and towers for their principal
defense against attack. When a keep was added to the castle complex, which occurred frequently, it was not rectangular in shape,
but was round or multangular in shape.

It was the round or multangular keep of the Crusaders which
made the earliest impact on European castles. So overwhelmingly
logical was the improved defense of this new castle style, and so
little did it change the cost or technology of the keep construction,
that it immediately began to alter all further castle building. Indeed, its impact away from the Holy Land occurred so quickly
that some historians have chosen to judge this to be a European
innovation without the influence of the Crusades.[177] Still, it is
difficult to deny what must have been a strong influence on the
many European Crusaders who saw as early as 1096 the impressive Byzantine circular towers on the walls of Constantinople or
in the keeps of the nearby castles at Romuli Hissar and Anadoli
Hissar which faced each other across the Bosporus Strait just north
of that city.[178]

The first multangular or "transitional" keep, as they are sometimes called, appeared in France as early as 1130 with the construction of the keep at Houdan. There a two-story tower was
built in a round shape with four projecting circular turrets or
contreforts added to the outside. Inside, the Houdan castle had a
square-shaped plan in both of its large stories. The bottom story
served as a store room and the upper as a great hall. Residential
chambers were in three of the turrets, while the fourth contained
a staircase to the battlemented roof. The only entrance to the
castle was into the second story through the north turret (6 meters
above the ground). It was reached by a drawbridge which led
from the bailey curtain wall-walk. The walls of the keep measured
3.5 meters thick.[179]

The size of the castle at Houdan was not impressive, nor were
its accompanying outer defenses; the castle measured only 30 meters high and 15 meters in diameter, not including the two-meter-
wide turrets. But it established a style which would be followed
by several later and often larger castles, including Provins, Gisors,
and Étampes in France and Orford, Conisborough, Chilham,

Odiham, and Longtown in England. These later castles, all built before 1200, varied little in style from Houdan. Provins and Conisborough were larger, containing four stories instead of two, and Gisors and Provins were built on top of mottes. Other differences included the shape and function of the inner residences and the amount and quality of the bailey defenses. However, the chief deviation from Houdan was in the turrets added to the keep. In this only Provins imitates the original. Étampes was built in a quatrefoil style, and Chilham and Odiham were octagonal. Orford, which may have served as a residence for Henry II, had three square instead of round turrets and all were taller than the keep. Finally, Gisors, Conisborough, and Longtown did not contain turrets in the functional sense; all instead had three or more buttresses added to the outside of the keep.[180]

The multangular keep marked a distinct change in European castle building strategy. The circular shape of the castle, the battlemented roofs and the guarded entrance to the keeps all meant that the architects of these castles emphasized the defensibility of the structure. A further step in this defensive evolution came in the early thirteenth century with the removal of all appendages, turrets or buttresses, from the outside of newly constructed keeps, leaving the round-shaped structure alone.

In England, the most notable example of this castle style was built at Pembroke c.1200 by the famous knight-errant, baron, and regent of England, William Marshal. William's keep was perfectly circular and relatively large, more than 24 meters high and 16 meters in diameter. It contained four stories, with three residential floors and a basement, and its only entrance was into the second story over a drawbridge. The walls were thick, measuring 4.6 meters, and were the same thickness throughout the entire structure. Stability was added to the keep by the infrequency of windows—only four were allowed throughout the building—which produced a dark, but very strong fortress. Outside defenses were negligible, with only a thin curtain wall strengthened by a few circular towers, as it is clear that William relied on the strength of the keep and the somewhat harsh terrain for the defensibility of the castle.[181]

In France, circular keep castles were much more popular than in England, especially as they seem to have been promoted by

King Philip Augustus. The castles at Dourdan, Falaise, Rouen, Issoudun, and Villeneuve-sur-Yonne all contained large circular keeps, but perhaps the two best examples of this French castle style were found at Aigues Mortes and at Coucy.

The circular keep at Aigues Mortes, known as the Tower of Constance, was not exceptionally large or impressive. Built in the mid-thirteenth century, it measured only 30 meters high and 22 meters in diameter, and contained just two residential stories and a small basement. But this structure clearly showed the new European emphasis on defense. The walls were 6 meters thick at their base and the foundations were 18 meters deep. Access to the keep was through a lone entrance guarded by machicolations and gained only by traversing a drawbridge over an encircling moat, and entering two heavy wooden doors and a portcullis. As well, only two small windows and a number of narrow arrowslits penetrated the walls. An 11-meter high curtain wall was later added around the keep as an extra defense.[182]

The Tower of Constance and the keep at Pembroke were dwarfed by the round tower at Coucy. This was by far the largest, strongest, and grandest of the European circular keeps. Built between 1225 and 1242 as the chief residence of Eugerrand III, the Sire of Coucy, it covered an area 31 meters in diameter and rose more than 55 meters high. It too had a very secure entrance, which although penetrating the ground floor contained all of the defenses present at Aigues Mortes: the moat, drawbridge, machicolations, doors, and portcullis. A second entrance, also protected by a drawbridge, led from the second story to the curtain wall-walk. The keep at Coucy, unlike other circular keeps, included powerful outer defenses. A large trapezoidal bailey wall, 20 meters high and flanked by four large drum towers, surrounded the circular keep and provided further protection to the already strong castle.[183]

The Castle Complex

More important even than the circular keep, the Crusaders' castles introduced the castle complex to Europe. As with the Crusaders' castle complexes, their European imitators always included extensive bailey defenses. High walls, large flanking towers, crenellated wall-walks with machicolations, and extensive, secure gateways all characterized these new buildings. Most were built on the summits of precipitous hill-tops or on high man-made mottes. However, unlike their Crusader cousins, the European models almost always added a keep to the complex, sometimes constructing the new fortress around an existing keep and at other times building an entirely new structure. When an existing keep was used it tended to be rectangular in shape; a new keep tended to be multangular or circular.

Although numerous, three of these complexes should suffice as examples of this castle building style. The first, the castle at Dover, was built by Henry II as a defense of the vulnerable southeast coast of England and also probably as a royal residence. The Dover Castle was an extremely expensive venture for the powerful English king who spent a recorded £6,400 on its construction, an expense which was added to later by his sons, Kings Richard the Lionhearted and John. The initial construction, between 1181 and 1187, saw the erection of a powerful keep. Built in the traditional rectangular style, it was very large, measuring almost 30 square meters at its base and rising to a height of 29 meters. It contained two stories and a basement. Both stories held a large hall, divided down the middle by a cross wall, a number of smaller chambers and garderobes, a latrine (which emptied its contents onto the outside castle yard), a well, and a chapel. The second story, which was twice the height of the first story, also included a gallery. Two spiral staircases, located in opposite corners of the keep, gave access to the two stories and also to the roof, which was skirted by a crenellated rampart and four crenellated square corner turrets which rose another 3.7 meters above the keep. The keep could be entered only through a forebuilding, containing three long flights of stairs, which was strengthened by three towers. The walls were well buttressed and varied at the base between 5.2 and 6.4 meters in thickness.

The keep was further protected by a tall bailey wall fortified by 14 square towers. There were two gateways, each guarded by two flanking towers, the largest of which was known as Constable's Gate. Each gate tower was equipped with an outer defensive structure, known as a barbican, which was placed in relation to the gateway so that an attacking force was exposed to maximum flanking fire.

The defenses of the Dover Castle were quickly put to the test as it came under siege in 1216 by the French Dauphin, later King Louis VIII. The castle walls held and the keep was not threatened. But the attack prompted the construction of a parallel outer wall, built between 1230 and 1260, which also contained a large number of towers, this time semi-circular in shape.[184]

A second example of the European castle complex can be found in the castle constructed at Najac in Aveyron. Begun in 1253 by Alphonse of Poitiers, the brother of King Louis IX, on the site of a small, early twelfth-century rectangular keep, the castle of Najac incorporated many of the characteristics of the castle at Dover. At the same time, it showed a further evolution in castle building strategy in that it did not regard the keep as the last defense of the castle, but instead saw it as a functioning part of the initial defenses. The keep at Najac, circular in shape, did not stand in the middle of the complex, but instead was incorporated into the bailey wall structure as its largest and most formidable tower.

The bailey wall was the most important defensive feature of the Najac Castle. It rose between 7 and 8 meters in height and had a thickness of 1 meter. It was also fortified not only by the keep at its southeast corner, but by two more round towers on the northeast and northwest corners, the old rectangular keep on the southwest corner and two semi-circular towers guarding the two gateways. The gateways were further guarded by barbicans and ditches. Along the wall was a walk which was equipped with an elaborate system of stairways and passages, some visible and some hidden, which could be isolated from the rest of the castle by barriers.

The Najac keep, while not as elaborate or as comfortable as the keep at Dover, was nevertheless impressive. It was 11 meters in diameter, 40 meters in height and contained three stories. Its walls were also very thick, measuring 2.2 meters in width, and were pierced only by arrowloops. The keep could be entered on the ground level from inside the castle yard, but this entrance was protected by both a moat and a drawbridge. Other entrances into the second and third stories were connected to the ramparts.

Perhaps the most imposing defense of the castle came from the harshness of its terrain. In imitation of the Crusaders' castles, the castle at Najac was built on the summit of a steep hill, 200 meters high, which presented any would-be attacker with an intimidating target. Consequently, there is no record of this castle ever being captured or even besieged during the Middle Ages.[185]

However impressive the castles at Dover and Najac might have been, perhaps the best example of a European castle complex was Chateau Gaillard. Built in 1196-98 at Eure in Normandy at the behest of the English king, Richard the Lion-hearted, Chateau Gaillard stood on a precipitous cliff, over 90 meters high, overlooking the Seine River. The castle consisted of three baileys arranged in a line, each surrounded by a large wall. The outer bailey had a triangular plan with its apex facing the valley below. Its wall was fortified by one large circular tower at the apex and three other smaller semi-circular towers, and it was completely surrounded by a moat, 17 meters wide and 15 meters deep. The middle bailey was located across the moat to the northwest of the outer bailey. Its wall was also fortified by three semi-circular towers, located on the two corners facing the outer bailey and on its northern face, and by one square tower on its southern face. The inner bailey, which was enclosed completely by the middle bailey, had no wall towers, but was built on a precipice rising more than 12 meters above the middle bailey. It too was surrounded by a moat. Access to the middle and inner baileys was possible only over a drawbridge connected with the outer bailey. The outer bailey in turn had only a single entrance, on its northwest corner, which was guarded by a flanking tower, and was accessible only by a drawbridge.

The keep, which may have been a later addition, was constructed on the edge of the cliff, mostly within the inner bailey, but also forming a part of the southeast face of the wall. The keep was circular in shape, with walls 3 to 4 meters thick, except for one thicker side which jutted out almost like a beak towards the courtyard in the direction most exposed to attack. The keep also contained machicolations supported by buttresses built along the wall adding further protection. It contained two stories, but was probably used only as a barracks for the troops garrisoned at the castle. Other courtyard buildings, constructed along the

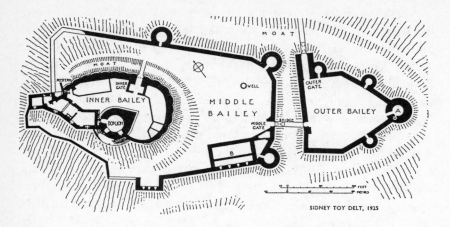

Castle complex: plan of the Chateau Gaillard.
[From Toy (1955).]

inside of the inner bailey wall, also served as barracks and other
domestic structures. The keep could only be entered by a long
flight of stairs which ascended from the courtyard to a guard room
in the upper story.

Chateau Gaillard was constructed very quickly, in the space
of only three years. It was also one of the most expensive castles
constructed during the Middle Ages, costing an estimated £21,203,
including the cost of materials and extraction, transportation, and
labor.

Because of the military conflict between Richard the Lion-
hearted and Philip Augustus over Normandy, Chateau Gaillard
was attacked less than five years after its construction. Philip
besieged the castle for more than a year and eventually captured
it, but not before suffering high casualties. It was also besieged
several times during the Hundred Years War: in 1418, the French
lost the castle to Henry V's English force after a six-month siege;
in 1420, the French regained the fortress, only to have it again
captured by the English before the end of the year; and finally,
in 1449, Charles VII restored it to French control.[186]

The castle complex style was so influential in the late twelfth
and thirteenth centuries that many castles built earlier, like that
at Najac, were added to in order to improve their outer defenses.
Such was the case with both the White Tower in London—which

continually saw its outer defenses rebuilt and strengthened, ultimately gaining two bailey walls, cylindrical flanking towers, a moat, a main gatehouse guarded by a barbican, and a series of lesser gateways—and the Counts of Flanders' castle at Ghent, which around 1180 had its early twelfth-century rectangular keep supplemented by an extensive crenellated outer wall fortified by several towers and a gateway reinforced with a barbican and machicolations. The Ghent Castle also added a water-filled moat surrounding the outer walls.[187]

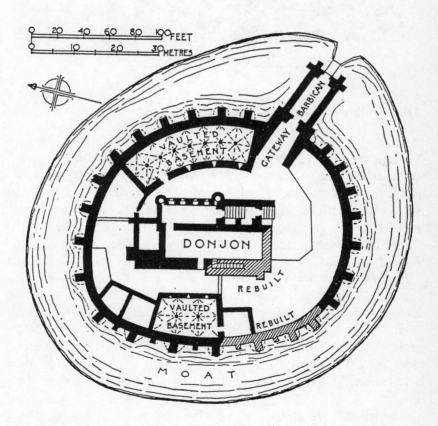

Castle complex: plan of the Count of Flanders' castle at Ghent. [From Toy (1955).]

Castle complex: The Count of Flanders' castle at Ghent.

The Welsh Castles of Edward I

Perhaps the most extensive medieval fortification building program came at the end of the thirteenth century when the English king, Edward I, constructed a number of castles in Wales in order to suppress rebellions there. Between 1277 and 1297 ten new royal and four new "lordship" castles were begun; added to these were three native Welsh castles which underwent major reconstruction. ("Lordship" castles were held by strong noble allies of Edward and were essentially under his control.) Edward's strategy in erecting these castles was certainly not new, as William the Conqueror had established the policy of facing insurgency and rebellion with fortifications. But unlike William's small and temporary motte-and-bailey castles, Edward I's castles were large, expensive, and permanent fortresses. They were also built in the complex style with powerful bailey walls fortified by a number of strong towers.[188]

Most of these castles were built in the north of Wales. These included the royal castles built at Flint, Rhuddlan, Ruthin, Hope, Conway, Caernarvon, Harlech, and Beaumaris; the four "lordship" castles at Hawarden, Denbigh, Holt, and Chirk; and two of the three reconstructed native castles, those at Dolwyddelan and Criccieth. Two other new castles, at Builth and Aberstwyth, and the other reconstruction, at Bere, were built in the middle of Wales. Five of the castles were also integrated with urban fortifications: Aberstwyth, Flint, Rhuddlan, Conway, and Caernarvon.

Because this was a systematic construction program, there was an attempt by Edward's architects, led by the famous Master James of St. George, to use a similar plan (a concentric plan).[189] Most were built in a quadrangular shape with two bailey walls, and all, with the exception of the castle at Flint, had no keep. The walls provided the primary defense for the castle, and these, especially the inner walls, were extremely large—Rhuddlan Castle's inner wall measured 10 meters high and 3 meters thick— and were fortified by ramparts, crenellations, and machicolations. As well, beyond, and sometimes between, the bailey walls were large moats.

To provide even further security, large circular towers, known as "drum towers," were built on the four corners of the inner wall with further towers added along the wall where needed. Towers were also used to guard the entrances to the castle, as only two castles, Harlech and Beaumaris, contained large gatehouses. (Harlech Castle had only one gatehouse, while the castle at Beaumaris had two.) As well, these towers served as the chief residential dwellings and barracks for the castles, although they were often supplemented by buildings built within the inner bailey which functioned as halls, kitchens, latrines, and stables.

Only when the terrain warranted a less fortified structure was there a deviation in the concentric design of these castles. For example, at Flint there was no need for an outer ring of walls as the castle was constructed near the Dee River and used its banks as a protective outer defensive curtain. And Rhuddlan Castle was built on top of a low bank next to the tidal river Clwyd and therefore only needed the protection of two bailey walls on three sides.

The two largest and strategically most important of the Welsh castles, Conway and Caernarvon, varied quite a bit from their other Welsh cousins, although this difference was seen only in the finished structure and not in the architectural thought on which it was based. Both of these castles remain relatively intact and are impressive fortifications.[190] The castle at Conway has been described by the distinguished historian, J. Goronwy Edwards, who devoted much of his career to its study, as "incomparably the most magnificent of Edward I's Welsh fortresses," and Caernarvon Castle is said to have elicited from Dr. Samuel Johnson the exclamation: "I did not think that there had been such buildings."

They were among the largest of English castles. Conway Castle enclosed an area of 91.5 by 30.5 meters with a town wall extending from the fortress for more than 1280 meters, and Caernarvon Castle's area measured 170 by 60 meters with an additional town wall of 731.52 meters.

In design these castles were much alike, as they shared the architectural genius of the Master of St. George. They were both irregularly-shaped castle complexes which adapted to and exploited the terrain on which they were built. The castle at Caernarvon was constructed on a low peninsula of rock projecting into the Menai Strait and situated between the Seiont and Cadmant Rivers, and Conway Castle was erected on an isolated spur of rock lying between the Conway River and its tributary, the Gyffin River. This latter site was judged to be of such strategic worth that the Cistercian Abbey of Gwynedd, which previously stood in its place, was appropriated and removed for the construction of the castle. Moreover, because of the natural defensibility of these sites, both castles did not require an outer bailey wall.

As with the other Welsh castles of Edward I, the castles at Caernarvon and Conway relied chiefly on their high and thick walls for defense. At Caernarvon, these walls measured 4.6 meters thick and 17 meters high. The walls were further fortified with arrowloops, crenellations, and ramparts. Caernarvon Castle even had two extra levels of firing galleries built into the walls below the rampart to provide three ranks of fire against any attacker.

As was conventional with all thirteenth-century castle complexes, huge towers lined the bailey walls. Conway Castle contained eight massive drum towers, four on each face, measuring 12.2 meters in diameter, with turrets added to the top of the four surrounding the inner bailey. At Caernarvon, there were nine large towers. However, they were polygonal, in a style which some historians claim was imitative of the fifth-century Theodosian Wall at Constantinople. Nevertheless, despite this minor stylistic difference, the towers at both of these castles provided flanking fire which succeeded in exposing all points on the bailey wall to intense crossfire. The towers also served as the residences for the castles' occupants.

Of the towers, none was more impressive than the largest one built at Caernarvon. Known as the Eagle's Tower, this powerful structure guarded the most vulnerable spot on the bailey wall, at the confluence of the two rivers, and was for all intents and purposes the keep of the castle, complete with several chambers, two chapels, and an escape gate, should the inhabitants of the castle discreetly wish to flee.

The entrances to these two castles received the traditional heavily fortified security. At Conway, the two gateways were each guarded by double drum towers with accompanying barbicans, while at Caernarvon two of the three entrances were guarded by elaborate gatehouses, named the King's and Queen's Gate, which

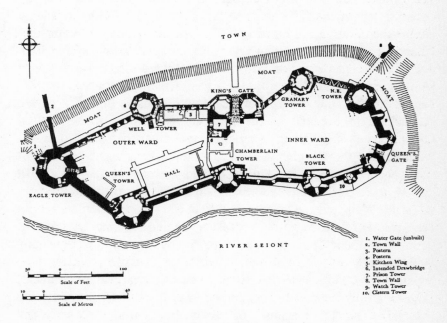

1. Water Gate (unbuilt)
2. Town Wall
3. Postern
4. Postern
5. Kitchen Wing
6. Intended Drawbridge
7. Prison Tower
8. Town Wall
9. Watch Tower
10. Cistern Tower

Castle complex: plan of the Caernarvon Castle.
[From Taylor (1986).]

were reminiscent of those built at Harlech and Beaumaris. A third entrance, leading from the river and thus known as Water Gate, did not have a gatehouse, but did lead to a wall, 4 meters thick, which jutted out into the river protecting the entrance's dock.

The yards of both castles were divided longitudinally into two wards of unequal sizes. At Caernarvon, there appears to have been no logical reason for this division, and in fact the dividing wall is quite thin, but at Conway, this separated the royal apartments, which formed the inner bailey (measuring 24.4 by 21.4 meters), from the rest of the castle's great hall and barracks. Furthermore, because both fortresses were built to house royalty, they have more ornamentation and decoration than the conventional medieval castle; Conway Castle was even completely whitewashed.

Perhaps the only significant difference between the castles at Conway and Caernarvon, besides the shape of the towers, was the time it took to construct each fortification. Conway Castle was quickly built, erected in five seasons of construction between 1283 and 1287, while Caernarvon Castle took much longer, erected between 1293 and 1323. Consequently, the castle at Caernarvon, at an estimated £20,000, cost much more to complete, than did the castle at Conway, which cost an estimated £14,086.

The Welsh castles of Edward I constituted the last large castle building project of the Middle Ages. Costing between £62,000 and £80,000, the enterprise was too expensive to be repeated elsewhere in England or on the continent. Most of the cost of these castles was supplied by the royal treasury, the "forinsec" accounts of the King's Wardrobe, a sum which was for the most part not available to the kings of Europe embroiled in the almost constant warfare of the fourteenth and fifteenth centuries.

The Welsh castles also took a long time to be completed, with construction on the castles at Caernarvon and Beaumaris extending into the 1330s. They were built by Savoyard artisans, especially imported by Edward I for their expertise in castle building, who controlled a large army of English masons, carpenters, diggers, and other workmen. In 1277 no fewer than 1845 diggers, 790 sawyers, and 320 masons worked on the castles of Chester and Flint; in 1295, 400 masons, 200 quarrymen, and at least 2,000 laborers worked on the castle at Beaumaris.[191] These too were luxuries impossible to repeat during the next two centuries. More importantly, it is uncertain whether the expense of skill, time, and money on these castles was necessary or valid. The Welsh insurgencies had ended long before the completion of all the castles, and although no further rebellions occurred there, it is impossible to know whether the fortifications were the determining factor in the termination of these insurrections.

Medieval society was also on the brink of change. In the thirteenth century, urbanization was rapidly occurring; the new cities could not be sufficiently protected by rural castles designed for the guarding of sparsely populated agricultural lands. Even the powerful castles at Conway and Caernarvon would have been unable to protect their urban populations had they not been accompanied by a large, heavily fortified town wall.

Furthermore, with this rapid urbanization came a new societal class, one which rose above the lower or peasant class but did not have the inherited privileges of nobility: a "middle class." Some of these people grew very wealthy, and they too desired fortified dwellings to protect their families and possessions. They did not need the extra defensive structures which comprised traditional castle complexes; instead, they desired more comfort, a luxury traditional medieval castles had given up to provide extra defense. These new castles were little more than fortified residences. This then was the future of medieval fortifications: town walls and fortified residences.

Urban Fortifications and Fortified Residences

To say that castles were not constructed during the fourteenth and fifteenth centuries would be misleading. Castles in the theoretical sense of the word continued to be built well into the early modern period, especially in those areas threatened by foreign invasion or civil war. But the perception of castles as fortified structures did change. No longer did medieval castle builders deem it necessary or even desirous to construct the heavily fortified complex which had been developed in the Holy Land during the Crusades and which then was extended to Europe.

Moreover, there was some question as to whether the castle complexes had truly fulfilled the defensive purposes for which they had been constructed. For example, within five years of its completion, even the powerful Chateau Gaillard fell to enemy forces after a siege of less than one year. Its defensive value continued to remain in doubt, as it was besieged and captured no fewer than three more times before the end of the Middle Ages.[192] Other castles met similar fates. At other times, enemy forces merely avoided the castles knowing that their garrisons were often not strong enough, or foolish enough, to leave their protective walls to pursue an evading army.[193]

Perhaps this is why so many earlier castles fell into disrepair by the fourteenth and fifteenth centuries. Everywhere in Europe during those two centuries there were reports of weak and derelict castles. Several examples show this. In 1341, Criccieth Castle in England was reported to be so weak that its doors could scarcely hold up to the wind, and this despite late thirteenth-century repairs to the structure.[194] In 1405, the ducal castle of Vannes in Brittany, known as La Motte, was in such disrepair that its walls were being used as a quarry for other construction projects in the town.[195] A similar use was found for the walls of the large castle at Worcester which had fallen out of use in the thirteenth century and was being quarried to repair the town walls in the fifteenth century.[196] In fact, the ruination of many once strong and powerful castles in England had become so evident in the early sixteenth century that when John Leland made a tour of the island he became obsessed with the plight of the once powerful and now derelict castles. He found himself unable to understand how so many monuments of medieval military strength had fallen into such disrepair. Of the 258 castles whose condition Leland comments on, 30 were partially derelict with 137 completely in ruin. Only 91 were still being used.[197]

Fortified Residences

Although castles continued to be built, castle builders began more and more to disregard the defensive aspects of the structure and to emphasize comfort and luxury in their place. A late medieval castle first had to be architecturally beautiful. No longer would a simple, plain keep or a castle complex hidden behind huge and ugly walls suffice to meet the aesthetic demands of its owner.[198] Even those fortresses built ostensibly as defenses against invasion, like Bodiam, Cooling, and Queensborough in England and Clisson, Rambures, Hunandaye, and Vincennes in France did not sacrifice comfort for defense.[199]

The outside of these new castles needed to be decorative, original in design, and opulent enough to impress the observer of the extraordinary wealth and high social standing of the inhabitants. Walls were often capped with decorative cornices, and the windows and mouldings were embellished with lavish sculpture and trim. Buttresses, crenellations, barbicans, and ramparts became more beautiful than functional. Moats, now often filled with water, included lilies and other water flora. Some even included a flock of swans or other water birds. Many castles even had hunting parks.[200]

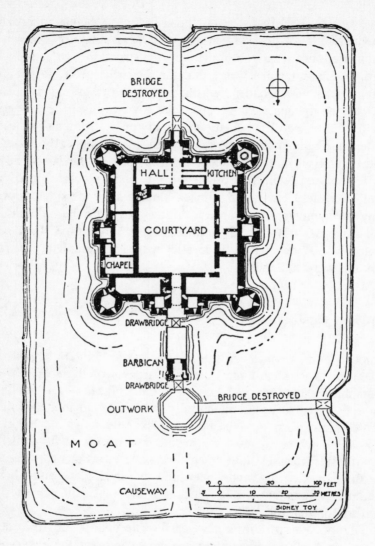

Fortified residence: plan of Bodiam Castle.
[From Toy (1955).]

The insides of these castles were also elegant. Halls were
large enough to accommodate banquets and other celebratory functions. They also were better lit than earlier castles with more and
larger windows built into the castle walls. Apartments were larger
and more comfortable, each usually having its own garderobe,

fireplace, and latrine. These apartments were also more numerous than in earlier castles, with as many as 40 and 50 being included in the larger residences.[201]

Other chambers, mostly new to castles, also exhibited the change in castle building attitudes. Most of the fortified residences had chapels, and because the chaplain had become a regular member of the household, they also included his lodgings.[202] Also, since these castles served as the administrative centers for their owner's business enterprises, they all contained elaborate offices for the lord and his staff.[203] As well, while garrisons of troops were most often missing from the late medieval castle, they had in most cases been replaced by an army of domestic servants, all of whose quarters were included in the building. Finally, as some castle owners were responsible for the administering of justice in their lands, their fortified residences often had small prisons located in the basements or lower levels.[204]

Defense was not entirely forgotten. Some rural fortified residences continued to be built in inaccessible places, and some bailey walls were still large, crenellated, and lined with towers. Entrances remained protected by barbicans and large gatehouses. In addition, large moats, far wider and deeper than earlier castle ditches, added to the overall defensibility of the building.[205] At the same time, there was the addition of gunports in many late fourteenth- and fifteenth-century castles. Still, most of these late medieval fortresses were but small imitations of earlier fortifications, and even those meant to withstand foreign attack or to inhibit civil war could not rival the castles built in the twelfth and thirteenth centuries.[206]

There were two styles of rural fortified residences built in the late Middle Ages. The first, and less numerous, resembled the earlier castle complex, although it was neither as large nor as defensible. However, like its earlier exemplars, it did consist of large bailey walls lined with towers, which sometimes enclosed a keep. Perhaps the most famous example of this type of fortification was built at Bodiam in England between 1386 and 1390. Erected by Sir Edward Dalyngrigge for the purpose of defending the region against a French assault, the castle attempted to combine the defensive qualities of earlier castle complexes with the comfort required by its aristocratic owner. Its walls were built in a rectangular shape with a projecting round tower on each corner. The east, west, and south walls were protected by square intermediate towers, with the southern intermediate tower also serving as a secondary entrance. In the middle of the north wall stood a large gatehouse flanked by two square towers guarding the primary entrance into the residence. This gatehouse, which was machicolated on the parapet level and contained gunports, held three sets of barriers each consisting of a portcullis and heavy door. Perhaps the most defensive feature of the castle was its large, water-filled moat which completely surrounded the structure. It was traversed either by a single L-shaped causeway which contained three drawbridges and a barbican leading into the main gatehouse, or by a narrower straight causeway with a single drawbridge into the secondary entrance.

There was no keep at Bodiam Castle. The owner's residence ringed a rectangular courtyard in a two-story series of apartments and offices which included a large hall, kitchen, buttery, pantry, and chapel. Some military quarters were also included, but these were quite small and may have only served to house Dalyngrigge's personal retinue rather than a garrison of regular troops. Although not as extravagant as some late medieval castles, the domestic quarters at Bodiam were quite comfortable. All chambers were quite large and well-lit and each contained its own garderobe. The most elaborate of these suites, located on the main floor near the gatehouse, was reserved for Dalyngrigge himself. There were several other apartments which provided lodging not only to Dalyngrigge's own family and servants, but also to a large number of guests.[207]

Another example of this type of late medieval fortification was built at Pierrefonds in France. Constructed at nearly the same time as Bodiam Castle, between 1390 and 1400, this castle served as the primary residence of Louis d'Orleans, Duke of Valois and brother of King Charles VI. Like Bodiam, Pierrefonds imitated the earlier castle complexes with high walls and projecting round corner towers. Round towers, 38 meters in height and named after classical heroes, also projected from the middle of each wall. It seems, however, that the builder of this castle had been much more conscious of defense. Although there was no large moat, Pierrefonds Castle was built on a promontory of land protected

Fortified residence: Bodiam Castle, Sussex.

on three sides by steep escarpments and surrounded by a thin
outer wall. At the same time, entrance into it was gained only
by climbing a ramp, entering a gate in the outer wall, traversing
a narrow terrace along the entire length of the inner wall and
crossing under a barbican and across a drawbridge.

It is evident that the Valois castle at Pierrefonds was perceived
to be a defensive structure, but, like its English counterpart, it
also emphasized the rich comfort expected by a powerful brother
of the king. It too contained a number of richly decorated, large
suites and halls ringing an almost-rectangular courtyard. But unlike
Bodiam Castle, Pierrefonds also contained a many-storied square
keep which jutted into the courtyard from the southern wall.[208]

A second, more numerous style of late medieval rural fortification was the tower house. Here the imitation was not of the
castle complex, but of the earlier rectangular castle keep. In essence, the tower houses of the late Middle Ages were, as the
name implies, residences built in a tower. Although there were
many variations, they were generally rectangular in shape and
stood two to five stories high with an area of between 6 and 18
meters square. They were also permanent residences, containing
several apartments and other chambers which were stacked on top
of each other. These rooms were all well-lit by many large windows and were elaborate in their size and decoration. Moreover,
although less numerous than the number of suites in the fortified
residence built around a courtyard, the quarters were sufficient
for the needs of most aristocratic owners and their servants.

Defense in these fortifications was almost entirely neglected.
Except for their size, crenellated roofs, and the often inaccessible
terrain on which they were built, these fortified residences provided little protection against an enemy attack.[209] However, as
they were frequently constructed in areas of potential warfare,
along the border of Scotland and in the duchies of Brittany, Picardy, and Gascony in France, their defensive worth may be underestimated.[210]

Again two examples, one in England and one in France,
should suffice to illustrate this style of fortified residence. In England, there may have been no finer example of a tower house
than that built in 1433-38 by Ralph Lord Cromwell at Tattershall
in Lincolnshire. It was a rectangular structure built of brick with

a stone base and stone dressings and measuring 18.3 by 24.4 meters in area and 36.6 meters in height. Inside there were five stories, including a basement. Each story consisted of a richly decorated and well-lit large hall, 12.2 by 6.1 meters in size, with several smaller chambers leading off it.

Defensibility at Tattershall seems almost non-existent. The structure was tall and contained four crenellated octagonal corner turrets rising from the roof, but the construction in brick with three poorly guarded entrances leading onto the main floor displayed little concern on the part of the builder for defense against attack. This is further shown by the lack of a kitchen in the main edifice, indicating that the cooking was done in another building apart from the fortified residence itself. The castle thus had little chance of surviving a prolonged siege.[211]

In France, an example of the tower house may be found at Rambures in Picardy. The Rambures Castle, begun in 1421 but not finished until 1470, was not a large fortress. Rather than being rectangular in shape, it was polygonal and consisted of six round towers attached to each other by a series of doorways. The four corner towers, more complete than the inner two, measured 12 meters in diameter and rose to a height of 20 meters, although when considering the depth of the surrounding moat, the entire height of the building was 35 meters. Each tower also had a conical roof and was connected to the others by a rampart. Inside the castle, there were six complete, but short stories, with two below the level of the ditch. The chambers, encompassing the entire area of each tower level, were large, but they were not as elegant or well-decorated as those of other tower houses.

At the same time, Rambures may have been better prepared for defense than its English counterpart, for not only was it surrounded by a large moat, it had also fairly thick walls (3 meters thick) with gunports added at the second floor level. As well, each of the six towers was easily able to shut itself off from the others and thus provide better protection for its inhabitants.[212]

During the late Middle Ages, fortified residences were also built in towns, where wealthy individuals, both noble and non-noble, desired a security for their families and possessions similar to that of the rural castle. These urban castles were like their rural cousins in many ways. For one thing, their functions were

similar. Although the urban fortified residence was not expected
to withstand a foreign invasion, the large amount of urban unrest
and the local governments' inability to keep the peace necessitated
some protection for its wealthy owner and his family. As well,
urban castles often served as centers of the political, economic,
and social power of the prosperous towns.[213]

Urban fortified residences were also built in a style similar to
the rural fortified residences, with some imitating tower houses
and others built around a courtyard. In most cases these urban
castles were much smaller than their rural models; however, when
built for a prince or another local governor, an urban fortified
residence might have been as large or larger than a similar fortification built in the country. For example, the residence of the
Sforza Dukes in Milan was a large walled fortress lined with
towers and surrounded by a moat (traversed by no fewer than 62
drawbridges). It also included a barracks large enough to house
between 800 and 1200 mercenary soldiers.[214]

Like their rural counterparts, the builders of urban fortified
residences also showed a preference for comfort over defense.
Clearly, the main purpose was to house the owner's family in a
style which indicated a wealthy and prosperous social standing.
Large and opulent lodgings, kitchens, halls, and servants' quarters
were all found within these castle walls. At the same time, many
urban fortified residences also included offices, shops, and ware-
houses in support of the owner's business.[215]

Even if their owners had desired, most urban fortified residences could not have duplicated the defenses which protected
rural fortifications. Because of the smaller confines of the town,
few of these urban fortresses could be guarded by outside walls,
moats, barbicans, or ramparts. However, this did not mean that
defense was totally neglected. Indeed, most urban fortified residences were protected by fortified gates and guarded entrances,
towers, gunports, and even holes in the walls and ceilings of
entrances through which boiling oil and pitch could be poured on
attacking enemies.[216]

Town Walls

Fortified residences were not the primary fortification construction of the late Middle Ages. This was instead the town wall. Before the fourteenth and fifteenth centuries, few new town walls had been constructed. Some towns relied on the old Roman walls to meet their defensive needs, while other urban areas were often only protected by a ditch and earthen rampart.[217] In Germany in 1200, for example, there were only twelve walled towns, and nine of these had old Roman walls.[218]

These fortifications seem to have met the needs of the towns, at least until the thirteenth century when they began to grow in number, population, and wealth. Even then, towns were often allowed to grow beyond their older defenses, forming unprotected suburbs.[219] Even Paris, the largest and most populated town of western Europe, went without a complete enclosure until the mid-fourteenth century.[220] By then, however, town governments began to recognize the need for new fortifications. Local violence, civil war, and foreign invasion all threatened the security and prosperity of those living within their boundaries. The answer was either to repair and extend old Roman walls, or, if this was not possible, to build new ones.[221]

At first this was done without much cost, using only the meagre resources of the town treasury. Masonry was salvaged from old buildings, lands were confiscated "for the public good," and the goods and services of many within the town, especially masons, were levied for the construction of these walls.[222] However, in many places this was insufficient to build the strong defenses most towns required. Usually extra funds were needed to completely enclose the town with a fortified wall. In these cases, money could be obtained by an added taxation of the townspeople. The walls at Caernarvon and Conway were paid for by a levy on goods sold within the town, and in Nantes, Rennes, and Fougères, the construction of the walls was paid for by a tax on alcoholic beverages.[223] Funds for building town walls also could be granted by the king or another governing person. The walls of Canterbury were built in part by a murage grant from the archbishop; and in 1367, the king of France allowed one-quarter of all royal taxes raised in a town building walls to be used for that construction.[224]

During the late Middle Ages so many towns built protective walls that by the end of the fifteenth century, few notable towns were without a sizeable fortification surrounding them. In England alone, perhaps the least populated medieval kingdom in western Europe, it is estimated that between 108 and 200 towns acquired walls during this period. The total number of walled towns in France, Germany, Italy, Spain, and the Low Countries was undoubtedly much higher.[225]

The principal defensive feature of these fortifications was the wall itself. Those surrounding London were 10.67 meters high, Caernarvon 8.53 meters high, Conway 7.32 meters high and Carcassone between 7 and 8 meters high.[226] They were very wide, most measuring nearly 2 meters in thickness.[227] They were also often extremely long. Those surrounding French towns were usually more than 2000 meters in length, with the walls of Amiens, Chartres, and Provins measuring more than 3000 meters long and the walls of Rouen measuring more than 4000 meters.[228] The town walls in England were often shorter, with the walls at Conway and Caernarvon measuring only 1280 and 731.52 meters respectively, although larger towns, like York and London, had walls which rivaled the length of those in France. The walls surrounding York were more than 4800 meters in length.[229] The areas enclosed were impressive. The walls at Yarmouth enclosed an area of nearly 54 hectares, at Winchester an area of nearly 56 hectares, and at Rennes an area of 62 hectares.[230]

Almost all town walls were crenellated and had ramparts wide enough to support archers or gunners.[231] Some walls were doubled,[232] and many were surrounded by wide and deep ditches which were frequently filled with caltraps, thick metal spikes, and other hindrances.[233] All of these features added to their defensibility, but the most important defensive addition were the towers which stood at regular intervals along the walls and the fortified gates which limited access to the town enclosure.

Most town walls incorporated a large number of towers placed at intervals of 40 to 60 meters. The walls at Canterbury had 24 towers, at Conway 21 towers, at Carcassone 25 towers, and at Southampton 29 towers.[234] These towers had various shapes, although most were circular, horseshoe, or square-shaped.[235] They were also often much taller than their walls, sometimes as high

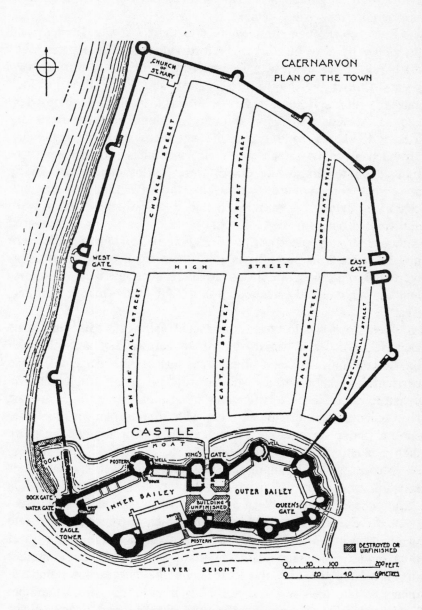

Town walls: plan of Caernarvon Castle and town walls.
[From Taylor (1986).]

as 20 to 30 meters taller, as at Carcassone, and were filled with arrow-slits and gunloops.[236] This allowed them to provide flanking fire against most siege attacks.

Entrance through these walls into the town was limited, and then only by way of a strongly fortified gate. These gates were often few in number, with Caernarvon entered only through two gates, Conway through three gates, and York through four gates,[237] although some towns with large markets or industries, such as Ghent and Southampton, needed and had more entrances.[238] Like castle gates, the entrances in town walls also provided a strong defense for their inhabitants. Some gates were flanked by towers, while others were towers themselves. Many were pierced by numerous arrow-slits and, after the late fourteenth century, gunloops, and most included a barbican. Doors were constructed out of heavy wood bolstered by iron bars and covered with leather to protect against fire. Placed in front of these were one or more iron portcullises.[239] Moreover, because these gates were the only part of the fortification seen by most travelers, many were opulently decorated as a sign of the town's prosperity.[240]

Most town walls were constructed using the same materials as castles—battered ashlar against an earthen rampart—although by the late fourteenth and fifteenth centuries some walls, like those surrounding the town of Hull, were built using bricks.[241] The construction of these fortifications often took a long time, at least five decades for most town walls, with some urban fortifications, such as those surrounding Coventry and Canterbury, taking more than a century before completion.[242]

Most town walls impressed late medieval observers with their strength and their defensive capabilities.[243] However, there is some debate among modern historians as to their defensive effectiveness. Some claim that the walls which surrounded most late medieval urban areas were weak defensively and failed to protect their towns' inhabitants. This is certainly seen in the large number of walled towns which fell to the numerous sieges and bombardments of late medieval warfare.[244] It is also recognized that, because the cost of these fortifications was so high, some towns were unable to complete their walls, or to extend them to cover their suburbs,[245] and those that did were unable to keep them in good condition, with the walls of Alnwick, Richmond, Warwick, Southampton, Chester, and even York falling into ruin before 1500. Indeed, Southampton's walls were in such poor condition in 1460 that a contemporary writer described them as "so feeble that they may not resist any gunshot, and so thin that no man may stand on them to make any resistance or defense."[246] Even Christine de Pizan, writing in the early fifteenth century, was forced to admit that most walls built to defend the towns of her time were not as good as those built by the Romans centuries before.[247]

Other modern historians are less critical of these fourteenth- and fifteenth-century town walls. Some believe that many towns did adequately defend themselves against the numerous sieges and bombardments of the later Middle Ages, forcing their attackers often to withdraw without conquering them.[248] Furthermore, the fact that many town walls continued in strength into the sixteenth and seventeenth centuries, and indeed remain the principal fortification of those centuries, does seem to denote a defensive achievement that cannot be criticized too harshly.[249]

The Influence of Gunpowder Weapons

One final question should be asked before ending a discussion on medieval fortifications: what effect did gunpowder weapons have on the construction of castles and town walls in the late Middle Ages? By the end of the fourteenth century, it was apparent that gunpowder weaponry would change siege tactics and with them fortification construction. From shortly after their invention, gunpowder weapons began to be used in sieges. They were possibly used in 1340 at the siege of Tournai and were certainly present at the siege of Calais in 1346-47. But on both of these occasions their use was minor in comparison to other siege machines.

Still, gunpowder weapons continued to be used to attack fortifications, and by the end of the century they began to have some successes in breaching them. In 1374, the French used them to bring down the town walls of Saint-Saveur-le-Vicomte; in 1377, Philip the Bold, Duke of Burgundy, used guns to break the fortress of Odruik; and in 1382, the rebellious Ghentenaars used their gunpowder artillery to breach the walls of the town of

Oudenaarde. In the beginning of the fifteenth century, no castle or town wall was safe from bombardment, and castles, such as Berwick in 1405, and towns, such as Harfleur in 1415, were easily taken by gunpowder weapons. Sieges were so quickly brought to a conclusion by gunpowder bombardment by the middle of the century, that where it once could take more than a year to capture a heavily fortified and well stocked town or castle, now it might take less than one month. Perhaps the most famous defeat by bombardment was the city of Constantinople, whose great walls were said to have fallen in 1453 to the continual attack of one large bombard, known as Urban's Bombard after its Hungarian builder, which was so large and took so long to cool down before reloading that it could only be fired six times a day.

Naturally, this threat of attack by gunpowder weapons influenced those responsible for the construction or maintenance of fortifications. It was quickly realized that traditional medieval castles and town walls with their tall, flat surfaces were easy targets for guns, especially for the large calibre bombards so frequently used in sieges. The tall walls of medieval fortifications had been built to withstand weapons which could not inflict the continual barrage on a single area as could the new gunpowder weapons, and in fact the weight and relative thinness of the base of these walls invariably made it easier to penetrate these fortifications.

It was both too expensive and time-consuming to rebuild all fortifications to meet the attacks of gunpowder weapons. Therefore, the initial move was to outfit these fortifications with guns as a defense. Gunpowder weapons began to be delivered to castles and town walls by the middle of the fourteenth century, but guns mounted on the tops of castle and town walls made little sense as they could not effectively defend the wall below them, an area which was most likely to be attacked.[250] This meant that the wall itself needed to be pierced with gunports so that defending fire could be more directly aimed at attacking artillery. This may have occurred as early as 1347 when the gate at the castle of Bioule was recorded as having been defended on its first floor by two men firing cannons,[251] but if so the idea did not become popular in England until at least 1365 and in France until after 1380. Germany, Italy, and Spain may not have constructed gunports in their fortifications until even later than this.

Once it did become popular in England and in France, however, the number of fortifications, both castles and town walls, which received gunports multiplied rapidly. In England, gunports were added to Quarr Abbey on the Isle of Wight in 1365-66 (perhaps their earliest English use), to Queensborough Castle in 1373, to Assheton's Tower at Porchester in 1379, to Carisbrooke Castle in 1379-80, to the Canterbury town wall in 1380, to Cooling Castle in 1381, to Southampton Castle in 1382-86, to Saltwood Castle in 1383, to Norwich town wall in 1385, to Bodiam Castle in 1386, and to the Winchester town wall in 1390.[252] In France, gunports were added more slowly and in fewer numbers. Besides those which may have existed at Bioule Castle, it is only the gunports in the town wall of Mont-Saint-Michel and at the castles of Blanquefort and Saint-Malo which can be confirmed to have been built before 1400.[253] Others were not built until after 1412, with the large towns of Paris and Rennes receiving their gunports in 1415 and 1418 respectively.[254] However, gunport construction in France continued until 1480, while in England it declined drastically after 1420.[255]

In the late fourteenth century most gunports were shaped like inverted keyholes with circular openings for guns below long vertical slits. This may indicate that they were initially nothing more than arrow-slits adapted for gunpowder weapons by adding a circular opening to the bottom, as fifteenth-century gunports were usually built without the vertical slit; however, some architectural historians contend that the slits were there merely to facilitate the sighting of the weapon.[256] Gunports were also quite small: the slits ranged in length between 381 and 813 millimeters and in width between 65 and 152 millimeters, while the circular openings ranged between 127 and 305 millimeters in diameter. They were also built near to the ground, generally no higher than one meter from the inside floor.[257]

The number and distribution of gunports around the fortifications varied greatly. Sometimes there was only one or two gunports in a fortress, while other fortifications, especially those built in the fifteenth century contained a much larger number. For example, Raglan Castle, built c.1450, contained no fewer than 32 gunports.[258] Most also were located in the fortification's gates and towers. This allowed them to provide some flanking fire along the wall and causeways, although such flanking fire may have been of limited effect, as most gunports allowed less than a 45° angle of fire.[259]

The small size of these gunports meant that they did not allow the use of large guns for defense of the fortification. This is seen also in the small size of the gunport embrasures on which these guns were mounted, most of which were less than 70 centimeters long. This allowed only the smallest of mounted gunpowder weapons, probably culverins, or hand-held guns to be fired from these gunports.[260]

Gunports could not supply sufficient defense against most gunpowder artillery bombardments. Although defensive guns provided some protection against enemy gunfire, the height of castles and town walls still afforded an ideal target to any force attacking with guns, especially as those guns by the early fifteenth century had evolved into more powerful and more accurate siege weapons. Other methods of improving defense were needed.

Some towns and castles tried to meet the threat of gunshot bombardment by thickening their walls with piles of earth behind them. While this did protect the walls from being easily breached in some instances, it was not always successful. The earthen rampart exerted a heavy pressure on the wall and frequently weakened the masonry instead of strengthening it. As Philip, Duke of Clèves, noted at the end of the fifteenth century, "whenever the guns batter the wall, the earth tumbles down with the masonry, which makes it all the easier for the enemy to climb into the breach."[261]

Other fortifications tried to thicken their walls with more masonry instead of earth. Or they added a sloping *glacis* of masonry to the front of their walls to produce glancing gunshots rather than direct impact on the flat wall. However, both of these additions were very expensive and thus not generally obtainable for many towns or castle owners whose resources were usually quite limited.[262] Still others tried to increase the size of the ditches surrounding their fortifications, noting the relative security against bombardment of large moated fortresses, like Bodiam, Kenilworth or Caerphilly Castles, but this too was more expensive than most towns or castles were able to afford.[263]

Some builders tried to increase the defense of castles and town walls by adding new fortifications to the existing defensive structures and then filling them with defensive artillery. In essence the theory behind these defensive additions was the same as that of gunports, facing guns with guns, except that they were separate from the castles and town walls themselves, and thus their defeat did not necessarily mean the collapse of a fortification. Generally, these were built in two styles. The first style was the low earth-work defense, known as a *boulevard*, which was generally placed before a vulnerable gate or wall. Its defense derived from its large number of guns (which increased the amount of defensive fire-power), its low height (which made it easier to fire) and its earthen walls (which more readily absorbed the impact of stone and metal cannonballs). It seems to have been particularly popular in mid-fifteenth-century France among fortresses which were more open to gunpowder artillery bombardment.[264]

boulevard

The second was the artillery tower. This was a newly constructed tower, again filled with a large number of gunpowder weapons, which was added to the most exposed part of a fortress. Its purpose was nearly the same as the *boulevard* both to increase the amount of defensive firepower and to add flanking fire to a vulnerable wall or gate, but it was generally much taller and constructed in stone. The artillery tower was also usually round in shape to provide no flat surfaces to enemy gunfire. It was the preferred artillery fortification added to English castles and town walls, and was in fact built into the sixteenth century. *Boulevard* construction ceased for the most part by the end of the fifteenth century.[265]

The artillery tower may have been the impetus behind the construction of larger round-shaped castles at Queensborough in England and at Rambures in France. However, only Rambures' dates (1421-1470) allow for a construction possibly conscious of the power of gunpowder weaponry.[266] Queensborough Castle, on the other hand, was constructed in the 1360s, which may have been before the time it was recognized that round walls were a viable defense against gunpowder artillery bombardment. Still, it is known that guns were an important early defense of the castle, together with non-gunpowder artillery, and that they were fired off in honor of a visit by Edward III in 1373. This may mean

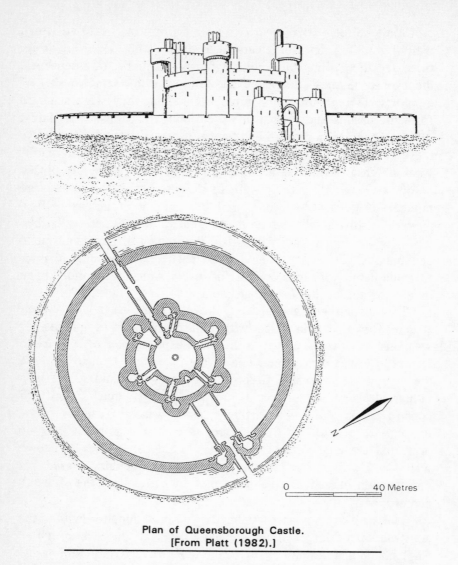

Plan of Queensborough Castle.
[From Platt (1982).]

that the builders of this castle did indeed perceive the anti-bom-
bardment defensive capabilities of this fortification style, although
if they in fact did it was not similarly recognized by other castle
builders of the late fourteenth and fifteenth centuries as its style
was never copied.[267]

    None of these additions to existing fortifications provided a
"complete" security against gunpowder artillery attack, and by the

end of the fifteenth century it was recognized that traditional medieval fortifications, even with a number of additions, could not provide an adequate defense against a gunpowder weapon attack on their inhabitants. A more elaborate system of fortifications was needed, a system whose walls could withstand the constant impact of stone or metal cannonballs while at the same time offering its own forceful gunshot bombardment against those besiegers.

Known as the *trace italienne*, because of its appearance in numerous late fifteenth- and sixteenth-century Italian city-states, this system of artillery fortifications originated in Leon Battista Alberti's *De re aedificatoria*, written in the 1440s (although it was not popular until after its 1485 printing). Alberti contends:

1) that fortification walls facing gunpowder weapons should be both short enough to easily see the ground below them and wide enough to withstand the impact of cannonballs,

2) that artillery towers projecting at an angle beyond the walls should be added to the fortification—this would not only protect the fortification itself but also keep offensive guns at bay and cover blind spots along the fortress walls,

3) that angled bastions projecting out at regular intervals from the fortress walls be built giving increased flanking cross-fire along the surface of those walls,

4) that as time passed further refinements should be added to the fortification: wide and deep ditches along the walls to keep enemy artillery at a distance and to cut down on mining with detached casements or bastions (called *ravelins*) built beyond those ditches to further impede enemy artillery attacks, and

5) that extensions should be built to these fortifications, complete with crownworks or hornworks, to protect outside strategic areas.[268]

The *trace italienne* completely changed the future of fortification construction. No longer would tall castles and town walls be built as defenses against foreign invasion or domestic rebellion. Already by the end of the fifteenth century, the Italian fortifications of Sarazana, Avezzano, and Ostia Antica began to adapt Alberti's ideas in their construction. However, it was not until after 1494 when Charles VIII's invasion of Italy would show the vulnerability of Italian strongholds to artillery bombardment that most *trace italienne* artillery fortifications began to appear, and they would continue to be built into the nineteenth century.[269]

Notes

1   Wright (1964):27.

2   Ferrill (1985):26-28.

3   Ferrill (1985):28-30.

4   See Ferrill (1985):44-53, 170-75 for discussions on the fortification problems
     of Egypt and Greece. See Wood (1985):114-18 for a discussion of the
     destruction of Troy VIIa, believed by many historians and archaeologists
     to be the Troy of Homeric legend.

5   K. White (1984):83 and Fino (1970):29.

6   Luttwak (1976):55-80.

7   There are a number of good and rather lengthy descriptions of Hadrian's
     Wall. I have used those found in Forde-Johnston (1977):59-64 and Toy
     (1955):6-49.

8   Luttwak (1976):68.

9   Lander (1984):5.

10   Fino (1970):56-63; Johnson (1983):9-27; and Butler (1959):26-27.

11   Johnson (1983):13-14.

12   Johnson (1983):20.

13   Forde-Johnston (1977):65-66.

14   Luttwak (1976):170-88; Petrikovits (1971):179-82; and Cary and Scullard
     (1975):534.

15   Luttwak (1976):160-61 and Petrikovits (1971):188-89.

16   Forde-Johnston (1977):66-69 and Johnson (1983):201-07.

17   Lander (1984):168-69.

18   Johnson (1983):82-225; Butler (1959):28-50; Lander (1984):168-262;
     Petrikovits (1971):189-218; Luttwak (1976):159-70; and Fino (1970):56-63.

19   As quoted in Contamine (1984):6. See also Petrikovits (1971):184-88.

20   E.A. Thompson (1952):122-23.

21 Contamine (1984):6. See also Johnson (1983):245-61 and Lander (1984):263-293.

22 Toy (1955):52-54.

23 On the barbarian invasions see Bury (1967); Lot (1961); E.A. Thompson (1982); Wolfram (1988); and Geary (1988).

24 Zosimus is quoted in Contamine (1984):6-7. For *De rebus bellicis* see E.A. Thompson (1952):112-13. Only the *Notitia dignitatum* claims that the Romans had more troops along the borders during the invasions than during Diocletian's reign, and its credibility on this calculation has been attacked rather forcefully. See Contamine (1984):7-9.

25 Wolfram (1988):141.

26 Wolfram (1988):151-55.

27 Bury (1967):127.

28 Bury (1967):147-49.

29 Bachrach (1972):9, 11-12.

30 Bachrach (1972):21-22, 26, 53-54, 55, 59, 60-61.

31 E.A. Thompson (1958):16.

32 Bachrach (1972):101, 105.

33 Bachrach (1972):37-38.

34 Contamine (1984):12-13.

35 Bury (1967):91-97; Wolfram (1988):155-61; and Lander (1984):293-97.

36 E.A. Thompson (1958):16-17.

37 On the ease of Belisarius' conquest see John Barker (1966):145-60.

38 Wallace-Hadrill (1962):32-33.

39 Gregory of Tours (1974):182-83.

40 Quoted in Guillerme (1988):23.

41 The best discussion of these rural fortifications is found in Fournier (1978):27-34.

42 Fournier (1978):31-32 and M. Jones (1981):157.

43 Sidonius Apollinaris (1963):I:262-83.

44 Gregory of Tours (1974):172-73.

45 Fournier (1978):32-34.

46 Fournier (1974)123-35; Bachrach (1974):9-10; and McKitterick (1983):51.

47 Fournier (1978):35 and Bachrach (1974):9-10.

48 On the fortifications and siege of Pavia see Bullough (1965):49-50. On the siege of Barcelona see Bachrach (1974):28. On the Saxon fortifications see Fournier (1978):36. And on the Avar fortifications see Bowlus (1978):17.

49 Bachrach (1978):23-25 and Bachrach (1983):183.

50 Bowlus (1978):22-25.

51 Fournier (1978):36-38.

52 McKitterick (1983):51.

53   There are several good accounts of the Viking raids. See in particular G. Jones (1968); Sawyer (1962); and Sawyer (1982).

54   Macartney (1930) and Musset (1965).

55   Quoted in Hamer (1970):27.

56   Riché (1983):42-46.

57   Fournier (1978):38; McKitterick (1983):233; and Vercauteren (1936):119-20.

58   Vercauteren (1936):120.

59   On Alfred the Great see Duckett (1956) and Stenton (1971):239-76.

60   Abels (1988):68-69. On Offa's Dyke see Forde-Johnston (1977):73-74 and Brown, Colvin and Taylor (1963):6-7.

61   The best introductions to this text are Hill (1969):84-92 and Bachrach and Aris (1990):1-17.

62   Abels (1988):68-78; Bachrach and Aris (1990):1-17; Forde-Johnston (1977):74-76; Brown, Colvin and Taylor (1963):8-10; Radford (1970):83-103; and Turner (1971):17-20 and *passim*.

63   Abels (1988):69.

64   Abels (1988):69-71.

65   Abels (1988):74-75 and Bachrach and Aris (1990):2-3.

66   Forde-Johnston (1977):74-75; Radford (1970):84-103; and Bachrach and Aris (1990):2-4.

67   Forde-Johnston (1977):74-75 and Bachrach and Aris (1990):3-4.

68   Abels (1988):76-78; Brooks (1971):71-73; and Hollister (1962):143.

69   Abels (1988):71-74. An excellent discussion of the military thinking and the use of archery in the defense of these fortifications is found in Bachrach and Aris (1990):5-17.

70   Abels (1988):92-93 and Brooks (1979):17-18.

71   Bowlus (1978):24-25.

72   Drew (1964):444-47.

73   Vercauteren (1936):121-23.

74   Vercauteren (1936):128-29.

75   Vercauteren (1936):123-24; Gillmor (1988):87-106; Dearden (1988):107-12; and Boyer (1976):21-27.

76   Boyer (1976):23-27 and Sawyer (1982):89.

77   Gillmor (1988):106.

78   Vercauteren (1936):123-28; Fournier (1978):38-39; and Sawyer (1982):89-90.

79   Fournier (1978):39.

80   Fournier (1978):39; Coulson (1976):29-36; and Binding (1972):23-34.

81   Vercauteren (1936):131; Coulson (1976):32-34; and Bachrach (1975):545.

82   Fournier (1978):51.

83   Fournier (1978):39-40.

84   See Bouard (1964):19-26.

85   Fournier (1978):67, 72-74; Fino (1970):103; Hope-Taylor (1956):247-48; and Renn (1973):4.

86   Fournier (1978):67; Renn (1973):3; Fino (1970):9; Brown (1976):34; King (1988):38; and King (1972):101.

87   Quoted in Brown (1976):60.

88   Fournier (1978):68-69; Renn (1973):4; Platt (1982):3-4; and Le Patourel (1976):304.

89   Fournier (1978):67; Le Patourel (1976):204-05, 305-06; and Douglas (1964):42, 140-41.

90   Douglas (1964):140-41.

91   Brown (1989a):222-25 and Stenton (1957):pl. 23-26, 28.

92   Le Patourel (1976):303-05; Platt (1982):2; and Stenton (1961):197-200.

93   Brown, Colvin, and Taylor (1963):I:19 and Brown (1989d):84.

94   Brown (1976):50; Renn (1973):27-28; and Stenton (1957):pl. 51.

95   Brown (1976):50-51 and Beeler (1956):584-86.

96   Beeler (1966): 36-37.

97   Beeler (1966):37.

98   Brown, Colvin, and Taylor (1963):I:21; Beeler (1956):pp. 585-86; and Addyman (1972):7-12.

99   Beeler (1966):51-53 and Beeler (1956):598.

100 Beeler (1956):598 and Le Patourel (1976):305.

101 Brown, Colvin and Taylor (1963):I:23-26; Beeler (1966):51-53; Le Patourel (1976):309-15; Brown (1989d):83-84; Douglas (1964):216-17; and Barrow (1956):47-48.

102 Ellis (1833):I:223-24.

103 Beeler (1956):586 and Painter (1935):322. King (1972):102 counts 741 motte-and-bailey castles, while Brown (1989b):65-66 estimates the number to be nearer to 1000.

104 Brown, Colvin, and Taylor (1963):I:29-32 and Brown (1989b):74.

105 Stenton (1957):pls. 23, 24, 25-26, 28 and 51; Brown (1989a):222-25.

106 Addyman (1972):9.

107 Hope-Taylor (1956):224-25 and Addyman (1972):9.

108 Brown (1976):55-56; Kenyon (1990):9-12; Hope-Taylor (1956):226; and King (1972):101-12.

109 Hope-Taylor (1956):226.

110 Brown (1989a):223-24 and Stenton (1957):pl. 28.

111 Abinger's tower was only 3.7 square meters in area (Hope-Taylor (1956):237). See also Brown (1976):34-35 and M.W. Thompson (1960):89-90.

112   Kenyon (1990):13-23; Brown, Colvin and Taylor (1963):I:23 and Stenton (1957):pl. 26.

113   Stenton (1957):pl.23.

114   M.W. Thompson (1961):305-06.

115   Hope-Taylor (1956):225.

116   Stenton (1957):pl. 26.

117   Hope-Taylor (1956):248.

118   M.W. Thompson (1961):306 and M.W. Thompson (1960):88.

119   M.W. Thompson (1961):306; Brown (1976):34; and Davison (1967):206-07.

120   M.W. Thompson (1961):306.

121   Hope-Taylor (1956):236-37; Brown (1989a):223; and Stenton (1957):pls.25-26.

122   Brown (1976):56-57; Brown, Colvin and Taylor (1963):I:23; and Hope-Taylor(1956):226.

123   Brown (1976):58-59; Kenyon (1990):31-38; and Hope-Taylor (1956):226-27.

124   Brown (1976):61 and Brown, Colvin, and Taylor (1963):I:23-24.

125   Brown (1976):61 and Stenton (1957):pls. 24-26, 28, 51.

126   Brown (1976):61.

127   King (1972):196-97.

128   Brown (1976):57-58; Brown (1989b):70-72; and Taylor (1958):103.

129   Taylor (1958):103.

130   Lindsay (1974):152.

131   Hope-Taylor (1956):233-34 and Taylor (1958):104.

132   Brown (1976):51-52.

133   Brown (1976):51 and Brown, Colvin, and Taylor (1963):I:24.

134   Brown, Colvin, and Taylor (1963):I:20.

135   Bachrach (1983):538-60.

136   Bachrach (1979):531-49.

137   Bachrach (1979):534-35 and Bachrach (1984):47-50.

138   Deyres (1974):7-28 and Verbruggen (1950):51, 54. Fournier (1978):69 agrees with this conclusion.

139   Bachrach (1979):534-41 and Bachrach (1984):47-62. Fino (1970):386-88; Contamine (1984):47; and Héliot (1966):504-05 agree with Bachrach in his contentions here.

140   Bachrach (1979):544.

141   Bachrach (1979):541-47 and Deyres (1974):7-28. Héliot (1966):505-06 agrees with Bachrach in this argument.

142   Bachrach (1979):549-54.

143   Bachrach (1979):554-59.

144   Lomax (1978):31-43 and Collins (1983):253-68.

145 Beeler (1971):163-64 and Araguas (1979):205-08.

146 Araguas (1979):208-23.

147 Contamine (1984):46, 109.

148 See Emden (1984):1-11.

149 Brown (1954):35.

150 Brown (1954):36.

151 Platt (1982):20.

152 Brown (1954):37-43 and King (1988):63-67.

153 Renn (1973):187-89; Platt (1982):22; and M.W. Thompson (1960):81-94.

154 On the Norman rectangular keep see Renn (1973); Brown (1954):35-59; Platt (1982):7-45; Kenyon (1990):39-54; Toy (1955):74-85; King (1988):67-74; Brown, Colvin and Taylor (1963):I:29-40.

155 There are numerous writings on the White Tower. Probably the best are two articles by Brown (1989g) and (1989f). See also Renn (1973):326-30; Brown, Colvin, and Taylor (1963):I:29-32; Platt (1982):10; Toy (1955):78; Forde-Johnston (1977):84-86; and Bonde (1984):84-91.

156 Renn (1973):151-54; Forde-Johnston (1977):86; and Toy (1955):78-79.

157 Brown (1954):52-54.

158 On Gisors Castle see Fino (1970):372-76 and Toy (1955):71. On Pfeffengen Castle see Toy (1955):72-73.

159 On Arques Castle see Toy (1955):80-81. On Loches Castle see Fino (1970):399-403 and Toy (1955):76-77. And on Ghent Castle see Fino (1970):368-71 and Héliot (1974):218.

160 On the numerical strength of the First Crusade and early Crusaders' kingdoms see Runciman (1964):I:336-41.

161 See Toy (1970):86-103; Müller-Wiener (1966); Boase (1967); Lawrence (1988); Smail (1956); Smail (1951):133-49; and Boase (1977).

162 Toy (1955):93 and Prawer (1980):104-12, 472-79.

163 Smail (1957):60, 204-07; Smail (1956):135-38.

164 Smail (1957):60-62, 205-14 and Smail (1956):135-45.

165 Smail (1957):214; Smail (1956):145-49; Boase (1967):41; and Prawer (1980):52.

166 Toy (1955):93-94; Smail (1957):217-18; Boase (1967):44-45; and Boase (1977):141-42.

167 Smail (1956):226-30.

168 Müller-Weiner (1966):51-52; Toy (1955):101; Boase (1967):60-61; and Boase (1977):145.

169 Müller-Weiner (1966):64-65; Boase (1967):45; and Boase (1977):144-45.

170 Toy (1955):86-93; Smail (1956):230-32; and Boase (1967):42-43.

171 Müller-Weiner (1966); Toy (1955):94-101; Smail (1967):215-16, 218-30; Boase (1967):49-67; and Boase (1977):145-62.

172 Lawrence (1988):77.

173   Müller-Weiner (1966):59-62; Toy (1955):99-101; Smail (1967):223-26; Boase (1967):51-56; Boase (1977):152-56; and Lawrence (1988):77-88.

174   Prawer (1980):483.

175   Boase (1967):63-66.

176   Toy (1955):104.

177   See, for example, King (1988):77-89.

178   Toy (1955):86-91.

179   Toy (1955):104-06 and Fino (1970):377-80.

180   Toy (1955):104-13; Platt (1982):32-45; Lawrence (1988):93-101; Brown (1954):52-57; and Fino (1970):356-57, 372-76, 416-20.

181   Toy (1955):133; Platt (1982):39; Forde-Johnston (1977):95-96; and A.H. Thompson (1912):180-81.

182   Fino (1970):307-10 and Toy (1955):139.

183   Fino (1970):343-47; Toy (1955):137-39; and Platt (1982):52.

184   Toy (1955):84; Platt (1982):43-46; Brown (1954):38, 49-51, 67-68, 83-84; Forde-Johnston (1977):86-77; Brown, Colvin, and Taylor (1963):I:65, 78; and Taylor (1958):113.

185   Toy (1955):136-37 and Fino (1970):408-11.

186   Toy (1955):128-31; Fino (1970):327-30; Dieulafoy (1898); and Heliot (1962):53-75. An itemized listing of the castle building costs for Chateau Gaillard can be found in Contamine (1984):110.

187   On the additions to the White Tower see Brown (1989f):168-76. On the additions to the castle at Ghent see Toy (1955):147 and Fino (1970):368-71.

188   Because of the importance of these castles several works have discussed them. See in particular Taylor (1986) (which is a reprinting of Brown, Colvin, and Taylor (1963):I:293-408, II:1027-39; Edwards (1946):15-81; Taylor (1977):265-92; Taylor (1961):104-33; Prestwich (1988):207-16; Toy (1955):164-72; Brown (1954):61-81; Forde-Johnston (1977):108-15; Platt (1983):63-79; Taylor (1958):111-19; and A.H. Thompson (1912):252-86.

189   On the Master James of St. George see Taylor (1950):433-57.

190   On Conway Castle see Taylor (1986):45-62; Edwards (1946):37-43; Toy (1955):167-68; Brown (1954):74; Platt (1982):71; Taylor (1958):115-16; and A.H. Thompson (1912):252-62. On Caernarvon Castle see Taylor (1986):77-103; Edwards (1946):43-52; Toy (1955):167-68; Brown (1954):74; Platt (1982):71-75; Taylor (1958):117-18; and A.H. Thompson (1912):252-62.

191   Prestwich (1988):214.

192   Mercier-Sivadjian and Sivadjian (1985):38. See also Toy (1955):161-62.

193   Allmand (1988):77.

194   Stenton (1960):119.

195   M. Jones (1981):153.

196   M.W. Thompson (1987):19-20.

197 M.W. Thompson (1987):104, 171-78. See also Dobson (1977):5.

198 Morley (1981):104-05 and Brown (1954):90.

199 M.W. Thompson (1987):17, 29-30; Brown, Colvin, and Taylor (1963):II:802; Fino (1970):421-23, 438-41; and M. Jones (1981):178-80.

200 Morley (1981):113.

201 Morley (1981):107-11 and Toy (1955):228-29.

202 Morley (1981):107 and Toy (1955):230.

203 Morley (1981):113.

204 Toy (1955):230-31.

205 Prestwich (1982):176 and D.J. Turner (1986):168-69. However, Vale (1986):136-37 and M.W. Thompson (1987):3 dispute this contention, claiming instead that defense was always of primary interest to the builder of these fortified residences.

206 Brown (1954):89-91; Turner (1986):268; and Vale (1986):138.

207 D.J. Turner (1986); Toy (1955):218-20; Brown (1954):94-96; Platt (1982):114-18; Forde-Johnston (1977):120-23; and Taylor (1958):121-22.

208 Fino (1970):412-15 and Toy (1955):222-23.

209 Toy (1955):212-28; M.W. Thompson (1987):17-18, 22-26; Forde-Johnston (1977):127; and M. Jones (1981):177.

210 On the Scottish tower houses see Cruden (1960):100-43; Brown (1954):91-92; Brown, Colvin and Taylor (1963):I:235-36; and Prestwich (1982):174-75. For France see M.W. Thompson (1987):3 and M. Jones (1981):172-80.

211 Toy (1955):225-26; Platt (1982):169-73; M.W. Thompson (1987):87-91; Forde-Johnston (1977):130-33; and M.W. Thompson (1981) :156-62.

212 Fino (1977):421-23 and M.W. Thompson (1987):29-30.

213 English (1984):175, 190-91.

214 Martines (1979):221-22. See Toy (1955):212-13, 216-18 for other examples of princely urban fortified residences.

215 English (1984):183-84 and Brucker (1969):35-38.

216 English (1984):185 and Eltis (1989):100.

217 Stephenson (1933):188-92; Kenyon (1990):183; Jones and Bond (1987):112; and Allmand (1988):77.

218 Stephenson (1933):12.

219 Stephenson (1933):24.

220 Stephenson (1933):26.

221 Stephenson (1933):23; Forde-Johnston (1977):134; Guillerme (1988):49; Frere and Stone (1982):91; and Rörig (1967):169.

222 Contamine (1978); Turner (1971):28-46; and Allmand (1988):77-78.

223 Forde-Johnston (1977):137 and M. Jones (1981):171-72.

224 Frere and Stone (1987):91 and Allmand (1988):77-78. See also Kenyon (1990):183-84; Dobson (1977):6 and Forde-Johnston (1977):134.

225 Kenyon (1990):183; Platt (1976):41; and M. Jones (1981):153-55.

226 H. Turner (1971):156, 211-13; Forde-Johnston (1977):134-36; and Fino (1970):334-35.

227 The walls of Conway were two meters thick (H. Turner (1971):212-13 and Forde-Johnston (1977):134-35), while the walls at Canterbury were 1.78 meters in thickness (Frere and Stowe (1982):91).

228 Guillerme (1988):49 and M. Jones (1981):153-55.

229 H. Turner (1971):141, 211-13 and Forde-Johnston (1977):134-36.

230 H. Turner (1971):141, 179 and M. Jones (1981):153.

231 H. Turner (1971):61-66 and Frere and Stowe (1982):91.

232 As at Carcassone (Fino (1970):334-35). See also Christine de Pizan (1932):136.

233 Christine de Pizan (1932):138; Kenyon (1990):197-99; Fino (1970):334; and Frere and Stowe (1982):91.

234 H. Turner (1971):60-62, 211; Forde-Johnston (1977):134-35, 141; and Fino (1970):334-35.

235 H. Turner (1971):59 and Kenyon (1990):195-97.

236 Fino (1970):334-35.

237 H. Turner (1971):66-72, 211-13; Kenyon (1990):191-95; and Forde-Johnston (1977):134-36.

238 Nicholas (1987):70 and Forde-Johnston (1977):141.

239 H. Turner (1971):66-72 and Christine de Pizan (1932):137-38.

240 Guillerme (1988):49.

241 Kenyon (1990):186-89; Frere and Stowe (1982):23; and Platt (1976):42.

242 Kenyon (1990):184; Platt (1976):44; and Frere and Stowe (1982):91.

243 See, for example, the description of Harfleur in 1415 given by the anonymous author of the *Gesta Henrici quinti* (Taylor and Roskell (1975):29-31) and the description of early fifteenth-century Arras given by Enguerran de Monstrelet ((1857-62):III:22).

244 Allmand (1988):79.

245 For example, Ipswich and King's Lynn in England (Platt (1976):42-43) and Fagnano and Venice in Italy (Mallet and Hale (1984):89).

246 Dobson (1977):6-7 and Platt (1976):44.

247 Christine de Pizan (1932):136.

248 M. Jones (1988):236.

249 Parker (1988):7-16.

250 O'Neil (1960):4-5, 10-11, 22 and Renn (1968):302-03.

251 Contamine (1984):202.

252 Kenyon (1981):206-12; Renn (1968):301-02; O'Neil (1960):9-11, 17-18, 20; Brown, Colvin, and Taylor (1963):II:594, 801-02, 844; Frere and Stowe (1982):23; and D.J. Turner (1986):270-72.

253 Contamine (1984):202; Vale (1981):133; and M. Jones (1981):174.

254 L. Douet-d'Arcq (1863-64):II:32-33 and M. Jones (1981):175.

255 Contamine (1984):202-03 and Kenyon (1981):232.

256 O'Neil (1960):12-13 and Kenyon (1981):207. Kirby Muxloe Castle does have fifteenth-century gunports which have the muzzle hole apart from the slit. See Toy (1955):237.

257 O'Neil (1960):7-11, 17-20, 29-30, 37; Kenyon (1981):207-08; Kenyon (1989):143-60; Renn (1968):301; Leguay (1988):185; and Frere and Stowe (1982):117.

258 Kenyon (1989):162.

259 Kenyon (1981):209 and Frere and Stowe (1982):117.

260 Kenyon (1981):207.

261 Duffy (1979):2 and Eltis (1989):94.

262 Contamine (1984):204.

263 Fino (1970):297-300 and D.J. Turner (1986):269.

264 Fino (1970):295-96; Contamine (1984):204; Leguay (1981):171-72, 185-86; M. Jones (1981):176; Vale (1981):133.

265 H. Turner (1971):60, 165; Contamine (1984):204; Brown, Colvin and Taylor (1963):II:606; Fino (1970):294-95; Vale (1981):133; Leguay (1981):187; M. Jones (1981):175-76; and Hale (1965):479.

266 Fino (1970):421-23.

267 M.W. Thompson (1987):36 and Brown, Colvin, and Taylor (1963):801-02.

268 Albert (1988). See also Hale (1965):471-81; Parker (1988):8-11; and Contamine (1984):204-05.

269 Hale (1965); Hale (1977); Pepper and Adams (1986); and Duffy (1979).

Part IV:

Warships

Introduction

The earliest ships were small vessels used solely for transportation and trade. These were probably rafts, floats, or dugout canoes, as Lionel Casson writes, "whatever [men] could find that would keep them afloat."[1] The technology was simple. Boats such as these were constructed using the most accessible materials—reeds, light wood, bark, or animal skins—and were fashioned with the most rudimentary skills. They were made to sail only on rivers or along coasts of seas and lakes, as their hulls were not constructed to withstand high waves or bad weather.[2]

Nor could they hold much cargo. But as the population of the ancient world began to increase, the need for larger trading ventures also increased, and the least expensive means of transportation for these ventures was on water. Therefore, larger ships were built to accommodate larger cargoes, and these vessels also began to take more risks, traveling where earlier ships had been unable to go. By the third millennium BC in Egypt, ships had become so large that they were able to ferry large blocks of rock along the Nile River from quarries to building sites, and a thousand years later similar vessels measuring more than 70 meters in length and 25 meters in width carried obelisks down the Nile from their quarries at Aswan.[3]

Initially, at least, these ships were constructed using similar materials to earlier vessels. Even when shipwrights and other shipbuilding craftsmen had become more expert in their construction and began using more substantial materials, ship design did not differ much from the earlier boats. The earliest planked ships were flat-bottomed and square-ended. They were constructed in the clinker-style: first a keel plank (or planks) was laid which formed the centerline of the hull, and from there, on both sides, other short planks were added, fastened to each other and to the keel planks by dowels, mortises and tenons, wooden clamps, or a combination of these. These short planks continued to be added until the shell of the vessel had been completed. Gunwales, crossbeams, and deck planks were then attached to the hull to strengthen it. A pole mast, equipped with a single, loose-fitting, square, papyrus or cloth sail, was also often present, although most ships were powered principally by oarsmen, paddlers or punters. Steering was accomplished by one or more steering oars placed near or at the stern of the ship.[4] This mode of construction remained popular until the Middle Ages.

It is difficult to determine when the first warships appeared in the ancient world. Some historians theorize that as cargo ships grew larger and trade became more prosperous, piracy also began to flourish. This theory may indeed be valid, but there is little evidence to support it, or in fact to defeat it. It is not until c. 1400 BC that an artistic source which possibly shows a warship is found; a painting on a Mycenaean vase from the eastern coast of Greece depicts a curved stempost characteristic of later Greek galleys.[5]

It is not until at least two centuries later that an Egyptian artistic source depicts a military engagement on sea: a large carving on the side of a temple portrays a naval battle fought on the Nile River between the Egyptian fleet and ships from barbarian invaders known only as "Sea Peoples." From this source it can be determined that the numbers and sizes of these ships were impressive, and that their hulls were no longer square-ended but rounded. They were also decorated, with a lion's head adorning most of the prow posts. Lookouts were placed on the top of the mast, and rowers were protected by a high bulwark attached to the hull. Perhaps most important was the fact that the loose-fitting sail common on all ancient ships was now outfitted with brails, lines for controlling the area of the sails exposed to the winds, which could be used to shorten the sails and add maneuverability. It should also be noted that both fleets as depicted in this carving were nearly identical. Moreover, no long-range weapon was depicted in this carving for use in battle on sea; the only means of fighting was the grappling of opposing ships, by means of a grappling iron or hook, and then hand-to-hand combat in imitation of a land battle on both decks.[6]

The first successful style of warship to appear in large numbers in the ancient world was the oared warship or galley. Although probably first invented by the Phoenicians sometime between 725 and 680 BC—they developed both a single-banked oared warship known as a *penteconter* and a two-banked warship known as a *bireme*[7]—this ship is best characterized by the Greeks, who, in the fifth century BC, perfected it by adding a third bank of oars (creating a *trireme*), and used it to control the Mediterranean Sea from then until long after Alexander the Great's Empire had split and fallen.

The first ancient oared warships were low-hulled and flat with crews of 25 oarsmen rowing on each side of the vessel (in combat the oarsmen became archers). However, this one level of oarsmen did not produce much speed, and therefore ships were equipped with several banks of oarsmen, creating biremes, triremes, and even larger vessels. The best and most common of these ships were the triremes. Triremes measured approximately 35 meters long and 3.5 meters wide and carried a crew of 170 oarsmen: 31 oarsmen on the top bank of oars and 27 on each lower bank. Larger ships—quadriremes, quinqueremes, sixes, twelves, sixteens, twenties, and even thirties—simply lost mobility, while their heaviness did not adequately increase their speed.

Why had speed become such a factor? The weapon of most ancient oared warships was not the grappling iron but the ram. The invention of the ram gave the oared warship added ability to attack an opposing ship. It is believed that the first ram was attached to a warship between 1200 and 1000 BC, but that it was not used effectively until 600 BC when the Greeks began to outfit all of their oared warships with them. Initially, the ram was simply an extension of the keel, but later this was changed both in shape and size, leading eventually to a down-turned, three-pronged ram covered with metal sheeting. The ram remained continually in use until AD 121-22, when the Romans discarded it as a naval weapon in preference for the grappling iron and pseudo-land battle for naval warfare. It would return to use in the early Byzantine Empire.

It should also be mentioned that our concept of ancient oarsmen/sailors as slaves or prisoners is mistaken. For the Greeks at least, much pride was taken in their rowing skill. Only the best athletes could be oarsmen for the triremes, and they frequently held competitions between ships to determine which crew was the strongest and fastest. Only later, during the Roman Empire, were oarsmen replaced by slaves and prisoners.[8]

Throughout the first centuries of Roman Republican domination there was little change in the warships common in the eastern part of the Mediterranean. These were the ships which opposed

each other in the large naval battle of Actium fought in 31 BC
between the Roman fleet of Octavian and the Roman/Egyptian
fleet of Marc Antony and Cleopatra. Octavian, mixing his triremes
with larger warships, known as "sixes," defeated Antony and
Cleopatra's triremes and "tens," securing for himself the sole
leadership of Rome—the emperorship.

Actium was the last large naval battle for 300 years. For most
of the history of the Roman Empire there was no need for a large
naval force. By the beginning of the first century BC, the entire
Mediterranean Sea was under imperial control (the Romans called
it *nostrum mare*, "our sea") and crossings of the English Channel
and Black Sea were unhindered by opposing fleets. The Roman
navy was used for little more than transportation, communication,
and control of piracy. For these duties, the trireme was too large,
bulky, and slow. A lighter, more maneuverable warship was
needed, and this was provided by the *liburnian*.

The liburnian, which took its name from a piratical tribe which
lived among the islands of the Dalmatian coast, was a sleek, fast
galley outfitted with two banks of oars and a main mast with
square sail. Its use in pirate attacks on imperial fleets had been
so impressive that by 36 BC the Roman navy began to build some
for their own use. Soon they were a primary ship of the fleet,
as evidenced by their frequent appearance on Trajan's Column
and other artistic sources. And although triremes reappeared for
a time during the civil wars of the early fourth century AD, the
liburnian remained the chief warship of the Roman Empire until
its fall.[9] It also became the archetype for the two-banked Byzantine
dromon, the primary warship of that Empire until its fall in the
fifteenth century. The dromon, 40 to 50 meters in length, contained two banks of 25 oars on each side.[10]

The initial barbarian invasions did not alter the Roman naval
strategy. With the possible exception of the Suevi, who began
their invasions on the southern shores of the Baltic Sea and may
have sailed to the northwestern shores of Iberia, all invasions of
the Empire were land-based and required no warships. It was not
until the Vandals crossed from Spain to North Africa and the
Visigoths from Italy to Spain in the early fifth century that the
Mediterranean was invaded, and it is unlikely that the ships used
in these crossings were built for naval conflict.[11] Similarly, the

invasions of Britain by the Angles, Saxons, and Jutes in the fifth century were probably accomplished by using ships only for transportation and not for naval engagement. A vessel like that uncovered at Sutton Hoo may have been used.[12]

Once established in North Africa, the Vandals did build a pirate fleet which preyed on Mediterranean shipping and which was used in the invasion of Italy in 455. It is uncertain what type of warships the Vandals used in these operations, or even whether they were similar to those used at the same time by the Romans. It is certain, however, that their tactics were different as a passage written by the Byzantine historian, Procopius, illustrates:

> But the Vandals...raised their sails and, taking in tow the boats which...they had made ready with no men in them, they sailed against the enemy [the Romans]. And when they came near, they set fire to the boats which they were towing, when their sails were bellied by the wind, and let them go against the Roman fleet. And since there were a great number of ships there, these boats easily spread fire wherever they struck.... And already the Vandals too were at hand ramming and sinking the ships, and making booty of such of the soldiers as attempted to escape, and of their arms as well.[13]

By 500, the Vandal naval threat had ended, defeated finally by the Byzantine forces under Belisarius.[14] The new threat in the Mediterranean, the Muslims, were still nearly two centuries from active naval opposition. In western Europe, the barbarians, unaccustomed to fighting on the sea, had established their kingdoms without navies. Even the great Charlemagne felt no need to outfit a navy until nearly the end of his reign, and it was not until the reigns of his son and grandsons that this navy was put into use against the Muslims and the Vikings.[15]

It was in fact these two threats from the East and from the North which again led to the construction of warships in medieval Europe. In the Mediterranean the naval threat to Europe came from Muslim fleets. While the barbarian tribes conquered the western part of the Roman Empire, the Byzantine Empire inherited the eastern part, including the Middle East. However, this dominance ended with the rise of Islam in the sixth and seventh centuries. By 710 Mohammed and his followers had conquered all of the Middle East, North Africa, Spain, Persia, and much of

India. Only the Byzantines and the Franks were able to stop their
further progress. In conquering these lands, many ports in the
Mediterranean were taken and with them many ships. These were
used later to attack other regions, as the Muslims (or Saracens
as they were known) continued their onslaughts on Europe.

The Muslim Navy

The first organization of a Muslim navy came in 651 when
Muawiyah—the governor of Syria (and later caliph)—organized
the ships captured in newly conquered Mediterranean ports. His
first target was the almost completely unprotected island of Cyprus; it fell quickly. Other Mediterranean targets were taken
equally as fast. Between 672 and 678, a large Muslim navy even
attempted an attack on the Byzantine capital, Constantinople, and
although this ultimately failed, and indeed almost completely destroyed the attacking fleet, it showed the strength and designs of
Muslim sea captains. A second attack on Constantinople followed
in 717-18, but it too proved to be unsuccessful.

The Muslim navy continued to play a major role in the Mediterranean until the end of the Middle Ages. The technology of
their early ships is difficult to ascertain as few illustrations of
them exist before the thirteenth century. According to contemporary sources, their tactics were similar to those of the Byzantine
navy, and perhaps their technology was like the Byzantines as
well. What is known is that the Muslim vessels were oared warships, especially built for raiding, and less well crafted for battle.
They also were limited both in number and size by the shortage
of wood available in the Middle East for constructing naval vessels.

This did not change until the early ninth century. Largely
because of Byzantine political unrest, which forced a decline in
naval power, the Muslims again began to exert their naval might.
Sicily, Crete, Cyprus (which had earlier been reconquered by the
Byzantines), Corsica, Sardinia, and the Balearic Islands all fell in
quick succession. In turn, more naval bases were established on
these Mediterranean islands from which frequent raids against the
rest of Europe, especially Italy, were undertaken. While it seems
that many of these ships, especially the larger ones, continued to

resemble the Byzantine *dromons*, others became smaller and even began to be powered primarily by the lateen (or triangular) sail rather than by the oar. Larger warships also began to use Greek Fire and catapults as weapons in battle. This was the nature of the Muslim fleet until the middle of the eleventh century.[16]

The Vikings

In the north, at the end of the eighth century, the Vikings began to attack the lands across the sea from their Scandinavian homelands. These attacks were completely unanticipated by a European populace which did not believe that it was possible to make ships capable of raiding their coasts. As the English scholar, Alcuin, wrote to Aethelred, the King of Northumbria, concerning the Viking raid on the Lindesfarne monastery in 793: "Lo, it is nearly 350 years that we and our fathers have inhabited this most lovely land, and never before has such terror appeared in Britain as we have suffered from a pagan race, nor was it thought that such an inroad from the sea could be made."[17] The raids were very profitable and continued, with varying intensity, for the next three centuries. The ship, as the primary means of transportation for the Viking raids, again gained significance in military matters.

Historians have many questions concerning Viking shipbuilding and naval tactics. Fortunately, not only are there a large number of written sources, especially Scandinavian sagas, which describe the adventures of Viking sailors/raiders, but the significant number of Viking ships excavated by archaeologists have added to our knowledge of their construction and use at sea.

Scandinavian ships were not always capable of raiding the coasts of other European lands. In the early Middle Ages, these vessels had little potential for open sea sailing and were probably not unlike boats constructed elsewhere in Europe. They had a relatively shallow hull, built in a clinker style, in a manner similar to the shipbuilding techniques of the ancients, with strong ribs placed inside for added support. Loose planks were laid between these ribs to serve as a deck. These ships also contained no strong keel, and thus were unable to carry a mast, so that the oar was their sole means of power. This changed in the early eighth century, when ships with stronger keels began to be built. This in-

novation allowed a deeper, flatter, and longer hull to be constructed. It also permitted the placement of a heavy mast, perhaps
as long as 12 meters. The new hull strength, depth, and length,
and the addition of a sail, made it possible for the raids which
began later in the century.

Many ships took part in the Viking raids over the following
centuries. They varied in size and, seemingly, in purpose. Some
were quite large in length and width—the Gokstad ship measures
23 meters in length and 5.2 meters in width, the Osberg ship 22
meters in length and 5 meters in width, and the Skuldelev longship
measures 28 meters long (its width cannot be estimated because
of the bad state of preservation)—but shallow in depth which may
indicate that they were built as warships. Others were considerably
smaller in length and width, but larger in depth, perhaps denoting
vessels used chiefly for transporting cargo. However, all Vikings
ships may have participated in the very profitable raids, as they
were only needed for transporting men to and from their raiding
destination and not for naval combat.

The Viking ship could be rowed, with most large vessels
equipped with 15 or more oarlocks cut into both sides of the hull.
This would accommodate as many as 50 to 60 sailors. But it was
also equipped with a large square sail. The sail did not add to

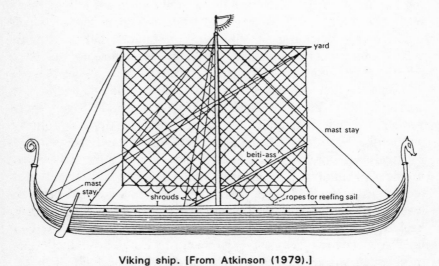

Viking ship. [From Atkinson (1979).]

the maneuverability of the ship, but did add considerable speed. The ship was steered by a single rudder attached to one side near the stern.[18]

Most Viking ships cannot be considered "true" warships as they did not fight naval battles, but were used solely for transportation. Indeed, such ships were used to transport settlers and their chattel to Normandy, Russia, northern England, Scotland, Ireland, the Orkney Islands, the Faroe Islands, Iceland, Greenland, and North America. One exception to this was the battle of Svolder, fought in 1000 between the powerful king of Norway, Olav Tryggvason, and a consortium of opponents which included King Svein Forkbeard of Denmark, King Olav of Sweden, and Earl Eirik, the Norwegian king's rebellious noble vassal. The tactics of the Viking forces at this battle were little different from those of the Romans.

The king of Norway had perhaps the greatest fleet of his day; included in it were such prize large longships (known collectively as *drekkars* or dragon ships) as the *Long Serpent*, *Short Serpent*, and *Crane*. However, this fleet had never been used in a naval battle. At Svolder, the consortium lured Olav into a trap and forced him into battle. The two fleets approached each other, grappled together, and then fought a long and violent battle with bows and hand weapons on the decks of all vessels. Arrows and spears flew, and axes were swung. Finally, the battle came down to a single combat between Olav's Norwegians on board the *Long Serpent* and Eirik's Norwegians on board his vessel, the *Iron Beard*. Ultimately, Eirik's forces gained the upper hand. Most of Olav's Vikings were slain, and he jumped overboard and was drowned.[19]

Because of the political turmoil of most European states during the centuries in which the Vikings raided, few competent attempts at naval opposition against them were made. Only the English were successfully able to counter the Viking navy by building ships of their own. This was begun as early as 851, when West Saxon ships opposed Viking raiders, but it did not become an earnest effort until the reign of Alfred the Great. Alfred, perhaps realizing the potential for naval defense against the Vikings, built a large fleet early in his reign. It was successful against a Viking flotilla in the summer of 875, and again in 882 and 885, and may

have been one of the causes of the peace between the English
and the Vikings which followed and which lasted for more than
a decade. Finally, in 896 as the Vikings threatened England once
again, Alfred's fleet was enlarged. The *Anglo-Saxon Chronicle*
reports:

> Then King Alfred had "long ships" built to oppose the Danish
> warships. They were almost twice as long as the others. Some
> had sixty oars, some more. They were both swifter and steadier
> and also higher than the others. They were built neither on the
> Frisian nor the Danish pattern, but as it seemed to himself that
> they could be most useful.[20]

No sooner were these ships constructed than they were used
in several successful naval conflicts against the Vikings. That these
ships were unlike those opposing them is recorded, but how different, or in fact what exactly they were like has not been confirmed by archaeological excavation.[21]

William the Conqueror's Fleet

The Viking threat diminished in the tenth and eleventh century.
But it did not end completely until 1066 when Harald Hardrada,
the king of Norway, led a large fleet across the sea in an attempt
to conquer England. He and most of his companions met their
death at the battle of Stamford Bridge, defeated by the king of
England, Harold Godwinson; the remnants of the Viking force
returned to their homeland in a much smaller fleet. This was the
last major naval undertaking of the Scandinavians. But it was not
to be the last attack on England that year. William, Duke of
Normandy, also attacked England in 1066, this time defeating
King Harold and conquering the kingdom.

For this journey, William needed many ships—contemporary
numbers vary between 696 and 3000—to transport an army of at
least 5000 and perhaps as many as 10,000 soldiers accompanied
by 2000 to 3000 horses. They were only troop and horse carriers,
however, as the once vaunted navy of the Anglo-Saxons had declined in power and thus provided little opposition to a naval
assault on the island.[22] It has been commonly thought that these
vessels were built by William the Conqueror in Norman harbors

using Viking cargo or transport ship designs,[23] but recently this view has been challenged.

Bernard S. Bachrach holds that William, in order to acquire the ships needed to transport his army, was faced not only with the difficulty of procuring vessels to transport his troops, but also, because his army was cavalry-based, of procuring vessels to transport their horses. This could be accomplished only by constructing an entirely new fleet of specially built horse transports or by using the same ships for both horses and men. The *Bayeux Tapestry* shows that men and horses traveled together in no specially constructed horse transport, but this source, especially in depicting the Norman fleet, is fraught with technological problems. For example, no horse stalls are depicted, although "these are absolutely necessary if horses are to be transported by sea without injuring themselves or each other."

Nor does it appear that the technology for transporting horses across the sea was known in northern Europe at this time. Certainly, Bachrach contends, there is no evidence to show that Viking ships were capable of this type of naval transport, nor were any others. Only the Byzantine shipwrights could construct horse transports, precisely what William desired. They were brought north to design his ships. The remainder of his troops were transported to England by more conventional vessels acquired from Norman and Flemish owners.[24]

A second article, written by Caroll Gillmor, while chiefly concerned with the number of William's ships, also discusses the type of vessels used for the Channel crossing. She holds that there is an "unreliability of standardization" to be faced when studying the Norman fleet of 1066. Based on archaeological evidence and the depiction of the transport vessels portrayed on the *Bayeux Tapestry*, the Norman invasion fleet must have been composed of sailing ships native to the Northern Sea coastal region (primarily from Normandy and Flanders) rather than rowed vessels similar to those of the Vikings, and it was definitely "not a necessity to import the designs of Mediterranean vessels." It also seems certain that most of these ships were procured rather than constructed for the invasion. Furthermore, this "lack of standardization" also meant that while "the number of ships cannot be established with any certainty," the numbers themselves should be lowered, perhaps as low as the Anglo-Norman chronicler Wace's estimate of 700, an estimate much lower in number than other contemporary chroniclers.[25]

Finally, with J. Neumann's article, "Hydrographic and Ship-Hydrodynamic Aspects of the Norman Invasion, AD 1066," the argument comes full circle. For, although Neumann is more concerned with the shape of the Norman ships and their capabilities against heavy channel winds than he is in the origin of their design and construction, he does conclude that they could have been designed after the traditional Viking transport ships of the day. Indeed, their dimensions—which he estimates to have been 12.5 meters in length with a length-to-beam ratio of 4.5 based on his hydrographic and hydrodynamic calculations—are not dissimilar to most of the Viking transport vessels which have been excavated. Nor is their estimated sail size—4 or 5 square meters set on a 7 to 8 meter high mast—different from the estimated sail size of the same Viking transport ships. Viking-style warships were too long and slender to have been used for transporting horses and men, although some ships of this design were probably used by William to protect his fleet.[26]

The Crusades

While the Viking invasions of Europe and the Norman Conquest of England were relatively small engagements, the Crusades represented a far greater medieval naval undertaking. The First Crusade proceeded to the Holy Land across land, requiring naval assistance from the Byzantines only in crossing the Bosporus Strait. Once the Crusaders captured Jerusalem and established their kingdoms, ships were required for delivering supplies, reinforcements, and pilgrims.[27] Although for the most part this requirement was filled by cargo and transport vessels, warships were needed to capture coastal towns and protect cargo fleets. Before the Crusades, western European lands had mostly failed to take advantage of the Mediterranean as a route of trade or commerce. Late Carolingian fleets were weak and small, with only the Pisans in Italy and the Catalans in Spain able to muster enough naval strength to make conquests of nearby islands: Corsica by the Pisans and the Balearic Islands by the Catalans. These were but short-lived conquests, as the islands were soon recaptured by superior Byzantine and Muslim naval forces.[28]

This began to change somewhat in the late tenth and early eleventh centuries when the port-cities of Venice and Naples-Amalfi began to construct fleets and develop trade links with Byzantine and Muslim lands in the Middle East and North Africa. The prosperity which this brought encouraged other Italian coastal cities to build their own fleets, and soon Pisa and Genoa had joined in the contest for the Mediterranean Sea. Although initially their entry was limited to piratical activities along the shores of Corsica, Sardinia, Sicily, and North Africa, by the late eleventh century they had also assisted in the Norman invasion of Sicily and southern Italy, including Naples-Amalfi.[29] This state of affairs continued throughout the first three Crusades, with all Italian naval powers, but especially Venice and Genoa, profiting extensively from the transport of men and supplies to the Holy Land.

Most of the ships used for this purpose during the Crusades were small vessels of various designs, commonly referred to as *coasters* because of their tendency to keep close to the shore. When open-sea travel was required, vessels capable of carrying larger and heavier loads for longer voyages were used. The Genoese and Pisans favored two-masted round-ships with lateen sails, called *nefs* or *naves* (similar vessels in the north were known as *hulks*), while the Venetians and Napolese preferred galleys, descended from Byzantine dromons, which used two banks of oars for power, but were also outfitted with either one or two masts of lateen sails.[30] Sometimes larger ships were known, such as Saladin's three-masted galley, which was capable of carrying "a hundred camel-loads of arms of every kind: great heaps of arbalests (crossbows), bows, spears, and arrows" as well as "seven Saracen emirs and eight hundred chosen Turks," and was equipped with Greek Fire. Ships of this size were extremely rare and usually only associated with the highest leadership.[31]

Because no specialized warships were constructed, these round-ships were often modified to allow for some offensive and defensive military capabilities. Rams were still found on galleys, but the chief weapon on almost all ships was the personnel sailing aboard them. All sailors were used as bowmen on their ships' decks, and by the end of the twelfth century crossbowmen also discharged their bows effectively from the rigging of their vessels. As well, both galleys and round-ships were often equipped with castles, wooden turret-like superstructures attached to the aft section of the ship, on which crossbows and sometimes even trebuchets could be operated against the enemy. Stones and other materials were also frequently thrown from these castles in an effort to damage an opposing ship or to disrupt its personnel.[32] Still, it should be understood that warfare carried out between ships before the thirteenth century was rare, with piracy, minor skirmishes, and amphibious operations being the chief military duties of naval vessels.[33] The only major naval conflicts occurred in 1123, when a Venetian fleet defeated the Fatamid Egyptian navy near Ascalon, and in 1191, when Richard I of England's ships defeated Saladin's fleet near Acre, including the destruction of Saladin's large and powerful ship mentioned above.[34]

One major technological innovation which began to alter and improve ships in the Mediterranean during the eleventh and twelfth

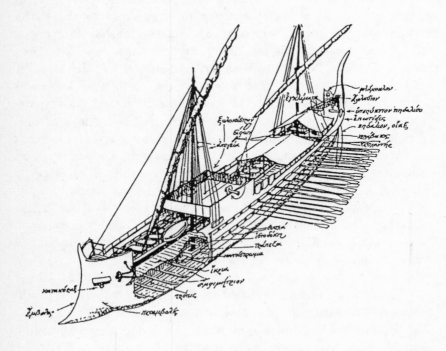

Mediterranean Galley. [From Unger (1980).]

centuries was the adoption of skeleton or carvel construction. Prior to this time all ships, both those used as warships and as cargo vessels, were built in the clinker style. But with the rise of maritime trade and the necessity for ships to carry more cargo, shipwrights began to recognize the need for larger cargo vessels. However, the size of ship was severely limited by the method of its construction, the hull only capable of rising to a height allowed by the strength of the planks forming its shell. Carvel construction reversed the order of building after the keel of the ship was laid; then instead of a plank shell attached directly to the keel, a heavy timber skeleton framework of ribs was attached on which the planks were affixed. This added great strength to the hull and enabled the construction of larger and deeper vessels. While it took nearly a century before most ships, including warships, began to be made in this manner—it still was not fully developed in 1250, with some northern ships, including the extremely large English warship, the *Grace Dieu* of Henry V, remaining clinker-built into the fifteenth century—it is clear that this shipbuilding innovation, perhaps more than any other, permitted the construction of the larger vessels needed for Atlantic exploration.[35]

Thirteenth-Century Ships

In comparison with the eleventh and twelfth centuries, the thirteenth century saw a number of naval conflicts, especially on the Mediterranean Sea. On the one hand, it is true that by the beginning of the century Naples and Sicily had declined in their naval seapower and that there was little activity between Muslim and Latin fleets in the Holy Land. However, the thirteenth century also saw the rise in naval conflicts over maritime trade between the remaining Italian seapowers, especially Genoa and Venice, and the entrance into this competition of new, powerful, and bellicose Aragonese fleets, especially those of Barcelona and Catalonia.[36] So powerful were these fleets, that by the middle of the century King James I of Aragon had captured both the Balearic Islands and Valencia.[37] As well, in the north, piracy and privateering, sometimes state sponsored, continued to be a frequent occurrence, with warships from England, France, Germany, Scandinavia, and the Low Countries preying continually on op-

posing ships and ports. Ultimately, in 1285, the piracy between
France and England developed into more serious naval warfare
which continued intermittently until the end of the century.[38]

Perhaps the demeanor of the century was established at its
very beginning when a combined land and naval attack of Constantinople succeeded in destroying the ships and naval power of
the Byzantine Empire, a blow from which it would never recover.
Called somewhat improperly the Fourth Crusade, the amphibious
landing and conquest of a number of western European warriors
against the ancient walls of the Byzantine capital not only put a
Latin king on the imperial throne until 1261, but also gave the
Venetian navy, the conveyors of the Fourth Crusaders, a complete
monopoly over the eastern half of the Mediterranean. The western
half was fought over by Venice, Genoa, Pisa, and Aragon, with
Genoa as the chief combattant.[39]

Between 1253 and 1270 Venice and Genoa fought several
naval engagements including large sea battles at Acre, Tyre,
Settepozzi, and Trepani; in these Venice achieved more victories
than losses, largely because of Genoese tactical ineptitude, although Genoa's assistance of the Byzantines in recovering Constantinople in 1261 may have far exceeded any defeats it suffered.
In 1281 the Genoese again struck a defiant blow for domination
of the Mediterranean when they provided the naval support for
Charles of Anjou's conquest of Naples and Southern Italy, a conquest won despite the destruction of the Angevin-French fleet by
the Aragonese at the Bay of Naples in 1282. Following this, in
1284, Genoa destroyed the Pisans at Meloria. Finally, between
1294 and 1299 the Genoese and Venetians fought a second naval
war with battles in such places as Lapazzo and Curzola, each of
which were won by Genoa.[40]

Almost all of the engagements in these wars were fought on
the open sea, the first such naval warfare. This has given rise to
the belief among some historians that modern naval strategy and
tactics originated here, although in a period before the invention
and use of naval gunpowder weapons.[41] More importantly, however, may be the question of what such incessant naval warfare
cost the Crusader kingdoms in the Holy Land. For without a
strong Mediterranean fleet, it was impossible for the Crusaders
to gain reinforcements and supplies. Jerusalem, it is true, fell in

1229, before most of the intra-Mediterranean warfare began, but most of the Crusader coastal cities were not recaptured until after 1260—Caesarea, Haifa, and Arsuf in 1265, Antioch in 1268, Tripoli in 1289, and Acre, the last vestige of the Crusader kingdoms in the Holy Land, in 1291. Their fall must have been influenced by the western European Mediterranean warfare.[42] As well, both of Louis IX's Crusades (sometimes referred to as the Sixth and Seventh Crusades), launched at Egypt and Tunis in 1248 and 1270, failed to win great victories probably because of the lack of naval ability to support them effectively.[43]

Galleys built in the thirteenth century were little changed in style and technology from those constructed the century previously, although they began to be made larger. These, known as great galleys, measured 39 meters long and 5.2 meters wide with a draught of 1.3 to 1.7 meters when fully laden. Their masts were 22 meters tall. They could carry 130 to 145 tons of cargo. These galleys were most frequently biremes, although the Vene-

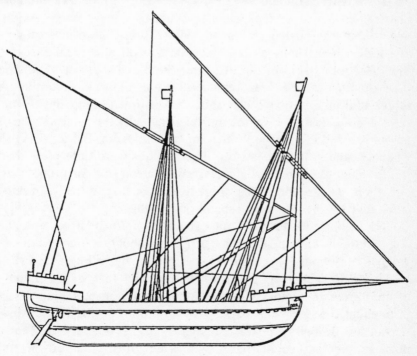

Two-masted round ship built for the Crusades of Louis IX.
[From Unger (1980).]

Medieval Military Technology

tians did construct some triremes, with one or two masts for sailed travel. Finally, these ships also generally carried a large crew, with Venetian galleys of the period, for example, carrying a crew of 158, 139 of whom manned the oars. Others on board served as captain, honor guard, and crossbowmen.[44]

Other thirteenth-century warships were the *galleons* (also called the *galea* and *galiottes*). This was a smaller vessel than the galley, and is sometimes known simply as a light galley. It also seems to have been built in the same way, with both oars and sails for propulsion, but it carried a smaller crew—Venetian galleons carried 126 men, 101 of whom were rowers.[45]

Galleys also served as cargo ships, capable of carrying sizeable cargoes at a relatively high speed. Most often these operated solely in the Mediterranean, carrying spices, Eastern goods, and pilgrims, but galleys from Flanders traveling along the Atlantic and Mediterranean coasts to Italy were known.[46] However, galleys as cargo ships were limited by the space needed for the large numbers of oarsmen and their personal possessions, so most cargo continued to be transported by round sailing ships. Two-masted nefs and hulks, sometimes as large as 500 or 600 tons, remained the dominant round-ship of the early thirteenth century, but by its end their dominance had been replaced by the *taurides* (or taride), a larger multiple-masted cargo ship of Muslim design, and by the *cog*, a ship designed in the north principally to transport large amounts of cargo through the much less calm Baltic, English Channel, and Atlantic seaways. The taurides were little more than larger versions of the earlier nefs, using lateen rigs for propulsion, and their construction was short-lived, as they quickly became surpassed by the superior capabilities of the cog.[47]

No medieval ship may have been as influential as was the cog. Little is known about its origin, although it may have developed out of smaller coastal vessels prominent in England, Friesland, and Scandinavia, but it is well known that by the middle of the thirteenth century it had become the dominant sailing vessel throughout the medieval world, both in the north and in the Mediterranean. Initially, it was smaller than its twelfth- and early thirteenth-century counterparts, with a length of 25 to 30 meters, a width no more than 9.5 meters and a draught of between 3 and 4 meters; yet it could carry as much or more cargo (sometimes as much as 300 tons) while operated by a smaller crew. It also had the potential to grow larger, and as the need arose, the size of the cog increased, without much increase in construction costs or crew size. Its single, large, square sail (sometimes as large as 355 square meters) also provided sufficient propulsion to deliver its load quickly, and yet its high freeboard also made it capable of withstanding the treacherous heavy winds and waves found in northern and Atlantic waters. Moreover, castles could be and were frequently added to both its fore and aft decks giving it sufficient defensibility to stand alone against pirates and other warships. Although it had little offensive naval capabilities, this made it practically a warship in its own right, cutting down markedly the need for a convoy to protect it. All of this added up to a striking savings in maritime freight costs.[48]

Naval Weapons

Weaponry on board thirteenth-century ships was little different from those of the eleventh and twelfth centuries, with personal arms of the crew still the dominant weapons used against opposing vessels. According to a 1225 Venetian law, these weapons were a helmet, shield, broad sword, dagger, and two lances or long lances; but this may not have been indicative of all sailors' arms of the period.[49] Crossbows certainly continued to provide most warships' firepower, and at least according to one author, Frederic C. Lane, it is important to recognize that the nautical use of the crossbow increased substantially with the use of the double-castled cog. This can be seen most clearly in the large number of regulations of the thirteenth and fourteenth centuries requiring that either a special body of crossbowmen be present on board all ships or that any mate or sailor above a certain rank be outfitted with a crossbow as well as his other personal arms. Some crossbows, called by the name *balistae*, may also have been mounted on the deck of these ships, although these should not be confused with the ancient Greco-Roman catapult.[50] A few ships also carried trebuchets on their castles, but the use of these, as was the case in the twelfth century, was limited to firing on fortifications or to hurling burning projectiles at distant ships.[51]

All grappled or close-order combat was fought solely by individual sailors. Such warfare is reported by the Spaniard Bernat
Desclot to have taken place in a battle within the port of Malta
between the Catalan navy and the southern French navy of Charles
of Anjou:

> And the battle was great and hard with lances, and with stones
> and lime [used to blind their opponents] and arrows from the
> crossbows; and it was mostly from the galleys of the Provençals
> that came so many lances and stones and so much lime on to
> the galleys of the Catalans, that all the galleys and sea were
> covered. Then the admiral of the King of Aragon said to the
> men of the galley he was in, and they said it from one galley
> to the other, that they should not throw any weapons, only
> arrows of the crossbows, and that they should think to cover
> themselves well and resist the missiles. This word got through
> all the Catalan galleys; and so it was that they did not throw
> any weapons, but they took cover and withstood the missiles
> which came from the galleys of the Provençals, of lances and
> stones and lime, so dense that it was frightful to see. But the
> crossbows of both sides shot; so that the snapping of the cross-
> bows was so strong that it was terrible to hear. The battle went
> on till noon [it had begun at sunrise] with neither one party nor
> the other knowing which had the advantage, until the galleys
> of the Provençals had exhausted the lances, the stones and the
> lime and began to throw the rammers and the mortars [used to
> pulverize the lime]. When the Catalans saw that they were
> throwing the rammers and mortars, they learned that they had
> exhausted all their weapons and then they cried: "Arago—via
> sus." And they took strength and fought them with great vigor
> and threw their lances of ash with hardened points...and hunting
> darts and hurled them so hard that neither defenses nor shields
> helped, all were pierced; even the deck of the galley was pierced
> one side to the other.[52]

Technological Innovations

Like the introduction of the carvel-built ship in the twelfth century,
the thirteenth century also saw numerous technological changes.
Two of these, the stern rudder and the compass, were of particular
importance and must be highlighted here, as both eventually played

an extremely important role in the African and Atlantic exploration which would take place in the later Middle Ages.

The sternpost rudder, which was an invention accompanying the development of the cog in the thirteenth century, quickly proved to be far superior to the traditional dual steering oars which piloted other ships. A ship could now be much more easily maneuvered through water, even the most turbulent waves. It also meant that lateen rigs were not needed, and that they could be replaced with more powerful square sails.[53]

Invented about the same time, the primitive boxed compass, its origins debated, completely changed the navigational method of medieval ships. Earlier navigation was based on the stars and inaccurate maps; ships had difficulty sailing on cloudy nights, and they ceased sailing in the winter. The compass permitted year-round sailing in almost any weather condition. It also allowed for the creation of accurate portolan charts, which enabled a vessel to sail more easily on open sea.[54]

Changes in Naval Warfare

Certainly in comparison with the thirteenth century, but also perhaps in comparison with the two centuries prior to the thirteenth, the late Middle Ages saw a paucity of naval warfare. It did not look like a time of peace at the outset, however, as the fourteenth century began as the thirteenth century had left off with naval warfare both in the Mediterranean and in the English Channel. In the eastern Mediterranean, Venice and Genoa fought two more wars, both ending in a draw, although Genoa did scare Venice greatly by appearing with full fleet in the Venetian lagoon. In the western Mediterranean, Genoa also fought a naval war, this one against the Catalans. Genoa was defeated and lost Sardinia. In the English Channel the fleet of Edward I of England and Philip IV of France continued to spar against each other with little decisiveness. Edward I and his son, Edward II, also used their navy against the Scots from 1296 to 1328.[55]

However, by the middle of the century naval warfare had began to decline significantly. Part of this was certainly due to the many natural and man-made disasters which seemed to define the century—the Black Death, the Bardi and Peruzzi bank failures,

the Hundred Years War, Flemish and Italian trade decline, etc.—
but not to be underestimated were the changes in design and construction which made attack on these vessels no longer a simple
feat. In the Mediterranean piracy continued almost unabated, especially with the resurgence of late medieval Muslim naval activity, but naval warfare such as that common during the thirteenth
century had virtually disappeared. Even though there would be a
slight rise in naval activity during the 1420s and 1430s, again
between Genoa and Venice, the Mediterranean remained relatively
calm into the sixteenth century.[56]

   This peace permitted Venice, Aragon and, at least until 1460,
Genoa to strengthen their maritime empires and even to recover
some of their lost territories. Venice especially grew strong, with
large mainland holdings along the Italian peninsula, on the Dalmatian coast, and in Greece and Cyprus, and her fleet grew to
an estimated 80 galleys and 300 sailing ships, clearly the largest
in the Mediterranean. Only Ottoman Turkey would eventually
compete with Venice in the eastern Mediterranean. Venice's
strength was nearly equalled by that of Aragon which controlled
much of the western Mediterranean, with Naples, Sicily, and Sardinia added to Valencia, Aragon, and Catalonia during the reign
of Alfonso V; Castile (which had taken Gibraltar in 1462) joined
this union with the marriage of Ferdinand of Aragon and Isabella
of Castile; Grenada was added in 1492. Finally, it cannot be
forgotten that it was with ships from the Aragonese fleet that
Columbus sailed to the New World.[57]

   The Mediterranean peace also gave rise to new maritime powers. Florence grew into a minor naval power after its conquest
of Pisa in 1406, while at the same time Southern France also
began to develop its own fleet. Yet, neither of these naval entities
duplicated the rise of Portugal. With the western Mediterranean
saturated with maritime activity, the Portuguese, under the able
leadership of Prince Henry the Navigator, took a new approach
to naval activity. Instead of venturing east into the Mediterranean,
the Portuguese went south toward the islands of the Atlantic, conquering Madeira, the Cape Verdes, and the Azores by 1410, and
toward North Africa, conquering Ceuta, on the Moroccan coast
opposite Gibraltar, in 1415. By 1471 Portugal had complete control of Tangiers and all the Moroccan ports south to Agadir. Nine

years later, the Portuguese had traveled to the coasts of Guinea, Ghana, Nigeria, and the Congo, and by 1487, Bartholomeu Diaz had landed at the Cape of Good Hope. Eleven years later Vasco da Gama sailed around Africa and landed in India.[58]

In the north, peace was harder to come by. The conflict of the late thirteenth and early fourteenth centuries between France and England developed into the Hundred Years War. From its onset naval warfare was a prominent feature. Indeed, the first major engagement, fought at Sluys in 1340, was a naval battle, with the navy of Edward III, now King of England, sweeping down on the moored French and mercenary Spanish fleet with, as contemporary historian Geoffrey le Baker writes, "the wind and sun at his back and the flow of the tide with him." The English prevailed, and the French fleet was either captured or destroyed. The English would prevail again over a much smaller French-bought Castilian fleet in 1350, at the battle of Winchelsea. Together these victories gave the English almost unhindered access to the channel, and they used this freedom to transport large armies to the continent, armies which won battles at Crécy, Calais, and Poitiers. But the French eventually recovered, again with the help of mercenary Castilians, and at the battle of La Rochelle, fought in 1372, they responded with an impressive victory against the English, destroying most of the latter's fleet, but also leaving their own fleet in ruin. This, coupled with French and English financial problems—after the death of Edward III, the English were forced to sell off many of their ships to pay the royal debts— meant the end of the naval phase of the Hundred Years War. This decline continued into the fifteenth century, with neither France nor England desiring to engage each other on the sea, although piracy and privateering continued between the two kingdoms until the end of the war.[59]

Fiftheenth-Century Advances

The cog continued to be the most prominent ship of the late Middle Ages, especially in the north, both as a cargo vessel and as a warship. So dominant was this ship in England, for example, that studies have shown that more than 57 of the vessels in that navy between 1337 and 1360 were cogs.[60]

Their popularity also extended to the Mediterranean, but there the great galley continued to be a most favored cargo and warship, as it would remain into the sixteenth century. Its long, thin shape was perfect for the relative calm of the Mediterranean, while its speed continued to be ensured by capable oarsmen and lateen sails. Some galleys also had square sails. Galleys were also known in the north, with several involved in the naval battles of the early Hundred Years War, but their popularity waned after the first decades of the fourteenth century.[61]

By the fifteenth century, other naval vessels began to appear. One was the *balinger*, a small oared cargo ship of indeterminate design, although probably similar to a barge, which served as a coastal cargo transport primarily along the English, French, and Low Countries coasts.[62] A second was the extremely large northern European herring *buss*, the principal fishing ship of the rising Dutch fleet.[63] And a third new ship was the *caravel*, a two-masted ship of Muslim influence which used lateen and square sails together to allow for both speed and maneuverability. Twenty to 30 meters long, 4 to 5 meters wide, with a shallow draught and a cargo capacity of 50 tons or more (150 to 200 tons by the end of the fifteenth century), it could also travel long distances with relative ease and was favored by the Portuguese and Spanish for their lengthy voyages of exploration, with Columbus' *Nina* and *Pinta* the most famous examples.[64]

However, the most famous new ship of the fifteenth century was the *carrack*. Essentially a modification of the earlier cog, the carrack (which was sometimes mistakenly called a nef in the fifteenth century) was a large ship carrying two and later three masts on which hung primarily square sails, although some lateen rigs were always included to give the ship added maneuverability. Its enormous size, sometimes as large as 38 meters long and 12 meters wide, with a cargo capability of 1000 to 1400 tons, made it an excellent cargo ship, capable of carrying heavy bulk cargoes, while its carvel construction, stern rudder, and multiple sails made it able to withstand both Atlantic and Mediterranean travel. And, like the cog, the carrack was capable of being both warship and cargo vessel, outfitted with the same fore and aft castle arrangement as its predecessor, on which could be set crossbowmen and cannons. By the end of the fifteenth century, the carrack, which counted Columbus' flagship, the *Santa Maria*, among its number, had already replaced the cog as the ship of choice among late medieval sailors, and it would become the model of the great sailing ship, the "floating fortress" of the early modern era.[65]

What made the carrack the great vessel that it became was that it took the discoveries of the compass, carvel construction, and the sternpost rudder, and added the innovation of full-rigging. Full-rigging, "the great invention of European ship design" in the words of Richard W. Unger, was the mixture of both lateen and square sails together on board the ship. Generally this meant that while the fore- and mainmasts of the carrack carried one or two large square sails apiece, giving the ship great wind velocity, the mizzenmast was outfitted with a lateen sail providing extra maneuverability. At the end of the century, a small square sail was also often attached to the bowsprit as a headsail for further handling control. Full-rigging enabled the ship to be controlled more easily and with greater power, features required for a vessel to endure the frequently inhospitable Atlantic coastal waters of Europe and Africa as well as the high waves and harsh winds of open sea travel.[66]

The world changed in the fifteenth century. In 1453 the Hundred Years War ended, marking the beginning of French European power and the decline of English continental designs (although Calais, at least for another century, would remain in English hands). In that same year the Ottoman Turks took Constantinople, ending the more than eleven centuries of Byzantine domination of the eastern Mediterranean, and at the same time capping a Turkish war of conquest of that region which had begun 200 years earlier. Their holdings included most of the Middle East, Persia, Asia Minor, the islands of the eastern Mediterranean, and the Greek peninsula. In 1492 Columbus set sail west across the Atlantic Ocean exploring several Caribbean islands; later voyages would take him to other islands and along the coast of South America. These voyages opened a floodgate of later western explorations. In 1494 Charles VIII took his army through Italy on a journey of discipline against the Kingdom of Naples, then rebelling against his cousin, the Duke of Savoy. Although not his primary purpose, his invasion forced the relatively free Italian city-states to realize that their independence was basically dependent on wars which kept the larger and more militarily dominant lands of Europe away from their vulnerable land mass. Finally, in 1498, Vasco da Gama circled Africa and landed in India. The East became closer, although the journey was still perilous. Trade, with its unfortunate side-effects, slavery and exploitation, now became possible with all coasts of Asia and Africa. All of these events affected the European concept of sea travel and shipbuilding. Moreover, with gunpowder weapons becoming more available and more practical, warships began to develop their offensive and defensive strategy around them. Hull openings permitted varying tiers of these weapons, which when used in unison could sink a ship in what would later be called the broadside. Never again would naval warfare be carried out as it had during the Middle Ages.[67]

Notes

1   Casson (1971):1.

2   See Casson (1971):3-10.

3   See Casson (1971):11-42 and Bass (1972b):11-36.

4   Casson (1971):13-16.

5   Casson (1971):31-32.

6   Casson (1971):36-38.

7   See Casson (1971):54-65 and Anderson (1962):1-5.

8   On the Greek oared warship see Foley and Soedel (1981); Casson (1971):77-140; Anderson (1962):6-30; Keith DeVries and Katzev (1972):37-64; and Steffy (1980). On the ram see Basch and Frost (1975) and Linder (1987). A Greek trireme has been reconstructed and is currently commissioned in the Greek navy. This has greatly increased our knowledge about its construction and sailing capabilities.

9   Casson (1971):141-47; Anderson (1962):31-36; and Unger (1981):236.

10 Dolley (1948):48-53; Unger (1980):43-46; Casson (1971):148-54; Lewis (1951):30-32, 72-75; van Doorninck (1972); Pryor (1988):57-61; and Anderson (1962):36-41.

11 Lewis and Runyan (1987):9-10.

12 Lewis and Runyan (1987):12 and Michael E. Jones (1987):62-69. On the Sutton Hoo boat see P. Marsden (1972):123-24.

13 Quoted in Lewis and Runyan (1985):10-11. See also Lewis (1951):18-19 and Rodgers (1940):6-9.

14 Rodgers (1940):9-14.

15 Lewis and Runyan (1987):62-63.

16 Lewis (1951):54-78, 100-15, 132-63, 192-98; Lewis and Runyan (1985):41-50; Nicolle (1989); Kreutz (1976); Unger (1980):99-100; Pryor (1988):28-29; and Rodgers (1940):30-40. On the Byzantine naval effort against the Saracens see Lewis and Runyan (1985):24-39; Unger (1980):52-55, 96-98; and Stratos (1980).

17   Hooper (1989):203 and Rodgers (1940):72.

18   See Atkinson (1979); Crumlin-Pedersen (1981); Binns (1981); Christensen
     (1972); Unger (1980):75-96; G. Jones (1968):182-90; Lewis and Runyan
     (1985):92-99; and Rodgers (1940):69-87. On the Viking sail specifically
     see Gillmer (1979) and Christensen (1979).

19   Atkinson (1979):41-44. See also Lewis and Runyan (1985):95-99. On the
     Long Serpent see Rodgers (1940):73-76. Other Viking naval battles include
     the battle of Hafrsfjord (c.872), Aarhus (1044), Nisaa (1062), and Gotha
     River (1159). See Rodgers (1940):80-86.

20   As quoted in Lewis and Runyan (1985):94.

21   See Hooper (1989):203-04; Hollister (1962):103; and Lewis and Runyan
     (1985):94.

22   See Hollister (1962):103-26 and Hooper (1989).

23   See, for example, Lewis and Runyan (1985):94-95 and Douglas (1964):189-
     90.

24   Bachrach (1985b).

25   Gillmor (1985).

26   Neumann (1989).

27   Lewis and Runyan (1985):64-65, 115; Rodgers (1940):53-58; and Unger
     (1980):120.

28   Lewis and Runyan (1985):62-63.

29   Lewis and Runyan (1985):63-64.

30   The most extensive discussions of the Crusader round-ship can be found in
     Pryor (1982); (1984); (1988):32-34; and (1990); Steffy (1981); Unger
     (1980):123-27; and Unger (1981):237-38. The best description of a galley
     built during the years from 1000 to 1250 can be found in Unger (1980):121-
     22. See also Lewis and Runyan (1985):66-68.

31   As quoted in Lewis and Runyan (1985):75-76. On the more traditional
     Muslim ship facing the Crusaders see Nicolle (1989):170-75.

32   Lewis and Runyan (1985):68-69 and Pryor (1988):75-76.

33   For a chronology of Crusader-Muslim naval conflict between 1099 and 1126
     see Hamblin (1986).

34   Lewis and Runyan (1985):75-76 and Pryor (1988):115-30. On the 1123 defeat
     of the Fatamid navy see Hamblin (1986):83.

35   Unger (1980):120-21, 129, 225-26 and Anderson (1962):43.

36   Lewis and Runyan (1985):69-70.

37   Lewis and Runyan (1985):69-70.

38   Lewis and Runyan (1985):121-23. See also Freeman (1980) and Rodgers
     (1940):81-95.

39   Lewis and Runyan (1985):70-72 and Dotson (1981):87. For a description of
     the naval operation at Constantinople see Queller (1980) and Rodgers
     (1940):117-28.

40   Lewis and Runyan (1985):70-76 and Rodgers (1940):128-42. On the first
      Genoese-Venetian war see Dotson (1981). On the Aragonese naval battles
      of the thirteenth century see Pryor (1983).

41   See, for example, Lewis and Runyan (1985):77.

42   Lewis and Runyan (1985):76-77.

43   Lewis and Runyan (1985):76-77 and Unger (1980):123-25.

44   Robbert (1969):142-43; Laures (1987):19-20; Mott (1990):110-11; Pryor
      (1988):64-66; Unger (1980):121, 176-82; Unger (1981):238-40; Lewis and
      Runyan (1985):74; and Rodgers (1940):110-16. On the Venetian construc-
      tion of triremes see Lane (1963b). On English galleys of the thirteenth
      century see Anderson (1962):42-51. The number of oarsmen differed
      greatly between vessels, with Flemish and Spanish galleys often having
      more oarsmen than their Italian counterparts.

45   Robbert (1969):143; Mott (1990):104-08; Pryor (1988):66-67; and Unger
      (1980):176-82. Numbers of crewmen also varied on these smaller oared
      vessels.

46   Unger (1980):176-82.

47   Pryor (1982):103-25; Lewis and Runyan (1985):74; Unger (1980):123-25;
      and Rodgers (1940):112.

48   Unger (1980):138-46, 150-51; Unger (1981):242-47; Ellmers (1979); and
      Lewis and Runyan (1985):74-75. On the defensibility of the cog see Unger
      (1981):235.

49   Robbert (1969):141 and F.W. Brooks (1928):126. A 1255 Venetian law
      altered this to require all seamen to be equipped with a sword, shield,
      dagger, three lances or javelins, a helmet or cap, and a battle jacket. See
      Lane (1969-70):162.

50   Lane (1969-70); F.W. Brooks (1928):121-25; and Laures (1987):26-27.

51   F.W. Brooks (1928):119-20 and Robbert (1969):143.

52   As quoted in Laures (1987):26.

53   Unger (1980):141-43 and Lewis and Runyan (1985):74-75.

54   Marcus (1956); Lane (1963a); Unger (1980):130-31, 174; and Lewis and
      Runyan (1985):74-75.

55   Lewis and Runyan (1985):77-78; Freeman (1980); and Reid (1960).

56   Lewis and Runyan (1985):78-81.

57   Lewis and Runyan (1985):79-82, 148-49.

58   Lewis and Runyan (1985):81, 145-48.

59   See Richmond (1971); Runyan (1986); Sherborne (1967); Rodgers (1940):95-
      105; and Lewis and Runyan (1985):123-28, 149. On the battle of Sluys
      see DeVries (1987):155-202. On the French use of Castilian mercenaries
      during the first part of the Hundred Years War see Lewis and Runyan
      (1985):133-34.

60   Unger (1980):162-71, 182-87; Lane (1934):37-50; Runyan (1986):93-96;
      Burwash (1947):117-21; Sandurra (1972):214; and Lewis and Runyan
      (1985):82-83, 137-38.

61   Mallett (1967); Dotson (1981); Tinniswood (1949); Anderson (1928); Mott
      (1987); Lane (1963c); Lane (1934):1-34; Unger (1980):176-82, 192-93,
      209-11; Anderson (1962):52-55; Sandurra (1972):209-10; Pryor (1988):66-
      70; Law (1987):114-17; and Runyan (1986):96-97.

62   Sherborne (1977); Burwash (1947):101-17; Unger (1980):171-72; Unger
      (1981):247-48; and Lewis and Runyan (1985):137-38, 158.

63   Unger (1980):206-09; Lewis and Runyan (1985):158-59; and Unger
      (1973):394-97.

64   Unger (1980):212-14, 231; Lewis and Runyan (1985):82-83, 159; and Law
      (1987):121-22. For English caravels see Burwash (1947):128-31.

65   Unger (1980):220-21,, 228-31; Lewis and Runyan (1985):82-83, 159-63; and
      Sandurra (1972):214. On the carrack's defensibility see Unger (1981):235.

66   Unger (1980):216-20, 226-27; (1981):247-48.

67   On the changes between medieval and early modern ships see Unger
      (1980):228-81; Guilmartin (1974); Parker (1988); Cipolla (1965); and Pryor
      (1988):165-92.

Bibliography

Abels, Richard P. 1988. *Lordship and Military Obligation in Anglo-Saxon England*. Berkeley and Los Angeles: University of California Press.

Addyman, P.V. 1972. "Excavations at Baile Hill, York," *Chateau Gaillard* 5:7-12.

Addyman, P.V., Nicholas Pearson and Dominic Tweddle. 1982. "The Coppergate Helmet," *Antiquity* 56:189-94.

Alberti, Leon Battista. 1988. *On the Art of Building in Ten Books*. Trans. J. Rykwert, N. Leach and R. Tavernor. Cambridge, Mass: MIT Press.

Allmand, Christopher. 1988. *The Hundred Years War: England and France at War, c.1300-c.1450*. Cambridge: Cambridge University Press.

Anderson, R.C. 1928. "English Galleys in 1295," *Mariner's Mirror* 14:220-41.

—————. 1962. *Oared Fighting Ships from Classical Times to the Age of Steam*. London: Percival Marshall.

Apollinaris, Sidonius. 1963. *Poems and Letters*. Trans. W.B. Anderson. 2 vols. Cambridge, MA: Harvard University Press.

Araguas, Philippe. 1979. "Les châteaux des marches de Catalogne et Ribagorce (950-1100)," *Bulletin Monumental* 137:205-34.

Ascherl, Rosemary. 1989. "The Technology of Chivalry in Reality and Romance." In: *The Study of Chivalry*. Ed. H. Chickering and T.H. Seiler. Kalamazoo: Medieval Institute Publications. 263-311.

Ashdown, Charles H. 1925. *Armour and Weapons in the Middle Ages*. London: The Holland Press.

Atkinson, Ian. 1979. *The Viking Ships*. Cambridge: Cambridge University Press.

Baatz, Dietwulf. 1978. "Recent Finds in Ancient Artillery," *Britannia* 9:1-17.

Bachrach, Bernard S. 1969. "The Rise of Armorican Chivalry," *Technology and Culture* 10:166-71.

—————. 1970a. "Charles Martel, Mounted Shock Combat, The Stirrup, and Feudalism," *Studies in Medieval and Renaissance History* 7:47-75.

—————. 1970b. "Procopius, Agathias and the Frankish Military," *Speculum* 45:435-41.

—————. 1972. *Merovingian Military Organization, 481-751*. Minneapolis: University of Minnesota Press.

—————. 1974. "Military Organization in Aquitaine under the Early Carolingians," *Speculum* 49:1-33.

—————. 1975. "Early Medieval Fortifications in the 'West' of France: A Revised Technical Vocabulary," *Technology and Culture* 16:531-69.

—————. 1976. "A Study in Feudal Politics: Relations between Fulk Nerra and William the Great, 995-1030," *Viator* 7:113-21.

—————. 1979. "Fortifications and Military Tactics: Fulk Nerra's Strongholds circa 1000," *Technology and Culture* 20:531-49.

—————. 1983. "The Angevin Strategy of Castle Building in the Reign of Fulk Nerra, 987-1040," *American Historical Review* 88:533-60.

—————. 1984. "The Cost of Castle Building: The Case of the Tower at Langeais, 992-994." In: *The Medieval Castle: Romance and Reality*. Ed. K. Reyerson and F. Powe. Dubuque, Iowa: Kendall/Hunt Publishing Company. 47-65.

—————. 1985a. "Animals and Warfare in Early Medieval Europe." In: *L'uomo di fronte al mondo animale nell'alto medioevo*. Settimane di studio del centro italiano di studi sull'alto medioevo, xxxi. Spoleto: Centro Italiano di Studi sull'alto Medioevo. 707-51.

—————. 1985b. "On the Origins of William the Conqueror's Horse Transports," *Technology and Culture* 26:505-31.

—————. 1988. "*Caballus et Callarius* in Medieval Warfare." In: *The Study of Chivalry*. Ed. H. Chickering and T.H. Seiler. Kalamazoo: Medieval Institute Publications. 173-211.

Bachrach, Bernard and Rutherford Aris. 1990. "Military Technology and Garrison Organization: Some Observations on Anglo-Saxon Military Thinking in Light of the Burghal Hidage," *Technology and Culture* 31:1-17.

Barber, Richard. 1982. *The Knight and Chivalry*. New York: Harper and Row.

Barbier, Pierre. 1968. *La France féodale*. Vol. I: *Chateaux-forts et églises fortifiées*. Saint-Brieuc: Les presses bretonnes.

Barker, John W. 1966. *Justinian and the Later Roman Empire*. Madison: University of Wisconsin Press.

Barker, Juliet R.V. 1986. *The Tournament in England, 1100-1400*. Wolfesboro: The Boydell Press.

Barker, Philip. 1987. "The *Plumbatae* from Wroxeter." In: *Aspects of the "De rebus bellicis": Papers Presented to Professor E.A. Thompson*. Ed. M.W.C. Hassall. BAR International Series, 63. Oxford: British Archaeological Reports. 97-99.

Barrow, G.W.S. 1956. *Feudal Britain*. London: Edward Arnold.

Bartlett, Robert J. 1986. "Technique militaire et pouvoir politique, 900-1300," *Annales: économies, sociétés, civilisations* 41:1135-59.

Basch, Lucien and Honor Frost. 1975. "Another Punic Wreck in Sicily: Its Ram," *The International Journal of Nautical Archaeology and Underwater Exploration* 4:201-28.

Bass, George F. (ed.) 1972a. *A History of Seafaring Based on Underwater Archaeology.* New York: Walker & Company.

Bass, George F. 1972b. "The Earliest Seafarers in the Mediterranean and the Near East." In: Bass (1972a):11-36.

Bautier, Anne-Marie. 1976. "Contribution a l'histoire du cheval au moyen age," *Bulletin philologique et historique* 209-49.

Beeler, John H. 1956. "Castles and Strategy in Norman and Early Angevin England," *Speculum* 31:581-601.

—————. 1966. *Warfare in England, 1066-1189.* Ithaca: Cornell University Press.

—————. 1971. *Warfare in Feudal Europe, 730-1200.* Ithaca: Cornell University Press.

Binding, Günther. 1972. "Spätkarolingisch-ottonische Pfalzen und Bergen am Niederrhein," *Chateau Gaillard* 5:23-34.

Binns, Alan. 1981. "The Ships of the Vikings, Were They 'Viking Ships'?" In: *Proceedings of the Eighth Viking Congress.* Odense: Odense University Press.

Bishop, M.C. and J.C. Coulston. 1989. *Roman Military Equipment.* Aylesbury: Shire.

Blair, Claude. 1958. *European Armour.* London: B.T. Batsford.

Bloch, Marc. (1961). *Feudal Society.* Trans. L.A. Manyon. 2 Vols. Chicago: University of Chicago Press.

Boase, T.S.R. 1967. *Castles and Churches of the Crusading Kingdom.* London: Oxford University Press.

—————-. 1977. "Military Architecture in the Crusader States in Palestine and Syria." In: Setton (1955-1990). IV:140-64.

Bonde, Sheila. 1984. "Castle and Church Building at the Time of the Norman Conquest." In: *The Medieval Castle: Romance and Reality.* Ed. K. Reyerson and F. Powe. Dubuque, Iowa: Kendall/Hunt Publishing Company. 84-91.

Bouard, Michel de Bouard. 1964. "Quelques données Françaises et Normandes concernant le problème de l'origine des mottes," *Chateau Gaillard* 2:19-26.

Bowlus, Charles. 1978. "Warfare and Society in the Carolingian Ostmark," *Austrian History Yearbook* 14:3-28.

Boyer, Marjorie Nice. 1976. *Medieval French Bridges: A History.* Cambridge, MA: Medieval Academy of America Publications.

Bradbury, Jim. 1985. *The Medieval Archer.* New York: St. Martin's Press.

Brodie, Bernard and Fawn M. 1973. *From Crossbow to H-Bomb.* 2nd. ed. Bloomington: Indiana University Press.

Brøndsted, Johannes. 1960. *The Vikings.* Trans. K. Skov. Harmondsworth: Penguin Books.

Brooks, F.W. 1928. "Naval Armament in the Thirteenth Century," *Mariner's Mirror* 14:114-31.

Brooks, Nicholas P. 1971. "The Development of Military Obligations in Eighth- and Ninth-Century England." In: *England Before the Conquest: Studies in Primary Sources Presented to Dorothy Whitelock*. Ed. P. Clemoes and K. Hughes. Cambridge: Cambridge University Press. 69-84.

—————. 1978. "Arms, Status and Warfare in Late-Saxon England." In: *Ethelred the Unready: Papers from the Millenary Conference*. Ed. D. Hill. BAR British Series, 59. Oxford: British Archaeological Reports. 81-103.

—————. 1979. "England in the Ninth Century: The Crucible of Defeat," *Transactions of the Royal Historical Society*. 5th series 29:1-20.

Brown, Elizabeth A.R. 1974. "The Tyranny of a Construct: Feudalism and Historians of Medieval Europe," *American Historical Review* 79:1063-88.

Brown, R. Allen. 1954. *English Medieval Castles*. London: B.T. Batsford.

—————. 1976. *English Castles*. 3rd ed. London: B.T. Batsford.

—————. 1989a. "The Architecture of the Bayeux Tapestry." In: *Castles, Conquest and Charters: Collected Papers*. Woodbridge: The Boydell Press. 214-26.

—————. 1989b. "The Castles of the Conquest." In: *Castles, Conquest and Charters: Collected Papers*. Woodbridge: The Boydell Press. 65-74.

—————. 1989c. "An Historian's Approach to the Origins of the Castle in England." In: *Castles, Conquest and Charters: Collected Papers*. Woodbridge: The Boydell Press. 1-18.

—————. 1989d. "The Norman Conquest and the Genesis of English Castles." In: *Castles, Conquest and Charters: Collected Papers*. Woodbridge: The Boydell Press. 75-89.

—————. 1989e. "Royal Castle-Building in England, 1154-1216." In: *Castles, Conquest and Charters: Collected Papers*. Woodbridge: The Boydell Press. 19-64.

—————. 1989f. "Some Observations on the Tower of London." In: *Castles, Conquest and Charters: Collected Papers*. Woodbridge: The Boydell Press. 163-76.

—————. 1989g. "The White Tower of London." In: *Castles, Conquest and Charters: Collected Papers*. Woodbridge: The Boydell Press. 177-86.

Brown, R. Allen, H.M. Colvin and A.J. Taylor. 1963. *The History of the King's Works*. Vol 1 and 2: *The Middle Ages*. London: Her Majesty's Stationary Office.

Bruce-Mitford, Rupert. 1974a. "The Sutton Hoo Helmet—a New Reconstruction." In: *Aspects of Anglo-Saxon Archaeology: Sutton Hoo and Other Discoveries*. New York: Harper's Magazine Press. 198-209.

—————. 1974b. "The Benty Grange Helmet and Some Other Supposed Anglo-Saxon Helmets." In: *Aspects of Anglo-Saxon Archaeology: Sutton Hoo and Other Discoveries*. New York: Harper's Magazine Press. 223-52.

Brucker, Gene. 1969. *Renaissance Florence*. Berkeley and Los Angeles: University of California Press.

Bruhn de Hoffmeyer, Ada. 1961. "Introduction to the History of the European Sword," *Gladius* 1:30-75.

—————. 1963. "From Mediaeval Sword to Renaissance Rapier," *Gladius* 2:5-68.

—————. 1966. "Military Equipment in the Byzantine Manuscript of Scylitzes in the Biblioteca Nacional in Madrid," *Gladius* 5:1-160.

—————. 1972. *Arms and Armour in Spain: A Short Survey*. Vol. I: *The Bronze Age to the High Middle Ages*. Madrid: Instituto de Estudios Sobre Armas Antiguas.

Brun, Robert. 1951. "Notes sur le commerce des armes à Avignon au XIVe siècle," *Bibliothèque de l'école des Chartes* 109:209-31.

Brunner, Heinrich. 1887. "Der Reiterdienst und die Anfänge des Lehnwesens," *Zeitschrift der Savigny-Stiftung für Rechtsgeschichte, Germanistische Abteilung* 8:1-38.

Brusten, Charles. 1953. *L'armée Bourguignonne de 1465 à 1468*. Brussels: Fr. van Muysewinkel.

Bullough, D.A. 1965. *The Age of Charlemagne*. New York: Putnam.

—————. 1970. "*Europae Pater*: Charlemagne and His Achievement in the Light of Recent Scholarship," *English Historical Review* 85:59-105.

Burne, Alfred H. 1955. *The Crecy War*. London: Eyre and Spottiswood.

—————. 1956. *The Agincourt War*. London: Eyre and Spottiswood.

Burns, Thomas. 1984. *A History of the Ostrogoths*. Bloomington: Indiana University Press.

Burwash, Dorothy. 1947. *English Merchant Shipping, 1460-1540*. Toronto: University of Toronto Press.

Bury, J.B. 1967. *The Invasion of Europe by the Barbarians*. New York: W.W. Norton and Company.

Butler, R.M. 1959. "Late Roman Town Walls in Gaul," *Archaeological Journal* 116:25-50.

Buttin, François. 1965. "La lance et l'arrêt de cuirasse," *Archaeologia* 99:77-178.

Carman, W.Y. 1955. *A History of Firearms from the Earliest Times to 1914*. London: Routledge & Kegan Paul.

Cary M. and H.H. Scullard. 1975. *A History of Rome down to the Reign of Constantine*, 3rd ed. New York: St. Martin's Press.

Casson, Lionel. 1971. *Ships and Seamanship in the Ancient World*. Princeton: Princeton University Press.

Chaucer, Geoffrey. 1951. *The Canterbury Tales*. Trans. N. Coghill. Harmondsworth: Penguin Books.

Chevedden, Paul E. 1990. "The Artillery Revolution of the Middle Ages: The Impact of the Trebuchet on the Development of Fortifications." Unpublished Paper.

Christensen, Arne Emil. 1972. "Scandinavian Ships from Earliest Times to the Vikings." In Bass (1972a). 159-79.

—————. 1979. "Viking Age Rigging, A Survey of Sources and Theories." In: *The Archaeology of Medieval Ships and Harbours in Northern Europe: Papers Based on those Presented to an International Symposium on Boat and Ship Archaeology at Bremerhaven in 1979*. Ed. S. McGrail. BAR International Series, 66. Greenwich: British Archaeological Reports.

Christine de Pisan. 1932. *The Book of Fayettes of Armes and of Chyvalrye*. Trans. W. Caxton. Ed. A.T.P. Byles. Early English Text Society. London: Oxford University Press.

Cipolla, Carlo. 1965. *Guns and Sails in the Early Phase of European Expansion, 1400-1700*. London: Collins.

Cirlot, Juan-Eduardo. 1967. "La evolucion de la lanza en occidente (piezas de hierro de hallstatt al siglo XV)," *Gladius* 6:5-18.

Cirlot, Victoria. 1985. "Techniques guerrières en Catalogne féodale: le maniement de la lance," *Cahiers de civilisation médiévale (Xe-Xiie siècle)* 28:35-43.

Clephan, R. Coltman. 1911. "The Ordnance of the Fourteenth and Fifteenth Centuries," *Archaeological Journal* 68:49-138.

Collins, Roger. 1983. *Early Medieval Spain: Unity in Diversity, 400-1000*. New York: St. Martin's Press.

Commynes, Philippe de. 1969. *The Memoires of Philip de Commynes*. Ed. S. Kinser. Trans. I. Cazeaux. Vol. 1. Columbia: University of South Carolina Press.

Comnena, Anna. 1969. *The Alexiad*. Trans. E.R.A. Sewter. Harmondsworth: Penguin Books.

Contamine, Philippe. 1972. *Guerre, état et société à la fin du moyen âge: Etudes sur les armées des rois de France, 1337-1494*. Paris: Mouton.

—————. 1978. "Les fortifications urbaines en France à la fin du Moyen Age: aspects financiers et économiques," *Revue historique* 260:23-47.

—————. 1984. *War in the Middle Ages*. Trans. M. Jones. Oxford: Basil Blackwell.

Coulson, Charles L.H. 1976. "Fortresses and Social Responsibility in Late Carolingian France," *Zietschrift für Archäologie des Mittelalters* 4:29-36.

Coulston, J.C. 1988. "Three Legionnaries at Croy Hill (Strathclyde)." In: *Military Equipment and the Identity of Roman Soldiers*. Ed. J.C. Coulston. Oxford: British Archaeological Reports. 1-15.

Coupland, Simon. 1990. "Carolingian Arms and Armor in the Ninth Century," *Viator*. 21:29-50.

Crossley-Holland, Kevin, ed. and trans. 1979. *The Exeter Book Riddles*. Harmondsworth: Penguin Books.

Cruden, Stewart. 1960. *The Scottish Castle*. Edinburgh: Nelson.

Crumlin-Pedersen, Ole. 1981. "Viking Shipbuilding and Seamanship." *Proceedings of the Eighth Viking Congress*. Odense: Odense University Press.

Davis, R.H.C. 1970. *A History of Medieval Europe from Constantine to Saint Louis*. London: Longman.

—————. 1983. "The Medieval Warhorse." In: *Horses in European Economic History: A Preliminary Canter.* Ed. F.M.L. Thompson. Reading: British Agricultural History Society. 4-20, 177-84.

—————. 1989. *The Medieval Warhorse.* London: Thames and Hudson.

Davison, Brian K. 1967. "The Origins of the Castle in England: The Institute's Research Project," *Archaeological Journal* 124:202-11.

Dearden, Brian. 1988. "Charles the Bald's Fortified Bridge at Pîtres (Seine): Recent Archaeological Excavations," *Anglo-Norman Studies* 11:107-12.

Deschamps, Eustace. 1878-1903. *Oeuvres complètes.* 11 vols. Ed. Q. de Saint Hilaire and G. Raynaud. Société des anciens textes Française. Paris: Libraire Renouard.

Deuchler, Florens. 1963. *Die Burgundebeute: Inventar der Beutestucke aus den Schlachten von Grandson, Murten und Nancy 1476/77.* Bern: Verlag Stämpfli & Cie.

DeVries, Kelly. 1987. *Perceptions of Victory and Defeat in the Southern Low Countries during the Fourteenth Century.* Unpublished Dissertation. University of Toronto.

—————. 1990a. "A 1445 Reference to Shipboard Artillery," *Technology and Culture* 31:818-29.

—————. 1990b. "Military Surgical Practice and the Advent of Gunpowder Weaponry," *Canadian Bulletin of Medical History* 7:131-46.

DeVries, Keith and Michael L. Katzev. 1972. "Greek, Etruscan and Phoenician Ships and Shipping." In: Bass (1972a):37-64.

Deyres, Marcel. 1974. "Les châteaux de Foulque Nerra," *Bulletin monumental* 132:7-28.

Dieulafoy, M. 1898. *Le Chateau Gaillard et l'architecture militaire au XIIIe siècle.* Paris: Libraire C. Klincksieck.

Dobson, R.B. 1977. "Urban Decline in Late Medieval England," *Transactions of the Royal Historical Society.* 5th series 27:1-22.

Dolley, R.H. 1948. "The Warships of the Later Roman Empire," *Journal of Roman Studies* 38:47-53.

Dotson, John E. 1981a. "Merchant and Naval Influences on Galley Design at Venice and Genoa in the Fourteenth Century." In: *New Aspects of Naval History.* Ed. C.L. Symonds. Annapolis: Naval Institute Press. 20-32.

—————. 1981b. "Naval Strategy in the First Genoese-Venetian War, 1257-1270," *American Neptune* 46:84-90.

Douet-d'Arcq, L. (ed.) 1863-64. *Choix de pièces inédites relatives au règne de Charles VI.* Société de l'histoire de France. Paris: Libraire Renouard.

Douglas, David C. 1964. *William the Conqueror.* Berkeley and Los Angeles: University of California Press.

Drew, Katherine Fischer. 1964. "The Carolingian Military Frontier in Italy," *Traditio* 20:437-47.

Dubled, H. 1976. "L'artillerie royale Française à l'époque de Charles VII et au début du règne de Louis XI (1437-1469): Les frères Bureau," *Memorial de l'artillerie Française* 50:555-637.

Duby, Georges. (1958). "La Féodalité? Une mentalité médiévale," *Annales: économies, sociétés, civilisations* 13:765-71.

————. 1980. "The Origins of Knighthood." In: *The Chivalrous Society*. Trans. C. Postan. Berkeley and Los Angeles: University of California Press. 158-70.

Duckett, Eleanor Shipley. 1956. *Alfred the Great: The King and His England.* Chicago: University of Chicago Press.

Duffy, Christopher. 1979. *Siege Warfare: The Fortress in the Early Modern World, 1494-1660.* London: Routledge & Kegan Paul.

Edwards, J. Goronwy. 1946. "Edward I's Castle-Building in Wales," *Proceedings of the British Academy* 32:15-81.

Ellis, Henry. 1833. *A General Introduction to the Domesday Book.* 2 vols. London: Eyre & Spottiswood.

Ellis Davidson, H.R. 1962. *The Sword in Anglo-Saxon England: Its Archaeology and Literature.* Oxford: Clarendon Press.

————. 1973. "The Secret Weapon of Byzantium," *Byzantinische Zeitschrift* 66:61-74.

Ellmers, Detlev. 1979. "The Cog of Bremen and Related Boats." In: *The Archaeology of Medieval Ships and Harbours in Northern Europe.* Ed. S. McGrail. BAR International Series, 66. Oxford: British Archaeological Reports. 1-15.

Eltis, David. 1989. "Towns and Defence in Later Medieval Germany," *Nottingham Medieval Studies* 33:91-103.

Emden, Wolfgang van. 1984. "The Castle in Some Works of Medieval Literature." In *The Medieval Castle: Romance and Reality.* Ed. K. Reyerson and F. Powe. Dubuque, Iowa: Kendall/Hunt Publishing Company. 1-26.

English, Edward D. 1984. "Urban Castles in Medieval Siena: The Sources and Images of Power." In: *The Medieval Castle: Romance and Reality.* Ed. K. Reyerson and F. Powe. Dubuque, Iowa: Kendall/Hunt Publishing Company. 175-98.

Engstrom, Robert, Scott Michael Lankton and Audrey Lesher-Engstrom. 1990. *A Modern Replication Based on the Pattern-Welded Sword of Sutton Hoo.* Kalamazoo: Medieval Institute Publications.

Enlart, Camille. 1916. *Manuel d'archéologie Française.* Vol. III: *Le costume.* Paris: Auguste Picard.

Esper, Thomas. 1965. "The Replacement of the Longbow by Firearms in the English Army," *Technology and Culture* 6:382-93.

Ferrill, Arther. 1985. *The Origins of War from the Stone Age to Alexander the Great.* London: Thames and Hudson.

————. 1986. *The Fall of the Roman Empire: The Military Explanation.* London: Thames and Hudson.

ffoulkes, Charles. 1912. *The Armourer and His Craft*. London: Methuen.

Fino, J.-F. 1964. "Notes sur la production du fer et la fabrication des armes en France au moyen-age," *Gladius* 3:47-66.

————. 1970. *Forteresses de la France médiévale*. Paris: Éditions A. & J. Picard.

————. 1972. "Machines et jet médiévales," *Gladius* 10:25-43.

————. 1974. "L'artillerie en France à la fin du moyen age," *Gladius* 12:13-31.

Flori, Jean. 1988. "Encore l'usage de la lance.... La technique du combat chevaleresque vers l'an 1100," *Cahiers de civilisation médiévale (Xe-XIIe siècle)* 31:213-40.

Foley, Vernard, George Palmer and Werner Soedel. 1985. "The Crossbow," *Scientific American* January:104-10.

Foley, Vernard and Werner Soedel. 1981. "Ancient Oared Warships," *Scientific American* April:148-63.

Foote, Peter G. and David M. Wilson. 1970. *The Viking Achievement*. New York: Praeger.

Forbes, R.J. 1955. *Studies in Ancient Technology*. Leiden: E.J. Brill.

Forde-Johnston, J. 1977. *Castles and Fortifications of Britain and Ireland*. London: J.M. Dent & Sons.

Fournier, Gabriel. 1974. "Les campagnes de Pépin le bref en Auvergne et la question des fortifications rurales au VIIIe siècle," *Francia* 2:123-35.

————. 1978. *Le château dans la France médiévale*. Paris: Aubier Montaigne.

Freeman, A.Z. 1980. "Wooden Walls: The English Navy in the Reign of Edward I." In: *Changing Interpretations and New Sources in Naval History*. Ed. R.W. Love. Jr. New York: Garland Publishing. 58-67.

Frere, S.S., S. Stow, and P. Bennett. 1982. *The Archaeology of Canterbury*. II: *Excavations on the Roman and Medieval Defences of Canterbury*. Maidstone: Kent Archaeological Society.

Froissart, Jean. 1888. *Chroniques*. Ed. S. Luce. Vol. 8. Société de l'histoire de France. Paris: Libraire Renouard.

Gaier, Claude. 1973. *L'industrie et le commerce des armes dans les anciennes principautés Belges du XIIIme à la fin du XVme siècle*. Paris: Société d'Edition "les belles lettres."

————. 1978. "L'invincibilité anglaise et le grande arc après la guerre de cent ans: un mythe tenace," *Tijdschrift voor gescheidenis* 91:378-85.

————. 1983. "Armes et armures dans l'oeuvre épique et historique de Jean d'Outremeuse (XIVe siècle)," *Gladius* 16:11-43.

Ganshof, François Louis. 1964. *Feudalism*. Trans. P. Grierson. 3rd ed. New York: Harper and Row.

————. 1968. *Frankish Institutions under Charlemagne*. Trans. B. and M. Lyon. New York: W.W. Norton & Company.

Garnier, Joseph. 1895. *L'artillerie des duc de Bourgogne d'après les documents conserves aux archives de la Côte d'Or*. Paris: Honoré Champion.

Geary, Patrick J. 1988. *Before France and Germany: The Creation and Transformation of the Merovingian World*. Oxford: Oxford University Press.

Giles of Rome. 1968. *De regimine principium libri III*. Frankfurt: Minerva G.M.B.H.

Gille, Bertrand. 1966. *Engineers of the Renaissance*. Cambridge, Mass: MIT Press.

Gillmer, Thomas. 1979. "The Capability of the Single Square Sail Rig: A Technical Assessment." In: *The Archaeology of Medieval Ships and Harbours in Northern Europe: Papers Based on those Presented to an International Symposium on Boat and Ship Archaeology at Bremerhaven in 1979*. Ed. S. McGrail. BAR International Series, 66. Greenwich: British Archaeological Reports.

Gillmor, Caroll. 1981. "The Introduction of the Traction Trebuchet into the Latin West," *Viator*. 12:1-8.

————. 1982. "European Cavalry." In: *Dictionary of the Middle Ages*. Ed. J.R. Strayer. New York: Scribners. II:200-08.

————. 1985. "Naval Logistics of the Cross-Channel Operation, 1066," *Anglo-Norman Studies* 7:221-43.

————. 1988. "The Logistics of Fortified Bridge Building on the Seine under Charles the Bald," *Anglo-Norman Studies* 11:87-106.

Giraud, J.B. 1895, 1899. *Documents pour servir à l'histoire de l'armement au moyen âge et à la Renaissance*. 2 vols. Lyon: J.B. Giraud.

Goodman, Anthony. 1981. *The Wars of the Roses: Military Activity and English Society, 1452-97*. London: Routledge & Kegan Paul.

Gregory of Tours. 1974. *The History of the Franks*. Trans. L. Thorpe. Harmondsworth: Penguin Books.

Guillerme, André E. 1988. *The Age of Water: The Urban Environment in the North of France, AD 300-1800*. College Station, Texas: Texas A&M University Press.

Guilmartin, John Francis, Jr. 1974. *Gunpowder and Galleys: Changing Technology and Mediterranean Warfare at Sea in the Sixteenth Century*. Cambridge: Cambridge University Press.

Gwei-Djen, Lu, Joseph Needham and Phan Chi-Hsing. 1988. "The Oldest Representation of a Bombard," *Technology and Culture* 29:594-605.

Hacker, Barton C. 1968. "Greek Catapults and Catapult Technology: Science, Technology, and War in the Ancient World," *Technology and Culture* 9:34-50.

Haldon, J. and M. Byrne. 1977. "A Possible Solution to the Problem of Greek Fire," *Byzantinische Zeitschrift*. 70:91-99.

Hale, J.R. 1965. "The Early Development of the Bastion: an Italian Chronology, c.1450-c.1534." In: *Europe in the Late Middle Ages*. Ed. J.R. Hale, J.R.L. Highfield and B. Smalley. Evanston: Northwestern University Press. 466-94.

—————. 1966. "Gunpowder and the Renaissance: An Essay in the History of Ideas." In: *From Renaissance to Counter-Reformation: Essays in Honour of Garrett Mattingly*. Ed. C.H. Carter. London: Jonathan Cape. 113-44.

—————. 1977. *Renaissance Fortification: Art or Engineering?* London: Thames and Hudson.

Hall, A.R. 1957. "Military Technology." In: *A History of Technology*. Ed. C. Singer et al. Oxford: Clarendon Press. II:695-730, III:347-82.

Hall, Bert. 1979. *The So-called "Manuscript of the Hussite Wars' Engineer" and Its Technological Milieu: A Study and Edition of "Codex Latinus Monacensis" 197, part 1*. Wiesbaden: Dr. Ludwig Reichert Verlag.

—————. 1983. "Cast Iron in Late Medieval England: A Re-examination." In: *Historical Metallurgy Notes: Early Ironmaking*. 76, #855:66-71.

Hamblin, William. 1986. "The Fatimid Navy during the Crusades: 1099-1124," *American Neptune* 46:77-83.

Hamer, Richard (trans.) 1970. *A Choice of Anglo-Saxon Verse*. London: Faber and Faber.

Hanson, Victor Davis. 1990. *The Western Way of War: Infantry Battle in Classical Greece*. Oxford: Oxford University Press.

Härke, Heinrich. 1989. "Knives in Early Saxon Burials: Blade Length and Age at Death," *Medieval Archaeology* 33:144-48.

—————. 1990. "'Warrior Graves'? The Background of the Anglo-Saxon Weapon Burial Rite," *Past and Present* 126:22-43.

Héliot, Pierre. 1962. "Le Chateau-Gaillard et les fortresses des XIIe et XIIIe siècles," *Chateau Gaillard* 1:53-75.

—————. 1966. "Les châteaux-forts en France du Xe au XIIe siècle à la lumière de travaux récents," *Journal des savants*. 483-515.

—————. 1974. "Origins du donjon résidential et les donjons-palais romans de France et d'Angleterre," *Cahiers de civilisation médiévale* 17:217-34.

Herben, Stephen J. 1937. "Arms and Armor in Chaucer," *Speculum* 12:475-87.

Hill, David. 1969. "The Burghal Hidage: The Establishment of a Text," *Medieval Archaeology* 13:84-92.

—————. 1979. "Siege-craft from the Sixth to the Tenth Century." In: *Aspects of the "De rebus bellicis": Papers Presented to Professor E.A. Thompson*. Ed. M.W.C. Hassall. BAR International Series, 63. Oxford: British Archaeological Reports. 111-17.

Hill, Donald R. 1973. "Trebuchets," *Viator* 4:99-114.

Hilton, R.H. and P.H. Sawyer. 1963. "Technical Determinism: The Stirrup and the Plough," *Past and Present* 24 (1963):90-100.

Hollister, C. Warren. 1962. *Anglo-Saxon Military Institutions on the Eve of the Norman Invasion*. Oxford: Clarendon Press.

Homer. 1950. *The Iliad*. Trans. E.V. Rieu. Harmondsworth: Penguin Books.

Hooper, Nicholas. 1989. "Some Observations on the Navy in Late Anglo-Saxon England." In: *Studies in Medieval History Presented to R. Allen Brown*. Ed. C.

Harper-Bill, C.J. Holdsworth and J.L. Nelson. Woodbridge: The Boydell Press. 203-213.

Hope-Taylor, Brian. 1956. "The Norman Motte at Abinger, Surrey, and its Wooden Castle." In: *Recent Archaeological Excavations in Britain.* Ed. R.L.S. Bruce-Mitford. New York: Macmillan.

—————. March, 1958. "Norman Castles," Scientific American. 198:42-48.

Hotz, Walter. 1981. *Pfalzen und Burgen der Stauferzeit. Geschichte und Gestalt.* Darmstadt: Wissenschaftliche Buchgesellschaft.

Hunt, Tony. 1981. "The Emergence of the Knight in France and England, 1000-1200." In: *Knighthood in Medieval Literature.* Ed. W.H. Jackson. Woodbridge: The Boydell Press. 1-22.

Huuri, Kalervo. 1941. *Zur Geschichte des mittelalterichen Geschützwesens.* Helsinki: Societas Orientalis Fennia.

[Inventaire]. 1855. "Inventaire de la bastille de l'an 1428," *Revue archéologique* 12:321-49.

James, Montague Rhodes, ed. 1913. *The Treatise of Walter de Milemete.* London: The Roxburghe Club.

Jones, Gwyn. 1968. *A History of the Vikings.* Oxford: Oxford University Press.

Jones, M.J. and C.J. Bond. 1987. "Urban Defences." In: *Urban Archaeology in Britain.* Ed. J. Schofield and R. Leech. London: Council for British Archaeology.

Jones, Michael. 1981. "The Defence of Medieval Brittany: A Survey of the Establishment of Fortified Towns, Castles and Frontiers from the Gallo-Roman Period to the End of the Middle Ages," *Archaeological Journal* 138:149-204.

—————. 1988. *The Creation of Brittany: A Late Medieval State.* New York: Hambledon Press.

Jones, Michael E. 1987. "The Logistics of the Anglo-Saxon Invasions." In: *Naval History: The Sixth Symposium of the United States Naval Academy.* Ed. D.M. Masterson. Wilmington: Scholarly Resources. 62-69.

Johnson, Stephen. 1983. *Late Roman Fortifications.* Totowa, N.J.: Barnes & Noble.

Justinian. 1987. *Justinian's Institutes.* Trans. P. Birks and G. Mcleod. Ed. P. Kruger. Ithaca: Cornell University Press.

Keegan, John. 1978. *The Face of Battle: A Study of Agincourt, Waterloo and the Somme.* Harmondsworth: Penguin Books.

Keen, Maurice. 1984. *Chivalry.* New Haven: Yale University Press.

Kenyon, John R. 1981. "Early Artillery Fortifications in England and Wales: A Preliminary Survey and Reappraisal," *Archaeological Journal* 138:205-40.

—————. 1987. "The Gunloops at Raglan Castle, Gwent." In: *Castles in Wales and the Marches: Essays in Honour of D.J. Cathcart King.* Ed. J.R. Kenyon and R. Avent. Cardiff: University of Wales Press. 143-60.

—————. 1990. *Medieval Fortifications.* New York: St. Martin's Press.

King, D.J. Cathcart. 1972. "The Field Archaeology of Mottes in England and Wales: Eine kurze überzicht," *Chateau Gaillard* 5:101-12.

—————. 1988. *The Castle in England and Wales: An Interpretative History.* Portland: Aeropagitica Press.

Kreutz, Barbara M. 1976. "Ships, Shipping, and the Implications of Change in the Early Medieval Mediterranean," *Viator* 7:79-109.

Kyeser, Conrad. 1967. *Bellifortis.* Ed. G. Quarg. Dusseldorf: VDI Verlag.

Landels, J.G. 1978. *Engineering in the Ancient World.* London: Chatto & Windus.

Lander, James. 1984. *Roman Stone Fortifications: Variation and Change from the First Century AD to the Fourth.* BAR International Series, 206. Oxford: British Archaeological Reports.

Lane, Frederic Chapin. 1934. *Venetian Ships and Shipbuilders of the Renaissance.* Baltimore: Johns Hopkins University Press.

—————. 1963a. "The Economic Meaning of the Invention of the Compass," *American Historical Review* 68:605-17.

—————. 1963b. "From Biremes to Triremes," *Mariner's Mirror* 29:48-50.

—————. 1963c. "Merchant Galleys, 1300-34: Private and Communal Operation," *Speculum* 38:179-205.

—————. 1969-70. "The Crossbow in the Nautical Revolution of the Middle Ages," *Explorations in Economic History* 7:161-71.

Larsen, Henrietta M. 1940. "The Armor Business in the Middle Ages," *Business History Review* 14:49-64.

Laures, Federico Foerster. 1987. "The Warships of the Kings of Aragon and their Fighting Tactics during the 13th and 14th Centuries AD," *International Journal of Nautical Archaeology and Underwater Exploration* 16:19-29.

Law, John. 1987. "Technology and Heterogeneous Engineering: The Case of Portuguese Expansion." In: *The Social Construction of Technological Systems: New Directions in the Sociology and History of Technology.* Ed. W.E. Bijker, T.P. Hughes and T.J. Pinch. Cambridge, MA: MIT Press. 111-34.

Lawrence, T.E. 1988. *Crusader Castles.* Oxford: Clarendon Press.

Leguay, Jean-Pierre. 1988. *Un réseau urbain au moyen age: les villes du duché de Bretagne aux XIVème et XVème siècles.* Paris: Maloine S.A.

Le Patourel, John. 1976. *The Norman Empire.* Oxford: Clarendon Press.

["Lettre"]. 1846-47. "Lettre sur la bataille de Castillon en Perigord, 19 juillet 1453," *Bibliotheque de l'école des chartes* 8:245-47.

Lewis, Archibald R. 1951. *Naval Power and Trade in the Mediterranean, A.D. 500-1100.* Princeton: Princeton University Press.

Lewis, Archibald R. and Timothy J. Runyan. 1985. *European Naval and Maritime History, 300-1500.* Bloomington: Indiana University Press.

Linder, Elisha. 1987. "New Evidence for the Study of Warships and Naval Warfare in Antiquity Based on the Discovery of the Athlit Bronze Ram." In: *Naval History: The Sixth Symposium of the United States Naval Academy.* Wilmington: Scholarly Resources. 20-25.

Lindsay, Jack. 1974. *The Normans and Their World.* London: Hart-Davis, MacGibbon.

Littauer, Mary Aitken. 1981. "Early Stirrups," *Antiquity* 55:99-105.

[*Livre des trahisons*]. 1873. *Le livre des trahisons de France envers la maison de Bourgogne*. In: *Chroniques relatives à l'histoire de la Belgique sous la domination des ducs de Bourgogne (textes Français)*. Ed. Kervyn de Lettenhove. Brussels: F. Hayez.

Lomax, Derek W. 1978. *The Reconquest of Spain*. London: Longman.

Lombares, Michel de. 1984. *Histoire de l'artillerie Française*. Paris: Charles-Lavauzelle.

Loomis, Roger Sherman and Laura Hibbard Loomis (trans.) 1957. *Medieval Romances*. New York: The Modern Library.

Lot, Ferdinand. 1961. *The End of the Ancient World and the Beginnings of the Middle Ages*. New York: Harper and Row.

Luttwak, Edward N. 1976. *The Grand Strategy of the Roman Empire*. Baltimore: Johns Hopkins University Press.

Lyon, Bryce. 1987. "The Role of Cavalry in Medieval Warfare: Horses, Horses All Around and Not a One to Use," *Mededelingen van de Koninklijke Academie voor Wetenschappen, Letteren en Schone Kunsten van België* 49:77-90.

Macartney, C.A. 1930. *The Magyars in the Ninth Century*. Cambridge: Cambridge University Press.

Mallett, M.E. 1967. *Florentine Galleys in the Fifteenth Century*. Oxford: Clarendon Press.

Mallett, M.E. and J.R. Hale. 1984. *The Military Organization of a Renaissance State: Venice c. 1400 to 1617*. Cambridge: Cambridge University Press.

Mann, James. 1933. "Notes on the Armour worn in Spain from the Tenth to the Fifteenth Century," *Archaeologia* 83:285-305.

————. 1957. "Arms and Armour". In: Stenton (1957). 56-69.

————. 1958. "Arms and Armour". In: *Medieval England*. Ed. A.L. Poole. Oxford: Clarendon Press. 314-37.

Marcus, G.J. 1956. "The Mariner's Compass: Its Influence upon Navigation in the Later Middle Ages," *History* n.s. 41:16-24.

Marsden, E.W. 1969. *Greek and Roman Artillery: Historical Development*. Oxford: Clarendon Press.

————. 1971. *Greek and Roman Artillery: Technical Treatises*. Oxford: Clarendon Press.

Marsden, Peter. 1972. "Ships of the Roman Period and After in Britain." In: Bass (1972a):113-31.

Martines, Lauro. 1979. *Power and Imagination: City-States in Renaissance Italy*. New York: Alfred A. Knopf.

McGuffie, T.H. 1955. "The Long-bow as a Decisive Weapon," *History Today* 5:737-41.

McKisack, May. 1959. *The Fourteenth Century, 1307-1399*. The Oxford History of England. Oxford: Clarendon Press.

McKitterick, Rosamund. 1983. *The Frankish Kingdoms under the Carolingians, 751-987*. London: Longman.

McNeill, William H. 1982. *The Pursuit of Power: Technology, Armed Force and Society since AD 1000*. Chicago: University of Chicago Press.

Mercier-Sivadjian, Eve and Sivadjian, J.-L. 1985. *Chateaux du moyen âge en France*. Paris: Libraire Larousse.

Monstrelet, Enguerran de. 1857-62. *Chronique*. Ed. L. Douet-d'Arcq. Société de l'histoire de France. Paris: Libraire Renouard.

Morley, Beric M. 1981. "Aspects of Fourteenth-Century Castle Design." In: *Collectanea historica: Essays in Memory of Stuart Rigold*. Ed. A. Detsicas. Maidstone: Kent Archaeological Society. 104-13.

Mortimer, Richard. 1986. "Knights and Knighthood in Germany in the Central Middle Ages." In: *The Ideals and Practice of Medieval Knighthood* I. Ed. C. Harper-Bill and R. Harvey. Woodbridge: The Boydell Press. 86-103.

Mott, Lawrence V. 1987. "Square-Rigged Galleys of the Late Fifteenth Century," *Mariner's Mirror* 73:49-54.

—————. 1990. "Ships of the 13th-century Catalan Navy," *International Journal of Nautical Archaeology and Underwater Exploration* 19:101-12

Müller-Wiener, Wolfgang. 1966. *Castles of the Crusaders*. Trans. J.M. Brownjohn. New York: McGraw-Hill.

Mumford, Lewis. 1934. *Technics and Civilization*. New York: Harcourt, Brace and Company.

Musset, Lucien. 1965. *Les invasions. Le second assaut contre l'Europe Chrétienne (VIIe-XIe siècles)*. Paris: Presses universitaires de France.

Needham, Joseph. 1976. "China's Trebuchets, Manned and Counterweighted." In: *On Pre-Modern Technology and Science: Studies in Honor of Lynn White, Jr.* Ed. B.S. Hall and D.C. West. Malibu: Undena Publications. 107-45.

—————. 1985. *Gunpowder as the Fourth Power, East and West*. Hong Kong: Hong Kong University Press.

—————. 1986. *Science and Civilisation in China*. Vol 5: *Chemistry and Chemical Technology*. Part 7: *Military Technology: The Gunpowder Epic*. Cambridge: Cambridge University Press.

Nelson, Janet. 1989. "Ninth-Century Knighthood: The Evidence of Nithard." In: *Studies in Medieval History Presented to R. Allen Brown*. Ed. C. Harper-Bill, C.J. Holdsworth and J. Nelson. Woodbridge: The Boydell Press. 255-66.

Neumann, J. 1989. "Hydrographic and Ship-Hydrodynamic Aspects of the Norman Invasion, AD 1066," *Anglo-Norman Studies* 11:221-243.

Nicholas, David. 1987. *The Metamorphosis of a Medieval City: Ghent in the Age of the Arteveldes, 1302-1390*. Lincoln: University of Nebraska Press.

Nickel, Helmut. 1982. "Bow and Arrow/Crossbow." In: *Dictionary of the Middle Ages* Ed. J.R. Strayer. New York: Scribner. II:350-54.

Nicolle, David C. 1980. "The Impact of the European Couched Lance on Muslim Military Tradition," *The Journal of the Arms and Armour Society* 10:6-40.

—————. 1988. *Arms and Armour of the Crusading Era, 1050-1350.* White Plains: Kraus International Publications.

—————. 1989. "Shipping in Islamic Art: Seventh through Sixteenth Century AD," *The American Neptune* 49:168-97.

Oakeshott, R. Ewart. 1964. *The Sword in the Age of Chivalry.* New York: Frederick A. Praeger.

—————. 1980. *European Weapons and Armour: From the Renaissance to the Industrial Revolution* . London: Luttersworth Press.

—————. 1991. *Records of the Medieval Sword.* Woodbridge: The Boydell Press.

O'Connell, Robert L. 1989. *Of Arms and Men: A History of War, Weapons, and Aggression.* Oxford: Oxford University Press.

Ogilvy, J.D.A. 1966. "The Stirrup and Feudalism," *The University of Colorado Studies: Series in Language and Literature* 10:1-13.

O'Neil, B.H.St.J. 1960. *Castles and Cannon: A Study of Early Artillery Fortifications in England.* Oxford: Clarendon Press.

Painter, Sidney. 1935. "English Castles in the Early Middle Ages: Their Number, Location, and Legal Position," *Speculum* 10:321-32.

Parker, Geoffrey. 1988. *The Military Revolution: Military Innovation and the Rise of the West, 1500-1800.* Cambridge: Cambridge University Press.

Partington, J.R. 1960. *A History of Greek Fire and Gunpowder.* Cambridge: W. Heffer & Sons.

Payne-Gallwey, Ralph. 1903. *The Crossbow.* London: Longmans, Green.

Peirce, Ian. 1986. "The Knight, His Arms and Armour in the Eleventh and Twelfth Centuries." In: *The Ideals and Practice of Medieval Knighthood.* Ed. C. Harper-Bill and R. Harvey. Woodbridge: The Boydell Press. 152-64.

Pepper, Simon and Nicholas Adams. 1986. *Firearms and Fortifications: Military Architecture and Siege Warfare in Sixteenth-Century Siena.* Chicago: University of Chicago Press.

Petrikovits, Harald von. 1971. "Fortifications in the North-Western Roman Empire from the Third to the Fifth Centuries AD," *Journal of Roman Studies* 61:178-218.

Platt, Colin. 1976. *The English Medieval Town.* London: David McKay Company.

—————. 1982. *The Castle in Medieval England and Wales.* New York: Charles Scribner's Sons.

Poertner, Rudolf. 1975. *The Vikings: Rise and Fall of the Norse Sea Kings.* London: St. James Press.

Powers, James F. 1988. *A Society Organized for War: The Iberian Municipal Militias in the Central Middle Ages, 1000-1284.* Berkeley and Los Angeles: University of California Press.

Powicke, Michael. 1962. *Military Obligation in Medieval England.* Oxford: Clarendon Press.

Prager, Frank D. and Gustina Scaglia. 1972. *Mariano Taccola and His Book "De ingeneis."* Cambridge, MA: MIT Press.

Prawer, Joshua. 1980. *Crusader Institutions*. Oxford: Clarendon Press.

Prestwich, Michael. 1980. *The Three Edwards: War and State in England, 1272-1377*. London: Weidenfeld & Nicolson.

—————. 1982. "English Castles in the Reign of Edward II," *Journal of Medieval History* 8:159-78.

—————. 1988. *Edward I*. Berkeley and Los Angeles: University of California Press.

Pryor, John H. 1982. "Transportation of Horses by Sea during the Era of the Crusades: Eighth Century to 1285 A.D.," *Mariner's Mirror* 68:9-27, 103-25.

—————. 1983. "The Naval Battles of Roger of Lauria," *Journal of Medieval History* 9:179-219.

—————. 1984. "The Naval Architecture of Crusader Transport Ships: A Reconstruction of Some Archetypes for Round-hulled Sailing Ships," *Mariner's Mirror* 70:171-219, 275-92, 363-86.

—————. 1988. *Geography, Technology, and War: Studies in the Maritime History of the Mediterranean, 649-1571*. Cambridge: Cambridge University Press.

—————. 1990. "The Naval Architecture of Crusader Transport Ships and Horse Transports Revisited," *Mariner's Mirror* 76:255-73.

Queller, Donald. 1980. "Combined Arms Operations and the Latin Conquest of Constantinople." In: *Changing Interpretations and New Sources in Naval History: Papers from the Third U.S. Naval Academy History Symposium*. Ed. R.W. Love, Jr. New York: Garland Publishing. 45-57.

Radford, C.A. Ralegh. 1970. "The Later Pre-Conquest Boroughs and their Defences," *Medieval Archaeology* 14:83-103.

Reid, W. Stanford. 1960. "Sea-power in the Anglo-Scottish War, 1296-1328," *Mariner's Mirror* 46:7-23.

Religieux de Saint-Denis. 1839-52. *Chronique*. Ed. L. Bellaguet. 6 vols. Paris: Crapelet.

Renn, Derek F. 1960. "The Anglo-Norman Keep, 1066-1138," *Journal of the British Archaeology Association*. 3rd series 23:1-23.

—————. 1968. "The Earliest Gunports in Britain?" *Archaeological Journal*. 125:301-03.

—————. 1973. *Norman Castles in Britain*. 2nd ed. London: J. Baker.

Riché, Pierre. 1983. *Daily Life in the World of Charlemagne*. Trans. J. McNamara. Philadelphia: University of Pennsylvania Press.

Richmond, C.F. 1971. "The War at Sea." In: *The Hundred Years War*. Ed. K. Fowler. London: Macmillan. 96-121.

Robbert, Louise Buenger. 1969. "A Venetian Naval Expedition of 1224." In: *Economy, Society, and Government in Medieval Italy: Essays in Memory of Robert L. Reynolds*. Ed. D. Herlihy, R.S. Lopez and V. Slessarev. Kent: Kent State University Press. 141-51.

Robinson, H. Russell. 1975. *The Armour of Imperial Rome*. New York: Scribner.

Rodgers, William Ledyard. 1940. *Naval Warfare Under Oars, 4th to 16th Centuries*. Annapolis: Naval Institute Press.

Rörig, Fritz. 1967. *The Medieval Town*. Berkeley and Los Angeles: University of California Press.

Ross, D.J.A. 1951. "Plein sa hanste," *Medium Aevum* 20:1-10.

—————. 1963. "L'originalité de 'Turoldus': le maniement de la lance," *Cahiers de civilisation médiévale* 6:127-38.

Runciman, Steven. 1964. *A History of the Crusades*. 3 vols. New York: Harper and Row.

Runyan, Timothy J. 1986. "Ships and Fleets in Anglo-French Warfare, 1337-1360," *American Neptune* 46:91-99.

Sandurra, Enrico. 1972. "The Maritime Republics: Medieval and Renaissance Ships in Italy." In: Bass (1972a):205-24.

Sawyer. P.H. 1962. *The Age of the Vikings*. London: Edward Arnold.

—————. 1982. *Kings and Vikings*. London: Methuen & Co.

Setton, Kenneth M. Setton et al (eds.) 1955-1990. *A History of the Crusades*. 7 vols. Philadelphia: American Philosophical Association Publications, and Madison: University of Wisconsin Press.

Sherborne, J.W. 1967. "The English Navy: Shipping and Manpower 1369-1389," *Past and Present* 37:163-75.

—————. 1977. "English Barges and Balingers of the Late Fourteenth Century," *Mariner's Mirror* 63:109-14.

Sherlock, David. 1987. "*Plumbatae*—A Note on the Method of Manufacture." In: *Aspects of the "De rebus bellicis": Papers Presented to Professor E.A. Thompson*. Ed. M.W.C. Hassall. BAR International Series, 63. Oxford: British Archaeological Reports. 101-02.

Smail, R.C. 1951. "Crusaders' Castles of the Twelfth Century," *Cambridge Historical Journal* 10:133-49.

—————. 1956. *Crusading Warfare, 1097-1193*. Cambridge: Cambridge University Press.

Soedel, Werner and Vernard Foley. (March) 1979. "Ancient Catapults," *Scientific American*. 150-60.

Steffy, J. Richard. 1980. "The Greek Ship: New Evidence through Nautical Archaeology." In: *Changing Interpretations and New Sources in Naval History: Papers from the Third United States Naval Academy History Symposium*. Ed. R.M. Love, Jr. New York: Garland Publishing.

—————. 1981. "The Medieval Cargo Ship: Evidence from Nautical Archaeology." In: *New Aspects of Naval History*. Ed. C.L. Symonds. Annapolis: Naval Institute Press. 13-19.

Stenton, Frank. 1957. *The Bayeux Tapestry: A Comprehensive Survey*. 2nd ed. London: Phaidon Press.

—————. 1960. "The Development of the Castle in England and Wales." In: *Social Life in Medieval England*. Ed. G. Barraclough. London: Routledge & Kegan Paul. 96-123.

—————. 1961. *The First Century of English Feudalism, 1066-1166*. 2nd ed. Oxford: Clarendon Press.

—————. 1971. *Anglo-Saxon England*. 3rd ed. Oxford: Clarendon Press.

Stephenson, Carl. 1933. *Borough and Town: A Study of Urban Origins in England*. Cambridge, MA: Medieval Academy of America.

—————. 1942. *Mediaeval Feudalism*. Ithaca: Cornell University Press.

Stork, Nancy Porter. 1990. *Through a Gloss Darkly: Aldhelm's Riddles in the British Library MS Royal 12.C.xxiii*. Toronto: Pontifical Institute of Mediaeval Studies Press.

Stratos, Andreas N. 1980. "The Naval Engagement at Phoenix." In: *Charanis Studies: Essays in Honor of Peter Charanis*. Ed. A.E. Laiou-Thomadakis. New Brunswick: Rutgers University Press. 221-47.

Strayer, Joseph R. 1965. *Feudalism*. Princeton: Princeton University Press.

—————. 1985. "Feudalism." In: *Dictionary of the Middle Ages*. Ed. J.R. Strayer. New York: Scribners. V:52-57.

Szwejkowski, W. Ted. 1990. "A Full Size Working Model of a Medieval Traction Trebuchet." Unpublished Paper.

Tacitus. 1970. *The Agricola and the Germania*. Trans. H. Mattingly. Harmondsworth: Penguin Books.

Taylor, Arnold J. 1950. "Master James of St. George," *English Historical Review* 65:433-57.

—————. 1958. "Military Architecture." In: *Medieval England*. Ed. A.L. Poole. Vol. 1. Oxford: Clarendon Press. 98-127.

—————. 1961. "Castle-Building in Wales in the Later Thirteenth Century: The Prelude to Construction." In: *Studies in Building History: Essays in Recognition of the Work of B.H.St.J. O'Neil*. London: Odhams Press. 104-33.

—————. 1977. "Castle-Building in Thirteenth-Century Wales and Savoy," *Proceedings of the British Academy* 63:265-92.

—————. 1986. *The Welsh Castles of Edward I*. London: The Hambledon Press.

Taylor, Frank and John S. Roskell (eds. and trans.) 1975. *Gesta Henrici quinti*. Oxford: Clarendon Press.

Thielmans, Marie-Rose. 1966. *Bourgogne et Angleterre: Relations politiques et économiques entre les Pays-Bas Bourguignonnes et l'Angleterre, 1435-1467*. Brussels: Presses universitaires de Bruxelles.

Thompson, A. Hamilton. 1912. *Military Architecture in Medieval England*. London: H. Frowde.

Thompson, E.A. (ed.) 1952. *A Roman Reformer and Inventor*. Oxford: Oxford University Press.

—————. 1958. "Early Germanic Warfare," *Past and Present* 14:2-31.

—————. 1982. *Romans and Barbarians: The Decline of the Western Empire*. Madison: University of Wisconsin Press.

Thompson, M.W. 1960. "Recent Excavations in the Keep of Farnham Castle, Surrey," *Medieval Archaeology* 4:81-94.

—————. 1961. "Motte Substructures," *Medieval Archaeology* 5:305-06.

—————. 1981. "The Architectural Significance of the Building Works of Ralph, Lord Cromwell (1394-1456)." In: *Collectanea historica: Essays in Memory of Stuart Rigold*. Ed. A. Detsicas. Maidstone: Kent Archaeological Society. 156-62.

—————. 1987. *The Decline of the Castle*. Cambridge: Cambridge University Press.

Thordeman, Bengt. 1939. *Armour from the Battle of Wisby, 1361*. 2 vols. Stockholm: Kungl. Vitterhets Historie och Antikvitets Akedemien.

Thorne, P.F. 1982. "Clubs and Maces in the Bayeux Tapestry," *History Today* 32:48-50.

Tinniswood, T. 1949. "English Galleys, 1272-1377," *Mariner's Mirror* 35:276-92.

Toy, Sidney. 1955. *A History of Fortification from 3000 BC to AD 1700*. London: Heineman.

Turner, D.J. 1986. "Bodiam, Sussex: True Castle or Old Soldier's Dream House?" In: *England in the Fourteenth Century: Proceedings of the 1985 Harlaxton Symposium*. Ed. W.J. Ormond. Woodbridge: The Boydell Press. 267-79.

Turner, Hilary L. 1971. *Town Defences in England and Wales: An Architectural and Documentary Study, AD 900-1500*. London: John Barker.

Unger, Richard W. 1973. "Dutch Ship Design in the Fifteenth and Sixteenth Centuries," *Viator* 4:387-411.

—————. 1980. *The Ship in Medieval Economy, 600-1600*. Montreal: McGill-Queens University Press.

—————. 1981. "Warships and Cargo Ships in Medieval Europe," *Technology and Culture* 22:233-52.

Vale, M.G.A. 1974. *Charles VII*. Berkeley and Los Angeles: University of California Press.

—————. 1975. "New Techniques and Old Ideas: The Impact of Artillery on War and Chivalry at the End of the Hundred Years War." In: *War, Literature and Politics in the Late Middle Ages: Essays in Honour of G.W. Coopland*. Ed. C.T. Allmand. Liverpool: University of Liverpool Press. 57-72.

—————. 1981. *War and Chivalry: Warfare and Aristocratic Culture in England, France and Burgundy at the End of the Middle Ages*. London: Duckworth.

—————. 1986. "Seigneurial Fortification and Private War in Later Medieval Gascony." In: *Gentry and Lesser Nobility in Later Medieval Europe*. Ed. M. Jones. Gloucester: A. Sutton. 133-58.

van Creveld, Martin. 1989. *Technology and War: From 2000 BC to the Present*. New York: The Free Press.

van Doorninck, Frederick. 1972. "Byzantium, Mistress of the Sea, 330-641." In: Bass (1972a):133-57.

Vaughan, Richard. 1962. *Philip the Bold: The Formation of the Burgundian State*. London: Longman.

—————. 1966. *John the Fearless: The Growth of Burgundian Power*. London: Longman.

—————. 1970. *Philip the Good: The Apogee of Burgundy*. London: Longman.

—————. 1973. *Charles the Bold: The Last Valois Duke of Burgundy*. London: Longman.

Verbruggen, J.F. 1947. "La tactique militaire des armées de chevaliers," *Revue du nord* 29:161-80.

—————. 1950. "Note sur le sens des mots *castrum*, *castellum*, et quelques autres expressions qui désignent des fortifications," *Revue Belge de philologie et d'histoire* 28:147-55.

—————. 1977. "De goedendag," *Militaria Belgica* 65-70.

Vercauteren, F. 1936. "Comment s'est-on défendu, au IXe siècle dans l'empire franc contre les invasions normandes?" *Annales du XXXe Congrès de la Féderation archéologique et historique de Belgique*. 117-32.

Vyronis, Speros, Jr. 1981. "The Evolution of Slavic Society and the Slavic Invasions in Greece: The First Major Attack on Thessaloniki, AD 597," *Hesperia* 50:378-90.

Wallace-Hadrill, J.M. 1962. "Gothia and Romania," in *The Long-Haired Kings*. New York: Methuen & Co. 25-48.

Webster, Graham. 1985. *The Roman Imperial Army of the First and Second Centuries*. London: A. & C. Black.

White, K.D. 1984. *Greek and Roman Technology*. Ithaca: Cornell University Press.

White, Lynn, Jr. 1962. *Medieval Technology and Social Change*. Oxford: Oxford University Press.

Williams, Alan R. 1977. "Methods of Manufacture of Swords in Medieval Europe: Illustrated by the Metallography of Some Examples," *Gladius* 13:75-101.

—————. 1980. "The Manufacture of Mail in Medieval Europe: A Technical Note," *Gladius* 15:105-34.

Wilson, David M. 1965. "Some Neglected Late Anglo-Saxon Swords," *Medieval Archaeology* 9:32-54.

Wolfram, Herwig. 1988. *History of the Goths*. Trans. T.J. Dunlap. Berkeley and Los Angeles: University of California Press.

Wood, Michael. 1985. *In Search of the Trojan War*. New York: Facts on File Publications.

Wright, Quincy. 1964. *A Study of War*. 2nd ed. Chicago: University of Chicago Press.

Index

(italicised page numbers indicate illustrations)